Orthodox
Russia
in Crisis

Orthodox
Russia
in Crisis

Church and Nation
in the Time of Troubles

Isaiah Gruber

NIU

PRESS

DeKalb

Illinois

© 2012 by Northern Illinois University Press
Published by the Northern Illinois University Press, DeKalb, Illinois 60115
Manufactured in the United States using acid-free paper.
All Rights Reserved
Design by Shaun Allshouse

Library of Congress Cataloging-in-Publication Data
 Gruber, Isaiah, 1977–
Orthodox Russia in crisis : church and nation in the Time of Troubles / Isaiah
Gruber.
        p. cm.
 Includes bibliographical references and index.
 ISBN 978-0-87580-446-0 (cloth: alkaline paper) — ISBN 978-1-60909-049-4
(electronic)
1. Russkaia pravoslavnaia tserkov'—History—17th century. 2. Russia—
History—Time of Troubles, 1598-1613. 3. Church and state—Russia—History—
17th century. 4. Orthodox Eastern monasteries—Economic aspects—Russia—
History—17th century. 5. Russia—Church history—17th century. I. Title.
BX490.G78 2012
281.9'47009032—dc23
2011036826

Maria Podkopaeva (b. 1981, Moscow), creator of *V Smutnoe vremia* (displayed both on the jacket
and as Fig. 1 in this book), belongs to the contemporary Russian realist school of painting. She is a
graduate of the historical studio of the Russian Academy of Painting, Sculpture, and Architecture.
Her works are exhibited in museums and private collections in Russia, Germany, Montenegro, the
United States, and elsewhere.

Contents

Illustrations and Tables

Preface

"The 'Time of Troubles'? Isn't that all of Russian history?" In Western countries I almost invariably encountered this question upon mentioning the topic of my research. Russian history has included an extraordinary amount of suffering by any standard. Yet in Russia the question tended to be different: "*Smutnoe vremia*? Isn't that now?" Russia's original "Time of Troubles" occurred at the beginning of the seventeenth century, but adversity and disillusionment in the post-Soviet period have made reference to a "new Time of Troubles" commonplace. It was partly my interest in contemporary Russia and the resurgent role of religion today that led me to research the history of the Russian Orthodox Church in the historical Time of Troubles. Some of the chapter epigraphs accordingly suggest a thematic continuity from then until now.

I have not attempted a comprehensive rewriting of the general history of the Troubles, on which numerous scholars have already labored. For the overall course of events, I frequently consulted standard works, such as those by Sergei Platonov, Ruslan Skrynnikov, and Chester Dunning. Recurring themes and debates in historiography have generally been presented briefly; in such cases further details concerning sources and interpretations may be found in the cited secondary literature. In treating my particular topic of the Church and national-religious identity, I strove to remain as faithful as possible to the primary sources. Some readers may be surprised that this book is not more focused on ikons, liturgy, doctrines, and other typically "religious" matters. The fact is that to Muscovites of the early seventeenth century, faith concerned all aspects of life. Even ecclesiastic sources largely dealt with what today would be considered "political" and "economic" matters, which could not be separated from Orthodoxy.

Transliteration from Russian, including unstandardized and variant spellings found in the sources, follows a slightly modified Library of Congress system. In the body of the text, I have used Anglicized forms of some common words (e.g., Moscow), often omitted the final adjectival ending *-ii* in the names of monasteries (e.g., Iosifo Volokolamsk), and modified some proper nouns to avoid awkward combinations and to aid in pronunciation (e.g., "Soloviev's" instead of "Solov'ev's"; "Fyodor" instead of "Fedor" or "Fiodor"). However, such modifications have not been made for transliterated citations in the endnotes and bibliography. I give Muscovite dates as they were recorded in the "Old Style" (Julian calendar), with years that reckoned time from the assumed moment of Creation (1 September 5509 BCE). Thus, "4 September 7108" in Moscow was the same day as "14 September 1599" in Vienna. For biblical citations I have simply used slashes to indicate alternate chapter and verse numbers. Thus, the single verse designated as Psalm 40/41:1/2 may be found as 41:2 in Hebrew, 40:2 in Greek (LXX), 40:1 in Slavonic and Russian, and 41:1 in English.

In this book, the term "literati" refers to the educated (literate) class of Muscovite Russians, particularly those who authored texts. "Ideologues" means state and church officials who formulated speeches, writings, and other expressions of the politico-religious outlook. In characterizing some such works as "propaganda," I mean that they were consciously designed for the intentional dissemination of ideas and information (whether true or false). I have tried to avoid customary but highly loaded appellations such as "First False Dmitrii" and "Second False Dmitrii." Whenever possible, I refer to these individuals instead as "Dmitrii I" and "Dmitrii II."

My research could not have been carried out without access to numerous archival and library collections, as well as interlibrary loan services. I am extremely grateful to the following institutions and their staffs: Rossiiskii gosudarstvennyi arkhiv drevnikh aktov (Russian State Archive of Ancient Acts); Gosudarstvennaia publichnaia istoricheskaia biblioteka Rossii (State Public Historical Library of Russia); Rossiiskaia natsional'naia biblioteka (Russian National Library); American University Libraries; Dartmouth College Libraries; Dumbarton Oaks Research Library; Georgetown University Libraries; George Washington University Libraries; Goucher College Library; Harvard University Libraries; Jewish National and Hebrew University Libraries; Johns Hopkins University Libraries; the Library of Congress; the State Library of New South Wales; Towson University Library; and University of Sydney Libraries.

Furthermore, I was privileged to receive financial support at various stages of the project from the Fulbright-Hays Fellowship Program; the International Research and Exchanges Board; the Georgetown University History Department; the Lady Davis Fellowship Trust at the Hebrew University of Jerusalem; Yechiel Bar-Chaim and Ernestine Gruber; and the Sir Zelman Cowen Universities Fund. Carl Foltz helped to cover some permission fees for artwork in this book.

Many colleagues, friends, and relatives read and commented on my drafts, advised on difficult questions, helped with translation or editing, aided in procuring materials, and provided moral support. My deepest thanks are due to the following individuals, each of whom invested significant time and effort in helping me to improve the manuscript: David Goldfrank, Chester Dunning, Catherine Evtuhov, Donald Ostrowski, Samuel Rausnitz, and the anonymous reviewers for Northern Illinois University Press. I also owe a significant debt of gratitude to many others: Yonatan Allon, Henriette De Bruyn Kops, Ariel Edery, Anton Fedyashin, Daniel and Susan Gruber, Charles Halperin, Daniel Kaiser, Tait Siddhartha Keller, Tomasz Kolodziej, Olga Kosheleva, Philip Longworth, George Majeska, Olga Meerson, Boris Morozov, Matthew Romaniello, Ariel Roth, Olya Samilenko, Mark Shelling, and Richard Wilkinson. A special thanks to my hosts in Moscow: Galina, Pyotr, and Volodya. It has been a pleasure to work with my editors: Amy Farranto, Susan Bean, and Aimee Anderson. The organizations and individuals named above are not responsible for any errors that may remain.

I dedicate this book to the souls who search for Truth in all its forms, from the tiniest details to the grandest ideas.

Mt. Scopus, Jerusalem
September 2011 [Elul 5771 / Muscovite 7520]

Orthodox
Russia
in Crisis

Introduction

Troubles, Then and Now

Вскую г[оспод]и отстоя далече, презриши въ бл[а]го время въ печалехъ.
(Why standest thou afarre off, O Lord? why hidest thou thy selfe in times of trouble?)
—Psalm 9:22/10:1 in the Ostroh Bible (1581) and
King James Version (1611)[1]

Our current situation today is not describable as anything but a "Time of Troubles."
—Major-General Aleksandr Vladimirov, Vice-President of the College of
Military Experts of the Russian Federation, 2002[2]

In the Muscovite year 7117 (1608–1609 CE), a provincial Russian Orthodox monk was startled by a vision of Moscow "cut up" by Polish-Lithuanian forces. To his great dismay he saw other parts of the Russian tsardom "in captivity and burned up." A voice instructed him to warn the tsar of this impending disaster. He traveled to the capital and conveyed the message—but to no avail. Over the next couple of years, the vision's horrors inexorably came true. Moscow fell to the invaders; many other towns and monasteries were looted, burned, and destroyed.[3]

In the middle of the bloody war, the Polish-Lithuanian commander Jan-Piotr Sapieha arrived with his troops at Rostov's Borisogleb Monastery, where the prophetic elder lived. Several lords in the foreign army began to accuse the old monk, saying that he stubbornly refused to pray for the Polish-Lithuanian king and candidate to the Muscovite throne, instead remaining loyal to the embattled Russian tsar. The old man did not back down. At the risk of his life, he proclaimed: "I was born and christened in Russia, and I pray to God for a

Russian tsar!" Upon hearing this, Sapieha replied, "Great truth is in the father: [a man] receives the tsar of whichever land in which he lives." The commander then listened humbly to the elder's advice before finally exclaiming, "Forgive, father!" (*Prosti, bat'ko!*). After bowing in reverence, Sapieha left in peace, sending a gift of five rubles and issuing orders not to despoil or damage the monastery in any way.[4]

So reads *The Life of the Venerable Irinarkh,* a text composed retrospectively by the monk's disciple of thirty years, Aleksandr (also Aleksei).[5] Written to glorify a potential saint, this biographical account reveals some key elements of the Russian mentality during the "Time of Troubles" (*Smutnoe vremia*). The experiences of Irinarkh (also Ilinarkh) demonstrate a strong association between Russian Orthodox piety and unshakable nationalism or patriotism. The tale furthermore promotes the spiritual superiority of the Russian national-religious ethos over its competitors, even those temporarily gaining the advantage of physical force. Texts such as this one reveal that the crucible of the Troubles forged a modern Russian identity, one rooted in a particular nationalist view of Orthodox Christianity. The story of this watershed period is not for the faint of heart, but it can hardly be surpassed for drama.

The Time of Troubles at the Beginning of the Seventeenth Century

Russia's first great Time of Troubles was a chaotic, violent, and tragic period of about fifteen years separating the two historical dynasties of Russian history. Moscow's branch of the ancient Riurikid or Daniilovich dynasty of Kiev died out in 1598, but the Romanovs did not begin to rule until 1613. In the interim the country experienced famine, civil war, numerous pretenders to the throne, concomitant revolts and coups, foreign invasion, rampant banditry, and finally the total collapse of the state itself. When all seemed lost, a dying Church patriarch managed to smuggle letters out of his prison cell pleading for all Russians to unite, to rise up and defend Orthodoxy. Surprisingly, it worked. A militia and provisional government formed in Nizhnii Novgorod managed to attract enough allies to reunite the land and recapture Moscow. Instead of the extinction of Russia at the hands of its religious and political enemies, the Time of Troubles resulted in the coalescence of a "national ideology"[6] and the setting of a trajectory toward Russia's position as a great world power during the modern age.

Despite or perhaps because of its extraordinary drama and importance, the causes and nature of the Time of Troubles have remained mysterious for four hundred years. At the close of the nineteenth century, Sergei Platonov devoted well over a third of his magnum opus on the Troubles to pre-1598 history, that is, to attempting to decipher the earlier roots and preconditions of the crisis.[7] In the early twenty-first century Chester Dunning wrote a major new reinterpretation in which he stated: "It was so complex and sources about it are so fragmentary and contradictory that to this day the Time of Troubles defies simple recitation of its basic facts, let alone satisfactory explanations of its nature, causes, and significance."[8] Partly as a result, numerous alternate periodizations have been proposed, including: 1584–1613, 1598–1618, 1601–1613, 1603–1613, 1603–1614, 1604–1613, 1604–1618, 1605–1612, and 1605–1613.[9]

The story of the Troubles begins sometime during the reign of Ivan IV Groznyi (1533–1584). His sobriquet has traditionally been translated as "the Terrible" or "the Dread" but almost certainly carried a positive connotation in sixteenth-century Muscovy. Ivan terrified his (non-Orthodox) enemies; this was a compliment of the first order. In English, a combination of *terrific* and *terrible,* or *awesome* and *awful,* might convey something of the same meaning.[10] In the 1550s, this fearsome Ivan conquered Kazan and Astrakhan, remnants of the mighty Mongol-Tatar empire founded by Chingis Khan in the thirteenth century. Muscovites referred to Kazan and Astrakhan as "tsardoms," meaning *khanates,* or steppe empires. These impressive conquests greatly increased the power and prestige of their state and ruler. Russia began to expand into Siberia, with its seemingly endless territory and resources.

The usual story, challenged by some historians,[11] is that something changed after Ivan's supposedly beloved first wife Anastasia died in 1560. The tsar moved from wife to wife until his death, never satisfied. His long, expensive, and futile Livonian War depressed both economy and society. In 1565, after abdicating or threatening to abdicate unless his demands were met, he set up the *oprichnina,* a large central region of the Russian state subject to his direct personal control. The officials of this new domain, the *oprichniki,* murdered potential opponents and terrorized the population for several years until the experiment was abandoned. In 1575 Ivan appointed a Chingisid (Simeon Bekbulatovich) as tsar and again made some confusing, temporary moves toward possible abdication. In 1581, back on the throne again, he killed his own son and heir, Ivan Ivanovich, in a fit of rage.

Historians have long debated whether Ivan IV's violence stemmed from a definite political purpose or from madness.[12] In either case, it weakened Russian society. The oprichnina and then a severe and prolonged economic downturn in the last decades of the sixteenth century led to an astonishing depopulation of the central regions of the state. Laws binding people to their obligations, including the imposition of formal serfdom, failed to solve these problems and in fact exacerbated them. Disaffected peasants, soldiers, slaves, petty landowners, and others fled to the southern borderlands, where they joined Cossack bands. Ivan's son Fyodor, who ruled in name only, died in 1598 with no surviving issue.

The late tsar's powerful regent, Boris Godunov, now claimed to have been chosen or elected to the throne by "all the land." According to contemporary witnesses, he was an intelligent and capable administrator. His rule seemed relatively secure until three consecutive years of crop failure and famine devastated the country in 1601–1603. According to some estimates, this horrific catastrophe wiped out an entire third of the Russian population. It also undermined Tsar Boris's legitimacy in the eyes of survivors, many of whom considered the famine a sign of divine displeasure. Not for the first time, rumors circulated that Boris had cleared his way to the throne by arranging the grisly and suspicious death of Tsarevich Dmitrii, Fyodor's half-brother, back in 1591.

In 1604 a man claiming to be this very Tsarevich Dmitrii gathered a small army in Poland-Lithuania and mounted a military and propaganda campaign to capture the Russian throne. According to his tale, he had miraculously escaped Boris's evil plot against his life: another boy had been killed instead. Despite the best efforts of the government in Moscow to discredit him as a runaway monk by the name of Grishka Otrepiev, the "tsarevich" quickly garnered mass support, particularly in the southwestern border regions of the Russian state. In mid-April 1605, with all-out war raging between the two camps, Tsar Boris died, and the throne officially passed to his young son Fyodor Borisovich. A large part of the new tsar's army almost immediately defected to Dmitrii, sealing the fate of the Godunovs. In June 1605 conspirators brutally killed Fyodor II and his mother, while Dmitrii entered Moscow in triumph.

The successful insurgent reigned for just under a year. In May 1606 he fell victim to a coup that coincided with the celebration of his wedding to Marina Mniszech, a Catholic and the daughter of his chief Polish backer. The lead conspirator, Vasilii Shuiskii, now ascended the throne. His four-year reign saw Russia degenerate into chaotic warfare, with numerous armies and gangs constantly roaming throughout the country. Bloody civil war began again almost immediately upon his succession. In the summer of 1606, a commander named Ivan Bolotnikov led a rebel army from the south—claiming to act in the name of "Dmitrii," who had supposedly escaped death by a miracle yet again.

Support for the new insurrection came primarily from the same border regions that had supported the first "Dmitrii." Eventually an impersonator of the former tsar materialized to claim leadership of the movement. In 1608 he established a competing government in Tushino, just northwest of Moscow, and besieged the capital. Numerous towns and regions transferred their allegiance to this "second false Dmitrii," and Marina Mniszech ostensibly verified that he was indeed her husband. In effect, the country had now split into two: each half had its own tsar and its own patriarch. Meanwhile, repressive measures by both sides and endemic banditry continued to exacerbate the suffering of the population.

Nor was this all. The rise and fall of the first Dmitrii stimulated new claimants to the throne. These pretenders (*samozvantsy*) attracted their own armies, often from among the Cossacks, and set out to control as much territory as possible. By the end of the Troubles, fifteen or so of them had surfaced, including a "third false Dmitrii," a *vorenok* or "Little Villain" (the infant son of Marina Mniszech); and a number of previously unknown "tsareviches" with names such as Ivan, Simeon, and Pyotr. As Platonov wrote: "Various bands of free Cossacks began to invent pretenders in great numbers. . . . A pretender was looked upon as the generally accepted method of mounting a revolutionary outbreak."[13] Many of these gangs brutally terrorized the countryside.

Knowing of the chaos in Russia, multiple Polish-Lithuanian forces invaded and joined the fray. An army commanded by Jan-Piotr Sapieha besieged the famous Troitsa Sergiev Monastery, located about seventy kilometers (45 miles) northeast of Moscow, for nearly a year and a half in 1608–1610. In 1609 King Zygmunt (Sigismund) III personally embarked on a siege of Smolensk, which finally capitulated in 1611. Meanwhile, his commander (hetman) Stanislaw Zolkiewski gained control of Moscow itself in 1610. Swedish intervention forces also fought in numerous battles, originally on the side of Tsar Vasilii. In 1611 they occupied Novgorod and its surrounding region.

By this time, both the Moscow and Tushino governments had collapsed. Oddly enough, the remnants of each camp had at different times offered the Russian throne to King Zygmunt's son Wladyslaw. While negotiations on this score dragged on, the zealously Catholic king plotted to conquer Russia outright and incorporate it into his own domain. The Orthodox Patriarch

Hermogen (also Ermogen, Germogen), who had been a staunch supporter of the deposed Tsar Vasilii, understood the danger. From his monastery prison cell, he sent out letters rebuking the people for having betrayed the "true faith" and their oaths of loyalty. He warned that unless Russians repented of their sins and stopped destroying their own fatherland (*ne svoe li otechestvo razoriaete?*), the country would suffer the same fate as Jerusalem at the hands of the Romans.[14] After a millennium and a half, the Jewish state still had not risen again from its destruction.

These appeals had an effect. Rallying to the defense of Orthodoxy, a new militia government and army coalesced in Nizhnii Novgorod under the command of Kuzma Minin and Dmitrii Pozharskii. Patriarch Hermogen died of starvation and abuse in his prison cell, but the "national liberation" army marched on Moscow and defeated the Polish-Lithuanian garrison in late 1612. An "assembly of the land" then selected sixteen-year-old Mikhail Romanov as the "God-chosen" candidate to the throne. His accession in 1613 marked the founding of a dynasty that would persist until the revolutions of 1917. Naturally, it took some time to quiet the internal and external conflicts, but by about 1619 Russia had regained a more "normal" state of affairs.[15]

Legacy of the First Russian Time of Troubles

It would be difficult to overestimate the significance, symbolic as well as practical, of the Time of Troubles (*Smutnoe vremia*). The painful memory of this period has never faded from the national consciousness and has in many ways defined it. In later periods, the Troubles frequently emerged as a paradigm for interpreting other extreme and prolonged crises. During one such turbulent period in the twentieth century, Mikhail Kovalenskii described the original Smutnoe vremia as an "unfathomable abyss" (*bezdonnaia propast'*) dividing two eras of Russian history.[16] Earlier the famous imperial historian Vasilii Kliuchevskii had defined the Time of Troubles as the boundary between medieval and modern Russia.[17] Numerous artistic, literary, and musical works also took their inspiration from the tumultuous drama of the early seventeenth century, thus reinforcing its symbolic power in the Russian mentality.

The very phrase "Time of Troubles" seems to pulsate with biblical overtones. Ancient Hebrew poetry from the Psalms and Prophets spoke often of a "day of trouble" (*yom tsara*), a "time of trouble" (*et tsara*), and "times of trouble" (*itot batsara*).[18] Yet Slavonic translations of the Bible, so important for Russian civilization, translated these phrases instead by such expressions as *den' bedstviia* (day of calamity) and *vremia skorbi* (time of sorrow). The Russian name for the Time of Troubles, *Smutnoe vremia,* arose from a different source.

In fact, the meaning of "Smutnoe vremia" and the shorter "Smuta" (Troubles) cannot be translated precisely into English. A now outmoded convention labeled the period Russia's "Epoch of Confusion."[19] Together, the two renditions give some sense of the Russian original. "Smuta" and related words derive from a Slavic root signifying the act of "shaking up" or "muddying" a liquid. One of the basic meanings of "smuta" was "disorder" or "muddle." By extension, this word also signified "agitation, disturbance, mutiny." In the sixteenth and seventeenth centuries, the Muscovite government meant something very specific when speaking of towns that had "become troubled" (*smutilis'*): that the subjects in question had rebelled against the tsar's authority. "Smutnoe vremia" (Time of Troubles) thus denoted a period of rebellion or mutinousness, as well as of confusion and turmoil. "Disturbed time," "rebellious age," and "troubled era" are all rough approximations. The early seventeenth century was shaken up, agitated, confused, and mutinous. Such is the literal meaning of the Russian term.[20]

The historical Troubles came by their name quite naturally, as an originally descriptive term evolved into an appellation. A Russian survey book dating from 1612–1613 recorded several items of the following nature: "the village of Elizarovo, and in it was a temple [i.e., church] of Nikolai the Wonder-Worker, and that temple burned down in the *smutnoe vremia* . . . and altogether [there are] 31 empty peasant places [in the district], and these peasants ran away in the *smutnoe vremia,* when villains [*vory*] came up to Nizhnii [Novgorod]."[21] Other contemporary sources featured variations on the same theme: *smutnoe priskorbnoe vremia* (disturbed, sorrowful time), *smutnoe i bezgosudarnoe vremia* (disturbed and sovereignless time), *smutnye gody* (disturbed years), and *smutnye leta* (disturbed years).[22] Words such as *gore* (grief, woe) and *beda* (calamity, disaster) were also used to characterize the period, but they did not figure into its eventual title.[23]

In the mid-seventeenth century, Grigorii Kotoshikhin, a Russian civil servant who had defected to Sweden, wrote a well-known description of Muscovy. Near the beginning of his book, he briefly alluded to "those troubled times" (*te smutnye vremena*) at the turn of the century. On this basis, historians have often mistakenly credited him with coining the name "Time of Troubles."[24] However, Kotoshikhin used the same description of "smutnoe vremia" (in the singular) to refer to the uprisings and crisis associated with a currency devaluation in 1656–1663. Other seventeenth-century authors also applied "smutnoe vremia" to that situation and then to the major Cossack rebellion led by Stenka Razin in 1670–1671.[25]

Unlike many other aspects of the national history, the Time of Troubles remained common knowledge in Russia for centuries, gaining rather than losing exposure in modern times. Literature, art, ceremony, and folklore all preserved and elaborated the notion of a severe and prolonged general crisis afflicting the entire nation, accompanied by warfare, grave uncertainty, and the collapse of the state. One seventeenth-century *bylina,* or long narrative folk song, wailed: "And for what did the Lord God become enraged against us / That the Lord God sent us the seducer / And villain Grishka Otrepiev the Defrocked?"[26]

In 1771 the Imperial Theater in St. Petersburg debuted Aleksandr Sumarokov's *Dimitrii the Pretender: A Tragedy.* Russia's national poet, the unmatched Aleksandr Pushkin, also took up the theme of the "first false Dmitrii," writing the poignant drama *Boris Godunov* in 1825. He judged it his best work.[27] A decade later, Mikhail Glinka composed his opera *Ivan Susanin,* also titled *A Life for the Tsar,* about the peasant hero credited with saving the life of Mikhail Romanov near the end of the Time of Troubles. In the second half of the nineteenth century, Modest Mussorgsky adapted Pushkin's play into the famous opera *Boris Godunov,* and Aleksandr Ostrovskii wrote his play *The Pretender Dmitrii and Vasilii Shuiskii.* Painters such as Ernest Lessner, Sergei Ivanov, and Vasilii Savinskii depicted scenes from Bolotnikov's revolt, the formation of the national militia, and other events of the Troubles. Since 1818 an impressive monument to Minin and Pozharskii, liberators of Moscow, has stood on Red Square in front of St. Basil's Cathedral. In other words, the heyday of Russian imperial culture did not pass before embedding the Smuta deeply into the national psychology and mythology.[28]

As it came to be understood, the Time of Troubles had been not merely a historical event, but rather a unique historical phenomenon with special features not always shared by other periods of extreme turmoil and suffering. The nineteenth-century historian Ivan Zabelin wrote: "*Smuta* represents a highly distinctive phenomenon. . . . It is only a deep shock [*glubokoe potriasenie*], a great 'reeling' [*velikoe 'shatanie'*] of the state itself."[29] Looking at the broad scope of Russian history, Zabelin considered extreme suffering among the people a very common phenomenon not sufficient in itself to constitute a "Time of Troubles." As E. V. Chistiakova explained at the close of the twentieth century, *S*mutnoe vremia stood as "a kind of symbol of breakdown, of the struggle of all against all, of the complete decomposition of authority in a country placed at the brink of ruin."[30]

Within historical literature, the Time of Troubles still figured as unquestionably "the stormiest epoch in the history of Russia" (*samaia burnaia epokha v istorii Rossii*) as late as 1911.[31] For decades already, officials of the tsar had been comparing their own rebellious age to the Smuta itself. Then in 1913, the Romanov dynasty's elaborate tercentennial celebrations pushed the Troubles to the very forefront of public attention. The Romanovs had begun to rule at the close of the Troubles, and they intended to capitalize on this fact in order to restore their decaying power. Period reenactments, pilgrimages to famous sites, numerous plays and books all canonized Russia's greatest moment, when unparalleled national heroism had conquered unimaginable national calamity.[32]

The last Romanovs had hoped to shore up their rule; instead, they ended up providing a model for its collapse. The First World War, the revolutions of 1917, and then the barbarous Civil War of 1917–1921 followed in brutal succession. Not surprisingly, many Russians both at home and in exile tried to make sense of the incredible turbulence and destruction by talking of a new "Time of Troubles." A number of published works demonstrate that the Smuta gained widespread currency as a paradigm for interpreting the ongoing disintegration of the state.[33]

Seventy years of communism brought no shortage of troubles, but it was the collapse of the Soviet Union that most reminded its citizens of the Smuta. In the 1990s ethnic conflicts, extortion, banditry, murder, and exploitation filled the void left by an ineffective government. An endless stream of articles in the Russian press, as well as other literature, drew direct comparisons to the original Time of Troubles.[34] For the third time Russia's state had collapsed, producing misery and uncertainty. In 2002 Russian Orthodox Patriarch Aleksii II joined the chorus of voices when he declared: "Surely the Time of Troubles brings to mind our [own] days, when attempts are being undertaken anew to Catholicize our compatriots, having forgotten about the thousand-year history of Orthodoxy in Rus'."[35]

In conjunction with the Orthodox Church, the government of the Russian Federation moved to refound the entire national mythos on themes from the Time of Troubles. In Soviet times the chief national holiday of November 7 commemorated the Bolshevik Revolution. In a feeble attempt to break with the past, President Boris Yeltsin simply renamed this the "Day of Accord and Reconciliation." The spectacular Soviet holiday metamorphosed into a mere day off from work, devoid of deeper significance and frequently ridiculed among the population. Then in 2005 Vladimir Putin moved the national holiday back a few days to November 4 and called it the "Day of National Unity." Reminiscent of observances under the old Romanov dynasty, this new festival commemorated the "salvation of the Russian land" at the end of the Time of Troubles. On November 4, 1612, a united Russian militia had finally recaptured the capital city of Moscow from the hated Polish-Lithuanian occupiers. Russia and Orthodoxy were saved.

At that time, Russians celebrated a miraculous victory and attributed it to the presumed efficacy of the Kazan ikon of the Mother of God. In Russian Orthodox tradition, November 4 (October 22 in Old Style) had been set apart for the commemoration of this particular image. In the twenty-first century, then, Orthodox Russians simultaneously observe a state holiday and a Church festival, both of which recall the same momentous event of the Time of Troubles of the early seventeenth century. The renewed observances on November 4 have stimulated patriotism and national pride, but also xenophobia and national-religious extremism.[36]

To date, the disasters of the post-Soviet period have not engendered the same magnitude of horrific suffering and slaughter as experienced during the first two Troubles. Still, the place of Smuta as a national rallying point continues to grow. The introduction of National Unity Day in 2005 featured the unveiling of a replica monument to Minin and Pozharskii in Nizhnii Novgorod. Artists of all styles, including Viktor Schupak, Pavel Ryzhenko, and Maria Podkopaeva, continue to find expression of their contemporary sentiments via interpretations of Smutnoe vremia. In 2007, Vladimir Khotinenko's blockbuster film *1612: Chronicles of the Time of Troubles* glorified a fantastic version of this history for a popular audience. Numerous new and reissued books on the period have surfaced to complement the media's frequent allusions to the Troubles.[37] Quadricentennial celebrations of the end of the Time of Troubles and the beginning of the Romanov dynasty are currently being planned for 2012–2013.[38]

What was this infamous Time of Troubles? Why has it become such a defining symbol for the current condition of Russia? What role did the Russian Orthodox Church play at the time? What, if anything, does that history tell us about the Church's post-Soviet resurgence?[39] These questions speak to the very heart of Russian national identity from the rise of Moscow during the twilight of the Middle Ages until today. Beyond question, the Troubles exerted a deep effect on the Russian psychology and left an indelible mark on the national consciousness. One may well imagine that tsar and Cossack, landowner and peasant, bureaucrat and revolutionary all paled at the sound of the words. Yet

1. Maria Podkopaeva, *V Smutnoe vremia* (*In Troubled Times*), 2008, oil on canvas. Reproduced by kind permission of the artist.

"Smutnoe vremia" clearly did not mean the same thing to everyone. For some, it denoted merely the rebelliousness of the lower classes, which had to be suppressed. For others, it conveyed some sense of the inexpressible suffering endured by the population. A few, especially during the second Time of Troubles, actually idealized the bloodbaths as a positive stage of "cleansing" and change. Nonetheless, the discordant voices all demonstrate that Russian identity cannot be separated from Smuta. The Time of Troubles left a legacy that continues to haunt Russia to this day.

Historiography of the Time of Troubles and the Russian Orthodox Church

Deeply engrained in the Russian consciousness, the Time of Troubles has produced a nearly unlimited flow of historiography. For four centuries, scholars have attempted to uncover the causes of the period's acute tensions and the true story of its tragedies. An equally large literature addresses the history of the Russian Orthodox Church, so important for all aspects of the Russian national experience. Nonetheless, their intersection—the history of the Russian Orthodox Church during the Time of Troubles—has never been studied thoroughly. The present book thus aims to remove a significant gap, to fill a critical void in the nation's history.

Standard Russian interpretations of the Time of Troubles arose during the imperial period, when the writing of national history acquired greater significance. Vasilii Tatishchev (1686–1750) and Mikhail Shcherbatov (1733–1790) both proposed that the mass uprisings of the period might have resulted from the imposition of serfdom at the end of the sixteenth century. The famous court historian of Alexander I, Nikolai Karamzin (1766–1826), emphasized foreign intervention and the loss of the tsar's authority. In his view, Boris Godunov served as "a sensible and solicitous Tsar" and "one of the most judicious Sovereigns in the world." At the same time this wise and legitimate ruler was a Russian Macbeth who had murdered to attain the throne. Karamzin assigned Tsar Boris much of the responsibility for the Troubles, remarking: "Was it not he . . . who more than all others furthered the disparaging of the throne, having mounted it as the murderer of a saint?" Karamzin followed seventeenth-century chroniclers in describing the "calamity" (*bedstvie*) that followed Boris's death in 1605 as God's just punishment of Russia.[40]

Karamzin's volumes on the Time of Troubles were his last, coming at the end of his life. By that time his place as a monumental interpreter of the Russian tradition had been assured. Concerning the earlier volumes of his *History of the Russian State,* Pushkin wrote: "The appearance of this book (appropriately) caused a sensation. . . . Ancient Russia seemed to have been discovered by Karamzin like America was by Columbus."[41] It was essentially Karamzin's version of events that Pushkin would eventually canonize in his classic drama *Boris Godunov.*[42] A long line of historians and other authors have repeated Karamzin's interpretations of numerous events, even when those interpretations stemmed from overly creative or fanciful utilization of the sources.[43]

The later nineteenth century saw unmatched development in Russian historiography generally, including scholarship on the Troubles. In his massive *History of Russia from the Most Ancient Times,* Sergei Soloviev (1820–1879) focused on the struggles between different groups within Russian society, particularly the Cossacks and the gentry. Nikolai Kostomarov (1817–1885) and Vasilii Kliuchevskii (1841–1911) each developed distinctive theories of how conflict among social classes had produced the Troubles. Kliuchevskii emphasized that the end of the old dynasty in 1598 had served as the catalyst or precondition for open struggle.[44]

The most renowned historian of the Time of Troubles, Sergei Platonov (1860–1933), created a synthetic model according to which the period consisted of three distinct phases: a dynastic crisis (1598–1606), a social struggle (1606–

1610), and a battle for national survival (1610–1613). Platonov wrote that "the top and bottom of Muscovite society lost the game, while the middle strata of society won it." He also pointed to longer-term causes, reexamining the oprichnina of Ivan IV and the crises of the later sixteenth century. Platonov's model remains influential to this day; a leading American textbook has long considered it "authoritative."[45]

The Bolshevik Revolution of 1917 altered trends in Russian historiography, infusing Marxist-Leninist thought into all forms of scholarship. Mikhail Pokrovskii (1868–1932) gained control of the central archives, postsecondary education, and the historical establishment. He allegedly used his power to eliminate rivals and create a new Soviet version of Russian history. George Vernadsky even claimed: "By his orders, a series of outstanding Russian historians were tortured to death in prison and exile (Platonov, Liubavskii, Rozhdestvenskii, Vasenko, Zaozerskii)."[46] Unsurprisingly, Pokrovskii's own textbook on Russian history asserted that the Time of Troubles represented an example of Marxist class warfare. Moreover, the supposed heroes Hermogen, Minin, and Pozharskii had merely displayed "a special form of class self-preservation." In reality, Pokrovskii asserted, the patriarch had not even written the letters that circulated in his name.[47]

Subsequent Soviet historians, including Ivan Smirnov, Aleksandr Zimin, and Vadim Koretskii, followed Pokrovskii's rejection of the term "Time of Troubles" and instead wrote about Russia's "First Peasant War." In their view, the Bolotnikov rebellion and other uprisings constituted a revolutionary movement against serfdom and the oppression of the upper classes. In a sense the older suggestions of Tatishchev and Shcherbatov had now been pressed into the service of modern ideological motives. This quasi-Marxist model dominated historiography within the Soviet Union until its dissolution in 1991; it still continues to influence many academics.[48]

However, the post-Soviet period has seen the emergence of a new interpretation of the Time of Troubles as Russia's "First Civil War." Ruslan Skrynnikov and Aleksandr Stanislavskii used this term in an attempt to move away from the "peasant war" model. In 2001 the American scholar Chester Dunning produced the most comprehensive reevaluation of the period since Platonov's classic work. In *Russia's First Civil War,* Dunning argued that the uprisings of the period had numerous causes but were fueled primarily by a genuine belief in Dmitrii as the legitimate, divinely anointed tsar. In his view, popular support for Dmitrii (in whatever guise he might appear) cut right through social distinctions and "united diverse elements of Russian society." There was in fact no "social revolution" and no peasant rebellion against serfdom.[49]

The causes and consequences of the Time of Troubles are likely to remain controversial. Serfdom and economic depression no doubt played their role, as did the all-important question of the tsar's legitimacy. The different schools of interpretation have resulted from emphasizing some one factor at the expense of another. Did rebels of the period actually believe they were supporting the legitimate, divinely authorized tsar—or did they use this rhetoric merely as a front for violently expressing their true grievances?[50] The Troubles apparently included examples of both types of revolt, as well as many that combined these two justifications into one. The explosion of discontent into chaotic and nearly constant warfare at least tells us that masses of people chafed at the situation in Russia. But who defined the good of the society? What was right and what was wrong?

Conjointly with the state, the Russian Orthodox Church held a monopoly on truth in Muscovite society. Ever since the Kievan adoption of Eastern Christianity in 988 or 989, the East Slavs had defined themselves in relationship to Orthodoxy. In Muscovy religion was inseparable from politics and provided the raison d'être and ideology of the state. Orthodoxy influenced every aspect of life, from literature and art to territorial exploration and prison wardenry. Although the extent to which the common people understood and adopted Christian teachings remains debatable, Russia was nothing if not Orthodox. In his classic interpretation of Russian culture, James Billington chose "the icon and the axe" as the two quintessential symbols of peasant life.[51] The axe, an everyday implement, cut the wood for the ikon, or holy painting, which symbolized Eastern Orthodox Christian civilization.

The Time of Troubles occurred within this political and cultural setting, so any interpretation of the period must grapple with the role of the Russian Church and Orthodoxy to some extent. Tatishchev wrote of the competition between ecclesiastic and secular landowners for peasant laborers at the turn of the seventeenth century; some later historians followed him in pointing to the Church's vast landholdings as an important factor in the crisis. Platonov began his classic work by describing the dominant role of the Solovetskii and other monasteries in the northern regions of the Russian state. Virtually all histories of the Troubles mention accusations of ecclesiastic speculation in foodstuffs during the Famine, Tsar Dmitrii's alleged failure to observe Orthodox customs, famous battles at monasteries, and the inspirational letters of Patriarch Hermogen.[52] In other words, standard histories of the period mention the Church and Orthodoxy frequently but incidentally; none of them considers the history of the Russian Orthodox Church during the Time of Troubles as a topic for investigation in its own right.

General histories of the Russian Orthodox Church also fail to present an adequate scholarly interpretation of its activity during the Troubles. The largest and best such works were written in the nineteenth century by Russian clerics and fervent Orthodox believers. These authors naturally adopted an almost invariably positive attitude toward the Church and tended to read the historical documents too uncritically. In addition, their primary interest lay in recounting the religious accomplishments of the Church's top hierarchs and other famous figures. As the introduction to a recent edition of one such work stated, "The history of the Church is first of all the history of the deeds and feats of the holy righteous men and zealous heroes."[53] By contrast, the enormous business activity of monasteries—which probably consumed a far greater amount of time and labor than working miracles, canonizing saints, or writing liturgies—generally merited little or no space. Several other histories of the Russian Orthodox Church either do not cover the Time of Troubles or contain at best a minimal amount of information.[54]

Metropolitan Makarii Bulgakov's twelve-volume *History of the Russian Church* represents the premier example of this kind of ecclesiastic historiography. Makarii assigned two roles to the Church, civil (or political) and religious, and he intermingled them in his account. In both instances, however, "the Church" meant essentially the heads of the Church. Makarii's chapter on the Time of Troubles was entitled "The First Three Patriarchs in Moscow and the Period Between Patriarchs" (*Tri pervye patriarkha v Moskve i mezhdupatriarshestvo*). Moreover, as a Church hierarch himself, Makarii occasionally included unflattering details but was inclined to justify the morally questionable actions of those he studied. For example, he conceded that Patriarch Iyov (also Iov, Iev, Job) may not have exercised impartiality in maneuvering behind the scenes to get Boris Godunov "elected" to the throne in 1598. Nonetheless, he argued that Iyov's actions accorded with the "general consciousness"—thus failing to explain why such strenuous efforts were needed in the first place, or why an apparent consensus would validate the patriarch's actions, especially since at least some voiced agreement only "unwillingly." Makarii further posited that Iyov could not have known about any "secret" wrongdoings, such as politically motivated murder, that Boris may have committed—thus belying the admittedly close association between the two men.[55]

Another creation of the mid-nineteenth century, Count Mikhail Tolstoi's *Stories from the History of the Russian Church,* adopted a similar tone. Tolstoi did not achieve the same level of scholarship as Makarii; his work was derivative and intended for a general audience. The *Stories* consisted mainly of tidbits that would please an Orthodox Christian readership: religiously inspired acts of charity, the physical and spiritual expansion of Orthodoxy, the deeds of saints. Tolstoi structured his narrative around political events, blithely accepting the witness of official documents and earlier historians. Following Karamzin, he described Boris Godunov as a regicide who had nonetheless been legitimately selected by "all the land" to rule, and then proceeded to quote the tsar's religiously laden interactions with Patriarch Iyov.[56]

More recent scholarship has furnished two additional categories of works related to the history of the Church during the Troubles. First, monographs and anthologies on religion in early modern Russia frequently cite the Time of Troubles as an enormously consequential moment in history, but with little or no consideration of the period itself. In his *Religion and Society in Russia,* Paul Bushkovitch termed the Time of Troubles a "watershed" separating two forms of Muscovite religiosity. Regardless, his presentation largely skipped the period *per se,* focusing instead on what came before and after. The same approach characterizes several other valuable collections of articles on Russian religion and culture.[57] The complexity of the Smuta and of the Church itself appears to have deterred historians from tackling the question head on.

The second group of recent works encompasses a number of articles produced by Russian scholars on specific topics related to the Church during the Troubles. In general these have been highly specialized studies treating such problems as the religious symbolism of a particular ceremony or the religious question in the negotiations concerning Prince Wladyslaw's candidacy for the Muscovite throne. Isolated chapters on the Time of Troubles in broader surveys also contribute much of interest but do not aspire to a complete history of the Church during the Troubles. The work of the Ukrainian scholar Vasilii Ulianovskii deserves special mention: his recent book *Smutnoe vremia* uniquely treats a range of questions regarding church-state relations in the years 1604–1606.[58]

In sum, an actual history of the Russian Orthodox Church during the Time of Troubles has, surprisingly, never been written.[59] Histories of the Troubles include some mention of the Church; histories of the Church contain some discussion of the Troubles. A variety of other works have nibbled at the edges of the topic or contributed important pieces of the puzzle. The goal of this book is to trace Russia's most important institution throughout the period of the country's greatest crisis. Such a task demands more than simply highlighting a few well-known events, which has often been done, or even examining selected problems in detail, which some scholars have done quite beneficially. The goal here is to paint a more comprehensive picture of the overall history of the Church during the Troubles, building upward from the details of surviving primary sources.

Difficult Questions

The history of the Russian Orthodox Church during the Time of Troubles alternately fascinates, stuns, alarms, and confuses. The first problem faced by the researcher is the labyrinthine quandary of how to approach the primary sources. The documentary remnants of the early seventeenth century yield nothing like a solid, secure, straightforward foundation for writing a well-rounded history of the Church. They lie instead at the opposite end of the spectrum: highly fragmentary, mostly lacking, and often unreliable or contradictory to boot. The complicated and deficient nature of the sources necessarily affects the questions that can reasonably be asked and answered about the history of the Church during the Troubles. The researcher must proceed with caution and creativity, much like a canny detective sifting meager clues and mulling the minutest of details in order to arrive at the truth. Certainty cannot always be attained; often it is possible only to hypothesize about this history.

The relative scarcity of sources has resulted partly from unfortunate events such as the great Moscow fire of 1626, which destroyed almost all the archives of the central government agencies (*prikazy*). As Konstantin Petrov remarked, "Documents of the sixteenth century and earlier that have been preserved until the present time represent, without exaggeration, only the pitiful remnants of the central departments' extensive record-keeping."[60] The chaotic nature of the Time of Troubles also hindered the production and preservation of documents, meaning that sources for this period are further reduced. Extant archival documents for the fifteen years 1598–1613 are considerably less plentiful than for either 1583–1598 or 1613–1628.[61]

Documents concerning the history of the Church during the Troubles include the written records of government decrees, business transactions, usufructuary rights, property boundaries, tax exemptions, donations to monasteries, legal appeals, liturgical matters, letters, speeches, wills, and travels. These kinds of sources deal with very specific and usually economic matters—for example, the sale of a cow, a monastery's ownership over some villages, the right to collect salt from a given mine, or the collection of dues from peasants. In total, the documents number one thousand or a little more. This sum should be placed in the context of a historical setting that included several thousand ecclesiastic institutions: hierarchical establishments from the patriarch on down, monasteries large and small, and local parishes. In other words, statistically we do not have even one document for every Church institution that existed during the Troubles. Moreover, the vast majority of extant documents concern only the fifteen or twenty largest institutions of the time (the patriarchate and major monasteries). Thousands of smaller monasteries and parishes are not mentioned at all in existing sources from the Time of Troubles.[62]

The translator G. Edward Orchard wrote, "The only bright spot in the almost unrelieved gloom [of the Time of Troubles] is in the realm of historical writing, in which the authors explored what lessons the dreadful events of past years held for Russia. . . . The accounts of foreigners who were present in Muscovy during these years admirably complement these annalistic writings."[63] The catastrophes of the Troubles did at least produce some extraordinarily colorful historical tales and stories, as well as biographical writings and even prophetic visions. Many of these texts represented significant innovations in the Russian historiographic tradition. Both Russians and foreigners—including Polish-Lithuanian commanders, French and German mercenary captains, and a Dutch merchant apprentice—felt compelled to record what they saw and heard during the tumultuous period. The historian must be grateful for these narratives, but their biases and frequent contradictions present another difficulty in deciphering history.[64]

The fact that perhaps ninety percent of archival documentation related to the Church during the Troubles concerns strictly economic matters means that this activity must be taken seriously. Although one might prefer a greater wealth of religious, literary, and cultural texts, honesty requires consideration of what exists rather than what one would like to exist. Yet the potential disappointment caused by this imbalance in the sources is offset by the discovery that ecclesiastic economic activity was an enormously important factor in the Troubles. Monasteries in particular contributed to the economic environment within which the Troubles occurred, and their trading pursuits influenced business patterns all through the period. Ecclesiastic economic interests also dictated political expediencies. These issues must be investigated. At the same time, it is necessary to avoid too facile a conclusion that it was "all about money."

Contemporary political documents were composed almost exclusively for propagandistic (i.e., publicity) purposes, a circumstance that forces reconsideration of the information they contain. All too often in historiography these documents have been cited as direct evidence of what happened during the Time of Troubles. In fact, however, they furnish highly selective or even distorted reflections of actual history. The researcher must read these sources "against the grain," wringing from them drops of evidence that actually run contrary to the original authorial or textual intention.[65] The same principle applies to many narrative sources, which were often compiled retrospectively in later decades.

During the Time of Troubles, the Russian Orthodox Church embraced both central and regional hierarchies, hundreds of monasteries and convents, thousands of churches or "temples," and (theoretically at least) millions of faithful Orthodox Russians. Its purview touched on everything from prayers to agriculture, from commerce to scholarship, from music to warfare, and from missionary expeditions to prison management. The difficulty of covering so many realms of activity on the basis of very fragmentary sources likely represents the principal reason that no one has yet produced a complete study of the topic in four centuries, despite widespread recognition of its significance. The sources unfortunately do not permit us as panoramic a view as we would like. They do, however, offer some glimpses or clues into each sphere of life. It is therefore possible as well as necessary to write a history of the Church during the Troubles that goes beyond merely a description of the top hierarchs and their activity.[66]

The period of Smutnoe vremia lies on a fault line in Russian history. The next great event would be the Church Schism (*Raskol*) of the mid-seventeenth century. A well-known historian of that crisis, Pierre Pascal, remarked: "We must go to the Time of Troubles to discover the germ of the great rupture [of the Schism]. The material and moral catastrophe vividly felt by the entire nation engendered an appetite for reforms."[67] A more recent historian of the Raskol, Georg Michels, has written: "It is not surprising that the Russian Orthodox Church became a significant target of popular hostility during the second half of the seventeenth century. The church was then one of the most vigorous institutions of Muscovite power under the new Romanov dynasty, for it had emerged from the Time of Troubles with its power base intact."[68]

What actually happened during the Time of Troubles to set the stage for the Schism and other socioreligious tensions in the second half of the seventeenth century? What precisely changed in the relationship between the Church and its people? Did the national disaster of the Troubles alter Russian mentality and faith? Put simply, what makes the Time of Troubles a watershed for Russian religion, culture, and society?

The sixteenth century represented the formative period of Russian national mentality, of a worldview that continues to influence the country to this day. In the words of one historian, "'Russian' history (as opposed to 'Rus' history) really began in the sixteenth century."[69] Yet at the most critical moment, the Troubles diverted the new stream of Russian ideology into unforeseen channels, both official and popular. Ecclesiastic ideologues hastily improvised to maintain the government's power in the midst of catastrophe; popular leaders and thinkers removed from the center of power appropriated select aspects of the new ideology for their own ends. When the dust settled, Russia had found a national identity that would both propel it into the modern age and also lay the seeds of unending conflict between elites and masses, and between conservatives and reformers.

Pascal characterized his entire investigation as an answer to the simple question, "What [was] the Schism?" (*qu'est-ce que le raskol?*).[70] Michels readdressed this same problem; his revised interpretation of history stemmed largely from a differing definition of the Raskol.[71] One may just as well ask, what was the Russian Orthodox Church during the Time of Troubles? The present study represents a reevaluation of the very meaning of the Russian Church and of Orthodoxy at this time in history. What was the Church's real place and role in Russian society? What do the primary sources tell us about ecclesiastic decisions and actions during a period of crisis? And how did the Russian people view Orthodoxy?

The Smuta hit the Russian nation with such force that its memory has remained vivid for centuries. Striking in its multivalence, the term became a symbol that still resonates strongly in the national culture today, much like the destruction of the Second Temple in Jewish memory. Yet extended periods of great suffering were not the only perceived links between Russians and Jews. The Time of Troubles took place at a time when, in the national-religious mindset, Russia *was* Israel, God's chosen people. This crucial belief provides the starting point for understanding the dark abyss of the Troubles.

CHAPTER ONE

Russia as "Israel"

The Muscovite Church-State

> The all-merciful Lord God who chose you as our sovereign—just as an-
> ciently Moses and Joshua and other liberators of Israel—may the Lord
> grant you as the liberator of us, the New Israel.
>
> —Patriarch Iyov to Tsar Boris, 1598[1]

> Moscow is the capital not merely of a state. It is the capital of history. And
> I did something highly foolish in leaving it: I fell out of history.
>
> —Aleksandr Zinoviev, *Homo Sovieticus,* 1982[2]

In the sixteenth and seventeenth centuries, Russia consciously
portrayed itself as the "New Israel" or simply "Israel." This self-image
acted as a constant lens through which all political realities and historical
events could be interpreted. In a clear and understandable manner, it linked
Russia's current realities to the whole of biblical and sacred history. The
notion of Russia as Israel also influenced the internal organization of the
country and affected its perspective on foreign relations. During the Time
of Troubles, the New Israel ideology readily provided a way to make sense
even of the unbearable disaster all around, and it grew in popularity as
a literary trope.[3] Although sometimes overlooked in historical studies,
Russia's national identification with ancient Israel courses through the
writings of both church and state and represents a key to the mentalité
of Russian society at the time. As shown in this chapter, these features of

Muscovy's ideological landscape played a leading role in shaping attitudes as the nation entered the Smuta.

What did it mean for Russia to "be Israel"? Within the Orthodox Christian context, this phrase unambiguously symbolized the exclusive, special status of God's "chosen people." The implications of such a claim were numerous and enormous. Like the sons of Israel in the Tanakh (Hebrew Bible), the Russian establishment saw itself as divinely "set apart" from surrounding ungodly and often enemy tribes. The meaning and substance of all human history could be found in the relationship between God and his people; thus, Moscow was the capital or center of history. All of life comprised a struggle between the "right way" (Orthodoxy) and various wrong ways, and so Russia's wars against Catholics, Lutherans, Muslims, and pagans were in reality God's wars. The Almighty was known to reward and punish his people according to their actions: piety therefore brought prosperity and victory, but any deviance from Orthodoxy invited calamity. Each of these components of the Russian worldview represented a "transposition" or altered reflection of earlier ideas contained in the Jewish Torah (Pentateuch).

Muscovy's lack of firm ideational and practical distinctions between religion and politics was another important corollary of the New Israel theory. In biblical history, the Davidic kingdom and Levitical priesthood had constituted separate institutions, but they were intended to function conjointly in pursuit of the same overall ends. Similarly, the Byzantine notion of "symphony" conceived of *sacerdotium* and *imperium* as indivisible: the warp and the woof of government, or two sides of the same coin. One scholar of the Empire has remarked, perhaps too optimistically: "No one today would still talk about Church and state as two institutions, or concepts, which common sense or history have conclusively taught us to distinguish. . . . The state is sacred and the Church is power."[4] According to James Billington, "In Muscovy the two were even more closely intertwined," without even the pragmatic divisions that had developed over the course of Byzantine history.[5] Donald Ostrowski disagrees, citing examples from the fifteenth to the seventeenth centuries that illustrate a certain mutual respect for distinct spheres of activity, ranging from temporal to ecclesiastic.[6] Yet in either case, church and state were seen to work together in harmony, with overlapping goals if not always jurisdictions. Indeed, the raison d'être of Russia's state could be described as religious—the preservation and expansion of Orthodoxy—and that of its church as political— the right ordering of the realm. Muscovy boasted not only a state church but also a church state; in Dunning's words, it had "no concept of a secular state."[7]

Acceptance of this unitary church-state model is critical for understanding Russian society on its own terms. All too often a Western mindset of "church vs. state" has distorted scholarship on Orthodox Russia. Many scholars have termed the Russian Church an "obedient handmaiden" of the state or tsar, that is to say, a fully subordinate servant.[8] The Soviet historian Nikolai Nikolskii proclaimed: "The patriarch and the bishops were, in essence, simple bureaucrats of the tsar. . . . Supremacy in the church in fact belonged in all regards to the tsar, and not the patriarch."[9] More recently, Pierre Gonneau repeated the very common understanding that the "Russian Church [was] always in the position of Caesar's servant," though he views it as breaking out of this role during the Time of Troubles.[10]

It is true that Russian heads of state (grand princes and tsars) did possess the physical power to adjudicate ecclesiastical matters or to get rid of troublesome heads of the Church (metropolitans and patriarchs). In 1568–1569, after Metropolitan Filipp repeatedly refused to bless Ivan IV in protest against atrocities of the oprichnina, the tsar had him deposed and probably ordered his subsequent strangling.[11] However, the reality of brute force did not mean that the "state" was dominant and the "church" subordinate. Church and state were at times inseparable, overlapping, or indistinguishable. Thus, to say that the Russian Church "failed" to obtain "independence" from the state distorts history. The Orthodox Church neither desired nor pursued something so antithetical to the goals of its own political ideology. That would have been anathema, unthinkable. On the contrary, the Russian Church sought not separation but rather near coalescence with its Orthodox state—that is, a constant symphony or joint-power arrangement. According to Catherine Evtuhov, even the first revolution of 1917 brought only "*unwilling* acceptance by the church of separation from the state."[12]

A look at Muscovite political rhetoric might even suggest that the church, or Orthodoxy, dominated the state. In the Orthodox mindset, the church—far from being inferior—actually overlay the state and furnished the principles that governed the state. All political actions had to be couched in terms of religion.[13] The tsar might be able to depose the patriarch, but he still bowed to him as "father." Vladimir Valdenberg, author of a study on the limits of the tsar's authority, argued that even the dreaded Ivan IV "recognize[d] something standing above the tsar—the Orthodox faith."[14] This may or may not have been the case; but the tsar reigned as God's ostensible representative on earth—and therefore had at least to appear pious.[15] In Russia of the sixteenth and seventeenth centuries, Orthodox Christianity thus represented a kind of official ideology on which both the system of tsarism and the authority of each individual tsar relied.

The old conundrum of the pen and the sword has some relevance here. Although the state wielded more physical and short-term power, the other partner in this holy or unholy marriage commanded greater ideological and long-term influence. The recent resurgence of the church in the post-Soviet period continues to demonstrate the staying power of Russian Orthodoxy. In the Muscovite period, Russia's theo-political system intended not a competition or conflict between church and state, but rather a harmonious cooperation and complete conjunction of interests. A long process of adoption and adaption of ideas and practices from earlier societies had given this unique politico-religious system the form it would assume during the Time of Troubles.

The Historical Development of Muscovite National-Religious Ideology

Russia did not invent its claim to be Israel. Christianity as it developed in the Roman Empire was supersessionist, positing a replacement of Israel by the Church. The Jews, according to this theory, were God's chosen people in the past, but having rejected Christ, they had now been rejected by God. The Christian collective stood in the place of Israel as God's new people. This "New Israel" claimed to inherit favorable biblical promises and covenants originally applicable to the first Israel. The focus of sacred history had shifted from one people to another, but a certain continuity was said to overlay the disjunction. Despite occasional modification, this theology of replacement has been foundational for most variations of Christianity, both Eastern and Western, ever since.

In Russia, the New Israel doctrine assumed a unique form due to the peculiarities of historical development. Instead of a general theory describing all Christians or "true" Christians, the balancing notions of replacement and continuity fused into a vision of the Muscovite state as God's Israel in the present. Somewhat unusually for Christians, Muscovite literati[16] accepted not only the blessings but also the curses of the Torah—warnings to the original Israel against disobedience—as directly and literally applicable to their society. With the possible or partial exception of Ethiopia, no other state in medieval and early modern times appears to have held such a view as its official and exclusive ideology. New Israel or "replacement" theology did influence all Christian societies to some extent. In Russia, however, the confluence of church and state produced a "self-image" governed by exclusive identification with ancient Israel.[17]

How did this happen? To the Muscovite mind, the line of sacred continuity followed a zigzag path from the Middle East to the north. Human history began in the Garden of Eden, but the first chosen people had its capital at Jerusalem. From there the mantle of destiny passed to Rome, center of Christianity. Not for long, though, as the Western Empire disintegrated and the New Rome, Constantinople, assumed its role as the standard-bearer of Orthodoxy. In some interpretations, Byzantium endowed Kiev with a special charisma. Yet the latter fell to the Mongols in 1240 and the former to the Ottoman Turks in 1453. Emerging from under the suzerainty of the Qipchaq Khanate in the fifteenth century, Moscow gradually laid claim to a special inheritance from both Byzantium and Kiev. By the time of the Smuta, Russians who called themselves "New Israel" regarded themselves as the continuation, and possibly even the culmination, of a consistent supernatural plan stretching back millennia.[18] Each stage of history had contributed something to their composite worldview, a process worth tracing briefly.

When Constantine I convened the Council of Nicaea in 325 CE, the specific question to be decided was when to celebrate *Pascha,* originally the Jewish Passover. This controversy over dates had been ongoing since at least the second century. Much more was at stake, however. Constantine and his allies within the church wanted to create an official, standardized, unified religion clearly separate from Judaism and just as clearly linked to the state. The impetus for such a move had also been building for centuries within Gentile Christianity; already in the mid-first century Saul or Paul had argued against an early form of separatism from Judaism.[19] "Like some heavenly messenger of God," Eusebius said, the Roman Emperor entered the assembly at Nicaea and greeted the bishops in Latin. In the ensuing discussion, however, he tried out his Greek in order to appeal to the great majority, who hailed from the Eastern half of the Empire. The bishops, at first viciously divided, were reportedly swayed by his arguments. All endorsed his judgment: "Let us then have nothing in common with the detestable Jewish crowd; for we have received from our Saviour a different way."[20]

By marking a clear departure from biblical custom and institutionalizing the distinct Christian Easter observance, Constantine entrenched three important principles that would influence all subsequent Christianity and especially the Muscovite politico-religious system. First, he linked church and state, presiding personally over the resolution of a religious dispute seen as politically important.[21] Over a thousand years later, Muscovite grand princes and tsars would also convene church councils to adjudicate the religious disputes of their day. Second, Constantine used "passionate hatred of the Jews" and of all Jewish practices as the deciding factor in a controversy over religious observance.[22] One perceives echoes of this policy in Muscovy's general anti-Jewish orientation, in the condemnation of some heretics as "Judaizers" in the late fifteenth and early sixteenth centuries, and in the nearly complete exclusion of Jews from Russia's borders until the Partitions of Poland at the end of the eighteenth century.[23] Third, the emperor formally established a mechanism for determining religious truth. In a letter sent "to the churches" after the Council, he wrote: "Whatever is determined in the holy assemblies of the bishops is to be regarded as indicative of the Divine will."[24] Like rabbinic pronouncements a couple of centuries earlier, this statement meant that an official council of hierarchs could authoritatively redefine the tradition, even if its judgments revised or altered the plain sense of written scriptures.[25] Muscovite Church councils had less freedom to revise fundamental doctrines, being circumscribed by earlier Orthodox rulings. Nonetheless, their judgments seemed just as critical to contemporaries and also claimed the status of authoritative truth.

The basic Constantinian theory of government that would eventually hold sway in Muscovy received further development in the Eastern Roman, or Byzantine Empire. Justinian I (r. 527–565), who regarded himself as a second Constantine, incorporated the guiding concept of *sumfonia* or "symphony" into his famous law code. Denoting literally a harmony or confluence of sound, as in music, in the political realm this word came to signify the official theory of joint church-state government. According to this doctrine, church and state had distinct domains but collectively represented a seamless whole, inseparable as two sides of a single fabric. If both church and state were ordered well, then in theory no conflict could arise between them. Practice, of course, might tell a different story. Ostrowski actually regards discord as part of the normal ebb and flow of the symphonic system, "one of the bases of harmony between Church and State," in that the head of the church and other "wise advisers" had the obligation to speak up against bad policies and evil rulers.[26] "But antagonism between the *imperium* and the *sacerdotium*," as George Ostrogorsky noted, "was not characteristic of Byzantium, where there was on the whole a close and intimate relationship between State and Church, a fundamental interdependence of the Orthodox Empire and the Orthodox Church which together formed a single political and ecclesiastical entity."[27]

The resonance of the "symphonic" concept in the East represents a principal difference from the West, where after the fall of Rome religious and political authority no longer coincided in a single, unified entity. Eastern Christianity thus remained truer to the original Constantinian conception.[28] According to George Majeska, historian of Byzantium and Muscovy:

> The new Christian Roman, or Byzantine, Empire was conceived as the physical counterpart of the Christian church, the body, as it were, of which the soul was the church. The state's existence was justified by its role as protector of the church, the Christian community that was seen as essentially coextensive with the empire. Church and empire were assumed to have the same membership and the same goal, saving souls.[29]

A combination of war, trade, diplomacy, and missionary activity spread the religion and ideology of Byzantium to Slavic peoples in the Balkan and Black Sea regions. By the time Prince Volodimer of Kiev (Kyiv) chose Eastern Orthodox Christianity in 988–989, *Slavia Orthodoxa* included a more or less comprehensive, ready-made political and religious system, with theology that would draw largely from John Chrysostom.[30] According to a famous legend, Volodimer's envoys said, "We knew not whether we were in heaven or on earth," when confronted with the sensory beauty of Hagia Sophia in Constantinople. For the East Slavs, this alluring Orthodox aura contrasted sharply with what they perceived as the more restrictive religions of Judaism, Catholicism, and Islam. The last of these would have even required abstention from drinking alcohol, which constituted "the joy of the Rus'"! The neighboring Khazars had adopted Judaism a century or two earlier, but their steppe empire was already crumbling. Moreover, the belief that God had banished the Jews from their historical homeland made that religion less appealing politically.[31] In a move that would eventually alter the course of world history, the Rus' prince therefore chose to make his people bearers of the "Greek faith," Eastern Orthodox Christianity. Ironically, a Jewish Khazarian tale may possibly have furnished the prototype for this Rus' narrative on choosing Orthodoxy, and Khazar institutions almost certainly exerted an influence on Rus' political culture.[32]

The new Orthodox metropolitanate of Kiev did not fit seamlessly into the structure of the Constantinople patriarchate, to which it was formally subservient. The Rus' state boasted its own national government, language, and ethnicity and did not look only to Byzantium for inspiration. According to Thomas Noonan, "the Rus' grand princes of Kiev . . . aspired to be recognized as successors of the Khazar *khagans*."[33] Their territory was geographically distinct and much larger than Constantinople's sixty or seventy other dioceses. Even from the beginning of their Christian history, the East Slavs had, in Jaroslav Shchapov's words, "a national state church organization" that stood out from among its peers.[34] These realities naturally stimulated a somewhat more independent orientation on the part of the Kievan Church vis-à-vis Constantinople.[35]

The first native Rus' metropolitan, Ilarion, made a decisive conceptual step in promoting the equality of the Kievan church-state as a Christian regime in its own right, rather than a dependency of Byzantium. During the reign of Iaroslav the Wise in the mid-eleventh century, he delivered his famous "Sermon on Law and Grace" (*Slovo o zakone i blagodati*). The occasion for this grand speech may have been the dedication of Kiev's own Cathedral of St. Sophia. Ilarion's composition demonstrated a mastery of the guiding principles of Eastern Orthodoxy and an ability to innovate within that tradition for specific political ends. Appealing to theology, history, and (sometimes misquoted) scripture, Ilarion asserted a new place for the Rus' people in the community of Christian nations.[36]

After Ilarion, the church continued literary and ideological endeavors aimed at distinguishing and elevating the Rus' polity. The *Primary Chronicle,* compiled by Orthodox monks in the eleventh and early twelfth centuries, developed the nascent national-religious identity of the East Slavs. Modeled after Byzantine chronicles, this important document—still our chief written source on Kievan Rus'—promoted a particularist vision of history. According to Janet Martin: "Like Hilarion's Sermon on Law and Grace, the Primary Chronicle conveyed the pride and self-awareness of a new nation, which by recording its history was proclaiming its place in the Christian community."[37]

At this relatively early stage Russian Orthodoxy could already be considered a national glue imbuing the state with cohesion and purpose and differentiating it from its neighbors. As Robert Crummey remarked, "Long before Moscow emerged as the political centre of north-east Russia, the Eastern Orthodox Church directed the spiritual and cultural life of the nation. *Being Russian meant, more than anything else, adhering to the Orthodox faith.*"[38] Although aspects of paganism would continue to flourish among segments of the population for centuries, the symphonic church-state system had taken root in Rus'. Any coherent image of the Rus', or Russian, nation had already become inconceivable without the Russian Orthodox Church.

The sack of Kiev in 1240 and consequent subjugation of Rus' by the Mongols presented the church with the basic question of what to do in the new situation. Political overlordship by foreign nonbelievers challenged the entire ideology of an Orthodox church-state. According to Charles Halperin,

"Russia had never before been subjugated by an alien, infidel power and lacked a historical theory to account for it."[39] In this thorny context the church decided to adopt a pragmatic approach. Instead of resisting Mongol suzerainty, it cooperated fully with the conquerors. In exchange for this support, the Mongols granted ecclesiastic institutions considerable privileges that greatly enhanced their economic and general standing.[40] To a certain extent, the same "symphonic" relationship continued to exist between church and state, despite the non-Orthodoxy of the Qipchaq Khanate.

Church writers also suppressed or omitted the uncomfortable political reality as much as possible, adopting what Halperin has called an "ideology of silence."[41] That may be a slight exaggeration. Ostrowski prefers the subtler term "conspiracy of silence."[42] David Goldfrank similarly suggests calling the Muscovite approach a "strategy of selective silence." In his words, "the self-contained, closed sphere of Rus Christianity, which persisted for centuries, enabled some of the Orthodox writers to treat the Mongol overlordship as a secondary matter."[43] Ostrowski additionally informs us that, surprisingly, "no chronicle entry that has an anti-Tatar bias can be dated to the period between 1252 and 1448."[44] The topic of foreign domination and oppression did appear in many sermons and chronicle entries of the Mongol period. However, it was generally parsed as divine punishment, essentially for not being Orthodox enough. Byzantium had preserved and passed on the notion that God's relations with the "New Israel" could result in punishments of this type.[45] Later, during the Time of Troubles, this form of historical interpretation would become even more pronounced.

Meanwhile, new currents of thought were stirring in the South Slavic lands. "At the end of the fourteenth century, a writer at the Bulgarian court hailed his royal patron, John Asen Alexander, as a Christian emperor (tsar) and called his capital, Trnovo, the new imperial city."[46] This Bulgarian innovation marked a further stage in the development of Orthodox continuity theories, also termed *translatio imperii,* the translation or transfer of empire. The Byzantine Empire still claimed to have succeeded Israel and Rome as the center of history. Yet Byzantium was in decline, and this opened up new opportunities for competition among Orthodox states.

Bulgaria's claim to inheritance of the mantle of destiny would influence the Russians, who had already begun to develop their own theory of *translatio.* As various local princes struggled for preeminence, the Rus' metropolitanate moved its residential headquarters out of Kiev to Vladimir in 1299–1300, and then from Vladimir to Moscow in 1322. Some historians believe that ecclesiastics soon developed a succession theory, positing continuity from Kiev to Vladimir to Moscow. In other words, each move represented not a break with the past, but rather a divinely ordained stage in a flawless historical progression. Others dispute this interpretation, arguing instead that the chronicles show an initial attempt at "eradicating it [Kiev] from historical memory."[47] In either case Muscovy's eventual formulation of its own identity would clearly incorporate both the Kievan heritage and a claim to inherit the divine callings of Israel, Rome, and Byzantium.[48]

Several major events of the mid-fifteenth century coincided to catalyze this crucial shift. In 1439, within the context of continual military losses to the Ottoman Turks, Constantinople explored a union with the Papacy. Viewed from Moscow, this act compromised its integrity as the leading center of Eastern Orthodox Christianity. In 1448, the Russian Church declared independence, meaning that its metropolitan would no longer be appointed formally by the patriarch of Constantinople. Then in 1453 the Byzantine capital succumbed to the Ottomans, who transformed the famous Hagia Sophia cathedral into a mosque. With Bulgaria and most of the rest of the Balkans also subjugated to Muslim rule, the nascent Muscovite state emerged as the only Orthodox church-state remaining in the entire world. Nowhere else did the symphonic system exist; no other known state preserved the "true faith." Russia gradually came to view itself as the lone "Israel" in a world of infidels.[49]

Other factors also combined propitiously to enable the introduction of a "messianist" flavor into the Russian ideological mindset, that is to say, the belief in a special national chosenness, redemptive purpose in universal history, and ultimate destiny.[50] Moscow's growing economic and military might had enabled it to unite the Rus' northeast and to lead the way out of the so-called Tatar yoke. From 1462 on, the grand prince no longer ruled by will of the khan. If the onset of Mongol-Tatar suzerainty had earlier signaled God's displeasure, then the reemergence of independence—and at such a portentous moment in history—certainly seemed proof of divine favor. According to Ostrowski, ecclesiastics now "had to work hard" in order to "fashion the khan into a basileus"; i.e., to refound Muscovite politico-religious legitimacy on inheritance from Byzantium rather than the sanction of Tatar overlords.[51] Moreover, an important side effect of all the changes taking place in the region was that the Rus' metropolitanate itself split into two. The Orthodox Church in the western Rus' lands, now under the control of Lithuania, functioned under a separate administration. Although such a split might be perceived as lessening the power of the Russian Church, in fact this undesired paring permitted the growth of a much more powerful Muscovite organization. By means of these circumstances, Russia almost unwittingly reestablished an Orthodox Christian regime in the Constantinian sense: one in which "the political and religious communities were [seen as roughly] identical."[52]

It did not take very long for ideology to catch up with the new reality. At the end of the fifteenth century, as Muscovy entered the "eighth millennium" according to its *anno mundi* reckoning, Metropolitan Zosima announced that Ivan III ranked as "the new Emperor [or Tsar] Constantine of the new Constantinople—Moscow [and its lands]."[53] Ivan had already married a Byzantine princess, Zoë Paleologue, in 1472. According to the standard view, he also had his court adopt some insignia and ceremonies directly from Byzantium. An alternate interpretation suggests that Ivan instead introduced such elements as the double-headed eagle "as a reaction to . . . diplomatic maneuvering of the Hapsburg rulers."[54] In either case, the new imperial style bolstered the prestige of state and ruler. Use of the title *tsar'* (a derivative of *caesar* used to translate both *khan* and *basileus*) with reference to the Muscovite monarch became more common during this period, prior to its official adoption by Ivan IV in 1547 "at the behest of the Church." Also during the reign of Ivan III, the monastic leader Iosif (Sanin) Volotskii or Volokolamskii worked out a kind of homegrown political theory. Borrowing directly from Deacon Agapetus, who wrote during the reign of the Byzantine Emperor Justinian I, Volotskii expressed a classically Orthodox position on the relationship of church and state.[55]

In the early sixteenth century, the monk Filofei of Pskov propounded the most infamous alleged formulation of Russian supersessionist claims. His rhetoric exultantly declared: "Two Romes have fallen; the third stands; a fourth there shall not be!" Russia, the "third Roman tsardom," thus appeared to claim superiority over all other political, ideological, and religious systems. The first and second Romes (Rome itself and Byzantium) were things of the past; Moscow had overtaken them as the capital of Orthodox Christianity, and therefore of history.[56] Yet a significant controversy exists over the correct interpretation of Filofei's striking phrase. Some scholars have detected an ominous, even apocalyptic note in Filofei's warning that there would never be a fourth Rome. Crummey extrapolated a common view: "As later generations were acutely aware, the fate of the entire universe depended on the purity of Russian Orthodoxy. If Russia lapsed into apostasy, the end of the world would inevitably follow."[57] On the other hand, Ostrowski argues that the "Third Rome" expression "had an explicitly anti-Muscovite resonance" and represented an attempt by the church to limit state power—not at all a declaration of Muscovite grandeur. He further contends that the notion remained of marginal importance in the context of Russian history.[58]

Without doubt, later historians have at times exaggerated the importance of the Third Rome idea. Particularly during the Soviet period some Western scholars portrayed it as an underlying factor in supposedly endemic Russian imperialism and expansionism. However, several commentators observed that Muscovite identity did not correspond well to this notion, which appeared infrequently in the sources. Building on the work of Bushkovitch, Ostrowski, Joel Raba, and others, in 1996 Daniel Rowland published a seminal article entitled, "Moscow—The Third Rome or the New Israel?" His contention was not that the two conceptions contradicted each other, but rather that historiography had inverted their relative significance: "Both themes were products of the Muscovite perception of history as a succession of chosen peoples: Israel to Roman Empire to Eastern Roman Empire (Byzantium) to Muscovy. . . . Yet the evidence overwhelmingly indicates that the Bible in general, and the Old Testament in particular, loomed far larger in the historical imagination of Muscovites than did any image of Rome."[59]

In Muscovy the terms "Israel" and "Russia" could even be used interchangeably, and during the Time of Troubles they frequently would be. Rowland points out that "not only the language of historical discussion but also the historical archetypes" at the root of the Muscovite worldview derived from biblical Israel, not Imperial Rome. For instance, sixteenth-century records of the coronation of Ivan IV (r. 1533–1584) cited the prophet Samuel's anointing of David as king over Israel. In the mouth of the Russian Orthodox metropolitan, this story served as a template for the contemporary divine choice of Ivan as "tsar over Thy people." Parallels of this type were extremely common in Muscovite literature. Prince Kurbskii (or perhaps pseudo-Kurbskii) chastised Ivan, "Wherefore have you destroyed the strong in Israel?" This allusion to 2 Samuel 1:17–27 required no explanation; "Israel" clearly meant "Russia."[60] An earlier letter, to Ivan III, had similarly used the phrase "sons of Israel" to refer to the Muscovite army.[61]

The Third Rome idea appeared occasionally in Russian sources, whereas the New Israel theory influenced the Russian elite much more deeply and constantly. After all, Rome's importance had lain merely in its temporary succession of Jerusalem as God's capital. In a quite literal sense, Russia considered itself to have permanently replaced (old) Israel and to *be* Israel—the new or real national Israel of the present. These conceptions eventually filtered down to

the popular level. In 1912 the philosopher and jurist Prince Evgenii Trubetskoi published some reflections on "old and new national messianism." He cited a "well-known" (but undated) Russian folk tale, a retelling of the story of Jesus and the Samaritan woman at the well (John 4). In the "Russified" version, the woman exclaimed: "How ever can I give you a drink, when you are a Jew?!" The "Christ" of this tale responded: "You are lying; I am pure Russian [*vresh',
ia chisto russkii*]."[62] The fact that Jewishness appeared at all demonstrates that this tale did not arise out of ignorance, but rather as conscious argumentation. Christ had been Jewish originally, but now he belonged only to the "true Israel," Russia. (Ironically, the original version in John specifically stressed the Messiah's Jewish identity vis-à-vis the Samaritans.[63])

The reign of Ivan IV expanded and entrenched Muscovite continuity theories as official Russian Orthodoxy. Church hierarchs choreographed an elaborate coronation ceremony in the Byzantine imperial style. Court ritual, dress, and rhetoric drew increasingly from Byzantine tradition in an effort to demonstrate that a new Orthodox emperor now held sway in Christendom. Most significantly from an ideological perspective, Metropolitan Makarii apparently labored for many years supervising the compilation of comprehensive historical and theological surveys known as the *Great Menology* (*Velikie Minei Chet'i*) and *Book of Degrees* (*Stepennaia kniga*). These volumes tied together all the strands of earlier Russian Orthodox politico-religious thought, making use of Ilarion's innovations, the "strategy of selective silence" from Mongol times, and of course translatio imperii. According to David Miller: "A myriad of texts in Makarii's compendium showed Moscow, often called the Russian empire, to be the center of God's world; the last of a series of divinely exalted empires . . . Jerusalem was the first world center, and the Jews were the first chosen people." In Miller's interpretation, the Orthodox metropolitan actually oversaw the invention of a modern Russian national consciousness, "born in the guise of religious messianism" and founded on "the triad of dynasty, Church, and land."[64]

Other events of Ivan's reign highlighted the process of Moscow coming into its own as the world's Orthodox Christian empire. In 1551, he and Metropolitan Makarii convened the Stoglav or "Hundred Chapters" Council of the Church. As the Orthodox tsar, Ivan IV ostensibly presided over ecclesiastic disputes much as Constantine had more than a millennium earlier. Just as at Nicaea, the main purposes of this council included standardizing religious practice and reinforcing church-state collaboration. The tsar's subsequent conquests of Kazan and Astrakhan were portrayed as great military and spiritual triumphs accomplished through the favor of God and on behalf of the Orthodox faith. An extraordinary ikon commemorated the expansion of Moscow's Christian empire with the title, *The Blessed Army of the Heavenly Tsar.* In this depiction, also called *The Church Militant,* the Archangel Michael and Tsar Ivan rode on horses at the head of their triumphant army, while Kazan burned in the background. A glorious welcome awaited them in the New Jerusalem, where the Virgin Mary sat with her infant son, flocked by attendant angels. The identification of Moscow with the heavenly New Jerusalem could not be missed; Ivan and his army naturally returned from Kazan to the earthly Moscow.[65]

In an intriguing twist, Russia even projected *translatio* onto its enemies. Contemporaneous with the development of theories positing sacred and universal continuity from Jerusalem and Constantinople, Muscovite bookmen argued for an intra-Slavic Kiev-Moscow continuity, sometimes expressed as Kiev-Vladimir-Moscow.[66] As Jaroslaw Pelenski has shown, this notion of Moscow as the second or third Kiev found reflection in the parallel supposition of Bulgar-Kazan continuity. Occupying roughly the same part of the world as the later Kazan khanate, the Muslim Volga Bulgars had represented a traditional antagonist of the Rus' until the thirteenth century. Muscovite texts of the fifteenth and sixteenth centuries referred to Muslim Kazan as a continuation of that Bulgar state. Phrases such as "the Bulgars who are called Kazanians" and "Bulgar which is Kazan" gave the impression that the current enemies of Russia also had a long history. Terming such enemies "Hagarites," after the biblical Hagar and Ishmael, projected this anti-*translatio* all the way back to the days of ancient Israel. Meanwhile, the developing sense of a fused national-religious identity justified and glorified the conquests. As Miller wrote: "National loyalty was synonymous with Orthodoxy."[67]

By the end of the reign of Ivan IV, the Muscovite state had seemingly raised itself from its origins as a relatively minor principality on the fringe of Christendom to the glorious heights of God's chosen people and the vanguard of Orthodoxy. Yet an uncomfortable and quite major problem inhibited the new self-image. While claiming superiority to all other peoples and lands, the Russian Church remained technically subservient to Constantinople, and only one of the dozens of metropolitanates within the Eastern Orthodox Churches. Russia might be "autocephalous," or independent in practice, with no peers challenging her status as the lone symphonic Orthodox state. Still, the venerable patriarchates of Constantinople, Alexandria, Antioch, and Jerusalem

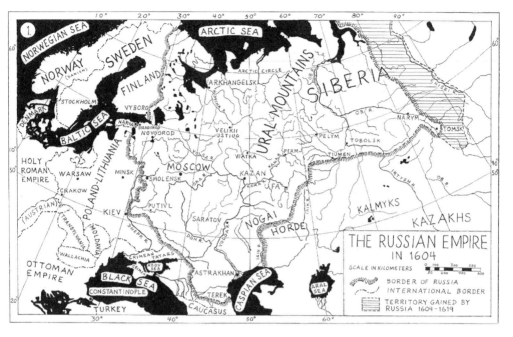

2. The Russian Empire in 1604. From *A Short History of Russia's First Civil War* by Chester Dunning. Copyright © 2004 The Pennsylvania State University. Reproduced by kind permission of Penn State Press.

ranked far higher in the Orthodox hierarchy and garnered more prestige in the Orthodox world. Equaling or superseding these former capitals required the elimination of this glaring discrepancy.

When Patriarch Jeremiah II of Constantinople traveled to Moscow on a fund-raising trip in 1588–1589, the Russian government did not miss its chance. With the capable and ambitious Boris Godunov already at the helm during this period of Tsar Fyodor's nominal reign (1584–1598), Moscow demanded an actual status commensurate with its rhetorical glory. Jeremiah had no desire or mandate to elevate Moscow to the status of a patriarchate. However, intimidation, confinement, harsh treatment, and economic incentive eventually broke him. The Muscovite regime simply would not let him go until he gave them a patriarchate. The result was of questionable legitimacy, but it could be made legal ex post facto. In 1589 Boris's close personal ally Iyov became the first Russian patriarch. A lavish ceremony, a sumptuous banquet hosted by Tsaritsa Irina, and other celebrations marked this momentous occasion in Russian history.[68]

Thus, just prior to the Time of Troubles, Moscow had arguably established itself as the vanguard of Orthodox Christianity. The lofty status now enjoyed by the Orthodox church-state must have seemed like the culmination of generations of striving. Centuries had passed since Ilarion of Kiev heralded the entrance of the Rus' onto the scene of world history. Now the Muscovite instantiation of East Slavdom seemed to clench the scepter of divine purpose, to carry the mantle of history. In Halperin's words, Russia stood as "the last remaining *tsarstvo* [i.e., true empire] on earth, on whose survival the very possibility of salvation depended."[69] The notion of "Russia as Israel" had in fact come to form the bedrock for an eclectic historiosophy shaping official Russian identity. Other societies, including in the West, proclaimed alternate teleological models of history. Yet none of those societies was Orthodox. Muscovite authors of the late sixteenth century would have understood what Aleksandr Zinoviev meant in the late twentieth century: to leave Moscow was to "fall out of history."

Literary Transpositions

Muscovy's distinctive New Israel ideology fueled a constant assimilation of biblical words, phrases, and concepts into Russian language and literature. Close identification with ancient Israel implied that biblical formulae remained the most suitable mode of expression even three millennia after Moses. Yet the language of the Torah was ancient Hebrew, not sixteenth-century Russian. Before making their way into Muscovite usage, biblical words and concepts necessarily underwent multiple "transpositions" via a series of linguistic and cultural translations: first from Hebrew to Judeo-Greek, from there to Christian Greek, then to Old Church Slavonic, and finally from Slavonic into Russian. A kind of archaeological layering thus separated the original textual meanings from their Muscovite incarnations.[70]

According to the hypothesis of D. M. Bulanin, a typical Old Russian author would compile a set of relevant quotations from authoritative biblical and patristic texts before sitting down to write his original composition. Lists of quotations have in fact been found and are presumed to have provided basic structures for early Russian literary creations.[71] In the sixteenth and seventeenth centuries biblical quotations and allusions invariably flooded the pages of Muscovite literary works. Just as the worldview of the day knew no distinction between religion and politics, so too the bookmen could not imagine separating Orthodoxy from history or literature. As Rowland wrote: "The Russian literary language . . . was still heavily influenced by Church Slavonic and usually contains a steady pattern of references in Church Slavonic to various Scriptural, liturgical, and patristic texts. . . . [It] developed in the closest relationship to these same texts and to Orthodox Christianity in general."[72]

Dating from the Time of Troubles, the "Tale of 1606" (*Povest' 1606 goda*) or "Other Account" (*Inoe skazanie*) illustrates the Muscovite proclivity for biblical quotations. The author or authors of this text purported to record recent history, but also kept up a running commentary by tying in biblical passages at each point in the story. By this means they could express approbation or, more frequently, condemnation of contemporary historical figures. Far from weakening their polemic, within the Russian cultural context the use of a rhetorical hammer two or three thousand years old intensified the poignancy and force of their criticism. Anyone displeasing the authors received a harsh evaluation, such as the following: "What the prophet states: Woe to the lawless, for evil will be cut [i.e., done] to them according to the deeds of their hands [Isaiah 3:11]."[73] Perceived character flaws, such as a lack of humility, also engendered a stern rebuke: "Not remembering the saying: Who knows the [things] of God, except God's Spirit? [1 Corinthians 2:11] and so forth; and again: Who has come to know the Lord's mind, or who has been a counselor to Him? [Isaiah 40:13; Romans 11:34; 1 Corinthians 2:16]."[74]

In addition to direct quotations, the Tale frequently made explicit reference to biblical passages with which readers would have been familiar. Almost immediately one encounters a striking instance of this device: "And this Boris [Godunov] was like the ancient serpent [Satan], which previously in paradise enticed Eve and our forefather Adam and deprived them of [the opportunity] to enjoy the food of paradise [Genesis 3]."[75] Shortly thereafter, the authors additionally compared Boris to Judas Iscariot, the betrayer of Jesus (Matthew 26; Mark 14; Luke 22; John 13; John 18).[76] Two more negative associations could not be imagined! Muscovite authors did not hesitate to denigrate opponents in the harshest possible biblical terms. These elements of contemporary style made for glaringly vivid, if somewhat awkward and disjointed, literary compositions.

The writings of Iyov, Russia's first patriarch, furnish similar examples of intertextual reference. In a letter intended to console or perhaps fortify Tsaritsa Irina after the death of her and Tsar Fyodor's baby daughter Feodosia, Iyov remarked: "Adam, how bitterly he cried over the body of his son Abel, but could not by tears restore him to life!"[77] Here Iyov mixed his biblical metaphors: in the Bible, it was David who cried bitterly over his dying infant son by Bathsheba, but to no avail (2 Samuel 12). The original story of Cain and Abel did not mention the tears that Adam may well have shed, though Eve's sorrow did make a brief appearance (Genesis 4). Perhaps the patriarch wanted to avoid mentioning King David's adulterous affair in connection with the holy royal couple of Moscow; or perhaps he was acquainted with an apocryphal reinterpretation that conflated the two tales, projecting elements of the David and Bathsheba narrative back onto the first human family.[78]

More common even than explicit references were allusions and the seamless integration of biblical words and phrases into a given narrative. According to his vita, the fourteenth-century monastic founder Sergii of Radonezh responded enthusiastically to the Orthodox liturgy from inside his mother's womb.[79] The story of John the Baptist (Luke 1) obviously underlay this trope, and in fact the parallel was drawn explicitly. Yet chroniclers often imitated the language and events of biblical accounts without explicitly mentioning them. The "Tale of This Book from Former Years" (*Povest' knigi seia ot prezhnikh let*) frequently made such remarks as "and God became enraged against him [cf., e.g., Deuteronomy 6:15, 31:17, 32:21; Judges 2:12]"; or "and the Lord had mercy upon His people [cf., e.g., Genesis 39:21; Deuteronomy 13:17; Isaiah 49:13]."[80] Not exactly quotations, these applications of biblical language pertained straightforwardly to specific historical events during the Time of Troubles. The Tale of 1606 employed a similar technique. At one point its narrator exclaimed: "Oh, how can I be silent about this? If we are silent, then the rocks will cry out! [cf. Luke 19:40]."[81]

Biblical language very nearly constituted a sine qua non for any passage expressing particularly strong emotion. The "New Tale about the Most Glorious Russian Tsardom and Great Muscovite State" (*Novaia povest' o preslavnom Rossiiskom tsarstve i velikom gosudarstve Moskovskom*) commenced a terrifying warning with the words: "I will tell you the truth, and I am not lying, that our enemies, who are currently in our [country] with our co-religionist traitors and with new apostates and blood-shedders and destroyers of the Christian faith, with Satan's firstborn, with the brothers of Judas the betrayer of Christ . . ."[82] We have already met with this manner of reference to Satan and Judas. In addition, the opening clauses of the quotation echoed Paul's words in Romans 9: "I am telling the truth in Messiah, not lying, my conscience witnessing with me in the Holy Spirit, that I have great grief, and my heart has continual sorrow . . ." Consciously or unconsciously, the Muscovite who penned the New Tale had absorbed a biblical form of expressing extremely turbulent emotion. When his own agitated feelings clamored for expression, the ink naturally flowed along nearly identical contours.

Quotations, allusions, and imitations of biblical language likewise saturated religious visions and prayers from the Time of Troubles period. One manuscript of the "Tale of a Certain Struggle, Lying upon Well-Honorable Russia Because of Our Sins" (*Povest'o nekoei brani, nalezhashchei na blagochestivuiu Rossiiu grekh radi nashikh*) included a gut-wrenching entreaty to God compiled by intermingling numerous biblical passages with the author's own words. The text did not cite biblical passages as examples or parallels; rather, it simply used biblical phrases as directly applicable to Russia in the present. Begging God to send mercy, deliverance, and military victory over the "enemies of Your cross," the author of this prayer borrowed freely from passages such as Daniel 9, in which the prophet cried out to God on behalf of exiled Israel.

> To You, Lord, is Your rectitude; but to us are shamed faces [Daniel 9:7]. And we did not walk in Your Law, and because of this there came on us the oath [or curse], written in the Law of Moses, Your servant [Daniel 9:11; cf. Deuteronomy 28]. . . . For You are our God, and we are Your people [Isaiah 64:9; Psalm 79:13, 95:7; 2 Chronicles 14:11; cf. Jeremiah 31:33; Hosea 2:23; Zechariah 13:9]; aside from You we know no other. For you, Ruler, are able, if You so desire: punish a little, but generously give much, inasmuch as Your most rich and human-loving, most divine womb shows favor. . . . And may Your Name, Israel's God, be blessed for ages [e.g., Daniel 2:20; Psalm 72:19, 113:2], for You are the Tsar of tsars [Daniel 2:37; Revelation 17:14].[83]

This excerpt expresses in a remarkable way what the New Israel ideology meant for Russia. To the modern reader, it may appear as a jumble of unrelated snippets from ancient texts. For Orthodox Muscovite bookmen, however, this manner of exploiting the Scriptures seemed perfectly natural. Passages written about Israel two or three thousand years earlier were seen as directly and literally applicable to Russia, the current "Israel." As the prayer frankly stated: "You are our God, and we are Your people." Even more strikingly, the deity was addressed simply as "Israel's God" (*Bog izraelev*). Back in the eleventh century, Metropolitan Ilarion had felt the need to modify his opening quotation of Luke 1:68 by interpolating a new name for God: "Blessed be the Lord God of Israel—the God of Christians—for He has visited and redeemed His people."[84] By the early seventeenth century, this was no longer necessary:

"Israel" and "Russia" had (in some contexts) become virtually synonymous in the Muscovite language. Vasilii Kliuchevskii explained that the biblical God of Israel was transformed into "the particular Russian God."[85] Muscovite authors could simply lift phrases from the literature of ancient Israel and use them without any qualification in their compositions about contemporary Russia. A century earlier the important monastic figure Iosif Volotskii had similarly quoted from the Pentateuch in this manner, applying ancient divine admonitions directly to Russia.[86]

The plight of Israel during the Babylonian exile had great resonance during the Time of Troubles. Texts spoke often of the *plenen'e* or "captivity" of the Russian land. Contemporary authors also feared an even greater catastrophe, similar to what they thought had been the Jews' final exile in the first and second centuries CE. Patriarch Hermogen warned in his famous missives of 1611 that Moscow, the new Jerusalem, would suffer the same fate as the old Jerusalem unless Russians repented of their sins.[87] This notion that the Troubles had come because of Russia's sins (*grekh radi nashikh*) represented the most common interpretation of the period, and it also stemmed from the prevailing New Israel ideology. In the Torah God had promised his people blessings for walking in his ways and curses for departing from them. The great catastrophes of the early seventeenth century seemed to indicate divine displeasure on a massive scale.[88]

After the destruction of Jerusalem's Second Temple, the "Psalms of Solomon" lamented, "But because of our sins sinners rose up against us; they assailed us and thrust us out. What You had not promised to them, they took away with violence."[89] In the mindset of ancient Israel, enemies often acted as instruments of divine punishment. Victory over one's foes symbolized God's favor; but any defeat revealed the presence of sin.[90] Muscovite literature imitated this element of the biblical worldview, projecting the corresponding features of a New Israel ideology onto the state's enemies. Just as Jews of the Roman period prayed for a messiah to expel the Gentile unbelievers from holy Jerusalem, so Muscovites in the Time of Troubles would petition God for a redeemer who would drive the Catholics, Lutherans, pagans, and other infidels out of holy Moscow.[91] In 1598 Patriarch Iyov acclaimed Tsar Boris as just such a liberator, one who would rescue the "New Israel" from the Crimean Tatars and other foes.[92]

The practices of quotation, allusion, and subsumption of biblical phrases and motifs would continue after the Time of Troubles and eventually influence the formation of a modern Russian literary language.

The famous Old Believer Avvakum made a name for himself largely by writing his own vita, "The Life of Archpriest Avvakum, Written by Himself" (*Zhitie protopopa Avvakuma im samim napisannoe*). In the analysis of the semiotician V. V. Vinogradov, biblical tropes color or "stain" (*okrashivaiut*) this entire narrative, imbuing each event of Avvakum's life with moral significance. Transposition of biblical themes underpinned his description of contemporary circumstances; "thus the ecclesiastic-biblical symbol [was] developed into a chain of realistic pictures." By freely mixing biblical language and allusions with popular idioms and expressions, the Old Believer outcast helped to develop a new literary language, stemming from the Orthodox tradition but neither official nor formal.[93]

A list of parallels between the texts of ancient Israel and those of medieval and early modern Russia could go on and on. Our examples represent but a tiny fraction of the extensive and constant borrowing that took place. Ceremony, architecture, and other cultural forms also emphasized transposed biblical concepts like "the idea of Moscow as a heavenly Jerusalem."[94] But what did Russian Orthodox monks inside their scriptoria think of the fact that so many of their ideas, expressions, and prototypes derived ultimately from ancient Hebrew texts? Contrary to a common misconception, Muscovite scribes were not completely ignorant of the process of linguistic and literary transposition that underlay their work. Though only a few knew Greek and none Hebrew, their manuscripts provide evidence of interest in the original meanings of biblical names, words, and phrases. Medieval copies of the Slavonic Pentateuch contain marginalia with reference to Hebrew *Vorlage*. The first Russian dictionaries, dating from the thirteenth century, were mere lists of Hebrew words with attempted translation—frequently inaccurate— into Russian. Glossaries of the sixteenth century included Greek, Arabic, and other languages.[95]

The concepts of sixteenth- and seventeenth-century Russian Orthodoxy had been shaped by a long ecclesiastic tradition in the Roman and Byzantine Empires, as well as the changing historical circumstances of Kievan Rus' and Muscovy. Yet for the church it remained important that these concepts derived ultimately from the Bible, from ancient Israel. Despite the typical Christian dichotomy of old vs. new, Jew vs. Christian, and Law vs. Grace, Russian Orthodox ideology functioned as though nothing essential had changed in God's relations with his people. The divine heritage had merely passed from one nation to the next, until it arrived in Russia.

The Legitimacy Question

The Time of Troubles launched a life-and-death struggle over the question of who was the rightful tsar.[96] Was it the "elected" Boris Godunov? The tsarevich Dmitrii, miraculously returned from the dead? The scion of an old noble family with ties to the old dynasty? In the expression of the day: who deserved the title of *pomazannik Bozhii*, "God's anointed [ruler]"? Like so many other facets of Muscovite rhetoric, this language derived from the Hebrew Bible. The priests and kings of ancient Israel had been anointed with olive oil as a sign of divine calling, authorization, and protection.[97] Muscovite use of this phrase symbolized the inseparability of political legitimacy from the all-encompassing purview of Russian Orthodoxy.

Due to the ideology of translatio imperii, Russian rulers received and demonstrated their legitimacy via imitation of the words and practices of Israel, Rome, Byzantium, and Kiev. The traditions of neighboring civilizations, such as the Khazars and Mongols, had also influenced Rus'. However, this influence was not formally acknowledged and promoted. In theory it was the Orthodox path that had made Russia what it was. Ceremony and rhetoric proclaimed a Christian emperor in Moscow who had acceded to the thrones of David, Constantine, and Volodimir. Underlying notions of legitimacy would emerge in the crucible of the Troubles as key weapons of the civil war. Muscovy's sixteenth-century revival of Byzantine ideology and concomitant trappings played an especially important role in setting the stage for this struggle. As Sergei Bogatyrev remarked, "The main source of Muscovite ideas associated with royal power was the Orthodox church."[98]

Lineage played a key role in the Russian mindset. The whole notion of an inherited mantle of destiny was itself a posited civilizational lineage. Muscovite ideologues felt that this universal paradigm should also be manifest in the ruler's personal pedigree, and so they created a fanciful genealogy linking the Riurikid dynasty to Caesar Augustus. When Vasilii Shuiskii came to the throne in 1606, he played up his family ties to the previous dynasty with rhetoric that had become standard in the sixteenth century. Vasilii styled himself "tsar and grand prince over the Russian state, which God did grant to our forebear Riurik, who was [descended] from the Roman Caesar."[99] This fictionalized claim to physical descent reflected the broader claim to a divinely ordained politico-spiritual heritage and was intended to enhance the ruler's prestige both at home and abroad. The tsars chose Rome instead of Israel for political reasons and because they believed the actual, physical Jews to have been dispersed irrevocably according to God's wrath.[100]

The tsar's alleged descent from Caesar meant that the Muscovite state needed imperial ideas and practices to match. According to Majeska, "in the pagan Roman Empire the emperor held his position by the consent of the army and the Senate representing the populace. In the Christian Byzantine Empire he held his post by the consent of the church, which was seen as representing the empire's citizenry."[101] During the Time of Troubles, the Russian Orthodox Church claimed a similar power of authorization or legitimization. The church saw itself as representing Orthodoxy itself, which formed the chief basis of legitimacy. The army and people usually lay dormant as sources of legitimacy, but as the Troubles would prove, they had not disappeared from the picture permanently.

The Church's legitimizing role was not a mere rubber stamp. Majeska continued to explain: "The emperor was not a tyrant free to do anything he chose. He had to behave as a Christian emperor or he would be thought to have lost God's mandate and would risk being replaced."[102] As the embodiment of Orthodoxy on earth, the church commanded great authority in certifying the presence or absence of a divine mandate. Michael McCormick noted that this function "gave the [Constantinople] patriarchate an influence that could sometimes stalemate imperial power."[103] In Muscovy, the power of the church to act independently and intervene in disputes over the throne may have seemed less, but this was at least partially due to the continued existence of a princely dynasty until 1598. Notably, in that year the church's candidate (Boris Godunov) won out over contenders with arguably more impressive noble pedigrees. Godunov also benefited from his marriage ties to the old dynasty and other elements of "kinship politics."[104] Yet the documents will show that patriarchal support did play a critical role.

In Byzantium, succession had generally passed from father to son, with sitting emperors frequently appointing their sons as "co-emperors" prior to their deaths. Yet rebellions erupted frequently: no fewer than 130 of them just in the century and a half prior to the year 1100. The track record of such revolts ominously foreboded Russia's predicament during the Time of Troubles. According to Leonora Neville, "Byzantine political theory allowed the success of a revolt to be proof that the deposed emperor was a tyrant. The leader of a successful revolt was God's agent in removing a tyrant and would rule as God's regent on earth."[105] Majeska similarly remarked, "If an emperor were toppled, it was a sign that God transferred his support to the new ruler. A coup was deemed successful if the church agreed to crown the new claimant to the throne, thus proving God chose him to replace the previous ruler."[106]

Thus ecclesiastic authorization had to furnish the stamp of divine approval regardless of the means of succession.

Muscovite literati were well aware of this Byzantine reality, as seen from the fifteenth-century "Hellenic and Roman Annalist" (*Letopisets ellinskii i rimskii*) and the fifteenth- or sixteenth-century "Russian Chronograph" (*Russkii khronograf*). Both texts described Emperor Phocas I (r. 602–610) as a tormentor or tyrant (*muchitel'*) who could properly be resisted, deposed, and executed, as indeed happened in the rebellion led by Heraclius I (r. 610–641). Phocas had himself usurped power from Maurice (r. 582–602) in order to gain the throne; as recorded by the Muscovite bookmen, this did not prevent him from ruling with church sanction for eight years. The successful revolt of Basil I the Macedonian (r. 867–886) against Michael III (r. 842–867) also produced a seemingly legitimate reign. In Muscovite documents of 1598, Basil would even appear as a positive proof case demonstrating that a tsar did not have to be born to the throne in order to be God-chosen and legitimate.[107] The Kievan Rus' state had kept these traditions alive not only via historical texts, but also through its own practice. Allowing the result of warfare to decide contests for the throne meant that "usurpation as such did not exist" in Kiev. Moreover, popular discontent could be viewed as legitimizing a rebellion.[108]

The sole Byzantine justification for revolt was also not lost on Russia. In Byzantium "a single limitation imposed itself on the action that the emperor exercised as holder of the supreme power, as ultimate judge, and as legislator: *he must be orthodox* and, if he could innovate, he was nonetheless submissive to the laws of the Church and must respect the traditions."[109] Lack of Orthodoxy represented the only just cause for rebellion against the sitting ruler. Iosif Volotskii, Muscovy's so-called "theorist of absolutism," echoed this Byzantine notion when he wrote that some rulers did not deserve to be obeyed. "The impious tsar [who] does not safeguard those under him"—meaning for Volotskii a ruler who refused to suppress heretics—"is not a tsar [or king] but a tyrant [*muchitel'*], and the evil bishop . . . is not a shepherd but a wolf." Regarding this "tsar-tormentor," Volotskii taught plainly: "Do not obey such a tsar or prince."[110] At stake for Volotskii was the purity of the Orthodox faith, preservation of which constituted the very raison d'être of the tsardom. The very first provisions in Emperor Justinian's *Codex* had in fact made heresy into an "offense against the state."[111]

Valdenberg's findings concerning the single entity greater than the tsar—Orthodox Christianity itself—thus do correspond to Byzantine and Muscovite theory and practice. During the Troubles Dmitrii's successful insurgency resulted in the denigration of the previous tsar, Boris Godunov, as a traitor, while the new tsar "was greeted in the Cathedral of the Assumption as the sacred ruler and defender of the Russian Orthodox Church."[112] The successful coup that toppled Dmitrii a year later used as justification the report that he "planned to destroy the Russian Orthodox Church."[113] Regardless of the real reasons for revolt, any legitimizing weight derived from claims of Orthodoxy and non-Orthodoxy.

Ancillary elements of Muscovite political rhetoric also drew heavily from Byzantine precedents. Simple association with the capital city, whether Constantinople or Moscow, helped to bestow prestige and legitimacy on a ruler. If "possession is nine-tenths of the law," as the popular adage avers, then holding the "center of history" indubitably aided a ruler's campaign for legitimacy.[114] Another major tactic for bolstering the legitimacy of Orthodox sovereigns was to attribute to them great military deeds in defense of the faith. Constantine had been the first to transform the cross into a symbol of military triumph (the *labarum*), thus linking Christianity to imperial warfare. By the time of Justinian, when the expansion of Christianity and the expansion or restoration of the empire could be portrayed as synonymous, military campaigns on behalf of Christendom represented a paramount indicator of the good and legitimate ruler. Subsequently, the defense and promotion of Orthodoxy by military means continued to figure prominently in the standard of behavior expected of a Christian emperor or tsar.[115]

Church-state symphony underlay the whole Byzantine system of legitimacy: the patriarch authorized the emperor, who in turn protected and promoted Orthodoxy as a matter of policy. Neither half of this symbiosis could be removed from dogma or ceremony. Already before Justinian new emperors had to be crowned by the Orthodox patriarch in order to be considered legitimate. Much later, in the twelfth century, the coronation ceremony evolved to include physical anointing with oil. The patriarch anointed the emperor as a sign of divine choice and sanction, imitating such biblical prototypes as the prophet Samuel's anointing of King David (1 Samuel 16). Moreover, the ceremony of anointing linked the emperor to Christ himself. Greek *christos* originally meant "smeared with oil" and stood for Hebrew *mashiakh*, "anointed one, messiah," in the Jewish-Greek Septuagint (LXX) translation of Tanakh. Byzantine cultic representations also portrayed the Christian emperor as very nearly God on earth. The emblem of the Palaeologus dynasty was a double-headed eagle with the motto *Basileus Basileon Basileuon Basileuonton* (in approximate translation: "King of Kings, Reigning over the Reigning"). Like other imperial titles, this grandiose motto was derived from biblical references to God.[116]

In biblical times, the status of *mashiakh* inspired awe and fear. Even after his own anointing, David twice refused to kill or harm his enemy and persecutor King Saul, "for he is the anointed of the LORD [*mashiakh YHWH*]" (1 Samuel 24 and 26). Later when Saul was severely wounded in battle, he begged his armor-bearer to kill him—but the servant refused "because he was sore afraid" (1 Samuel 31). When another man appeared claiming to have killed Saul, David had him put to death for slaying God's anointed (2 Samuel 1). Other Scriptural passages warned: "Do not touch My anointed; and to My prophets do not do evil" (Psalms 104/105:15; 1 Chronicles 16:22). Physical anointing with oil was understood to represent God's choice of an individual for a special and important task, with concomitant protection. The recipient of divine calling and charisma could even be termed *mashiakh* without physical anointing (Isaiah 45:1).

In McCormick's view the introduction of actual anointing with oil into the imperial coronation ceremony marked a zenith in the evolution of Byzantine ideological expression. "Religious legitimacy was indispensable. . . . The emperor's personal piety and Orthodoxy confirmed and allowed his Christomimetic rulership."[117] Muscovite churchmen eventually adopted this Byzantine practice and interpretation of anointing as they culled useful tools from the Orthodox tradition. "The God-chosen tsar, anointed with the holy oil," became almost a kind of incantation during the Time of Troubles, the pronouncement of which was supposed to establish a ruler's unchallengeability.[118] An idea birthed (or at least expressed) three millennia earlier in a completely different society thus symbolized Muscovite notions of legitimacy.

The historical documents furnish an almost endless supply of such Muscovite adaptations of Byzantine Christian interpretations of ancient Jewish texts. It is difficult or impossible to know precisely what motivated peasant and Cossack armies to fight to the death over the identity of *pomazannik Bozhii*. However, the curious genealogy of this concept provides us with a clue. Translated from Hebrew into Greek, transposed into Slavonic, the reverberations of biblical notions provided a constant backdrop for Russian Orthodox thinking and thus commanded great ideational force. The extreme crisis of the Time of Troubles would once again force churchmen to make drastic innovations within this complex tradition.

Russian Orthodoxy on the Eve of the Troubles

Transposition of ancient Israel represented a ubiquitous aspect of Russian Orthodoxy. The manifestations of this phenomenon were not confined to literary reflections but permeated all elements of religious life. The Orthodox calendar, like the Jewish one, began from the assumed creation of the world; its year commenced in the fall, like the Jewish Rosh Hashana; its day began at sundown, like the Creation-inspired Jewish day. The vestments of Orthodox clerics were based on the garments prescribed for ancient priests of Israel; the Orthodox rite featured cyclical readings of scripture, as in the synagogue; the Orthodox liturgy consisted of biblical passages intermingled with other prayers, as in the Jewish siddur; and the evening, morning, and midday services hearkened back to Israel's Temple worship. Most of this was common to all of Eastern Orthodoxy. Yet the special form that New Israel ideology assumed in Muscovy gave Russians a unique political understanding and national identity.

Metropolitan Makarii had drawn together many centuries of flux into a single grand interpretation of history with Russia at the fore. Boris Godunov saw to it that Russia gained its place as a supreme and independent Orthodox patriarchate, not a subordinate metropolitanate. At the end of the sixteenth century, official Muscovite ideology had finally come into its own as a justification for the majestic power and glory that seemed to lie ahead. The Time of Troubles would come as a shock of unprecedented proportions—shaking, shattering, but ultimately not destroying Moscow's carefully constructed visions of grandeur.

At the time, most churchmen probably had only a vague idea of what "official" ideology claimed. According to all accounts, the mass of Russian clerics remained uneducated—often illiterate—and of questionable comportment (to say the least). No less an authority than Patriarch Iyov denounced the situation he encountered in the 1590s: priests and deacons languishing in ignorance, not doing their jobs, getting drunk, behaving immorally. Iyov tried in vain to bring the ecclesiastic structure into accord with the provisions of the Stoglav Council that had taken place in 1551.[119] Foreign travelers to Muscovy were similarly taken aback at the extent of the ignorance and vulgarity within the Church. Giles Fletcher claimed to have spoken with a *bishop* who could not tell him how many gospels were in the New Testament! Fletcher further remarked: "As for preaching the word of God or any teaching or exhorting such as are under them, they neither use it nor have any skill of it, the whole clergy being utterly unlearned both for other knowledge and in the word of God."[120]

Among the general population, education had made even less headway. With no formal schooling, Russians who could read and write were scarce. Foreigners unanimously deplored the poor condition of learning in the country. Fletcher stated blankly, "The whole nation is utterly unlearned."[121] In the words of Jacques Margeret: "Ignorance is so great among the people that there is not one out of three who knows what the Lord's Prayer or the Apostles' Creed is. Indeed, one may say that ignorance is the mother of their devotion. They abhor any kind of studying."[122] Simple people, Margeret claimed, called their ikons *Bog,* meaning "God."[123] Isaac Massa chimed in, speaking of "the Muscovite youth, sunken in ignorance and barbarism."[124] Given such conditions, and even allowing for exaggeration by foreign observers, it is doubtful that many commoners understood translatio imperii or other elements of Muscovite historiosophy prior to the Time of Troubles. Crummey argued that such "theories of the uniqueness of Russian Orthodoxy" took time to "filter down" to the popular level. In his opinion, the later *Raskol* proves that "these rather esoteric theories took hold" at some (indeterminate) point prior to the middle of the seventeenth century.[125]

Although other historians might challenge some of Crummey's conclusions, evidence does exist that a transformation in the popular mindset took place during the Time of Troubles of the early seventeenth century. Constant struggles for power seem to have actualized the ideology in the hearts and minds of many Russians. Once official notions seeped into the popular consciousness, they shaped a broader national-religious identity that would arguably inform the Russian mentality for centuries. Transposition of ideas from ancient Israel allowed Russians to make sense of the turmoil all around them during the Troubles. Most commonly, the suffering was interpreted as God's anger, divine punishment for the sin of his people "Israel." Apparently some Muscovites also developed biblical messianic ideas from Isaiah and Daniel. At least according to Billington, some "ordinary Russians saw Muscovy as the suffering servant of God and looked to the monasteries for the righteous remnant."[126]

Looking to the monasteries seemed like a good idea at the time. The fifteenth and sixteenth centuries had seen an extraordinary expansion of monasticism in Russia. Hundreds of old and new monasteries lay scattered throughout the land, ranging from hermitages with a few simple brothers to stone fortresses housing veritable armies of monks and servants. Among the many activities of monasteries, their economic interests and pursuits would constitute one of the most significant factors directing the course of the Time of Troubles.

CHAPTER TWO

Profit and Piety

Russian Orthodox Monasteries as Economic Corporations

This Abbaie or howse of monkes hathe the reputacon to be the richest place
this daie in the worlde.
—English report on the Solovetskii Monastery, early seventeenth century[1]

As soon as he received the inheritance, he immediately started an endless
lawsuit with the monastery over some fishing privileges or woodcutting rights.
—Fyodor Dostoevsky, *The Brothers Karamazov,* 1879[2]

The Russian Orthodox Church did not restrict itself to political
ideology or overtly "religious" matters. Church institutions participated in
all aspects of Russian life, from territorial exploration and colonization to
the maintenance of armies and prisons. For large monasteries in particular,
economic activity represented a principal occupation and concern. Major
abbeys jealously guarded and zealously expanded their extensive rights to salt
mines, fishing spots, and a host of other natural resources. Combined with
immense landholdings and control of local peasant labor, such resources
ensured financial prosperity. The annual commercial activity of a large
monastery could amount to tens of thousands of rubles, roughly equivalent to
tens of millions of U.S. dollars in terms of purchasing power today.[3]

The hypothesis presented in this chapter is that pursuit of economic profit by ecclesiastic institutions played an important role in shaping the Time of Troubles. Many large monasteries of the late sixteenth and early seventeenth centuries acted like megacorporations, exploiting privileges granted by the tsar in order to expand lucrative landowning and trading ventures. Profit was also a factor in stimulating the founding of dozens of new monasteries in the resource-rich northern and northeastern territories of the Russian state. Meanwhile, a general economic depression and growing oppression associated with the onset of serfdom pushed masses of commoners and impoverished secular landowners in precisely the opposite direction—to the "wild" borderlands of the south and southwest, where they joined Cossack bands. This north-south fault line would become a consistent feature of the Troubles, with the southern and western borderlands repeatedly rebelling against Moscow, while the north and northeast remained loyal.

Dissolving a Theoretical Contradiction

How did this state of affairs arise, given that Christian monasticism originally sought a withdrawal from the corrupting influences of the world? Why did service to Mammon—which according to the Scriptures precluded service to God[4]—become such an essential component of the functioning of Orthodox monasteries? Generations of historians believed that two antagonistic factions formed within the Russian Church at the turn of the sixteenth century. Iosif Volotskii, the founder of a major monastery at Volokolamsk, allegedly headed the group that advocated "Church wealth." Nil Sorskii, inhabitant of a humble *skit* or hermitage, led the opposition and argued for "monastic poverty." These parties of "possessors" and "non-possessors" seemed comparable to the so-called Conventual and Spiritual Franciscans known to West European history, who had split acrimoniously over the same issue. In Russia, as in the West, the "possessors" won out, a result of seemingly "epochal significance."[5] Monetary profit was accepted as a legitimate and central pursuit of the monastery, which by its very existence still claimed to constitute a pinnacle of spirituality.

As it turns out, this traditional view may have been exaggerated. Recent reexamination of the writings of Iosif and Nil has led to significant historiographic revision. Many specialists now maintain that the two monastic leaders were not antagonists but rather colleagues who shared the same basic view of the Church and its purposes. Iosif and Nil may have emphasized different aspects of Orthodoxy or diverged on some elements of practice, but overall they agreed more often than not. Neither man argued that wealth should become the chief goal of the Church, but they dealt with the dilemma of economic support differently. Nil clearly feared attachment to worldly profit, yet still happily benefited from his hermitage's connection to the immensely rich Kirillo Belozersk Monastery. Iosif fostered poverty and asceticism for individual monks, but openly lauded and promoted his cloister's wealth-producing enterprises and capital. For him, the ideal repudiation of *private* property did "not imply in any way a materially poor life-style."[6]

The issue of "church wealth" therefore did not cause long-lasting theological battle lines to be drawn up in Russia. Unlike Western theology, Russian Orthodoxy had little tendency toward intricate intellectual controversies over minute issues of dogma. If in the West *orthodoxos* signified "right thinking," its Russian calque *pravoslavie* nonetheless meant literally "right worship." Russia's Great Schism of the mid-seventeenth century would not result from competing philosophical interpretations but rather conflict over an oppressive ecclesiastic administration and details of ritual. In Russian religious culture of the sixteenth and seventeenth centuries, monasteries could not deviate from prescribed ritual and still fall within the Orthodox fold. However, their economic status and practices could and did vary.[7]

By the Time of Troubles the economic life of monasteries had come to be marked by extreme variation. At one end of the scale, huge landowning corporations controlled massive amounts of wealth and manpower. The Englishman Fletcher remarked, "Besides their landes, (that are verie great) they are the greatest marchants in the whole countrey, and deale for all manner of commodities."[8] The Troitsa Sergiev Monastery in central Russia owned in the range of 200,000 to 250,000 hectares (about 500,000 to 600,000 acres) of land strewn throughout the country.[9] Nearly half of all arable land in the Moscow district was owned by monasteries.[10] The Solovetskii Monastery, an island fortress-town inhabited by nearly three hundred monks and over a thousand workers ("servants") and soldiers, functioned as a "state within a state" over a vast territory in the far north.[11] In the 1620s even the urban Spasskii Monastery in Yaroslavl owned more than 500 villages, with concomitant arable lands, hayfields, and forests.[12] At the opposite end of the spectrum, a few humble brothers might catch some fish and grub a few vegetables from the soil in order to sustain life in their remote hermitage. Hundreds of middling cloisters lay in between the two extremes.[13] All of these varied monastic communities belonged to Russian Orthodoxy; no *theological* barrier divided small from large, poor from rich.

Yet the remnants of early Christian ideals could still hinder commercial activity, at least from a psychological perspective. A large part of the original raison d'être for monasteries in both Eastern and Western Christianity had been to promote separation from such corrupting, money-grubbing influences of the world, enabling devotion to prayer and charitable activities instead.[14] Paul had written to Timothy in the first century CE: "Those who want to get rich fall into a temptation and a snare and many foolish and harmful desires which plunge men into ruin and destruction; for the love of money is a root of all kinds of evil!"[15] These principles contrasted with the nature of many business- and profit-oriented Russian monasteries.

The result was curious. According to Natalia Zarubina, "in Russian culture, there solidified a non-uniform, ambivalent conception of the merchant, the manufacturer, the entrepreneur. He is perceived as a person externally pious, but in point of fact far from God. Together with this, in the culture one meets with attempts to link religious and economic life."[16] In other words, according to this view, Russian Orthodox culture had conditioned some people to distrust commercial activity and those who engaged in it as unspiritual and defiling. Ivan Timofeev, an eyewitness to the Troubles, wrote that merchants and foreigners—many of whom came for reasons of trade— "exhausted" the Russian state instead of benefiting it.[17] Yet a singular "loophole" apparently allowed explicitly spiritual institutions to act as businesses without falling under any stigma. Since monasteries by definition already symbolized spiritual pursuits, no reservations hindered their pursuit of temporal profit. On the contrary, the richest monasteries were generally also the most prestigious. The more wealth a cloister acquired, the more it seemed to be contributing to the building up of Orthodoxy.[18]

What then of the original ideals of monasticism? Did major Russian monasteries pursue wealth in order to provide social services for the poor? Iosif had argued in favor of such an approach; Nil against it. Evidence exists that some communities regularly fed hundreds each day. For much of the sixteenth century, the Iosifo Volokolamsk Monastery operated an orphanage and helped run a sickhouse. The Kirillo Belozersk Monastery built an infirmary. The Troitsa Sergiev may also have built several hospitals during the Time of Troubles. However, in relative terms the level of charity could be shockingly low—a trend that would continue during the Troubles, when the starving and needy abounded. According to their accounting registers, most

Russian monasteries expended only a miniscule percentage of their income on helping the poor, even during crises.[19]

Tom Dykstra has offered an intriguing double-sided explanation for this unhappy reality. On the one hand he argues that monasteries did not consider themselves responsible for society as a whole, but rather for their own community. In his words, "the monastery is all about the spiritual welfare of the monks who live in it. . . . [Iosif's] Rule is not interested in any one else's welfare other than its own community's members."[20] According to Dykstra, charitably inclined heads of monasteries had to try to force through proposed nonprofit expenditures over the objections of other elder monks—much like a CEO answering to his growth-hungry board for making unnecessary philanthropic donations. Far from existing in order to provide free social services, "the monastery *as an institution* effectively tended to minimize such expenditures."[21]

On the other hand Dykstra points to the discrepancy between ideals and realities, theory and practice, that exists at all times and in all societies. To his mind, "the fact that many if not most Americans are overweight and underexercised does not prove they reject the ideal [of a physically fit body] *as an ideal.*" So too with Russian monasteries of the sixteenth century. Though the communal Rule set high expectations for moral purity and self-denying behavior, it also "constantly leaves the impression that many or most monks had to be badgered to fulfill even the most basic requirements—let alone lofty ideals—of monastic life." Pointing to common problems such as theft within the monastery, Dykstra concludes that most monks were not "spiritual athletes" but rather "very clearly espoused the ideal of non-possession while just as clearly living a 'capitalist' life."[22] In fact, monks and nuns from noble backgrounds could continue to own private property outside the monastery, receiving profits from agricultural and fishing enterprises in their names.[23]

This pragmatic synthesis meant that only a very rare monk would have "ever lost any sleep worrying about possible 'corrupting influence' from monastic landholding."[24] The rules of the game had changed. The ancient ideals of Christian monasticism regardless, major Russian monasteries of the sixteenth and early seventeenth centuries did not exist primarily for charitable reasons or to be "separate from the world." Thousands of documents demonstrate a constant and spirited pursuit of economic profit. No doubt many men and women chose tonsure for religious reasons. But others became monks and nuns as a way of "going into business." The "M.B.A." of the day could be earned within the walls of the elite and wealthy cloisters.

A Monk's Work

What then did most monks do? To answer this question accurately, we must be willing to give up many of the usual associations with the words "monk" and "monastery." The documents bear witness to such extensive business, trading, and administrative activity—and often to so little else—that these must have been the chief realms of occupation for a great many monks, at least in the major monasteries. Platonov emphasized that the "monk-landowner, [monk]-industrialist, and [monk]-merchant ruled [*gospodstvoval*]" in large areas of the northern White Sea regions.[25] Estate administration, resource exploitation, and trading must therefore have consumed much of the time of these "hyphenated" monks. Dykstra remarked that very few monks worked in the realm of ideology (or theology), but very many were "scribes writing up deeds, administrators supervising bailiffs, treasurers writing out receipts, stewards ordering grain for the kitchen, or cooks preparing meals."[26] The written remnants of the past bear witness to the fact that by the Time of Troubles, many Russian monasteries had merged their functions as religious institutions with increasingly large-scale business ventures.[27]

The most prominent monasteries operated very similarly to modern corporations. They had, in effect, a CEO, CFO, and board of directors chosen from within the ranks of the senior monks. They collaborated closely with government departments (*prikazy*) in order to secure access to resources and favorable trading conditions. When disputes arose with other landowners or commercial operations, they sent representatives to defend their interests in court. They went on business trips, kept detailed accounting records, and produced yearly financial reports. They lent money and took collateral security into their vaults. A large part of the job of any monastic administration was simply to look after the financial well-being of its monastery.[28]

Coincidentally, monasteries held a status equivalent to that of a modern "non-profit religious organization," benefiting from extensive tax exemptions—including on commercial activity—and from the ability to collect donations (*vklady*) in a religious-minded society. Impelled by Orthodox sentiment and other interests, everyone from the royal family on down to indigent peasants contributed to monasteries. Tsars and commoners alike gave gifts of gold, silver, grain, horses, cows, homesteads, lumber, books, bells, pearls, utensils, fabrics—anything and everything that had a value. Working with published documents from 1600–1710, Richard Hellie found that monetary donations "ranged from the relatively trivial sum of 2 kopeks (half a day's pay) to the grandiose sum of 7,500 rubles." Noble families often patronized specific institutions that in turn honored them greatly, thus enabling the establishment and strengthening of clan networks.[29]

In sum, major Russian monasteries such as the Troitsa Sergiev, Iosifo Volokolamsk, Kirillo Belozersk, and Solovetskii constituted "megacorporations"—each one a conglomerate comprising (at least) multiple for-profit businesses, a banking concern, and a religious arm attracting donations from all strata of the populace. Official "rankings" of the time preserved in Church documents recognized Troitsa Sergiev as the most prestigious Russian monastery.[30] Miller claims that this cloister's "enormous economic empire" made it the richest entity in Muscovy aside from the state.[31] Isolde Thyrêt spoke of the "Muscovite equivalent of a modern corporate raider" in describing aggressive takeovers of smaller monasteries by the Borisogleb Monastery of Torzhok in the seventeenth century.[32]

The extensive commercial activities of monasteries did not preclude the possibility of religious activity as well. The larger institutions maintained libraries of scripture, ecclesiastic liturgy, ascetic literature, and other religious writings. The very existence of such texts implies that some monks, apart from any monetary considerations, must also have been interested in hesychasm and spiritual pursuits. David Goldfrank has argued that the Iosifo Volokolamsk Monastery had at least one treasurer (business agent) who was also an active religious bookman.[33] However, the sheer scale of economic activity appears to have often overshadowed purely spiritual pursuits inside the largest monasteries.

In consequence, the vast majority of documents that remain from ecclesiastic archives of the late sixteenth and early seventeenth centuries deals with very specific economic matters. We find deeds, contractual records, survey books, loan and lease records, purchase and sales receipts, accounting books, tax documents, and donations records.[34] The prototypical monasterial document of the period was a "bestowal," signed by the tsar, of usufructuary rights or ownership over particular salt mines, fishing waters, forests, or peasant villages, usually with a large tax exemption for trade generated from those resources. Monasteries had to pay sizable fees to obtain such letters from the government, but the fees were nothing in comparison to the enormous profit that they could unlock.[35] Incidentally, the official Church hierarchy of the patriarchate, metropolitanates, archbishoprics, and bishoprics also participated vigorously in this economic system, but not to quite the same extent as the great monasteries.[36] Comparatively, far fewer documents have survived concerning their commercial activities.

The hegumen (father superior) and senior elders of a major monastery may or may not have been great religious figures, but they were also the chief economic officers of a wealthy corporation. Nowhere is this seen more clearly than in the documents they signed. The top elders had to give their stamp of approval (literally) to all the most important financial records. One typical example from early in the Troubles reads as follows:

> On the 30th day of January of the 7109th year [1601 CE], Hegumen Isidor of the Solovetskii Monastery, with the conciliar elders, [i.e.,] with the cellarer Elder Isak, and with the treasurer Elder Arkhip, and the priest Elder Feodosei, and Elder Kapiton, and Elder Protasei, and Elder Trifon, and Elder Dionisei, and Elder Isaiia, calculated according to these books of Elder Flavian; and the income that he had [recorded there] tallied with the expense. And Elder Feoktist signed the books.[37]

A common way to certify records was for the whole council of elders to spread their signatures out over all the leaves of a book. Cyclical patterns could be used to authenticate each single page and its place in the whole, so that in theory nothing could be changed or removed. With slashes representing page breaks, a sample certification in the margins of an accounting register progressed as follows: "To these books, / of the Solovetskii / Monastery / Igumen / Antonii / [his] hand / placed. / Treasurer / Elder / Protasei / [his] hand / placed. / Elder / Arkhip / [his] hand / placed[.] / Black monk / Ilia . . ."[38]

If the "lords" of the monastery thus directed a wide range of commercial activity, the lesser monks actually carried it out. Iosifo Volokolamsk "owned" an estimated 10,000 peasants, who were organized into various "departments" or "districts." Each of these had its own monastic bureaucracy for rent collection, record keeping, and a host of other economic functions.[39] Solovetskii mined, transported, and sold around 100,000 poods of salt per year—about 1.64 million kilograms or 1,800 U.S. tons.[40] Obviously a large staff of monks and nonmonastic "servants" was needed to supervise and carry out such large-scale ventures. Some monks rarely set foot in their own monasteries; instead they lived and worked at "branch offices" (*podvor'ia*) in other parts of the country or traveled incessantly. As Evgenia Kolycheva remarked, "Trading-commercial activity imposed an imprint on the whole daily life of a monastery. A significant portion of the monks were torn away for a long time from the monastery, where they were present only episodically."[41] Even at smaller monasteries and wilderness hermitages, much of a monk's time had to be devoted to agricultural or other economic activity, for the sake of sustenance if not great profit.

Did Russian monks have time for prayer? The short answer is yes, but that was often a business too. Very many prayers said in the monastery had been purchased by outside persons, often for commemoration of deceased relatives. According to researchers such as Ludwig Steindorff and David Miller, extensive "cultures of commemoration" developed at numerous Russian holy sites, sometimes threatening to overwhelm the abilities of the monks to keep up with all the required prayers. A wide range of memorial "packages" could be obtained via donations to monasteries. A temporary mention at the end of a list might cost only a few kopeks, but more prestigious and permanent remembrances could run into the thousands of rubles. Donors expected the monasteries to follow through on their incurred obligations to perform the appropriate rituals, particularly as the prayers were believed to have salvific or immortalizing power for ancestors and kinsmen. Monasteries, like parish churches, also charged fees for a wide range of liturgical and life-cycle services (christening, marriage, burial, etc.). Like other commodities, the professional prayers of monks in a monastery could be bought and sold. Some monks must have worked in for-profit "prayer departments," just as others worked in salt trading, logging, agriculture, or administration. None of this excludes the possibility of monks engaging in private, voluntary prayer motivated by personal piety or nonprofit communal prayer services. Yet prayer-as-a-business—sometimes accompanied by "aggressive" solicitation, in Miller's words—clearly constituted a basic component of the day-to-day life of the main monasteries.[42]

The economic documentation of Church institutions occasionally differs in a few particulars but not in any essential attributes from that of nonecclesiastic economic actors. The primary difference is simply that Church institutions received more privileges and tax exemptions from the throne and thus enjoyed an impressive economic advantage. Yet there seems to have been no inherent difference between, say, ecclesiastic and nonecclesiastic salt-mining, or ecclesiastic and nonecclesiastic landholding. Both types were businesses conducted for the sake of self-sustentation and profit, and both required the same written instruments and practical solutions.[43]

Dykstra agrees with this inference: "Iosifov as an institution was primarily interested in its economic self-interest. . . . In general monasteries acted as market-driven, for-profit institutions not fundamentally different from secular landowners in their ordinary business dealings."[44] He even pushes the analysis a step further, arguing that Russian monasteries should not be viewed as fundamentally different in any way from the broader society. Rather, monks "did take seriously Orthodox religious culture, but not in a way that would sharply distinguish them from their countrymen outside the cloister walls," and monasteries "acted more as a reflection of their social, religious, and political environment than as an influence on that environment."[45]

Although Dykstra's conclusions may be somewhat debatable, they probably held true for many cloister residents. True, most laymen did not compile collections of ascetic literature—but then again, neither did most monks! A committed piety thus did not figure as one of the prerequisites of coenobitic (communal rule) life; rather, it was a personal choice of some cloister residents. The regulated daily life of monks and nuns was likely to be different from that of laymen: they were supposed to attend services and eat at the communal refectory. Yet, as noted above, many monks spent much of their time away from the monastery, and it is highly unlikely (given frequent reports of abysmal ecclesiastic discipline) that the rules were always enforced even at home.[46]

As the Time of Troubles approached, most Russian monasteries bore little resemblance to the ideals laid down by early Christian ascetics or even much later native pioneers such as Iosif and Nil. The fundamental character of the monastery had changed.[47] Russian monks and monasteries of the late sixteenth century were not "withdrawn from the world," not particularly devoted to spirituality or prayer, and not more active in charitable work than other landowners.[48] The major institutions were enormously profitable business enterprises offering career monks a variety of possible occupations with apprenticeship and the opportunity for advancement. They even allowed for some social mobility.[49] Few comparable options existed outside the monastery.

In the Russian context, monasteries were also distinctive in that they operated very much like public corporations of today. No private owner(s) controlled the monastery or bore responsibility for its actions. Though some small- and medium-sized monasteries remained affiliated with particular noble families, others received largesse from multiple sources. The biggest and most powerful monasteries certainly acted as independent forces in the economy. Each one clearly identified and pursued its own interests under the direction of its appointed chief economic officers. In the absence of shareholding per se, prospective monks paid variable fees in order to join the organization—whether to begin their careers, retire from secular occupations, or even receive deathbed tonsure for religious reasons. Given these realities, Russian monasteries were also prone to many of the same problems as modern corporations, including profit-motivated behavior that might easily disregard the common welfare.

The Lure of the Forest

In the second half of the sixteenth century, Russia expanded dramatically. The conquests of Ivan IV, intense exploration of Siberia, and further settlement in the north all pushed the effective boundaries of the state outward. The Russian Orthodox Church did not stand idly by, but rather helped to spearhead the process of colonization. On the heels of explorers came monks who founded dozens of new monasteries, especially in the far northern and eastern regions of the incipient empire. Sometimes the monastic founders were explorers in their own right, canvassing the virgin forest in search of seclusion and/or natural resources to fuel commercial enterprises.

Five main factors contributed to the Church's expansion at this time. The first was a natural growth progression and the general desire for growth. As a massive and powerful institution, the Orthodox Church had a continual supply of new recruits and an unquenchable thirst for expanding its domain in tandem with the physical expansion of the state. The second impetus came from the state or "secular" government itself, which recognized that ecclesiastic ideological influence and social infrastructure were necessary in order to bring new lands truly under control. With overwhelmingly non-Orthodox populations in newly won territories, religiously motivated missionary activity represented a third reason for expansion. A fourth came from the indeterminate minority of monks who still sought *uedinenie* or solitude, a facilitator of spiritual reflection in the hesychastic tradition.[50] Given the widespread commercialization of Russian monasteries, these idealists had to look further and farther afield in order to find the remote wilderness isolation they craved.

The fifth factor, arguably the most important, arose out of that same commercialization. Ecclesiastic pursuit of profit also fueled the search for new lands to exploit economically. A finite geographical area could not support high profit margins for an increasing number of economic actors. Monasterial corporations therefore gazed hungrily at the prospect of access to more resources, particularly raw forest products that could be traded on the market. By the 1580s the seemingly unending expansion of the monasterial juggernaut did prompt legislation restricting further land acquisitions and commercial tax exemptions.[51] Even after these decrees, however, new monasteries could still be founded and receive sizable grants of land and resources. The ranks of Russian monasteries continued to swell right up to and indeed all the way through the Time of Troubles at the beginning of the seventeenth century.[52]

During these decades, the Church was usually quick to take advantage when war and exploration opened up new regions and travel routes. The conquest of Kazan in the East immediately stimulated both economic and ecclesiastic expansion. The city's first archbishop, Gurii (Grigorii Grigorevich Rugotin) promptly recruited his former pupil German (Grigorii Polev) to start up a new monastery in the region. The two knew each other from the days when both had belonged to the famous Iosifo Volokolamsk Monastery. In 1555 German did found the Bogoroditskii Uspenskii Monastery on Sviiazhsk, an island-town at the confluence of the wide Volga and Sviaga Rivers about thirty kilometers (roughly twenty miles) upstream from Kazan. Later German would succeed Gurii as second archbishop of Kazan. In 1556 his colleague Varsonofii (Ioann) founded the Spaso Preobrazhensk Monastery in the center of Kazan itself. Several additional monasteries appeared in the immediate vicinity throughout the second half of the sixteenth century and the first half of the seventeenth century.[53]

Cossack military expeditions into Siberia in the last quarter of the sixteenth century likewise engendered rapid ecclesiastic expansion. Peter Armstrong noted that the Church was "quick to establish a presence" in the new territories of Western Siberia:

> Within a few short years of Yermak's campaign, the first church in Siberia was raised in Tiumen in 1586 and the first monastery was founded at Tobolsk in 1588. Whenever new towns were founded a church was among the first buildings to be erected. After Tiumen, churches were built in Tobolsk (1587), Pelym (1595), Verkhoture (1598), Turinsk (1601), Mangazeia (1603) and Berezov (1605). By 1621, Narym, Tara, Surgut, Ketsk, Tomsk, Kuznetsk and Eniseisk also had churches, so that within forty years of establishing a permanent presence beyond the Urals, every major Russian town had its own house of worship.[54]

Before 1640 there would be a Russian Orthodox church as far away as Buryatia, on the eastern shores of Lake Baikal—more than 4,000 kilometers or 2,500 miles from Moscow.[55] Within another decade and a half, the famous "Old Believer" Archpriest Avvakum would wander with his family across Siberia, living a tortured life in exile for his dissident views.[56]

The Stroganovs, the great merchant family that played an instrumental role in the economic and military "opening" of Siberia, themselves founded or endowed multiple monastic communities in the northeastern territories they dominated. Around 1560 they established the Pyskorsk Spaso Preobrazhensk Monastery on the Kama River, a little south of Solikamsk and just shy of the Urals. In 1565 it was the Vvedenskii Monastery in Solvychegodsk. In the seventeenth century they set up the Sretenskii female monastery (convent), also in Solvychegodsk. The Stroganovs were probably also behind the founding of the Bogoroditskaia Uspenskaia Vvedenskaia *pustyn'* or "wilderness hermitage" in Okhansk, near Perm.[57]

Similar examples abound. In 1604 an adventurous monk named Iona could be found constructing a monastery "in the name of the holy wonder-worker Nikola and the holy passion-sufferers Boris and Gleb" in Verkhoturie, the recently founded outpost situated about ninety kilometers (fifty-five miles) east of the Urals. He had managed to gain the ready support of Tsar Boris, who wrote a letter instructing the local *voevoda* (commander) to provide Iona with logs and boards free of charge. It seems the Verkhoturie civil servants did not see the construction of a monastery as their top priority and had previously refused to give the monk enough materials for his building. The tsar saw things differently.[58]

Some months later the same *voevoda,* Neudacha Ostafevich Pleshcheev, reported the transfer of ecclesiastic property to Tobolsk and Tiumen—further evidence of the Church's energetic expansion into the new Siberian territories.[59] The official ecclesiastic hierarchy did not lag far behind the monasteries in expanding into the distant northeast. New archbishoprics appeared in Velikii Ustiug about 1613 and in Tobolsk in 1620–1621. The Velikii Ustiug archbishopric may even have been founded earlier, but its earliest surviving documents date from the period just after the Time of Troubles. Churchmen had certainly been active in the area for quite a long time; a famous vita relates Orthodox missionary activity there in the late fourteenth century.[60]

Although the Church sought to expand into all new territories and to increase its presence in the Russian heartland as well, documentary evidence shows a disproportionate expansion toward the north and east. In the second half of the sixteenth century, many new monasteries appeared along the great arc stretching from Novgorod to Perm and beyond, into Siberia. It was the taiga that most attracted monks willing to leave the center. The ideal locale for a new monastery was rich in natural resources (furs, honey, timber, salt, fish, and so forth), with a relatively sparse human population that could provide labor but would not consume too much of the valuable resources. Enterprising monastic founders went prospecting for just such sites all throughout the northern and northeastern regions of the Russian state. This process continued through the Time of Troubles and well into the seventeenth century.[61]

Ecclesiastic expansion toward the south was much less successful, and most of what did occur was concentrated in the southeast rather than the southwest. The problem was not a shortage of new territory. Astrakhan, conquered in the 1550s, lay on the Volga delta almost 1,300 kilometers or 800 miles southeast of Moscow—more distant from the capital than Perm or Arkhangelsk. The tsar's government had also been fighting and pushing its way south toward Crimea, which represented a constant security threat. According to Dunning, "between 1584 and 1599, the border of Russia moved south more than five hundred kilometers [i.e., over 300 miles]."[62] Yet despite a vast territory, the pace of monastic expansion in these new southern regions was much slower than in the new northern and eastern territories.

Nor was there a lack of perceived need for the Church to move into the steppe regions. On the contrary, here the need was far more acute. The frontier zones in the south and southwest played home to a large, roving, militarized population with grievances. The ranks of the Cossacks were continually being swelled by thousands of discontent peasants, slaves, soldiers, impoverished secular landowners, and other disaffected persons fleeing from the heartland to the "Borderlands" (*Ukraina*) and "Wild Field" (*Dikoe pole*). Many of the Cossacks were Orthodox, but both state authority and Church institutions remained weak or absent. Muslim Tatars and other non-Orthodox peoples filled out the ranks of the steppe inhabitants.[63]

The Muscovite government recognized that it had to jump-start ecclesiastic expansion in the south if there was to be any hope of social control and stability. Russian Orthodoxy represented a key integrating force of the empire. In 1568 Tsar Ivan IV ordered the foundation of the Troitskii Nikolaevskii Monastery in Astrakhan for the purpose of spreading Orthodoxy among the largely Muslim population. However, it was not until the beginning of the seventeenth century that the authorities formally established a bishopric in the city (although Sarai had received a bishop in the thirteenth century). In the meantime only one additional monastery had been founded, the Spasskii (Preobrazhenskii) in 1597. In the early seventeenth century only eighteen ecclesiastics (monks, priests, and deacons) resided in Astrakhan, out of a population of more than 700 permanent and more than 800 temporary residents.[64]

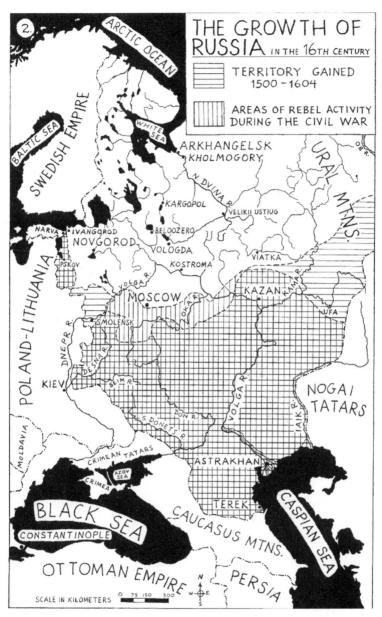

3. The Growth of Russia in the Sixteenth Century. From *A Short History of Russia's First Civil War* by Chester Dunning. Copyright © 2004 The Pennsylvania State University. Reproduced by kind permission of Penn State Press.

Such was the situation in an important town specifically targeted for state-sponsored and state-subsidized church growth. According to Andrei Dubakov, "Boris Godunov and Patriarch Iyov . . . assigned a special role to the Astrakhan ecclesiastic organization. It was supposed to become an important conductor of governmental influence on the spiritual life of Cossackdom."[65] Out on the "Wild Field," ecclesiastic expansion was even weaker—or more usually, completely nonexistent. By the time of Boris Godunov's regency at the end of the sixteenth century, the efforts of the state to stimulate ecclesiastic expansion in the south represented a case of "too little, too late."

A possible exception to this general pattern may have been the Kursk region, 450 kilometers (280 miles) south-southwest of Moscow. In 1597 the Korennaia Rozhdestvo Bogoroditskaia *pustyn'* appeared less than thirty kilometers (twenty miles) from the city.[66] According to at least one source, the Znamenskii Bogoroditskii Monastery at Oboian was originally founded in 1612 in Kursk to commemorate the liberation of that city from a Polish-Lithuanian siege.[67] Several other monasteries sprang up in the vicinity of Kursk either at the end of the sixteenth century or in the first half of the seventeenth century, but their dates of founding are uncertain or debated.[68] As a result, it is possible that the Kursk region did have a more visible ecclesiastic presence during the Time of Troubles, compared to other areas in the south and southwest. However, Kursk was not exactly unexplored territory for the Church. This city was mentioned in chronicles of the Kievan period, and only a bit more than one hundred kilometers (sixty miles) closer to Kiev, the Molchanskaia Rozhdestvo Bogoroditskaia Sofronieva *pustyn'* had existed since the thirteenth or fourteenth century.[69] The real frontier lay beyond Kursk, further south, where Cossacks and Tatars patrolled a swath of "unchurched" land hundreds of kilometers wide.

What was the reason for the discrepancy between ecclesiastic expansion in the north and in the south? Why did monasteries mushroom in the northern and northeastern forest regions, but sputter on (at best) in the southern and southwestern borderlands? The physical expansion of the state in the second half of the sixteenth century had made it possible for the Church to expand in a number of directions. The government built new towns and fortresses in the north and in Siberia—Arkhangelsk (originally Novokholmogory) in 1584, Tiumen in 1586, Tobolsk in 1587. Simultaneously, it reinforced and expanded southern towns and defenses. According to Dunning, "at the same time Russia was expanding rapidly to the east, on the southern frontier there was literally a frenzy of town and fortress construction."[70] Thus, a great deal of new territory lay open to the north, south, and east. Monastic founders could move in any of these directions. They could have, for example, furthered the shoring up of the southern territories. Instead, considered collectively, they much preferred to head north and east. Why?

Political and security considerations dictated that Church expansion should have been concentrated in the southern borderlands, but even with considerable incentives and subsidies the strategy never really materialized. Political and religious considerations revealed the need for missionary and conversion activity in the south and east both—but most missionaries chose the east. In the Kazan region, Gurii, German, and Varsonofii apparently expended much effort in the gradual process of seeking to convert local pagan tribes to Orthodoxy; all three came to be honored as saints by the Russian Orthodox Church.[71] According to Vasilii Zverinskii, another monastery of "great missionary significance" existed prior to 1608, all the way out on the Great Ob River in Siberia, 1,800 kilometers (1,100 miles) northeast of Moscow near the modern-day city of Niagan.[72] In areas like Penza and Tambov, only a few hundred kilometers further south than Moscow, monks did seek converts among the East-Finnic Mordva.[73] Yet missionary work among the Tatars and missionary-pastoral work among the Cossacks in the southern and southwestern frontier zones continued to be seriously lacking.

Some scholars have argued that after an initial stage in the 1550s during which Orthodox Muscovites vaunted their triumphs over the "godless pagans" of Kazan and Astrakhan, tore down mosques or transformed them into churches, and zealously pursued converts, a more "pragmatic" approach took hold. According to this view, Russians drew back from missionary activity directed at Muslims in order not to upset the Ottomans. D. S. Mirsky wrote, "This zeal for conversion did not last long and after the first flush of victory Islam was allowed to live on unmolested."[74] Willard Sunderland similarly remarked that "the steppes around the Lower Volga and 'beyond the Kama' were claimed without being appropriated."[75] This interpretation may offer a partial explanation for the observed incongruity between missionary activity in the east and in the south. However, it should be kept in mind that Russian Orthodoxy believed in the ultimate, universal triumph of the "true faith" and was simultaneously pursuing converts in other new territories. Moreover, this explanation does not address the lack of ecclesiastic presence in lands inhabited by Orthodox Cossacks.

What about the few hesychastic idealists who desired peaceful solitude? True isolation could be hard to find in the major monasteries with dozens or hundreds of brothers, extensive business ventures, significant administrative responsibilities, multiple religious services and prayer recitals, political intrigues, bookmaking, prison wardenry, and many other activities.[76] The windswept southern steppe certainly offered lonely and picturesque landscapes that could appeal to the more spiritual monastic types. Yet these founders also chose the north, leaving the towns and busy monasteries for the beautiful river-strewn forests of northern Russia. In 1600 a certain Evfrosin departed the Bolshoi Bogoroditskii Monastery in Tikhvin, "where the monastic life seemed noisy to him," and founded the Troitskaia Sino(e)zerskaia *pustyn'* on a lakeshore off of the Chagodoshche River, about 180 kilometers (110 miles) further east. Yet the Smuta reached even to isolated abodes, and sadly Evfrosin became a casualty of the Polish-Lithuanian invasion on March 20, 1612.[77]

Most of the factors contributing to ecclesiastic expansion in the second half of the sixteenth century simply cannot explain the disproportionate appeal of northern areas for monasterial founders. Political, social, and religious motives would all have tended to push many new monasteries further south. It is rather economic factors that provide an adequate explanation of why so many monks spread into the northern and eastern regions. The road to profit led in that direction. Products reaped from the forests, rivers, and lakes and then traded on the domestic and foreign market could make a new monastery instantly viable and profitable.[78] Even the urgent need to gain control of the south could not compete with the economic incentives of resource-rich forest zones. Miracles were generally said to lead to the founding of new monasteries at specific sites; but in actuality many seem to have arisen from much more mundane causes.

The Astrakhan region had a huge supply of salt and fish, but even substantial privileges in these trades could not solve the economic problems of local Church institutions. As Dubakov noted, "The most authoritative monastery in the region—the Troitskii—for a long time was sustained to a significant extent at the expense of state subsidies [*ruga*]."[79] Moreover, the few church institutions that did exist in Astrakhan were neither homegrown nor spontaneous developments. A weak hierarchy, a few monasteries, and several churches had all been called forth "at the initiative of the state," not out of religious sentiment or ecclesiastic intention.[80]

While the northern and eastern forests offered a wide variety of profitable market goods ripe for the picking, the principal occupations in the steppe borderlands were banditry, raiding, and small-scale plot farming. Theoretically, agriculture was also possible for monasteries, but the local population was far too strong and independent to be brought into subjection. Thus, monks would have had to till the soil themselves and give up any hope of monetary profit. Moreover, crops and lives would always be in danger from marauders. As Dubakov stated, "In the Lower Volga Region, land did not have value, since it was impossible to occupy oneself with agriculture on it, by force of the constant military danger."[81] Northern monastic founders also faced danger from free peasants, who had no wish to be subjugated or driven out, and some suffered injury or death as a result.[82] However, a few isolated villages in the forest did not represent the same threat as armed bands of Tatars and Cossacks. The danger was much greater in the south.

In short, the lure of profit drew explorative monks toward the north and northeast while concern for personal safety kept them away from southern frontier zones. Meanwhile, many Russians were running in exactly the opposite direction—away from the center to the wild border regions in the south and southwest. These contradictory trends split Russian society and helped to cause the Troubles. Virtually all of the *smuty* (uprisings, rebellions) of the period would originate in those very territories where the Church had failed to establish a significant presence (see figure 3). A bloody civil war pitting north against south rose on the horizon.

Prosperity and Poverty on the Eve of the Troubles

The Cambridge scholar-poet Giles Fletcher the Elder traveled to Russia as Queen Elizabeth's ambassador in 1588–1589. Tsar Ivan IV was dead, his oprichnina experiment having been abandoned as a bloody mess. The Russian economy, exhausted by his wars and rapine, was sliding ever further into a deep crisis. Still, it would have been hard to predict the utter chaos and unthinkable tragedies that would ensue in a little over a decade. For the time being, Ivan's fervently religious but "weak-minded" son Fyodor occupied the throne, his intelligent brother-in-law Boris Godunov ruling as regent. The Russian government was just in the process of securing for itself an Orthodox patriarchate and the concomitant glories of a great empire. To all appearances the wealth and power of the state were assured.

Fletcher, who seems not to have enjoyed his stay in Russia very much, recorded his observations at this critical historical moment in what has been called "unquestionably the most important English work on Russia before the reign of Peter the Great" and "the most systematic account of Muscovy ever written."[83] His book *Of the Rvsse Common Wealth* frequently criticized the

Orthodox Church, prompting an endless debate over possible bias.[84] In a typical passage he expressed disapproval of Russian monasticism, stating, "Of Friers they haue an infinit rabble farre greater the[n] in any other countrey, where popery is professed. Euery city, & good part of the countrey, swarmeth ful of them. For they haue wrought (as the popish Friers did by their superstition and hypocrisie) that if any part of the Realme bee better and sweeter then other, there standeth a Friery, or a monastery dedicated to some Saint."[85]

Fletcher's stridently negative tone offended many, but a couple of centuries later the Russian court historian Nikolai Karamzin would write that the Englishman had "said much that was fair and of interest about the condition of our society at that time."[86] The Russian lands did abound with monasteries new and old—probably well over five hundred institutions.[87] Moreover, these cloisters did often occupy the most desirable real estate. In his magisterial survey of Russian monasteries, Zverinskii repeatedly commented on the "exceptionally beautiful" locations that many of them boasted. Elena Romanenko, author of a recent book on the everyday life of medieval Russian monasteries, likewise remarked: "The majority of Russian cloisters were situated in places of wondrous beauty."[88] However, Fletcher probably exaggerated in these and some other claims: monks and nuns remained a relatively small minority among the Russian population.

Monasteries managed to become numerous and well situated in Russia because most functioned as for-profit ecclesiastic businesses in a religiously saturated society. Free from the usual stigma associated with commercial activity, monasteries continually expanded their business operations. Despite periodic attempts to check ecclesiastic wealth and a possible decline in the religious "charisma" of coenobitic institutions,[89] the sixteenth century saw a remarkable growth in the number, size, and wealth of Russian monasteries. By the early seventeenth century one foreign observer believed the Solovetskii Monastery to be "the richest place this daie in the worlde," with "springes of Treasor" flowing "from sundrie fountaines"—an assessment that prompted the English crown to weigh the merits of an invasion.[90]

If foreigners salivated over the lucrative monasterial economy in Russia, what was the situation domestically? Even prior to the Time of Troubles, the economic crisis reached absolutely catastrophic proportions. The policies of Ivan IV had no doubt weakened the country, but some analysts place most of the blame on the so-called Little Ice Age that arguably caused a general malaise across Eurasia.[91] Whatever the reasons, the crisis became so severe that agriculture ground nearly to a complete halt. Disease, famine, and flight from onerous taxes and corvée combined to produce an extraordinary depopulation of the central regions and some other territories. Scholars have estimated that only one quarter of peasants remained to work the land in the Moscow and Tver districts. In the Novgorod region some areas were completely abandoned. The situation in the towns was no better. *Posadskie liudi* (townsmen) also ran away to the south and to places like Nizhnii Novgorod.[92] Had the early part of the seventeenth century not been even worse, perhaps the last decades of the sixteenth would have been remembered as the "Time of Troubles."

On the eve of the Troubles, Russian economic actors found themselves fighting to survive. Competition became extremely fierce. Unlike most secular landlords, however, the great monasteries were actually well placed to deal with such an extreme crisis as this. In addition to agriculture and trade, they also benefited from religiously motivated donations, a source of income that could even increase in troublous times. Northern monasteries continued to sell their highly profitable goods to foreign merchants as well as to domestic customers. Not surprisingly, in Goldfrank's words, "by around 1600 . . . Kirillov's own enterprises (*promysly*) proved more profitable than the land worked by peasants, and this was where the cloister's economic future lay."[93]

Here was another way in which Russian monasteries were moving in a different direction from the general populace. Life had become impossibly difficult for most of the lower and middling classes and even some previously wealthy landowners. Yet major monastic corporations were still going strong and even looking to improve their profit margins. A partial recovery in the 1590s mainly benefited the top echelon of society. George Vernadsky put it this way: "The granaries of the owners of large landed estates and of the monasteries were filled with surplus grain. But the position of the peasant tenants had worsened. . . . Profiting by the situation, the landlords were demanding heavier work or rent from the tenants."[94] In a grim foreshadowing of the Troubles, the general downfall actually meant a windfall for some ecclesiastic institutions, as, in Vladimir Picheta's words, "much land passed into the hands of the bank of that time—the monastery."[95]

Peasant indebtedness also increased severely, as many of the poorer classes simply could not meet the obligations imposed on them by landowners. In November 1591 the Antoniev Siiskii Monastery in the Kholmogory (Arkhangelsk) region collected *obrok* (land rent or dues) for the recently completed Muscovite year 7099. Of the monastery's poorest subjects, termed *bobyli,* only a handful of households could pay a full ruble and absolve their debt for the year. Most paid only a half-ruble or less and thus carried over much of their assessed payment to the following year. Fourteen households of ninety-six in the list of Judicial Monk Gerasim received a distinct classification as the very poorest of the poor and paid only six *den'gi* (0.03 rubles)—apparently the minimum annual lease on continued survival.[96] With this inescapable entrapment in ever-increasing debt, such peasants often had no choices other than to flee or to succumb to a de facto condition of unfreedom.

For at least a century already monasteries had been at the forefront of the gradual onset of serfdom in Russia. An infamous 1497 law that restricted peasant movement to a two-week period after the end of harvesting and threshing arose out of the complaints of the Kirillo Belozersk Monastery, whose agricultural workers tended to leave at "inconvenient times." The prescribed moving time around "cold St. George's Day" (*Yurii kholodnyi,* November 26) became a symbol of remnant freedom, but probably most peasants—even if they were judged to have fulfilled all obligations and could afford the mandatory fee—were not physically able to move at this time when winter weather would have already set in. The constant expansion of monasteries into the northern forest regions also meant the loss of liberty for peasants who had formerly been free and independent. By the end of the sixteenth century, only the most northerly regions still had some free peasantry. In addition, the institution of "forbidden years" meant the suspension of even the limited freedom of movement permitted to bound peasants after harvest time. Vasilii Kliuchevskii's interesting conclusion was that Russian serfdom was "not created by the state, but only with its participation"; monasteries and other landowners constituted the driving force.[97]

New edicts designed to stop peasant flight amidst the economic crisis would later evolve into full-fledged formal serfdom but had only a limited effect in the short term. A law dated November 24, 1597, stated that peasants who had run away from secular or ecclesiastic landowners in the last five years, and whose masters had taken steps to search for them, were to be found and brought back and confined to where they had previously lived. Those who had left earlier or had not been sought were exempt. Nevertheless, "the edict did not have any great practical significance."[98] Peasant flight to the southern periphery continued unabated—one of the most critical preconditions of the incipient social tornadoes about to sweep back to the center.

The tsar's government continued to back the monasteries in multiple ways as economic pressures produced rising friction and conflict. In 1592 the same

Antoniev Siiskii Monastery obtained a special exemption from military levies of its peasants because it was constructing a stone cathedral, the Troitskii, which would not be finished until 1607 or 1608.[99] In 1596 Hegumenia (Mother Superior) Evnikeia of Suzdal's Pokrovskii Convent complained repeatedly to the tsar about serious mistreatment of "her" people by government officials. In one case certain tax collectors—"Stepanko, nicknamed Zhichka, and his fellows"—were said to go around beating up the monastery's poor peasants and petty craftsmen, preventing the latter from selling "their little wares" in the market. These thugs also forcibly exacted "taxes" from monasterial subjects who should have been exempt. In another of the monastery's holdings on White Lake (Belozero), Muscovite couriers habitually appropriated whatever transport they happened to require, while refusing to pay for this service. According to Evnikeia's complaint or "petition," the monastery's lands were "growing empty" as a result, as peasants—not to mention boats, carts, sledges, and horses—were taken off to various places. In both instances the tsar ordered the abuses stopped.[100]

But could documents signed and sealed in Moscow change individuals' behavior in the distant north? Lawsuits and complaints like Evnikeia's were common in the sixteenth century.[101] Monasteries sought to defend their own economic standing and authority, to protect "their" peasants and sources of income from competitors. They did not want others exploiting the lands, people, and resources they had fought hard to obtain. One wonders if convents, directed by women instead of men, were especially susceptible to infringement and abuse. The tsar's bureaucrats seem to have heard from Evnikeia more frequently than they would have liked: one missive from the central government instructed the civil servants, with a touch of annoyance, to start behaving better "so that Hegumenia Evnikeia with [her] sisters would not petition us about this any more"![102] Yet on the eve of the Troubles, it is doubtful that such edicts always produced the desired effect. Cutthroat competition and lawlessness would soon displace official documents as the order of the day.

Meanwhile, the political situation grew dicier. According to both foreign and domestic accounts, Boris Godunov was a talented and capable administrator. Yet Tsar Fyodor and Tsaritsa Irina continued to rule with no heir; their daughter and only child Feodosia had died in early childhood.[103] Fyodor did have a young half-brother Dmitrii, whom Fletcher described as already manifesting cruel and bloodthirsty inclinations at the age of six or seven. Fletcher also noted that rumors placed Dmitrii in danger of assassination by "some that aspire to the succession, if this Emperour die without any issue."[104] Within only a couple years, the prince lay dead of a knife wound to the throat, widely believed to be the work of Boris Godunov's henchmen. An official government investigation asserted that the boy had died in an epileptic fit while playing with a knife. But what was the truth of the matter? And was he really dead? In an extraordinary twist of events, these would become the defining questions of the Time of Troubles. Virtually every year a new "tsarevich" popped up, either Dmitrii seemingly returned from the dead or some other allegedly long-lost member of the royal family.[105] The angry masses of the borderlands rallied around each new pretender (*samozvanets*) with gusto and warred against the "establishment."

Ecclesiastic pursuit of economic profit had helped to create the context for revolt. Following the trail of monetary gain, monasteries had expanded to the north and east, while an increasingly indigent population fled southward. The Cossacks who inhabited the frontier zones remained largely beyond the reach of church and state propaganda; they were not tied in to the system. Fiercely guarding their independence, they showed signs of Orthodox piety and donated to monasteries on occasion. Yet during Yermak's campaign in Siberia, Cossack detachments had proven uninterested in disrupting paganism among the native peoples, and their attachment to Orthodoxy did not necessarily imply a corresponding acceptance of its official manifestations.[106] The official church could not sway their minds, and the state would also prove unable to conquer them militarily. Ecclesiastic economic interests had thus done much to shape the initial context for the Troubles. They would continue to exert a powerful influence on the course of events all throughout the coming turbulence.

CHAPTER THREE

Vox Dei, Vox Populi, and *Vox Feminae*

Delaying the Crisis of Legitimacy in 1598

Гласъ бо народа гласъ Божий.

(For the voice of the people is the voice of God.)

—Official Muscovite ideology, 1598–1613[1]

This is called "the voice of the people," with an addition,

"the voice of God." A sad and lamentable delusion!

—Konstantin Pobedonostsev, Supreme Procurator of the Holy Synod, 1896[2]

If the economic crisis of the late sixteenth century laid the groundwork for the "great reeling of the state" known as the Time of Troubles,[3] political developments are usually said to have provided the trigger. In Sergei Platonov's classic formulation, the year 1598 ushered in a "dynastic crisis," as Tsar Fyodor died childless and his regent, Boris Godunov, attained the throne without the traditional pedigree. Boris had to outmaneuver and overcome other candidates with closer blood ties to the old dynasty, such as Fyodor Nikitich (Romanov), a relative of Ivan IV's wife Anastasia.[4] Other historians claim that the real Troubles did not begin until later. The Great Famine devastated the country in 1601–1604, and then in the following year civil war broke out over the political question of who was the rightful tsar.[5]

Both interpretations express a significant degree of truth. In 1598 Patriarch Iyov and other top Muscovite ideologues acted to forestall the crisis of legitimacy that could have erupted at the time. Because the new tsar lacked hereditary legitimacy, they created an alternate paradigm for justifying the rule of an Orthodox sovereign. While emphasizing divine providence and the authority of the Church, the new approach replaced traditional dynastic bequest with notions such as *vox populi* (the voice of the people) and *vox feminae* (the voice of a woman). In the Muscovite context this model was quite novel, and it did not emerge overnight. A careful reading of the documents demonstrates that the ideologues produced several different "draft" justifications for Tsar Boris's rule before synthesizing them into a comprehensive statement around the time of his coronation in late 1598. This freshly minted paradigm only served to delay the crisis of legitimacy, which would be reawakened by Dmitrii Ivanovich's dramatic return from the grave.[6] Nonetheless, the new model would not only persist but become dominant and serve as a template for subsequent accessions, such as those of Fyodor Borisovich (1605) and Mikhail Romanov (1613).

An Old Tune: The Language of Legitimacy Prior to 1598

The new model invented in 1598 stands in marked contrast to what preceded it. In the half-century before the Time of Troubles, a clear formula existed for legitimizing each new ruler. The official record of the coronation of Ivan IV (1547), possibly compiled several years after the event, asserted that the ancient custom of Russian grand princes was to bestow the rulership on "their firstborn sons" (*synovom svoim pr"vym*). Placing these words in the mouth of Orthodox Metropolitan Makarii, the text continued by announcing that Vasilii III had therefore "blessed" (*blagoslovil*) his son Ivan to rule "and to be anointed and crowned with the God-crowned crown of the tsars."[7]

The document could hardly have been more straightforward in its ideological message. Ivan IV had inherited the throne by right of primogeniture and had received this inheritance through bestowal or "blessing" (*blagoslovenie*) from his father.[8] The transfer of power had been accomplished in accordance with God's will and sanctioned by the Church hierarchy. The framers of the document felt no need to appeal to any other sources of legitimacy, and hardly a word was said about "the people," except that the attending multitude "stood each in his place, with fear and trembling and with much heartfelt joy."[9]

The coronation of Tsar Fyodor in 1584 followed precisely the same formulaic template, albeit with some updates to reflect Ivan's conquests and the increasingly Byzantine practice of the court. However, the speechmakers omitted the word "first" or "firstborn" in speaking about heredity, since Fyodor was Ivan's third son. The eldest, Dmitrii, had died as an infant, and the second brother, Ivan, had fallen victim to the tsar's rage in 1581 (as immortalized in Ilya Repin's famous canvas). Arguably, primogeniture had never been formally established in Muscovy, even though it had become the custom. This time, then, Metropolitan Dionisii asserted merely that "the tsars and grand princes gave the Tsardom and Grand Principality of Russia to their sons [*synom svoim*]." He claimed that Fyodor had been predestined by God to take the throne; Ivan IV had reified this divine desire by blessing Fyodor to rule, "to be anointed and crowned with that crown and diadem of the tsars . . . [as] your father's heritor [*otchichem*] and your grandfather's heritor [*dedichem*] and the heir [*naslednik*] of the Russian tsardom."[10]

The official legitimation of Fyodor thus did not shy away from customary justifications of heredity despite the fact that he was not Ivan IV's firstborn son. To the contrary, the authors of the accession document overcompensated for this potential deficiency by the extensive addition of other hereditary terminology (*naslednik, otchich', dedich'*) and the claim that God had "fore-prepared" or "fore-ordained" this particular son of Ivan IV for the throne. Once again, the Church hierarchy sanctioned the bestowal accomplished by God and the new tsar's father. The "people" had no voice whatsoever—real or alleged—in elevating Fyodor to the throne.

Such was the accepted pattern of legitimizing a new tsar prior to the Time of Troubles. Clearly hereditary in nature, the legitimation scheme claimed the triple sanctity of divine will, ancient custom, and ecclesiastic approval. The method of accomplishing succession was paternal bestowal, generally performed at the end of the previous ruler's life.[11] "God's voice," in other words, manifested itself in the royal pedigree and became actualized by the tsar and Church jointly. This fit well with the classical notion of "symphony" between church and state that underlay official Christianity in the Roman and Byzantine Empires.[12]

In principle, heredity alone did not have to dictate who would ascend the throne in Moscow. The Kievan Rus' heritage included mention of inviting a foreign prince, Riurik, to come and rule, as well as the subsequent system of princely seniority and lateral selection. Orthodox rhetoric from the Kievan, Mongol, and early Muscovite periods assigned some legitimizing force (albeit secondary) to military success and popular consent.[13] The great nineteenth-century historian Sergei Soloviev pointed out that Ivan III (r. 1462–1505) held the attitude, "What if I am displeased with my grandson or with any of my children? I will give the rulership to whomsoever I please."[14] In 1576 Ivan IV reportedly indicated to an agent of England's Russia Company that his appointed "Tsar" Simeon (Bekbulatovich) had not been confirmed in office by any consensus—a possible hint at something like vox populi.[15]

Other commentators have raised the possibility that a *zemskii sobor* (land council or assembly of the land) may have "confirmed" the accession of Fyodor in 1584. The zemskii sobor was a quasi-representative body convened sporadically by Russian rulers of the sixteenth and seventeenth centuries and arguably derived from the steppe *quriltai*.[16] The Muscovite conception of a "land council" may also have been influenced by biblical precedents, such as the notion of *am ha-aretz* ("the people of the land"). According to Rabbi Joseph Hertz, this Hebrew term frequently designated a kind of ancient parliament or council of elders. For example, in Genesis 23:7 it described "the Council of the Hittites in session . . . the local Hittite national Council."[17] Yet Fyodor's legitimacy did not actually require or depend upon any such conciliar confirmation; he received it by right of inheritance.

At most, the pre-Smuta historical sources give only hazy hints of the possibility of nonhereditary legitimacy. Moreover, in practice neither Ivan III nor any of his descendants acted in the manner suggested. Instead, as the official documents made clear, they always bestowed the tsardom on their "firstborn sons" or their "sons." Even had Ivan or some other tsar attempted to assign rulership to someone other than his natural heir, the purported legitimacy of this act would have rested on the autocratic power of the grand prince—perceived as God's representative on earth—and certainly not on any form of vox populi or vox feminae. Yet the end of the Riurikid Daniilovich dynasty in 1598 would necessitate significant modifications to that paradigm. In the new situation, seven centuries' worth of hereditary and familial legitimization stretching back to the formation of the Rus' state proved inadequate.

A New Tune: The Initial Accession of Boris Godunov

The conventional story of Boris Godunov's accession in 1598 tells how a zemskii sobor or "assembly of the land," comprised of representatives from all strata of society, "elected" him to the throne. Due to the former tsar's lack of surviving issue, Patriarch Iyov took the logical step of summoning these representatives to choose "whom God would will." Various interpreters have seen in the actions of this body a greater or lesser amount of machination behind the scenes, a greater or lesser "democratic" composition, and so forth.[18] This is not surprising, for Patriarch Iyov owed his position at least partly to Boris Godunov, and the two had long been close allies. According to Makarii's *History of the Russian Church*, "Iyov advantageously promoted Boris' selection to the throne."[19] This may be putting it mildly. By whatever means, however, the assembly did choose Boris, and his authority to rule seemed to rest solidly on this "election."

This traditional story suffers from three main flaws. First, it accepts too uncritically an account given in official documents that were clearly compiled for propaganda purposes. Several scholars have in fact questioned this version of events, and historiography has swung back and forth like a pendulum when dealing with the issue. According to Platonov:

> One may now consider definitively abandoned the previous view of the 1598 selection of a tsar as a crude "comedy" and of the Assembly of the Land that selected Boris as a "toy" in the hands of a cunning ruler [*pravitel'*, a title Boris held already during Fyodor's reign]. . . . If we can assure ourselves that the Assembly of 1598 consciously and freely spoke out in favor of selecting precisely Boris, we will be obligated to consider his ascension to the throne a legal and correct act of the popular will.[20]

Yet a hundred years later, Chester Dunning has written, "The new tsar had himself 'elected' after the fact by a sham zemskii sobor." In fact, Dunning claims that the boyars originally wanted to call an assembly in order to choose a new tsar, but Boris prevented them. Then later the new tsar used the very same concept to legitimize his accession, which had actually been accomplished by other means.[21] Unending debates of this type are common for Muscovite history generally and for the Time of Troubles particularly. A close reading of the documents suggests that much of the confusion or controversy evident in historiography derives from confusion present at the time. It may be that Patriarch Iyov and his associates—the chief ideologues or "spin doctors"[22] of the realm—simply did not know at first what version of events to proffer.

A second problem pervades English-language narratives, since "election" is misleading today as a translation for *izbranie* (or *obiranie*). The Russian word implied only "choice" or "selection." Early modern English did commonly employ the word "election" in this sense, as when the King James Bible remarked on the "election of God."[23] Early modern Muscovite documents used "izbranie" in a similar sense: they spoke of Boris's izbranie by the assembly and also his izbranie by God. Such texts were not claiming that any election (in the modern democratic sense) had taken place. Rather, they were simply asserting that both God and the zemskii sobor had made a choice. Roman and Byzantine notions of "electors" who carried out the will of God in "acclaiming" new emperors likely influenced the Muscovite conception of izbranie.[24] Regardless of the actual history of succession in Muscovy, Orthodox ideology had thus preserved a method in principle for God, the Church, and the people (however conceived or defined) all to participate in the "election" or "selection" of a new ruler. This theory would come to the fore during the Time of Troubles.

The third major problem with the usual story of Boris's accession is that the earliest documents relating to this event actually give several different versions of what happened to bring him to the throne. It seems that at first no one had any clear idea of how to go about legitimizing the nonhereditary accession. The formulation of a new legitimation scheme—including a basic account of what had happened—was a gradual process that occupied the better part of a year. Patriarch Iyov and the other ideologues innovated continually, adding and subtracting various plot elements and ideological arguments as they attempted to produce a convincing Orthodox justification for Russia's first nonhereditary ruler. The final product, apparently prepared in time for Boris's coronation in September 1598 (the beginning of the Muscovite year 7107), contained a radically new paradigm unique to the Time of Troubles.

This new paradigm of legitimacy emerged in a few distinct stages. In March 1598—allegedly after the zemskii sobor had selected Boris, according to the traditional version—the patriarch issued a circular giving the church-state regime's first official version of the accession. According to this document, a large procession of churchmen, boyars, "the Christ-loving army," and "all Orthodox Christians of the Russian state" (*vse pravoslavnye khristiiane, vsenarodnoe mnozhestvo vseia zemlia rosiiskago gosudar'stva*) had gone with ikons and crosses to the Novodevichii Monastery outside Moscow, where Fyodor's widow Irina Godunova and her brother Boris had retired after the death of Tsar Fyodor. "Plunging their heads to the ground," they "petitioned and pleaded" that Irina (or Aleksandra, the name she took upon accepting monastic vows) would bestow the tsardom on Boris and that he would accept it. Eventually all their tears and cries met with success.[25]

Although the patriarch did not explicitly list the bases of Boris's legitimacy, his presentation suggested five sources. First and foremost, Iyov highlighted Irina's status as tsaritsa, wife of the former tsar. He bolstered her personal legitimacy by claiming that everyone wanted her to rule and implying that it would have been perfectly regular for her to do so. Having established Irina's authority, Iyov asserted that she had "blessed" Boris to rule—i.e., had bestowed on him the tsardom. Simply put, Irina had, by virtue of her status as tsaritsa, effectively succeeded Fyodor upon his death; hence, her "blessing" of Boris made him the legitimate tsar. In addition, Iyov tried to link Boris as closely as possible to the now-defunct dynasty by pointing out his family ties to Irina and Fyodor. These techniques correspond to the aspects of traditional Byzantine and Muscovite justifications for rule that had been based on lineage and bestowal.

Second, Iyov repeatedly invoked God as the driving force behind Boris's accession. Irina had not wanted to give in to the people's pleas, but she submitted to "God's will." Boris had not wanted to rule, but he "gave himself up to God's will." Not the Church, not the boyars, not the people, but God Himself had chosen Boris to be tsar. Constant references interspersed throughout the narrative to religious elements such as prayers, holy days, liturgical services, crosses, ikons, saints, and so forth all heightened the impression of God at work to provide for "his people." This notion of divine selection was consistent with Byzantine and Muscovite conceptions of the divinely ordained Christian emperor.

Third, Iyov's letter assigned the initiative and leadership in effecting the accession to himself as patriarch, followed by the rest of the Church hierarchy. The churchmen, determinants or interpreters of God's will on earth, had recognized his will and had led the boyars and the people in asking for Irina and then Boris to rule. According to the document, Iyov, as head of the Church, took it upon himself to pronounce and declare Boris "Sovereign, Tsar, and Grand Prince of All Russia."[26] This ecclesiastic component of legitimacy also drew from earlier imperial and Muscovite precedents.

Fourth, the patriarch took care to link the new tsar to the prestige of Moscow, describing his triumphal entry into the capital. In the Byzantine Empire also, simple association with the capital had often served to help shore up emperors' legitimacy.[27] Iyov's phrasing implied that Moscow itself possessed a special status lending legitimacy to its possessor—an understanding undeniably central to contemporary Russian ideology. To ascend the throne in the fourth Jerusalem, the third Rome, the second Constantinople, and the *first* Moscow—

the first divinely appointed "center of history" with no successor—was a weighty matter. The patriarch presented Boris's accession in Moscow as a fait accompli, a technique that appears calculated to forestall the voicing of any doubts about his legitimacy.

Fifth and finally, Iyov's letter hinted at the role of the Orthodox army and people ("all Orthodox Christendom") in bringing about the new tsar's accession. As of yet, there was no mention or discussion of an assembly of the land per se, only the bare statement that Iyov and his "sons"—the metropolitans, archbishops, bishops, archimandrites, hegumens, the "whole sanctified council," the boyars, and an "all-national multitude of all Orthodox Christians"—had "created a council" (*sovet sotvorshe*) prior to embarking on their pilgrimage to the Novodevichii Monastery.[28] Iyov's letter did not make much of the common people's presence and certainly did not assign to them the right to choose a tsar. In addition, this "council" did not deliberate, as in later versions, to consider who would be the best candidate. Indeed, it assembled *after* the whole multitude had already been petitioning Irina to bestow the rulership on Boris, without success. This initial letter actually gave the impression that the council was summoned only in order to determine the best *means* of convincing Irina to "bless" Boris, not to "elect" or "select" a ruler.[29] Some thought the Church had planned to "excommunicate" Boris and to suspend all religious services until he agreed to accept the throne.[30]

Clearly, the patriarch's first public legitimation of Boris's accession rested heavily on the assumption that Tsaritsa Irina held the rulership and could bestow it as she saw fit. Some historians have accepted this notion as fact. Precedents in the chronicles of Kievan Rus' did include a tenth-century female regent (Olga) as well as a few female provincial rulers. Platonov stated confidently, "If Irina had wanted to retain power in her own hands, no one could have contradicted her."[31] Dunning also argued that Irina had been Fyodor's "coruler" and thus "had a very real claim to the throne."[32] Isolde Thyrêt argued intriguingly that Irina's Orthodox piety and links to female saints bolstered her political legitimacy, with the result that "by the late sixteenth century an elaborate ideology had developed that proclaimed the acceptability of a female ruler in Muscovite Russia."[33]

However, the fact remains that the precise situation had not arisen previously in Muscovy. Elena Glinskaia, mother of Ivan IV, had apparently served as regent during her son's infancy in the 1530s, yet this did not entail actual succession to the rulership.[34] Thus, claims of what would have happened had Irina chosen to succeed her late husband may be stretching the case somewhat.

Indeed, if the acceptability of a female ruler rested on Irina's own personal piety, as Thyrêt's work implies, then it would be a mistake to think that any woman in the same position could have ascended the chief throne as a matter of course. Vox feminae, the authorizing voice of a royal woman, represented a significant innovation in official politics when it appeared in the Time of Troubles. Although Irina notably did *not* become the principal ruler of Russia, her status did provide the main justification for Boris's accession in early 1598. This legitimizing role—shared by several other women of the period—may have been a transitional stage in preparing the way for later female rulers of Russia.[35]

Active Interlude: The Crimean Affair

The next important stage in the lengthy process of legitimizing Boris's accession occurred in the summer of 1598, when the suppression of a real or imagined Crimean Tatar invasion catapulted the new tsar to a zenith of popularity and power. Boris set off on an ostensible military campaign to the south, while Patriarch Iyov publicly lauded him as the ideal Orthodox Christian ruler, both zealously and humbly pious, chosen by God for the throne, a mighty crusader for the faith and a terror to the infidel enemy. Boris fought no battles and barely got within a thousand kilometers of Crimea, but he returned triumphantly to Moscow as a hero and the unquestioned tsar of Orthodox Russia.

The contemporary witness Jacques Margeret claimed that this entire Crimean affair had been manufactured solely for the purpose of shoring up Boris's legitimacy. Margeret asserted that Boris intentionally circulated false rumors of an impending Crimean Tatar invasion specifically in order to lead an army south and thereby enhance his public image. With great pomp and a large army the new tsar proceeded to Serpukhov—about a tenth of the way to Crimea. There he received a Crimean ambassador and agreed on an allegedly prearranged treaty. Then Boris triumphantly returned to the capital, claiming to have frightened off the Tatar khan.[36]

The famous nineteenth-century historian Nikolai Karamzin adopted Margeret's account, scathingly attacking Boris for this manipulative deception. "With a cunning mind dominating the movements of his heart," wrote Karamzin, Boris had gathered a huge army, sent a "friendly letter" to the khan, and then "entertained with dinners, and each time no less than ten thousand men, on silver dishes, under tents . . . [as] the guards, nowhere seeing the dust, nowhere hearing the tramp of horses, dozed in the silence of the steppes." This "war" represented nothing but a clever intrigue. "Instead of [the expected] clouds of enemies, peaceful ambassadors of Kazy-Girei appeared with our couriers in the southern regions of Russia."[37]

As Karamzin observed, Boris made good use of an ostensibly dangerous situation to gain the overwhelming support of the Russian "army"—meaning primarily the aristocratic commanders, but perhaps also the rank and file. This was important for obvious practical reasons but also for ideological ones. Boris could now claim something akin to Roman imperial acclamation, when the army had voiced its support for a particular ruler (generally in exchange for gifts and favors). Meanwhile, Patriarch Iyov took care of the home front, unfailingly describing the tsar as a great Orthodox military champion, a new Constantine or Justinian.[38]

Did Boris and Iyov intentionally sound a false alarm in order to secure their position? Later in the nineteenth century Sergei Soloviev adopted a more cautious approach. He did not accuse Boris of contriving the whole affair but still pointed to its beneficial effects for the regime. The scale of Boris's triumphal return to the capital suggested that he had "conquered an entire foreign realm." Patriarch Iyov praised Boris in front of the assembled crowds as "our good and Christ-loving shepherd, beloved and highly favored by God." The clergy led the people in bowing to the tsar, with tears, and welcoming Boris "to his sovereign patrimony [*votchina*], to the throne of the tsars and to all the dominions of the Russian land." Thus, according to Soloviev as well, the Crimean affair clearly strengthened Boris's grip on power.[39]

Sergei Platonov also staked out a middle position, arguing that Boris had exaggerated a potential threat in order "to seek popularity and support for his throne among Muscovy's military forces."[40] In the later twentieth century, however, Ruslan Skrynnikov rejuvenated the position of Margeret and Karamzin. In his view the council of boyars was working against Boris "to establish a boyar regime" with Simeon Bekbulatovich, to whom Ivan IV had already given titles of "tsar" and "grand prince," as their puppet ruler.[41] Boris knew of these schemes and devised the Crimean affair as a means of gaining the upper hand over the boyars. The new tsar spread false rumors of an attack and then led his army southward, where "there was no enemy attack for the ruler to repel." Skrynnikov calls this "a decisive stage in Boris Godunov's election campaign" and credits it with gaining him official recognition from Crimea and also England.[42] In sum, "the Serpukhov campaign was unquestionabl[y] the cleverest move in his entire election struggle. . . . Godunov managed to have the Moscow and a majority of the provincial gentry recognize him as the *de facto* tsar."[43]

We know that Tsar Boris and Patriarch Iyov did see Bekbulatovich as a significant threat. They may have ordered him blinded, and eventually they exiled him. Later, Tsar Dmitrii would have him tonsured and imprisoned in the faraway north. Remarkably, however, both governments continued to accord him the title of "tsar"![44] Boris, of course, insisted that everything had been aboveboard during the Crimean campaign: Khan Kazy-Girei had heard of Moscow's relations with "all the great states"—including the Habsburg Empire, Persia, Spain, and France—and therefore asked "to be with us in friendship and in love."[45]

Skrynnikov's arguments to the contrary did not convince Chester Dunning. Emphasizing the credibility of the Crimean Tatar threat, he remarked, "There is little evidence . . . that Boris contrived this threat as a means to gain support for his election. The charge has been rejected by many scholars as just one more false report spread by Boris's enemies."[46] Dunning also maintained that "Boris Godunov was himself, first and foremost, one of the leading boyars. . . . Contrary to the traditional interpretation of his struggle for power, the bulk of the Russian aristocracy did not oppose Godunov's accession."[47] The debate thus continues.

The question of whether Boris's government actually did fabricate the threat of a Crimean Tatar attack is, like so many other questions of the period, unsolvable. Neither option can be discounted out of hand. Certainly the Crimeans did have the potential to mount a serious attack on Muscovy. In 1571 they had looted and burned parts of Moscow itself. Twenty years later they again penetrated all the way to the capital. In 1592 Crimean Tatar forces "devastated the regions of Riazan, Kashira, and Tula and brought back numerous captives."[48] Understandably, defense against Tatar raids in the Russian borderlands and heartland had to constitute a prime concern of the Muscovite government—and of its people—in the last three decades of the sixteenth century.[49] However, this merely shows that warnings of a Crimean invasion could easily appear credible, not that the particular warnings issued in 1598 were genuine. If Boris and Iyov did manufacture the crisis, they did so by jabbing a nerve with the potential to provoke real fear in the hearts of the population. The dispersion of the apparent threat, unsurprisingly, produced a concomitantly strong sense of gratitude and adoration in those same hearts.

Whether Boris and Iyov acted in good or bad faith during the Crimean affair, one thing is certain: the ostensible "victory" dramatically improved the new tsar's hold on power in the summer of 1598. Gaining the support of commanders in the field presented obvious advantages. However, Patriarch Iyov's efforts in the capital cannot be considered of lesser significance. By means of a very public correspondence with Boris throughout the course of the Crimean campaign, the chief ecclesiastic tied the new tsar in to the whole sacred history of Orthodox Christianity. Makarii, who accepted the correspondence more or less at face value, nonetheless remarked that it was "highly scanty in content, but then rich in verbosity and saturation of expressions."[50] However, the ostentatious rhetoric flowing back and forth between tsar and patriarch served a vital function. Official documents and oaths of loyalty already threatened any potential rebels with excommunication and damnation.[51] Yet such threats did not always constitute a sufficient deterrent—as indeed the subsequent history of the Troubles would repeatedly demonstrate. A successful usurper could always reverse the blessings and curses. The Crimean affair permitted the new government to strengthen its deterrent to revolt. Pious and humble, blessed and anointed by God, the "champion" and "liberator" of the "New Israel," Boris had defended the "true faith" and instilled fear in the "godless infidels." To challenge such a man would be tantamount to fighting against Orthodoxy itself.[52]

A sample from one of the patriarch's letters may illustrate this point. His missive of June 2 lauded Boris as "the inflexible true champion of the unblemished Orthodox Christian faith" and "son of the holy Church." According to Iyov, the new tsar's actions demonstrated that he concerned himself solely with protecting the Orthodox faith, the Orthodox Church, the Orthodox land, and the Orthodox people. Boris had set out to defend these against "the enemy of the cross of Christ," those "instruments of the devil," the "godless Hagarites" (a derogatory Muscovite term for unbelievers, especially Muslims).[53] God would therefore "send him a rod of strength from Zion" and "break iron bars" before him. These expressions came primarily from Isaiah 45, a famous prophecy addressed to "God's anointed" Cyrus I of Persia. Like many great military figures in biblical and Russian history—Abraham, Gideon, Prince Volodimer, Aleksandr Nevskii—Boris had set out on a holy mission that, the patriarch claimed, could not fail:

> Now then, that same all-merciful Lord God, who chose you as our sovereign, even as anciently [he chose] Moses and Joshua and others who liberated Israel— so then may the Lord grant you as the liberator of us, the new Israel, the people called by Christ's name, from this damned and utterly proud pagan Tsar Kazy-Girei who boasts against us; and [may] the Lord subdue his grandiloquence

and all your enemies under your feet; and [may] he send you as abettors his holy angels and the holy martyrs, and [may] they confound [*smiatut*] them, and [may] they perish![54]

The patriarch's other letters were replete with similar phrasings. Boris, proclaimed God's chosen head of the "New Israel," responded in kind. His answering letters described Iyov as "God-inspired [*bogodukhnovennyi*] . . . supernatural [*vysheestestvennyi*] in spiritual exploits." The term "God-inspired," or more literally "God-breathed," was a term applied to holy writings in 2 Timothy 3:16 (Judeo-Greek *theopneustos*). Application of this specialized term to Iyov implied that the patriarch's every word proceeded directly from God and should be regarded as absolute truth. Boris demonstrated his own submission to God and the Church by rhetorically bowing to "my great father and Sovereign," the "first patriarch" and "firm pillar of Orthodoxy." He honored Iyov as *pervoprestol'nik,* meaning the occupant of the premier (ecclesiastical) throne. Later he also called him *soprestol'nik* (co-ruler) on the two thrones of Muscovy. When Boris returned to Moscow in July at the head of his army, Iyov hailed him with the following words: "O chosen by God, and beloved by God, and honored by God, and gifted by God, pious and great Sovereign, Tsar, and Grand Prince Boris Feodorovich [Fyodorovich], Autocrat of All Russia!"[55] These exchanges between tsar and patriarch represented a supreme example of Orthodox "symphony" in practice.

The firmer establishment of Boris's sovereignty as a result of the Crimean affair had two aspects: the practical side of courting the army commanders and soldiers, and the ideological campaign directed by the Church, which installed the new tsar among the pantheon of great biblical and Orthodox Christian heroes. It is for this reason that the Crimean affair represented a turning point in Boris's accession. Hereafter, the ideologues would be free to innovate without compunction, accorded a greater flexibility by the securer position of the tsar. During the Crimean campaign the Church had already expressed its desire that the tsardom would pass from Boris to his "sons' sons for generation after generation forever."[56] Now it would set about attempting to make this goal a reality by inventing a thoroughly new paradigm of legitimacy unique to the Time of Troubles.

Second Movement: The Ideology of Boris's Coronation

The new government wasted no time in utilizing its newly won freedom of action. In the following months of 1598, Patriarch Iyov seemingly presided over a key transformation in the rhetoric concerning Boris's accession. The so-called "Conciliar Determination" and "Confirmatory Document" both gave explicit rationales for Boris's legitimacy and, most importantly, included what would later become the accepted version of events, repeated by generations of historians: his "selection" (*izbranie*) by a kind of representative assembly, commonly identified with the zemskii sobor (although not always called by that name in the documents). Formulated just in time for the coronation and anointing of the new tsar, this novel paradigm of legitimation would have a lasting impact.

The Conciliar Determination (*Sobornoe opredelenie*), despite its customary name, may actually have been a draft declaration rather than the official record of any council. This document of mid-1598 introduced several major modifications of earlier rhetoric: First, Boris's sister Irina disappeared from the story entirely. Instead of focusing on her "blessing," the document alleged a kind of bestowal of the tsardom on Boris by both Ivan IV and Fyodor, the previous (male) tsars. Second, the authors of this document repeatedly emphasized that God had "fore-chosen" or "pre-selected" Boris to rule. Third, instead of all the previous tears and "pleas" to the tsaritsa to appoint her brother as the new tsar, this time the "council" portrayed itself as a legal, constituent assembly entrusted with the task of confirming God's own selection of Boris. By its "selection" (*izbranie*) of the tsar, the whole Russian Orthodox people had obligated itself to obey him. Everyone in the whole empire "from end to end"—beginning with ecclesiastic hierarchs and boyars on down to merchants and peasants—was said to be represented in this assembly. Fourth, the document advanced an ostensibly "democratic" or popular form of legitimacy, making the extraordinary claim that "the voice of the people is the voice of God" (*glas naroda glas Bozhii*). In other words, public opinion—in this case, popular acclaim of Boris—allegedly represented an expression of the divine will! Fifth, the document also listed numerous biblical and historical precedents intended to demonstrate the appropriateness of Boris's accession and the "orthodoxy" of the new justifications for his rule.[57]

The major new modifications included in the Conciliar Determination demonstrate that instead of working ad hoc with whatever ideological elements seemed to fit the situation, the patriarch and his associates were now conducting fairly serious research in order to find completely new foundations for Boris's rule. The unprecedented use of *vox populi, vox Dei* was their most remarkable innovation—all the more so since its source remains mysterious. The Latin phrase is itself of obscure origin: the first surviving attestation dates not from classical antiquity but from the eighth century CE. In a letter to Charlemagne, Alcuin of York advised disregarding the saying as illegitimate, "since the riotousness of the crowds is always very close to madness." William of Malmesbury (ca. 1095–1143) also argued against vox populi, vox Dei, which in its original meaning apparently implied only that the voice of the people—correct or not—was too powerful to be resisted. However, in the fourteenth century Walter Reynolds, Archbishop of Canterbury, finally utilized the striking proverb in legitimizing the supposedly "popular" deposition of Edward II. The people's voice, he claimed, really should be respected as the voice of God. Nonetheless, in the mid-seventeenth century Sir Thomas Browne included vox populi, vox Dei as one of the widespread "vulgar errors" refuted in his *Pseudodoxia Epidemica.*[58]

In the absence of any known Byzantine, Kievan, or Muscovite usage prior to the Time of Troubles, one wonders if perhaps Russia's ideologues borrowed this phrase, together with its political implications, from Western Europe. Diplomatic and trade relations could have provided the vehicle of transfer.[59] In any event, the saying had not previously formed part of the toolbox of Russian Orthodox legitimacy. Precisely how anomalous it was for all of Russian history may be seen from the epigraph at the beginning of this chapter: at the close of the nineteenth century, representatives of the Russian regime would still be arguing vehemently against the very idea of associating the "people's voice" with "God's voice." In the early seventeenth century, it ironically seems to have been employed in the interest of fostering obedience among the people.

To return to the Conciliar Determination, a second noteworthy innovation at this stage of the game was a rather thorough culling of biblical and imperial history—"Israel and the Greek domain," as the Muscovites put it. Their historical presentation sought to demonstrate that Orthodox sacred history knew many instances of legitimate rulers arising from less than royal origins. Among those not born to the throne, the Muscovite ideologues counted "Tsar" David, the preeminent king of ancient Israel, and Joseph "the Beautiful," the son of Jacob who was sold into slavery but later rose to become prime minister of Egypt. The document claimed that Joseph had "reigned in Egypt" (*tsar'stvova vo Egipte*), even though in the biblical story Pharaoh expressly continued to occupy the throne.[60] Other alleged precedents for the "selection" of Boris included Constantine I the Great—"equal to the apostles, shining with Orthodoxy like the sun"; Theodosius the Great, termed predestined or "preselected" (*pred'izbran*) for his imperial role as "champion of piety, exposer of impiety"; Marcianus Augustus—"a great tsar of piety and faith"; Michael I

Rhangabe—that iconophile "of very blessed faith and piety"; and Basil I the Macedonian, who was "anointed to the tsardom by Patriarch Photius."[61]

As might be expected, the text did not treat all these figures accurately or evenly; for instance, it conveniently omitted Basil's murder of Michael III and the removal of Photius upon his objection to this act. Yet the overall point was eminently clear: Boris did not have to be of royal stock to be chosen by God to rule over his land. Moreover, the patriarch and church hierarchs could verify and reify "God's choice." The historical examples were followed by numerous Scriptural quotations and references to the authority of the Holy Spirit working through his earthly representatives. Anyone who would speak a word against the decisions of the Church in this case was "foolish and cursed" (*nerazumen i prokliat*) and would be judged by God.[62]

The Confirmatory Document or Charter of Affirmation (*Utverzhdennaia gramota*) purported to be an official record of the land assembly and provided a much-expanded official version of events. Dated August 1, 1598, one month before the new tsar's coronation ceremony, it represented a synthesis of all the previous attempted and proposed means of legitimation. Some scholars have questioned the veracity of this date, pointing to apparent contradictions with other elements of the historical record.[63] One possibility is that the Confirmatory Document was originally composed around this time and then edited and reedited over a period of several months. The Confirmatory Document is probably the most cited source on the accession of Boris Godunov. Despite the fact that it clearly represents a piece of carefully constructed propaganda, its version has essentially dominated historiography for four hundred years. The more appropriate approach, however, is to consider this document in the context of evolving legitimation of Boris's accession, rather than as a reliable historical record. The document expressed ideas that coalesced, just prior to Boris's coronation, into the authoritative, Orthodox justification for his rule.

Lev Cherepnin characterized this extraordinary composition as "both a legal document and a political tractate" that reinforced the defense of Boris's power. He described how "the thesis of the three sources of Boris' competence to be tsar (divine foreordination, the will of the people, the bequest of [Ivan IV] Groznyi) received further development."[64] One may add that the Confirmatory Document merged all of the previous justifications for Boris's accession into a single, comprehensive presentation: First, the theme of God's "fore-choosing" of the new tsar received extensive treatment and dominated the narrative. From start to finish, it was claimed, this had been "God's affair, not man's."[65] Second, the Church leadership confirmed "God's will." Third, Tsaritsa Irina reentered the picture; her "blessing" was again seen as necessary for Boris's accession. Nonetheless, at the same time this final formulation continued to rely on a quasi-bestowal of the tsardom by both Ivan IV and Fyodor, expressed somewhat differently than in the Conciliar Determination. Fourth, in the Confirmatory Document, the "whole land" again played an important role in persistently supplicating Irina and Boris to accept "God's will," and great lengths were taken to portray the council as a properly constituted, electoral body. However, the document shied away from assigning Boris's accession to popular election per se, preferring to focus on "God's will" and the alleged "unanimity" that reigned among all sectors of the population even prior to the convening of an assembly. In other words, there had been only one candidate ever eligible for "election." Fifth, the "Christ-loving army" made an appearance, as did Boris's allegedly great victories over the Crimean khan. Sixth, the Confirmatory Document also lauded Boris's personal characteristics, pointing to his capable administration and foreign policy successes during the reign of Tsar Fyodor.

Among Boris's alleged virtues his supposed reluctance to accept the throne ballooned into a major evidence of his fitness for the throne. The promulgation of this theme occupied page after page of the document and bordered on the absurd. The goal was to drive home the point that Boris had never thought of ruling, had never wanted to rule, and had finally consented to rule only in submission to God's will and in service to the country.[66] In all the above respects, the Confirmatory Document synthesized official legitimation rhetoric of the previous six months. The ideologues had decided to "cover all the bases," so to speak, to use virtually everything they had thought up since the death of Tsar Fyodor in January 1598. They only had to make sure to adjust each argument enough so that it did not conflict glaringly with any of the others.

Tsar Boris's coronation at the beginning of September 1598 put this final synthesis of legitimation strategies to good use. An extravagant affair, the ceremony placed special emphasis on the biblical and Byzantine notions of anointing, which served to distract attention further from Boris's lack of hereditary or dynastic legitimacy.[67] In the tsar's prepared speech to the patriarch, he recounted that Tsar Fyodor had been anointed (*pomazalsia*) after receiving the "blessing" to rule from his father Ivan IV. He then concluded, "And you, our father, according to God's will and according to your choice [*po vashemu izbraniiu*], should bless and anoint [*b"... blagoslovil i pomazal*] and place and crown me with that crown of the tsars, according to the ancient procedure of the tsars, [to rule] over that great state, over the great state [or dominion] of Vladimir and Moscow and Novgorod."[68]

Patriarch Iyov, the spiritual "father" of all Orthodox Russians, including the tsar himself, could thus legitimize Boris as Ivan IV had Fyodor. Iyov's answering speech to the new tsar also highlighted anointing as a key component of succession.[69] Boris Godunov, the erstwhile servitor, had now become God's anointed ruler (*pomazannik Bozhii*), on a par with King David or any number of other figures from Orthodox sacred history. In the coming years Patriarch Iyov would author a propagandistic *Life of Fyodor* that further attempted to tie Boris in with the previous dynasty and with Russian Orthodox piety. Iyov's encomium for the deceased tsar described the new one as surpassing all others in wisdom and bravery.[70]

Tsar Boris soon issued instructions for three days of national prayer on behalf of himself and his family, for a peaceful and victorious reign. Churches and monasteries throughout the land were to arrange the singing of predetermined prayers, at which attendance was obligatory.[71] Government officials also administered a new oath of loyalty that incorporated the recently devised story of Boris's accession. The population was required to "kiss the cross" to the truth of this version and to foreswear any contact with "Tsar Simeon"—who had recently and suspiciously "become blind."[72] As usual, the citizenry bound itself with curses against all possible forms of lèse majesté (thought, word, and deed):

> I kiss this holy and life-creating cross of the Lord to everything written in this record. . . . And [if] I do not undertake to serve and act rightly toward my Sovereign, Tsar, and Grand Prince Boris Fyodorovich of All Russia, and his tsaritsa, and their children, my sovereigns, according to this cross-kissing, or [if] I do anything that is evil, violating this cross-kissing; then let there not be upon me the favor of God and the Immaculate Mother of God and the great Russian wonder-workers Peter and Aleksei and Iona and all the saints, and let there not be upon me the blessing of the most holy Patriarch Iyov of Moscow and all Russia, and of the metropolitans and archbishops and bishops and archimandrites and the whole sanctified universal [Church] council.[73]

The contemporary witness Ivan Timofeev later wrote that this oath to Boris had represented a transgression of the edicts of previous tsars and blasphemy or heresy against God himself.[74] His comment illustrates the extent to which Patriarch Iyov and his assistants had created a new and different political orthodoxy (Orthodoxy) during the course of 1598. In retrospect, their official edicts could be perceived or portrayed as running completely counter to the earlier stream of Muscovite tradition. Yet it was the development of that tradition that had enabled Iyov's innovations. His new paradigm of legitimacy drew extensively from the flourishing of Byzantine ideology that had reached its zenith under Ivan IV. Boris's active pursuit of a patriarchate during the reign of Fyodor I had also made possible an exalted view of the top churchman's role in the political sphere, so central to the 1598 legitimation strategies.

In foreign affairs, too, the government presented a version of Boris's accession that synthesized its earlier legitimation strategies. In 1599 Boris sent an embassy to Emperor Rudolf II of Habsburg, one that succeeded in securing recognition for him as "autocrat" as well as "tsar." The documents of this embassy gave the following reasons for his accession: (1) the will of God; (2) the "order" (*prikaz*) of Tsar Fyodor; (3) the "blessing" of Irina/Aleksandra; and (4) the "petition and request" of the patriarch, the leading churchmen, "the whole consecrated ecumenical council of the Russian state" (*vsego osviashchennogo vselenskogo sobora rosiiskogo gosudarstva*), the vassals of Muscovy, the nobility, the service class, and "all Orthodox Christendom" (*vsego pravoslavnago khrest'ianstva*).[75] According to Bantysh-Kamensky, Rudolf's answering letter of 1600 contained the first reference by a Habsburg emperor to a Muscovite tsar as "utterly illustrious" (*presvetleishii*).[76] The syncretic approach of Boris and Iyov, which included unprecedented utilization of vox populi and vox feminae, would be imitated in legitimizing several subsequent rulers of the Time of Troubles.

Theme and Variation: The Attempted Accession of Fyodor Borisovich

In order to understand how the 1598 paradigm became established in the politico-religious ideology of the period, it will be useful to skip ahead for a moment to 1605. As the insurgent Dmitrii's forces were pressing the capital, Boris died and his sixteen-year-old son officially ascended the throne. Fyodor Borisovich Godunov barely had time to break in the royal vestments before losing his life in a coup. Nonetheless, his accession had a very significant effect in both revising and perpetuating the new forms of legitimation originally invented for his father.

Although the young Tsar Fyodor II had essentially inherited the throne from his father, Boris Godunov, official rhetoric concerning his accession followed the template created in 1598. Rather than heredity—the true source of his claim to the throne—Fyodor's legitimacy rested, according to the leading ideologues, on divine will, Church sanction, bestowal by the late tsar, bestowal by the widowed tsaritsa, and popular acclaim.[77] This combination had been extraordinarily novel in 1598; in 1605 it was purely mimetic.

As reproduced in an April 1605 letter from Metropolitan Kirill of Rostov and Yaroslavl, the accession story devised for Fyodor II began by claiming that before his death Boris had "ordered and blessed" his son to rule.[78] The document's formulators appealed to God's will, the sanction of the Church and the Orthodox faith generally, and the blessing or bestowal of the former tsar. Hereditary succession remained half-implied, but too much emphasis on this point would have been problematic, calling Boris's own legitimacy into question. After all, a rival was then at the gates of Moscow with an army heralding him as the true tsar due to his claimed paternity! As a result, the authors did not assert, as before 1598, that "the tsars and grand princes gave the tsardom and grand principality of Great Russia to their sons." To do so might actually have damaged rather than strengthened Fyodor's case.

Although Fyodor II had clearly come to the throne simply by inheritance, his accession was portrayed in the documents in almost exactly the same terms as his father's. The leading churchmen apparently wanted to give the impression that the nonhereditary justifications of 1598 represented an actual norm for Muscovy and that this "norm" had now been followed to the letter in 1605. The ecclesiastic account continued:

> And upon the decease of our Great Sovereign, Tsar, and Grand Prince Boris Fyodorovich, Autocrat of all Russia, the most holy Iyov, Patriarch of Moscow and all Russia, and with him in the Holy Spirit we his sons, the metropolitans and archbishops and bishops, and the whole sanctified universal council, and the boyars and nobles and chancery people and the whole tsar's cabinet [*sigklit*],[79] and the great merchants and trading people, and the all-national multitude of the Russian state pleaded [*molili*] with tears and requested mercy of the great Sovereign, the pious Tsaritsa and Grand Princess Maria Grigorievna of all Russia, that the Sovereign [Lady] would grant, [and] act mercifully, [and] not leave us orphans to be destroyed to the end . . . [that she would] bless her well-born son, our Great Sovereign, Tsarevich Prince Fyodor Borisovich of all Russia, to be over the Russian state as tsar and autocrat of all the Russian land.[80]

The above motifs had obviously been drawn directly, and nearly verbatim, from the story of Boris's izbranie. The Church leadership assumed a role of national leadership upon the tsar's death, acting "in the Holy Spirit." The entire nation allegedly participated in the process of selecting a new tsar, from ecclesiastics to boyars to merchants to the "multitude." According to the document, all these different social groups shared the same unanimous opinion of what was to be done. Dunning, drawing on the work of other scholars, interpreted this to mean that "documents were even faked to make it appear that the new tsar had been chosen by a zemskii sobor."[81] The authors, as often happened, were "fudging the books": without explicitly talking about a constituent assembly, they used the same terminology that had been devised in 1598 in order to "prove" broad support for the accession among all segments of the Orthodox population.

Continuing on the same theme, the document claimed that the patriarch and the nation as a whole tearfully "pleaded" with the former tsar's widow to "bless" a male relative (in this case, her son) to rule as tsar over the Russian state. This corresponded precisely to Irina's "blessing" of her brother Boris. Some nominal rule was assigned to the tsaritsa in order to enable her to fulfill this role. The prominence assigned to the title "autocrat," present to some extent in 1598 but also enhanced by Boris after his accession, constituted another important element. Fyodor was to be not only tsar but also *samoderzhets,* ruling independently of any suzerainty: this merited special emphasis in the document.[82]

What are we to make of this? Strange as it may seem, the Church had by now actually created an entirely new model for the accession of a Muscovite tsar. The old dynastic pattern, followed for centuries, had been scrapped—very quietly and very subtly. Without attributing legitimacy to any single factor, the ideologues justified Fyodor Borisovich's accession on the basis of the combination of factors concocted in 1598. Nor was this all; the rest of the official version of Fyodor's accession continued to imitate the 1598 synthesis:

And our Great Sovereign, the pious and Christ-loving Tsaritsa and Grand Princess Maria Grigorievna of all Russia, did not despise our tears and pleading [*molenie*]. . . . She blessed and commanded her son, our Great Sovereign, Tsarevich Prince Fyodor Borisovich of all Russia, to be tsar and autocrat over the Muscovite state and over all states of the Russian tsardom, just as also his father, the Great Sovereign, Tsar, and Grand Prince Boris Fyodorovich, Autocrat of all Russia, had been tsar over the Russian state.[83]

Like Irina's concession to the pleas and tears of the patriarch and the people in 1598, this passage highlighted vox feminae, the blessing to rule by a female authority figure. This time around Tsaritsa Maria was to continue to play a role as ruler—although precisely what role was not specified. Given these circumstances, it is especially significant that Dmitrii's allies killed not only Fyodor but also his mother—although not his royal sister Ksenia (Xenia)— when carrying out their coup d'état.[84] Perhaps this gruesome act demonstrates how entrenched the new paradigm of legitimacy had become in just a few short years. Not only the tsar but also the female authority figure had to be eliminated. In fact, upon ascending the throne Dmitrii would himself rely heavily on a form of vox feminae even while claiming hereditary legitimacy.[85]

The last part of Fyodor II's accession document described his own acceptance of the ostensible will of the "entire land" and the ensuing validation of his accession by Church and nation.[86] This was a fitting conclusion, again reminiscent of his father's accession. In sum, the official rhetoric of 1605 clearly perpetuated the nonhereditary forms of legitimation adopted in 1598. More than that, Fyodor's accession established a new Muscovite "norm." According to this new standard, portrayed as long-standing Orthodoxy, God directed the Church hierarchy in selecting a new monarch. The populace of all ranks cooperated in this process of selection, and then "all Orthodox Christendom," with the patriarch at its head, petitioned the tsaritsa to "bless" or appoint her male relative to rule. The new legitimation paradigm—which reflected striking innovation and improvisation—may thus be understood as a conscious combination of vox Dei, vox populi, and vox feminae. Official Orthodoxy throughout the rest of the Troubles, no matter which tsar was in power, would always be influenced by the unique and anomalous stratagem devised by Patriarch Iyov and his associates in 1598.

CHAPTER FOUR

In Hunger and Pain

The Response of the Church to Famine and
Civil Warfare

Глад же съодоле на земли.
(Yet the famine intensified in the land.)
—Genesis 43:1 in the Ostroh Bible, 1581[1]

For the sake of our sins and those of all Orthodox Christendom, God allowed in an enemy and profaner of the Christian faith.
—Letter of Patriarch Iyov, 1605[2]

The reinvention of politico-religious legitimacy that enabled Boris
Godunov's accession in 1598 could only postpone, not prevent, the Troubles.
After an initial period in which Tsar Boris's rule seemed relatively stable, a
dreadful famine hit in 1601 and did not let up for three years. If Russia was a
divinely ordered realm with the tsar at the top, representing God on earth, then
something must have gone terribly wrong. With the dead and dying lying in the
streets, rumors spread that Boris had not been "chosen" by God after all—and
that the "true tsar" was still alive. Frightening apparitions and perceived omens
of evil further delegitimized Boris.[3] When a man claiming to be Dmitrii, son
of Ivan IV, appeared in the Polish-Lithuanian borderlands, he quickly raised a
large army and marched on Moscow. The bloody civil wars that ensued would
plunge Russia into what many considered the darkest years in its history.

Although Boris and his son Fyodor claimed vox populi as the basis for their legitimacy, in actual fact they lacked the necessary popular support to establish their dynasty. Ironically, "Dmitrii" wrenched power from the Godunovs on the strength of a popular movement but rejected such "democratic" justifications for rule. His official legitimation scheme was a simpler and more traditional one, based on purported heredity. The Orthodox Church sanctioned and propagated each of these conflicting justifications for power, demonstrating that a dangerous political question had been left unresolved. What was the role of the people in choosing a tsar? And could their physical power be restrained by official ideological decrees?

In the economic realm, the monasteries and other ecclesiastic institutions continued to receive charters and tax exemptions for rights to land, people, and resources. This patronage relationship with the tsar's central government remained highly profitable in the first years of the Troubles. As a result, Church institutions continued to support whoever occupied the throne in Moscow, regardless of how it had been attained. But the stream of money did not flow in only one direction. The civil war throttled customary royal donations to monasteries (vklady), which had often reached into the thousands of rubles. Now the tsars began to impose huge war levies on the monasteries. Facing a depletion of their treasuries, the latter ever more stubbornly defended their economic privileges against the surrounding masses. The years of famine and warfare saw numerous conflicts as peasants and townspeople struggled to survive and ecclesiastics fought to maintain the foundations of their institutional wealth. Nonetheless, most commoners continued to look to Orthodoxy as their hope for salvation.

The Calm Before the Hurricane

"On the 28th day of June of the year 7107 [1599 CE], the Great Sovereign, Tsar and Grand Prince Boris Fyodorovich, Autocrat of all Russia, sent his envoy, Conciliar Secretary Afanasii Vlasiev, to his brother, the Great Sovereign, the Roman Emperor Rudolf [II]."[4] So begins the official account of the first Muscovite embassy to the Habsburg Empire after the accession of Boris Godunov. Having been crowned tsar by Patriarch Iyov in Moscow, Boris now needed external endorsement of his accession. As the "senior sovereign of the continent," the Holy Roman Emperor played a key role in European diplomacy of the period, acting as an arbiter of legitimacy. Rudolf's acceptance of any new ruler's claims could be taken as confirmation of the latter's right to rule. Conversely, his rejection of such claims would tarnish any attempts at legitimization.[5]

In Pilsen the Russian envoy Afanasii Vlasiev reported to the emperor's court the story of Boris's accession that Patriarch Iyov and the other ideologues had devised over the course of the previous year. This version of events apparently satisfied Rudolf. After some haggling over titles, he did recognize Boris as the rightful "tsar" (caesar) and also as "autocrat" (i.e., ruler *sui juris*). Boris desperately wanted to obtain endorsement of these claims, which would ostensibly give him the same status as hereditary rulers with unquestioned legitimacy. In his subsequent letter of 1600, the Habsburg emperor went further and for the first time referred to the Muscovite tsar as "utterly illustrious."[6] Supported by the Russian church domestically and recognized internationally by the Habsburg emperor, the new tsar had passed the most important hurdles of his young reign and could rest easier.

Vlasiev's embassy of 1599 also illustrated the central role devoted to Orthodox Christianity in the Russian conduct of foreign affairs at this time. The tsar professed great support for the Habsburgs in their "Long War" against the Ottoman Turks, while stressing that the disputed lands in southeast Europe truly belonged to the realm of Orthodoxy. The "liberation of Orthodox Christendom from the hands of the infidel" would remain a key pursuit of Russian foreign policy all the way through the nineteenth century. Following the text prepared for him in Moscow, the Russian envoy also repeatedly vilified the hated Polish-Lithuanian (Catholic) Rzeczpospolita as "unconcerned about [the fate of] Christendom," "friendly with the foe of all Christendom," and even "bribing the Turkish sultan and the Crimean khan against Christians."[7]

Back at home, Tsar Boris set about removing his domestic enemies. Known opponents and potential rivals among the aristocracy were arrested and exiled. Dunning argues that "Godunov's heavy hand in dealing with his political foes had disastrous consequences for his dynasty and for Russia. It apparently drove the remaining Romanovs, Bogdan Belskii, and possibly the Nagoi clan into a secret alliance against him."[8] Yet Boris was more lenient than many of his predecessors, and for the time being his rule seemed assured. The ambitious tsar even initiated a type of "Westernization," recruiting European doctors and professors in German cities. He sent young boyars to study in England, France, and Germany and planned to open an academy in Moscow.[9] This unusual step did not call into question his Orthodoxy; Boris's close alliance with and munificent gifts to the Russian Church were common knowledge.[10]

In these first years of Boris's reign, small- and large-scale monastic businesses apparently functioned well. Ecclesiastic institutions continued to receive their numerous charters for rights to land, villages, resources, tax exemptions, judicial privileges, and so forth. The tsar viewed all Russian monks and nuns as "his intercessors to God" (*bogomol'tsy svoi*), and his government actively participated in mediating their interaction with the broader society. Moscow had a clear motive in arranging matters so that the monasteries remained strong and profitable: these institutions acted as pillars of stability in a country with a relatively sparse national administration.

At the same time, the tsar and his bureaucrats did not allow the monasteries a completely free hand. In 1599 Stepan Vasilievich Godunov, a high-ranking second cousin of the tsar, instructed the Pokrovskii convent in Suzdal to allow the widow Mavra Yokovlevskaia (Shefrova) to live in the nun's cell that she had legally inherited. Sofia Pleshcheeva had previously purchased the cell for thirty rubles, a sizable amount, and then left it in her will to her daughter Mavra. The convent had sought to deny this inheritance, claiming the right to put the cell up for sale anew. Essentially the government ruled in this case that property inside a monastic institution could be privately passed on within a family, provided that the recipient was willing to live by the community rule.[11] In 1600 Moscow ordered the same Pokrovskii convent to accept a certain Semenka Loginov into its service.[12]

In conflicts over land and natural resources, monasteries triumphed in the tsar's court virtually without exception—or so it seems from the admittedly incomplete and potentially biased source base. In early 1601 the "honey-gatherer" Vaska Elizarov formally complained that the Pecherskii Monastery in Nizhnii Novgorod had appropriated the lakes and rivers where he and his father had always fished and trapped beaver. Elizarov claimed to have already paid the annual dues (obrok) of four rubles plus assorted fees for the current use of these resources. It seemed a clear-cut case, and the government officials originally ordered that Vaska be allowed to hold on to the fishing and trapping grounds. However, the monastery quickly submitted its own *chelobit'e* (petition or complaint). Archimandrite Trifan's staff of monks produced a document from the time of Tsar Fyodor, granting the resources in question to the Pecherskii Monastery in perpetuity for obrok of 3.675 rubles per year. This charter bore the signatures of three witnesses, including a *kniaz'* (prince or duke) and a *d'iak* (government secretary). In light of this development, Tsar Boris's government reversed its decision, now ruling against Elizarov and in favor of the monastery.[13]

Ecclesiastic institutions benefited from an uneven playing field. Elizarov's case was a typical one at the beginning of the seventeenth century. Monasteries often received grants and official charters for lands and resources that local peasants had utilized for generations. Armed with these documents they then had every legal right to exclude others from their new properties. Aggrieved parties complained frequently to the tsar but almost never won. Without official documents they had no way of convincing the government to side with them. Since the vast majority of peasants were illiterate, they could not comprehend, let alone acquire, the necessary legal instruments. In the case of Elizarov, his documents were trumped by the monastery's, leading to the same result. The documentary record strongly suggests that monasteries made themselves quite a number of enemies as a result of such practices.[14]

Although such tensions could perhaps be viewed as an indication of greater trouble to come, in reality all this signaled business as usual for the Muscovite state. The tsar's authority sufficed to settle most disputes, almost always to the advantage of his wealthy clients, the monasteries. The resentment of various lower-class individuals in the face of this biased system probably did not cause much consternation in Moscow. The documents suggest that Tsar Boris's regime was functioning more or less normally, despite the significant crises that had appeared by the late sixteenth century. There is therefore no reason to assume that it necessarily would have failed had not catastrophic natural phenomena intervened.

The Great Famine and the Russian Orthodox Church

The chronicles tell us that during the winter of 1600–1601 some areas of the Russian state experienced unusually mild weather, while other regions endured extraordinarily heavy and prolonged snowfall. For the next decade, summers would be uncommonly rainy and short, with frost and snow often coming too early to allow for normal harvesting. These manifestations of the "Little Ice Age," a climatic shift observed across Eurasia in the late sixteenth and early seventeenth centuries, would have particularly disastrous effects in Russia.[15]

In the summer of 1601, uninterrupted rains were quickly followed by frosts in July and August. Without sun, the grain had not ripened well, and much of it died standing due to the frost. Snow was already falling on September 1, the first day of the Russian year 7110 and three years after Boris's coronation. According to contemporary sources, not only grain but also "all vegetables" perished. The year 1602 was even worse, with a severe winter followed by rain, frost, and more snow in the summer. Starvation gripped the entire country, with thousands dying every week. In the words of Isaac Massa, a Dutch merchant apprentice living in Moscow, "God sent such a harsh time and famine into the whole land of Moscovia as was ever recorded by a history writer . . . so great was the hunger and misery in the whole land. Yes, mothers even ate their children."[16]

The famine and the cannibalism continued in 1603. The weather had improved somewhat, but many fields lay unsown for lack of grain. Dreadful epidemics also spread. Contemporaries estimated that one-third of the Russian population had been wiped out. Some regions, especially in the north, lost up to two-thirds of their inhabitants. Villages became ghost towns. Tsar Boris earnestly tried to relieve the incredible suffering and devastation by opening his treasuries and distributing food and money, but these measures only made the famine worse: officials embezzled most of the funds; masses of people flocked to Moscow and other cities only to die in the streets, while back home the arable land lay useless; speculators got hold of free bread and drove food prices up further; and public order disintegrated. Given Russia's politico-religious ideology, all this certainly seemed like God's punishment for some horrible sin.[17]

Finally, in 1604, the dreadful famine came to an end, at least in most areas of the country. But adverse weather patterns continued, with the result that bad harvests and famine persisted in certain regions for several more years. In addition, brigandage had become rampant and would remain endemic through the remaining Troubles. In the political realm Tsar Boris's legitimacy lay in tatters and desperately needed reconstructing. The Church's reputation had also taken a hit, largely because of widespread rumors of grain speculation.[18] Massa stated:

> [Those] who had provisions to last three or four years wanted the scarcity to continue; they hoped to sell their grain at enormous profits, not thinking that the famine would overtake them in turn. Right up to the patriarch himself, the head of the clergy, a man regarded in Moscow as an exemplar of sanctity, there was no one who did not announce that he would hold on to his copious reserves until grain had reached an even higher price. . . . In fact, there was enough grain in the country to feed all the population for four years, but the people were hungrier than ever. . . . Lords, convents—which are very numerous—and many rich people had full granaries, so much so that being shut up there for years, the grain became mouldy.[19]

Massa was by no means the only witness to record such claims, but historians have long debated their accuracy. Contemporaries reported that most Muscovites (not only churchmen) "tore each other apart" with price gouging.[20] Some contrary evidence exists that the patriarch and others gave away stores of grain during the famine.[21] Yet whatever the extent of ecclesiastic charitable efforts, they certainly were not sufficient to counter negative rumors that flew through the streets. Vadim Koretskii asserted on the basis of monasterial records that public almsgiving was only a thin smokescreen to hide ecclesiastic greed. He pointed out that "the monks of Iosifo Volokolamsk Monastery expended only about 0.5% of their annual monetary income on charity," while those of Kirillo Belozersk gave only 1% of their grain supplies to the poor and starving.[22] In Dunning's words the general impression that churchmen were hoarding and speculating in grain, "coupled with increased obligations imposed on serfs living on monastic estates during the famine years, eroded the reputation of the patriarch and other church leaders and generally undermined the authority of all well-fed leaders of famine-struck Russia."[23]

That some were quite well fed while others starved is certain. Surviving archives of major monasteries testify to food surpluses even during the famine. Zoia Dmitrieva studied the records of the Kirillo Belozersk Monastery and concluded that this institution continued to flourish in the first years of the seventeenth century, with full granaries and enough fodder to feed hundreds of animals. The monastery's own regular inventories of its possessions during the famine, now held at the Russian National Library in St. Petersburg, repeatedly mention huge stores of grain and other foodstuffs. The Solovetskii Monastery's accounting books from the same period recorded food purchases in the thousands of rubles, roughly equivalent to millions of dollars today. The Iosifo Volokolamsk Monastery's books tell a similar story.[24]

It is thus hardly surprising that a negative perception of monasteries and ecclesiastics developed among the starving population. Even if most of the rumors of speculation were unfounded, many monks and nuns still had plenty of good food while their neighbors ate rotten hay and dead (or living) bodies. The fragmentary nature of extant documentation precludes a comprehensive analysis of all ecclesiastics and all ecclesiastic institutions during the famine. What seems likely from the sources we do have is that churchmen behaved— as usual—quite similarly to the general population. Most were concerned primarily for their own welfare and closed their eyes to the rest. Some may have gone further and callously speculated in grain, trading lives for money out of pure greed. A few probably did their best to help as many as they could—perhaps even sacrificing their own needs, as in the story of the folk heroine Iuliania Osorina of Murom. According to her son, this pious woman gave away everything she had, even her last crumb of bread, but still trusted peacefully in God until succumbing in January 1604.[25]

Less obvious, but probably more significant and widespread, than speculation in grain was the practice of buying up homes and property during the famine. In normal times monasteries regularly purchased livestock and real estate from various strata of the population and for various reasons. The documents from the famine period suggest a sudden rash of such transactions, which is not surprising. Sizable monasteries held enormous cash savings at the time, while most of the country was desperate to find any means of buying food at prices that could easily be twenty or more times higher than usual. Thus, a sample document of the Iosifo Volokolamsk Monastery from 1602 recorded the purchase of a private homestead (*dvor*) for fifteen rubles. If it is indeed true that such purchases increased dramatically in the famine years, they accompanied an estimated nine-fold rise in slave sales that occurred at the same time. Peasants and impoverished landlords often had no choice but to sell all their belongings as well as themselves in an attempt to survive. The purchasers would necessarily be the great lords and monasteries, whose wealth not only insulated them from the effects of the famine but also enabled them to grow richer as a result of it.[26]

Ecclesiastic documents from the end of the Great Famine continued to bear witness to great wealth. At the same time they naturally reflected the disastrous consequences of the catastrophe. A simple, noncomprehensive enumeration of the land holdings of Moscow's Novodevichii Convent compiled in September 1603 covered the front and back of 101 leaves. This famous institution, where Boris Godunov and his sister Irina had stayed in 1598 after the death of Tsar Fyodor, obviously commanded extensive economic resources. However, a very large number of its villages had become depopulated due to famine and peasant flight. This may be seen from the listings for various regions, which often read as follows: "The empty place [*pustosh'*] that was the village Briukhanova . . . The empty place that was the village Kuprino . . . The empty place that was the village Dereviagino . . . The empty place Dubrovki . . . The empty place Diatlova. . . . And in all [in this district]: a small town [*selo*], and two villages, and a living clearing [*pochinok zhivushchei*], and twenty-two empty places."[27]

In this context of widespread devastation, the Church could be expected to lose income, even if not actual wealth. Competition for resources became ever fiercer, both among the general population and with respect to the monasteries. *Spornye dela* or lawsuits were the rule of the day. In November or December 1603, Kandrashka Pavlov, a fairly well-off peasant of Suzdal's Pokrovskii Convent, complained to the tsar that he had been beaten and robbed while taking his son to a wedding in another village. According to Pavlov's complaint, the gang led by Ivashko Dokuchaev had inflicted physical injuries and stolen horses, clothing, and money worth 23.37 rubles.[28] A year later the boyar Stepan Godunov adjudicated a conflict between Suzdal's Spaso Evfimiev Monastery and peasants from the small town of Borisovskoe. The peasants charged the monastery with seizing forest meadows or stubble-fields by force (*nasilstvom*). Predictably, however, the monastery could prove its rights to these meadows by means of official documents. Godunov discovered that the peasants of Borisovskoe had already tried unsuccessfully to recover these very meadows from the monastery three times previously: in the years 1555–1556, 1583–1584, and 1599–1600—or about once per generation. Not surprisingly, the peasants lost this case, too, in a judgment dated November 10, 1604.[29] The fact that they tried again after only a few years demonstrates the desperation and possible naïveté of these peasants, who may have looked to the tsar as their father and protector (*tsar'-batiushka*).[30]

The Great Famine caused unprecedented death and destruction, the depopulation of entire regions, and the disruption of all normal patterns of daily life.[31] Those among the poor masses who survived led a precarious existence, facing not only starvation but also the danger of marauding bandits. Competition for scarce resources led to conflicts, fights, thefts, and murders.[32] Given these facts, a loss of income on the part of ecclesiastic businesses would have seemed natural. Yet the documents reveal that some monasteries continued to make huge profits from their commercial activity all throughout the famine. So far from suffering deprivation, they actually increased their revenues during this period of catastrophe.

How could this be? The salt trade of the Solovetskii Monastery during the Muscovite years 7108–7113 (September 1599 to August 1605) provides an instructive example. The sales records of the monastery's branch office (*podvor'e*) in Vologda have been preserved intact and thus make possible a statistical analysis. In these six years the monks at Vologda sold about 600,000 poods of salt, which corresponds to almost 10 million kilograms or well over 20 million pounds. The total price paid for this vital commodity reached nearly 40,000 rubles, an enormous sum.[33] Table 1 summarizes the data (with slight rounding).

Table 1
Income of the Vologda Office of the Solovetskii Monastery, 1599–1605

Muscovite year	Sales volume	Average price	Sales revenue
7108 (1599–1600)	87,878 poods	0.0525 rubles/pood	4,617 rubles
7109 (1600–1601)	108,431 poods	0.0565 rubles/pood	6,129 rubles
7110 (1601–1602)	88,418 poods	0.0494 rubles/pood	4,366 rubles
7111 (1602–1603)	102,504 poods	0.0904 rubles/pood	9,262 rubles
7112 (1603–1604)	72,255 poods	0.1006 rubles/pood	7,268 rubles
7113 (1604–1605)	134,060 poods	0.0520 rubles/pood	6,969 rubles
Total for 6 years	**593,546 poods**	**0.0669 rubles/pood**	**38,611 rubles**

As the chart illustrates, the monastery's income from salt sales reached a zenith during the height of the famine (1602–1603). At this point, the wholesale price for salt was nearly double what it had been previously. The monastery continued to reap above-average income from the autumn of 1603 to the autumn of 1605. It would be impossible to surmise from these figures alone that the country was experiencing a dire crisis at the time. In fact, the general catastrophe meant a windfall for this monasterial business—even in the hard-hit northern regions of the state.[34]

One of the responsibilities of the Vologda office of the Solovetskii Monastery was to purchase supplies for the home base at Solovki. The Vologda elders would use much of the income from salt sales each year to buy great quantities of grain, fodder, equipment, and so forth. The amounts they recorded are summarized in Table 2.[35]

Interestingly, the lowest expense total occurred in 7111 (1602–1603), the same year (of the six) that the monks had their highest income. In the midst of the famine, these businessmen not only exacted higher sales revenue but also cut costs significantly. Hence, their net profit also increased. Documents of this nature show that wealthy Church institutions did not suffer during the famine. On the contrary, they could even benefit financially from the crisis. Furthermore, they continued to take in thousands of rubles in donations (vklady) from the general population, especially for commemoration of deceased relatives.[36]

Table 2
Expenditure of the Vologda Office of the Solovetskii Monastery, 1599–1605

Muscovite year	*Expenditure*
7108 (1599–1600)	6,224 rubles
7109 (1600–1601)	5,712 rubles
7110 (1601–1602)	5,211 rubles
7111 (1602–1603)	3,875 rubles
7112 (1603–1604)	7,935 rubles
7113 (1604–1605)	7,143 rubles
Total for 6 years	**36,100 rubles**

The Great Famine had a dehumanizing effect on Russian society. According to the German mercenary Konrad Bussow:

> The famine in the land was even more severe than at the siege of Jerusalem. . . . It cannot be reckoned how many children were slain, hacked to pieces, and cooked by their parents, parents by their children, guests by their hosts, or hosts by their guests. Human flesh, cut into small pieces and cooked in *pirogi* (that is, baked pastries), was sold in the market as the flesh of other animals and eaten, so that a traveler at this time had to take great care with whom he lodged.[37]

The economic activity of the Church during the famine must be understood within this historical context. The widespread perception of ecclesiastic speculation in grain may have been partly or even largely unfounded. After all, some churchmen did attempt to alleviate the ubiquitous starvation. No doubt poorer monks and priests suffered along with laymen. Yet, at the same time, monks from wealthy monasteries had more than enough food throughout the crisis. In addition, they defended their institutional wealth at every turn, clashing with a desperate population that diminished in size every day. Moreover, at least some ecclesiastic institutions actually increased their business profits during the famine and experienced no lack of money or supplies at all. The extreme contrast between these wealthy, satiated monks and a population starving to death explains the many negative rumors that circulated about the

Church during the famine. Nonetheless, the fact that people from all social strata continued to donate to monasteries demonstrates an Orthodox piety not dependent on the behavior of churchmen. This apparent ability to distinguish between personal Orthodox faith and the institutional Orthodox Church would have enormous consequences during the rest of the Troubles.

The Fall of the House of Godunov

In 1603 a young man claiming to be Tsarevich Dmitrii, son of Ivan IV of Russia, made his move to topple Boris Godunov from the throne. He announced his pretensions to powerful Polish-Lithuanian magnates whose estates bordered Russia—such as Prince Adam Vishnevetskii and Palatine Jerzy Mniszech—and cleverly negotiated for their support. He pledged to marry Mniszech's daughter Marina, to cede border territories once he became tsar, and to compensate his benefactors in other ways as well. After an audience with King Zygmunt (Sigismund) III, Dmitrii underwent a possibly insincere conversion to Catholicism and made further promises about promoting "the Latin religion." In exchange the Polish-Lithuanian lords drafted and hired a small army that assembled in the fall of 1604. Though the king's government had by now decided to oppose this dangerous scheme, Dmitrii's few thousand forces benefited from the spontaneous support of Orthodox Christian Ukrainians and managed to reach the Russian border. They crossed into southwest Russia in October 1604, starting a war against Muscovite forces.[38]

In the disaffected border region of Severia, peasants, slaves, townspeople, and soldiers eagerly joined Dmitrii's cause. With the help of the local population, Dmitrii quickly captured or gained Moravsk, Chernigov, and Putivl. The growing oppression of serfdom amidst a previously free population, bitter conflicts with monasteries for control of resources—which the monasteries seemingly always won in the tsar's court—and a general hostility toward Boris Godunov all played a role in sparking this revolt against Moscow.[39] Dmitrii's forces swelled with new recruits, and Tsar Boris mustered his army on an emergency basis to counter the very serious threat materializing in the southwestern border regions. By early 1605 a brutal civil war was in full swing. The two armies fought major battles as more and more southern towns rebelled against Moscow's authority. Boris sent Prince Vasilii Shuiskii to carry out a reprisal raid in Severia, with ghastly results. The army slaughtered residents and destroyed property in a brutal manner: "Men were hanged by one foot from trees, then burned alive or used for target practice. Women were raped, tortured, and then impaled. Little boys and babies were drowned, and older girls and young women were sexually assaulted and then carried off to be sold as slaves."[40]

These gruesome measures failed to check popular support for the "true tsar" Dmitrii. Facing incredible odds, the upstart survived, and the news of him spread throughout the country. The Famine had caused Boris's perceived legitimacy to sink, with rumors of God's punishment for his crimes. Dmitrii's strength lay not so much in his army as in the readiness of the Russian people at this particular moment in history to believe that Boris was a usurper who deserved to be overthrown. Moreover, support for Dmitrii automatically suggested an explanation for the horrors of the past few years: God could not sanction the "false tsar" and had therefore sent just punishment on His people: "Israel."[41] Rebellion in the name of Dmitrii thus offered the hope of national redemption.

Boris knew that the minds of his subjects had become the main battlefield, and he launched an intense propaganda campaign. His chief ally in this endeavor was the Russian Orthodox Church, headed by his old friend Patriarch Iyov. In 1589 Godunov had obtained the patriarchate for Iyov; in 1598 Iyov had arranged the tsardom for Boris. Throughout his reign the tsar had generously supported the monasteries and bishoprics. He unfailingly backed them in their battles for lands and resources, and he personally bestowed large sums of money and other gifts on them. The Iosifo Volokolamsk Monastery was one of many Church institutions to record numerous donations from Boris. When he came there on a pilgrimage with his son Fyodor, the monastic records lauded him as *blagovernyi* ("pious, of blessed faith"). The French mercenary captain Jacques Margeret remarked, "He had the good quality of ordinarily giving great alms and much property to the clergy, who were all devoted to him."[42]

The sources agree that the Russian Church hierarchy remained extremely devoted to Tsar Boris, largely out of economic interest, even as Dmitrii made considerable inroads among the rest of the population. According to Massa, the tsar for his part also "believed the priests and monks more than his most faithful lords," consulting them on all important matters.[43] Such contemporary witnesses suggest that during Boris's reign the upper echelon of the Russian Church enjoyed an even more prominent role in the state than usual.[44] This iron bond linking Boris Godunov with the Russian Orthodox Church was quite obvious even to the pretender. In the interpretation of Vasilii Ulianovskii, Dmitrii did not even try to appeal to the clergy in his campaign for recognition as the rightful tsar. Ignoring the advice of his Polish-Lithuanian backers, he recognized that the ecclesiastics would do nothing to disturb their highly profitable arrangement with the current ruler.[45]

The Russian Orthodox Church did everything possible to combat Dmitrii by pen and by sword. Monasteries and bishoprics contributed troops, horses, money, and supplies for the war effort.[46] Patriarch Iyov wrote and circulated missives denouncing the "villain, fugitive of our state, defrocked black monk Grishka Otrepiev," said to be posing as the (supposedly deceased) son of Tsar Ivan IV. The pretender was vilified as a runaway heretic and a lying puppet of the wicked and bloodthirsty Catholic King Zygmunt III. His invasion allegedly represented a "demonic plot" to obliterate the true Orthodox Christian faith by "destroying God's churches" and instead constructing chapels for "Latins, Lutherans, and Yids."[47] Poland-Lithuania at this time had a large Jewish population, which Russia passionately wanted to exclude from its own borders due to religiously motivated antipathy.[48] The commonwealth was also known for its religious diversity and pluralism. The Russian Church portrayed the uprising against Boris as a kind of Catholic-Protestant-Jewish conspiracy to annihilate Orthodox Christianity.[49]

In their public statements Boris and Iyov consistently characterized Dmitrii as anti-Orthodox and anti-Christian. He was described as a "tool of the devil" who dealt in "black-bookery" (i.e., sorcery or black magic). Boris wrote again to Rudolf II to try to ensure that the emperor would still support his legitimacy and reject Dmitrii's claims. He also tried to negotiate with Zygmunt III. The main thrust of Boris and Iyov's strategy was to remove the pretender beyond the pale of acceptable religion. Within Russia citizens were told that they must support Boris if they cared at all about the preservation of Orthodoxy. Outside Russia the tsar's envoys insisted that to recognize Dmitrii was to support a plot of Satan against Christendom.[50]

The strategy did not work. Monks traveled far and wide to "expose" Dmitrii—but occasionally ended up joining him instead. Cossacks, peasants, refugees, and military servitors continued to swell the ranks of the revolutionary army. Dmitrii gave outward signs of being Orthodox (such as offering prayers and receiving blessings) and insisted that he was the "true tsar." His message was appealing, and the propaganda emanating from Moscow unconvincing. Orthodox believers ignored Patriarch Iyov's order of excommunication for anyone who supported the pretender, again demonstrating an ability to distinguish in their own minds between personal attachment to Orthodoxy on the one hand and the official Church on the other. One possibility is that they were revolting in favor of Orthodoxy but against the Church. In Dunning's opinion, "by 1605 lots of people really did believe Tsar Boris was a regicide and usurper who had managed to bring down the wrath of God on Russia."[51] In this case they must also have viewed the Russian Orthodox Church as the evil ruler's accomplice.

In early 1605 Tsar Boris saw the end coming. Entire regions of the country had rebelled against him; his army rarely won any battles now and faced a growing problem of desertion; and he himself grew seriously ill. For about a year monasteries and churches had been reciting a special and unusually long prayer on his behalf—but apparently without effect. Perhaps as a result, the tsar lost his nerve and consulted astrologers, mediums, and spiritists. Nonetheless, he retained the staunch support of Patriarch Iyov and the Russian Orthodox Church. Just before his unexpected death on April 13, 1605, he received tonsure and took the monk's name Bogolep. Rumors quickly spread in the streets: Boris had killed himself out of guilt; he had been murdered; he had secretly escaped and was still alive in hiding. Church hierarchs sent out instructions regarding the standard forty-day requiem for a beloved Orthodox tsar. Massa reported that commemorative services were carried out "in all the monasteries" for six weeks. Ulianovskii found evidence that prayers for Boris and his family continued for nearly a century in some monasteries—such was the strength of ecclesiastic attachment to the deceased tsar.[52]

Boris's death essentially solved the military confrontation: it now became clear who would win. But there was another brief chapter to be written first. With the firm support of Patriarch Iyov and the Church, Fyodor Borisovich Godunov immediately succeeded his father as tsar of "all Rus'," while his mother served as a kind of co-ruler or regent.[53] He came to the throne in highly unpropitious circumstances, to say the least. The talented and educated sixteen-year-old could not control mutinous boyars or prevent military commanders from going over to Dmitrii's camp. His reign would last less than two months, and his life would be cut tragically short by the civil war he had inherited from his father.

The Russian Orthodox Church propagandized for Fyodor II just as it had for Boris. The method of legitimizing his rule, devised or at least approved by the patriarch, has been described in chapter 3. Instead of citing the real reason for his accession (heredity), the ideologues simply imitated the new syncretic paradigm invented for Boris in 1598. Officially, Fyodor's legitimacy rested on his election by God, the sanction of the Church, bestowal by the late tsar, bestowal by the widowed tsaritsa (vox feminae), and popular acclaim (vox populi). Not only the form, but also the content of the documents was the same: the authors did not neglect to include even the "tears and pleas" of the crowds who allegedly begged Tsaritsa Maria to "bless" her son Fyodor to rule. All this was simply a duplication of the 1598 template, according to which the people's tears and pleas had finally convinced Irina to bless her brother Boris for the tsardom.[54]

It is unlikely that many Russians actually cried for Fyodor to take the throne or took other steps attributed to them in official documents. The ideologues chose this legitimation scheme because they dared not suggest that true legitimacy came via paternity. If that were the case, then Boris himself would have been illegitimate—just as the pretender claimed. Moreover, Fyodor could not have inherited the throne legitimately from an illegitimate ruler. Hence, the documents drawn up for his succession probably related an entirely fictional version of events. They did mention that Fyodor would reign as tsar and autocrat "just as also his father" had, but they carefully avoided justifying his accession on these grounds.[55]

According to their own account, the Church hierarchs initiated and oversaw the process of accession from start to finish. The patriarch and his subordinates themselves blessed Fyodor to rule and administered an oath of loyalty to the populace. Russians "kissed the cross," swearing fealty to Fyodor, his mother, Maria, and his sister, Ksenia. Clerics throughout the land received instructions to publicize the official story of Fyodor's accession. They were also to conduct three days of prayer services for the new tsar and his family, asking for victory over the "Latin" and "Besermen" (Muslim) tribes; for peace, quiet, and a lack of calamities; and for the health, salvation, and prosperity of the rulers.[56]

Through no fault of his own, Fyodor II proved unable to reciprocate the support accorded him by the Church. His government no longer had the authority to enforce its decisions amidst the maelstrom of political, social, economic, and of course military pressures. As a result the monasteries had to orient themselves in the midst of increased lawlessness with less help from the center. A document of the Razboinyi prikaz (Brigandage Office or Chancellery) dated May 20, 1605, illustrated this trend toward anarchy. A long and complicated series of robberies and reprisals involving monasterial and secular peasants, civil servants, and at least one priest had resulted in several deaths and much damage. In the course of the vendettas, certain peasants had come to the town of Bykovo, owned by the Kashinskii Sretenskii Convent, and, with the aid of one of the monastery's caretakers (*monastyrskago dvora dvornik Timoshka*), had stolen and slaughtered a red cow. The town priest Fyodor was so incensed by this that he formed a posse of the monastery's peasants and tracked down the alleged perpetrators of the crime. This group of vigilantes captured their intended targets, kept them "in chains and irons" for a week at the monastery, and furthermore decided to exact reparations of seventy rubles and five cows. They tortured and beat a few of their prisoners nearly to death, drowned (*posadili v vodu*) their own traitorous caretaker, and let the rest go. Needless to say, this was not the end of the matter. When a city judicial official, Bulat Kashkarov, decided to get involved, he came to Bykovo and allegedly beat the monastery's peasants and tortured them with spears. Kashkarov also arrested a monastic servant and a church sexton and kept them locked up for five weeks, after which time they were in danger of starvation. More reprisals, violence, and numerous depositions to the authorities followed. The central government obviously wanted to restore order and a sense of its legal authority, but it was not entirely clear how this could realistically happen.[57]

As Dmitrii continued to gain strength and drew closer to Moscow, the unfortunate Fyodor Borisovich saw a dramatic change in the Church's orientation. In Ulianovskii's words: "The Church completely changed its attitude toward the Pretender and recognized him as the lawful tsar."[58] Essentially the lone holdout was Patriarch Iyov, who had been closely linked to the Godunovs for years and would go down with them. On May 7, 1605, in a carefully planned insurrection, most of the tsar's army defected. A few days later Ivan Golitsyn treacherously surrendered the entire army to the pretender. Throngs of Russians now cheered Dmitrii as he made his way toward the capital.

On June 1, 1605, pro-Dmitrii conspirators launched a riot in Moscow, which resulted (as planned) in the murder of Tsar Fyodor and his mother. Patriarch Iyov was deposed, cursed, denounced as a "Judas," and sent to a monastery to be locked up. According to some, Fyodor's older sister Ksenia was captured and held to be raped by Dmitrii after his triumphal entry into the capital on June 20.[59] The Church, the boyars, and the whole Muscovite population had allegedly wept for Fyodor to take the throne, but they betrayed him almost immediately. Concerning the army, Bussow remarked, "They held to their oath as long as a hungry dog keeps a fast."[60] Thus ended the short-lived Godunov dynasty of Russia.

The Church's Role in the First "Dmitriada"

In early 1605, as the Polish Sejm (parliament) discussed the Dmitrii affair, Hetman Jan Zamoiski exclaimed, "By God! Is this a comedy of Plautus or

Terence?" (*prze Bog! czy to Plauti, czy Terentiuszowa comaedia!*).[61] Four centuries later we can still have no confidence about the identity of the enigmatic "Dmitrii" who swept into power that year, carried by his own determination and a massive popular revolt. Just one man, Prince Vasilii Shuiskii, publicly proclaimed no fewer than three completely different versions of the Dmitrii story. As head of the investigatory commission sent to Uglich after the tragedy of 1591, he confirmed that the tsarevich had killed himself accidentally while playing with a knife. He repeated this version of events to Boris toward the end of the latter's life. As a principal instigator of the coup against Fyodor Borisovich in 1605, he stood before the crowds in Red Square and announced that the boy Dmitrii had escaped Boris's murder plot years before and was now returning to his rightful throne. After seizing power from Dmitrii in May 1606, Vasilii declared that Boris had in fact murdered Dmitrii and that the pretender who ruled in Moscow had been an imposter. Meanwhile, many Cossacks and Russians believed that Dmitrii had literally risen from the dead in order to right the wrongs of Russia.[62]

Whether the actual son of Ivan IV who had lived in hiding since at least 1591, another lad who had been raised to believe he was the tsarevich, the former monk Grigorii Otrepiev, or someone else altogether, "Dmitrii" came to symbolize the Time of Troubles. The question of who he was had already destroyed Boris Godunov's regime, would soon doom his own regime, and would torment and bring down his successor's regime as well. Until recently, most historiography presented the so-called first false Dmitrii as an anti-Orthodox or at least not fully Orthodox tsar whom the Russian Orthodox Church opposed. In fact, this portrayal had little truth to it. Tsar Dmitrii continually appealed to Orthodoxy, even if his wife Marina—chosen for reasons of political expediency—was a fervid Catholic. The Russian Church, so far from opposing him, cooperated fully with him and sanctioned his rule just as for other Orthodox tsars. During his short reign the official politico-religious line reversed itself completely. The ideologues now asserted that Dmitrii was himself the legitimate continuation of the previous dynasty, having been born in 1582 to Ivan IV and his seventh wife, Maria Nagaia. Orthodox canon law actually allowed a maximum of three wives, but this did not provoke significant opposition to Dmitrii.

As he rode toward the capital to begin his short reign, Dmitrii posed as the defender of the Orthodox faith and the restorer of Truth. He ordered the *Znamenie* ("Our Lady of the Sign") ikon brought to him from Kursk and reportedly prayed before it passionately every day until he reached Moscow. In letters of June 1605, he proclaimed his reclamation of "the Orthodox throne of

4. The Uspenskii (Dormition) Cathedral in the Moscow Kremlin. Reproduced by kind permission of Elizaveta Skriabina.

our forebears, the Great sovereigns, the Russian tsars." He claimed (apparently disingenuously) that the Orthodox patriarch, metropolitans, archbishops, and other hierarchs had recognized him as "their born sovereign" (*prirozhennyi gosudar' svoi*). He urged the Russian people to "remember the true Orthodox Christian faith" and therefore swear allegiance to him. His successful revolt against the Godunovs allegedly represented the triumph of good over evil, of Orthodoxy over heresy, of truth over lies.[63]

According to the contemporary Arsenii Elassonskii, a Greek who reached the rank of archbishop in the Russian Orthodox Church, Dmitrii's first acts in Moscow were all devoted to Orthodox Christian ritual. Upon his triumphal entry (June 20), an impressive delegation of Church hierarchs met him with crosses, ikons, candles, and incense burners. They blessed him and recited prayers, before taking him to the Kremlin's Uspenskii Cathedral. Inside the symbolic heart of Russian Orthodoxy, Dmitrii "bowed to the saints," kissing the venerable ikons in a prearranged spectacle. From there he moved to the nearby Arkhangelskii Cathedral, which housed the coffins of Russia's past rulers. He bowed to these as well, kissing more ikons and weeping openly. In front of the fascinated crowds, Moscow's new master delivered an emotional—and propagandistic—address to the sarcophagi of his purported father Ivan IV and brother Fyodor I. A carefully orchestrated religious service reinforced his claims of Orthodoxy and rightful rulership. Finally, Dmitrii proceeded to the palace and seated himself on the throne, "and all the boyars, the whole court council, and all the army that had come with him, and all the people bowed to him."[64]

The early part of Dmitrii's reign thus had hints of acclamation by the populace and the army, a key element of the innovative legitimation strategy devised for Boris in 1598. God's choice and the sanction of the Church remained strong features of his public justification for rule. In addition, the new tsar made extensive use of vox feminae. At every turn, he publicized the testimony of his ostensible mother, Maria Nagaia, who had "recognized" him as her long-lost son. Certification of legitimacy from a tsaritsa now became a virtual sine qua non for all rulers and pretenders of the period. Yet Dmitrii's chief legitimization technique was quite simple: a reversion to the seven-hundred-year-old tradition of hereditary succession in Orthodox Rus'. He claimed to be "tsarevich and heir" to the throne of Russia. In effect his propaganda equated Orthodox Christianity with hereditary legitimacy, thus contradicting the Church's official statements of the previous seven years.[65] The effect of Dmitrii's succession was therefore to modify, complicate, and perpetuate the unique synthesis of legitimation techniques characteristic of the Time of Troubles.

The onset of Dmitrii's reign also brought about a vilification and desacralization of the previous sovereign, Boris Godunov. Rather than a blessed ruler of Orthodox Russia, a defender of the faith and pious caretaker of the chosen people, Boris now appeared as a brutal usurper—a "false tsar" with no right to the throne. According to some (but not all) Byzantine and Muscovite political theology, the overthrowing of such a "tsar-tormentor" could be a righteous act, approved by God. By helping to delegitimize Boris ex post facto, the Russian Church now bolstered Dmitrii's perceived legitimacy as an Orthodox hero fighting injustice. It is quite unlikely that most Muscovites knew or understood the political ideas of Iosif Volotskii or other theorists who wrote of "true" and "false" tsars. However, they may well have hoped that Dmitrii's triumph would end the nation's great "sin" and thus turn away God's wrath from "his people."[66]

Tsar Boris's body had been laid to rest in the traditional burial chamber of the Russian grand princes and tsars, the Arkhangelskii Cathedral in Moscow's

Kremlin. Dmitrii promptly ordered it removed. "Without any ceremony," the corpse of Russia's first nonhereditary ruler was tossed into a pauper's grave at the small Varsonofievskii Convent. The remains of Boris's wife and son soon joined his. This denigration of the Godunovs even in death demonstrated the utter contempt that the new regime wished to cultivate toward the previous tsar.[67] Yet, at the same time, Dmitrii shrewdly furnished a convenient "out" for the masses of the population who had previously sworn fealty to Boris and Fyodor II. Since they had not even known of Dmitrii's existence, they had not done any evil in accepting those "false" tsars.[68]

The same clemency could not be extended unconditionally to the Church, which had claimed to act on God's behalf. The new regime needed a scapegoat, easily found in the person of Patriarch Iyov. This close ally of the Godunovs was portrayed as a "false" patriarch, just as Boris had been a "false" tsar. Even before Dmitrii entered the capital, his coconspirators deposed the patriarch in disregard of Orthodox canon law. In a public "anti-ceremony," Iyov was permitted or forced to conduct some last rituals of his office before being stripped of his priestly robes, nearly lynched, and led away to confinement in a monastery. Russia's first patriarch was denounced as a "false priest," a lying impostor who had "tempted" the Church. Resentment at the Church's role during the Famine may have played some role in the venom directed at Iyov. Dmitrii's executives now claimed to have "cleansed" the Church of this "impurity" and "evil." The new tsar installed his own man, a Greek Cypriot by the name of Ignatii who had been bishop of Riazan. Within a few days Russia had a new Orthodox patriarch, who would lead the Church in legitimizing and sanctifying Dmitrii. The people were supposed to believe that this prelate would speak God's truth whereas the other had lied continually.[69]

This strategy allowed for the vast majority of ecclesiastics, like civil servants, to keep their posts and to function under Dmitrii just as they had under previous tsars. With Iyov out of the way, the Russian Orthodox Church devoted itself to the new tsar without objection. Instead of waiting as usual for the Muscovite New Year in September, Dmitrii wasted no time in proceeding to the grand Orthodox coronation and anointing service. Patriarch Ignatii and other top churchmen conducted this ritual sometime in July 1605. For Russians the ceremony represented a public demonstration of divine and ecclesiastic legitimization. Archpriest Terentii's address to the new tsar drove home the new ecclesiastic orientation toward the rebel previously branded a "tool of Satan." Terentii blessed God for having sanctified Dmitrii "in your mother's womb," for having kept him safe from those who sought to kill him, for having restored him to his rightful throne, for "crowning your God-crowned head with glory and honor." He lauded the new tsar in customarily extravagant terms, calling him "beloved of God . . . autocrat of all Russia, firm guardian and champion of the holy Orthodox faith, zealot and adorner of Christ's Church . . . God's anointed." Oozing obsequiousness, Terentii promised that "we have never created and will never create evil to your power as tsar."[70]

The Church had pronounced many of these very same words to Boris Godunov seven years earlier. Now it had reversed itself completely. By claiming that Dmitrii had been chosen by God even while still in the womb, Terentii was drawing a comparison to the prophets Isaiah and Jeremiah and especially to John the Baptist.[71] By anointing him with oil and terming him *pomazannik Bozhii* ("God's anointed"), Patriarch Ignatii and the other hierarchs stressed how dreadfully wrong it would be to oppose him. In the Bible righteous David would not harm even the evil and murderous King Saul, because the latter was "the anointed of the LORD" (in Hebrew, *mashiakh YHWH*). Linguistically, this title was equivalent to "Messiah" or "Christ"—a fact that was known to Russian literati of the time. The Orthodox Christian coronation ceremonies thus underlined the tsar's "Christomimetic" rulership. According to official Church teaching, Tsar Dmitrii now stood in the place of Christ to his people.[72]

Propaganda written after the overthrow of Dmitrii in 1606 invented the idea of strong Church opposition to his rule. Supposedly Russian Orthodox clerics could not stomach the alleged lackey of King Zygmunt and tool of the Jesuits. However, even literature from that later period of revision demonstrates the falsity of such a claim. The "Filaret Manuscript" (*Rukopis' Filareta*), composed shortly after the Time of Troubles, admitted, "Patriarch Ignatei wavered and united himself with Grisha the Unfrocked; the metropolitans and bishops of Russia likewise dozed off."[73] In other words, according to this text, Russia's churchmen failed to be attentive to Dmitrii's "heresy" and did not resist him.

For most of the past four centuries, historiography has repeated the myth of ecclesiastic opposition to Dmitrii's rule. Yet even Metropolitan Makarii Bulgakov acknowledged in his *History of the Russian Church* that "some" (*nekotorye*) clerics accepted "the first false Dmitrii" as the true tsar. More recently, the research of Ulianovskii, Dunning, and others has shown the need to revise this longstanding assessment. It seems likelier that virtually the entire Church adopted a policy of complete collaboration with Dmitrii. So far from a bitter war between a "heretic-tsar" intent on destroying Orthodoxy and faithful clerics devoted to the "true faith," the situation was one of general acceptance. Stories about heroic resistance to "that villain" on the part of valiant ecclesiastics turn out to have been fabricated after the fact. According to his vita and later historians, Archbishop Feodosii of Astrakhan "denounced [the pretender] to his face." Yet in actuality he supported Dmitrii to the tune of 1,700 rubles and may have received his high rank as a reward! Feodosii also participated in the tsar's marriage to the Polish Catholic Marina Mnizsech, with the approval of the "Sanctified Council" of the Russian Orthodox Church.[74]

The economic documentation of Dmitrii's reign records this collaboration between tsar and church and makes clear the main reason for it. As during earlier periods, ecclesiastic business pursuits took priority. The monasteries needed the tsar to certify their vast and motley collections of trading rights, tax exemptions, fishing and salt collection rights, and so forth. Monks and nuns paid homage, gifts, and fees to Tsar Dmitrii, just as they were accustomed to do for all rulers since at least the Mongol period. In exchange they received charters for property, assets, and usufructuary rights.[75] Ecclesiastics did not really "doze off" or have a lapse of concentration in 1605–1606, as the author of the "Filaret Manuscript" would have us believe. Rather, they intentionally protected their business interests in the ordinary manner. As a result, in Ulianovskii's assessment, "the economic position of the Orthodox Church did not worsen during the reign of the Pretender."[76]

In mid-1605 Hegumen Antonii and Elder Protasii of the titanic Solovetskii Monastery traveled to Moscow to meet their new tsar. Along the way they took in over 1,000 rubles from various sources: vklady (donations given by nobles, churchmen, and commoners); a loan from another monastery; and the sale of materials such as rawhides and cow suet. The trip itself cost 58.7 rubles, which went toward transportation and supplies for the whole company (e.g., boats, carts, horses, ferries, polls, axles, reins, horseshoes, boots, cloth, hay, fish, barrels, cucumbers, paper, spoons, vinegar, furs). Yet Antonii and Protasii also conducted business on the go, so their total expenditure while traveling amounted to nearly 500 rubles. The main purpose of their journey was expressed in a few important ledger entries:

* Bought golden silk cloth [*otlas zolotnoi*]; gave seventy rubles. Also bought forty sables; gave thirty rubles. And that silk and [those] sables [we] carried to Sovereign, Tsar, and Grand Prince Dmitrei Ivanovich of All Russia.

* Bought violet silk cloth [*kamka bagrova kufter*]; gave ten rubles. Also bought forty sables; gave twenty rubles. And that silk and [those] sables [we] carried to Sovereign, Tsaritsa, and Grand Princess, Nun Marfa Fyodorovna of All Russia.

* Bought two pair of sables; gave four rubles 20 *altyn* [= 4.6 rubles]. And those sables [we] brought to the Most Holy Patriarch Ignatii.[77]

Anthropologists, sociologists, and historians have long debated the function and meaning of gifts such as these in societies throughout history and around the globe. Many scholars consider that "the gift" embeds an individual or entity within a socioeconomic network, thus entailing specific obligations and responsibilities. Gift-giving can both spring out of and define identities and relationships, including those within clan, family, or patronage networks. At the same time the boundary between exchange of "gifts" and "commodities" is often quite fluid, since many ostensible gifts actually oblige the recipient to reciprocate. Moreover, gifts appear in a multitude of forms and have varied purposes; some "gifts" actually form part of a competitive exchange with the goal of profit. Every society seemingly develops its own "theory and practice" of gift-giving with regard to a whole spectrum of interactions ranging from the most "intimate" to purely "economic."[78]

In the case of the Solovki monks, their gifts no doubt reflected perceptions of propriety and de facto obligations within a social, political, and economic network. At the same time, the marked differentiation among recipients clearly accorded with the purpose for which these gifts were given: the obtaining of profitable economic charters and privileges. The tsar himself received lavish presents valued at 100 rubles. The elders knew that his stamp of approval on their economic charters would be worth many times that amount. Muscovite charters always described privileges as emanating directly from the person of the tsar, even though bureaucrats usually bore responsibility for issuing them. The monks' other two gifts were less costly and actually formed part of showing allegiance and honor to the tsar. His royal mother Marfa (Maria Nagaia) was gifted with silk and sable fur worth 30 rubles. In this manner Antonii and Protasii attested that they did not question her testimony concerning Dmitrii's legitimacy. In other words they proclaimed themselves loyal subjects of the new tsar. Nor did these monastic representatives forget Patriarch Ignatii, who bestowed on Dmitrii the sanction of the Russian Orthodox Church. However, their gift to him was worth only five rubles—a large amount for any commoner, but not for these fabulously wealthy oligarchs. The head of the Russian Orthodox Church bore only a tangential relationship to the current objective of these monks, which was to secure the right to exploit valuable resources for profit. This may be one reason for their relatively small gift to the patriarch.

After paying homage to the new tsar, the Solovetskii elders visited the appropriate government offices and obtained seven official documents (*gramoty*) granting economic rights and privileges. They had to pay for special paper, seal wax, and inflated certification fees. These expenses amounted to 64.09 rubles, more than the travel costs of the 2,000-kilometer (1,250-mile) round trip. Again, however, the price of these charters would be well worth the enormous potential profit they unlocked. The chief elders of one of Russia's greatest monasteries obviously had no compunction about doing business with the erstwhile pretender, nor did they object to the new patriarch. Though Ignatii would later be vilified by the Church for his alliance with Dmitrii, and his patriarchal legitimacy called into question, this document referred to him normally as "the most holy patriarch" (*s[via]teishei patriarkh*).[79]

At the end of the ledger, an impersonal entry read: "To the poor was expended 5 *altyn* 2 *dengi* [= 0.16 rubles]."[80] This sum represented 0.03% of the monks' total expenditure on the trip and probably reflected the relative place of almsgiving in their business plan. After three years of famine and one of war, it could not have been a dearth of poor people that prevented the monks from giving more. Antonii and Protasii were neither brave heroes of Orthodoxy come to challenge an imposter and heretic nor philanthropists devoted to relieving the suffering of the general population. Rather, they were businessmen on a business trip, come to mine gold in the very same legal system that had worked so well for them under Tsar Boris.

Numerous additional documents illustrate the same kind of arrangements between Tsar Dmitrii and other monasteries. Moscow's Simonov Monastery paid fees of more than seven rubles for a new charter to its fishing grounds and other water resources in the Northern Volga region.[81] Moscow's Novodevichii Convent was able to restore its interrupted right to import salt, fish, and caviar from Kazan, Nizhnii Novgorod, and Astrakhan without taxes or tolls of any kind. Dmitrii even made the size of the exemption nearly fourfold what it had been under Ivan IV. The total monetary value of the new privileges was recorded at 3,000 rubles, or something like $4.5–6.7 million in terms of purchasing power today.[82]

Dmitrii's government dealt with smaller matters as well, adjudicating the ecclesiastic economy as under previous tsars. Rent and fees for a section of the Motra River, held by Murom's Borisoglebskii na Ushne Monastery, were set at the rate of 0.6375 rubles per year.[83] The Ambrosiev (Nikolaevskii) Dudin Monastery, located about 40 kilometers (25 miles) southwest of Nizhnii Novgorod on the Oka River, had taken on the responsibility of restoring a smaller agricultural cloister wiped out by disease. The tsar's bureaucrats confirmed its right to work the other monastery's lands free of tax.[84] When Ivan Nikitich Godunov, a third cousin of the late Tsar Boris, forcefully took over some lands claimed by the Borisoglebskii na Ushne Monastery, the regime ruled in favor of the monastery. The disputed real estate amounted to two-thirds of a village and about 14 hectares (35 acres) of medium-grade arable land. By order of the tsar, the following was to be read out to the affected peasants: "And you, all the peasants who live in those two-thirds of the village, must obey the [monastic] builder Zakharii and the brotherhood, plough the fields for them, and pay them revenue."[85]

The situation in the ecclesiastic economy under Tsar Dmitrii could be described as "business as usual," with a couple of minor exceptions. During his reign the government seems to have charged significantly higher fees for ecclesiastic economic charters than had been customary. Moreover, charters were more often rewritten rather than simply reconfirmed. Due to the fees charged by the bureaucracy, rewriting an official document was a much more expensive proposition than simple recertification (the latter meant only adding the new tsar's signature below the previous signatures). The fees for rewriting one brief charter of the Simonov Monastery in September 1605 amounted to more than seven rubles.[86] It therefore seems likely that the tsar approached the ecclesiastic economy strategically. He granted huge tax exemptions to major monasteries, key pillars of the socioeconomic system, but nonetheless found a way to recoup a small portion of these sums through higher fees. Alternately, one could speculate that the monasteries themselves requested these new documents, suspecting that in the future it might become uncomfortable for them to have recognized Dmitrii as a legitimate tsar and to have benefited from his patronage. After his reign older documents could and would be trotted out again to be recertified by Tsar Vasilii—thus skipping over Dmitrii and expunging his name from the record whenever possible.[87]

Like Boris, Dmitrii also exacted large forced loans from monasterial treasuries, partly to support foreign mercenary troops. In September 1605 tsarist officials wrote to the Iosifo Volokolamsk Monastery inquiring how much cash lay in the monastery's vaults. Subsequently, Prince Vasilii Mosalskii demanded a loan of 3,000 rubles in the tsar's name. He promised that the money would be repaid from the royal treasury "in the future," although it is questionable whether that actually happened.[88] Similar demands were placed on other monasteries: 30,000 rubles came from the fabulously wealthy Troitsa Sergiev Monastery, which had already sent 15,400 rubles to Tsar Boris's treasury; at least 5,000 rubles from the Kirillo Belozersk Monastery; 1,000 rubles from the Novodevichii Convent; 200 rubles from the Fyodorovskii Monastery; and so forth.[89]

Most such "loans" were never repaid, but some were. In addition, monasteries often received new grants from the tsar that helped to compensate for the depletion of their treasuries. Even as he demanded large sums of money from them, Tsar Dmitrii continued to recycle substantial donations right back into the monasteries throughout his reign. The distant Solovetskii Monastery recorded receipt of a donation of 2,000 rubles on May 19, 1606. Since this was two days after the uprising in which Dmitrii was overthrown and (reportedly) killed, the monies must have been in transit during the upheaval in Moscow. Monasteries also loaned to each other.[90] Taken as a whole, the system was not without its logic. The tsar granted the monasteries enormous tax exemptions, which was a simple way for him to deposit large sums of money into their treasuries without actually transferring any cash. The monasteries kept the money safe in their vaults, which were naturally scattered all around the realm for greater security. In time of need, these institutions had no right to refuse "loans" to the crown, since their wealth derived in the first place from the tsar's grants and charters of immunity.

In sum, Tsar Dmitrii promoted the ecclesiastic economy and monastic wealth no less than his predecessors, even while seeking to make sure that the state benefited as well. For their part Russian churchmen continued to "play the game," reaping the benefits of their extensive privileges within the system. The Church's behavior under the new tsar could be symbolized by the actions of an individual far removed from Russia—the Orthodox Patriarch Sophronius (Sophrony) of Jerusalem. Upon the accession of Tsar Boris, this foreign hierarch had offered his exuberant congratulations, thus acknowledging the new ruler's legitimacy. He then requested money. In 1605 Sophronius quickly adopted the "new Orthodoxy," expressing hope that Dmitrii would "receive the throne of his father, Tsar Ivan Vasilievich, without war or bloodshed." Once again the patriarch's main interest seemingly lay in obtaining funds.[91] Similarly, the Russian Church seems to have accepted and legitimized the accession of Dmitrii without any fuss, largely as a result of economic considerations.

Tsar Dmitrii did frequently surprise Muscovites by not following all of the traditional customs and adopting a more casual attitude toward Orthodox ritual. He wore Western clothing and entertained foreign ideas. That he brought Jesuits to Moscow and allowed them to have a church in the capital were also circumstances that could be used against him later. The ambitious Vasilii Shuiskii was especially eager to demonize the current tsar as a Catholic agent of Satan. In the generally xenophobic environment of Muscovy, Dmitrii's choice to consult with foreign (especially Protestant) as well as Russian advisors could be taken as confirmation of this charge. Makarii expressed what remains a common opinion today: "In spirit he was Latin [i.e., Catholic], but [outwardly] he appeared Orthodox and visited Orthodox churches."[92]

The question of Dmitrii's inner sincerity is a difficult one to judge. The young tsar seems to have been less devoted than most Muscovites to religion in general. His "sacral world" comprised a mix of ideas gleaned from Russian Orthodoxy, Western imperial and Catholic religious ideology, and the Bible (in accordance with the "New Israel" interpretive paradigm). Russians of the sixteenth and early seventeenth centuries were raised to view Orthodox Christianity as the only truth and to hate other religions with vehemence. Having lived in Poland-Lithuania, Dmitrii had developed a much more tolerant attitude toward a multiplicity of confessions. He was also a reformer interested in "modernizing" Russian government and culture to some extent. Dmitrii made extensive use of Orthodoxy for political ends but demonstrated no particular interest in exterminating other faiths. Since the latter was an expected form of "piety" for a Russian tsar, his "tolerance" made some suspicious. Nonetheless, the bulk of the Church and the boyars continued to collaborate with Dmitrii without compunction.[93]

Dmitrii certainly did appreciate the grave danger that any charge of heresy or unorthodoxy would carry in the Russian context. Reportedly he ordered men killed who spread rumors that he was "destroying the faith."[94] Yet he did not shy away from doing things that were unusual and therefore suspect. According to Bussow, Dmitrii "kept a joyful table," complete with singers and musicians. He dispensed with "many awkward Muscovite customs . . . namely that the tsar must incessantly make the sign of the cross and have himself sprinkled with holy water." He mounted horses without aid. He often walked alone or "with one or two companions," but without the customary "crowd of princes." In Bussow's words these practices "shocked the Muscovites" so much that "they drooped their heads as if they had lice behind the ears."[95]

Dmitrii's most controversial departure from Russian Orthodox custom was unquestionably his marriage to the Polish Catholic Marina Mniszech, daughter of his chief foreign backer. The deposed Patriarch Iyov claimed that this step proved Dmitrii wanted to destroy the Orthodox Christian faith. The future Patriarch Hermogen may have objected to the marriage as well, although the other Russian Church prelates sanctioned it.[96] The wedding of Dmitrii and Marina actually took place twice: in November 1605, in Krakow, according to Catholic ritual, with Ambassador Afanasii Vlasiev standing in as proxy for the tsar; and then in early May 1606, in Moscow, according to

Orthodox Christian ritual. This duplication greatly complicated matters—both for contemporary witnesses describing the event and also for later historians attempting to understand what happened. Based on a careful reading of the source base, Boris Uspenskii argued that Dmitrii actually played a "game" of deliberate ambiguity as he attempted to satisfy two diametrically opposed camps—Polish Catholic and Russian Orthodox. For example, many Russians thought that the Polish ceremony had been merely a "betrothal" (*obruchenie*) instead of a "wedding" (*venchanie*). In fact, however, Dmitrii and Marina had been formally married under the aegis of the Catholic Church and the Pope for half a year prior to their Moscow wedding.[97]

Patriarch Ignatii and Archpriest Fyodor conducted the elaborate Orthodox wedding of Dmitrii and Marina, together with the participation of the metropolitans and other Church hierarchs. The official description of the event, compiled later, specifically mentioned that Ignatii had overseen the union (*venchal evo*).[98] By combining the wedding with Marina's coronation, the tsar and patriarch could further develop their strategy of intentional ambiguity. According to Uspenskii, the unusual ordering of the multiple rituals—betrothal, coronation, anointing, and then wedding—had been intentionally designed to convey thoroughly contradictory messages to the two camps. The Poles believed that Marina ascended the Muscovite throne as a Catholic; whereas Muscovites perceived her "anointing" (*pomazanie*) as a sign of conversion to Orthodoxy. In fact, Marina did not convert. She nonetheless received the crown as a sovereign in her own right—apparently the first woman in Russian history to be so elevated. In describing Marina's accession, the Piskarevskii Chronicle invoked as precedents the roles played by Boris's sister Irina Godunova in 1598 and his wife Maria Skuratova-Belskaia in 1605.[99] Marina's accession thus clearly demonstrated the newfound authority of vox feminae in Russian politics.

The fact that the tsar married an already crowned Catholic tsaritsa was not the only anomaly that day. As is usual for sources of the Smuta period, contradictions abound in the contemporary accounts. Yet, at least according to some witnesses, many of the Russian Orthodox rites were not carried to completion. Marina was anointed and crowned—but not with the traditional *shapka Monomakha* (hat of Monomakh). She appeared to undergo parts of the conversion ritual—but not all of them. The new royal couple was offered the sacrament of Eucharist upon the pronouncement of their union, but one or perhaps both of them declined. The wedding also took place on Friday, a traditional fast day, but was accompanied by extensive feasting and celebration.

The ceremony began at a time forbidden by Orthodox tradition. Marina wore Polish dress that seemed offensive to the Muscovites. Moreover, the usually hated Polish Catholics were not only accorded great honor and permitted inside the sacred Uspenskii Cathedral but even given a place in the ceremony itself. Dmitrii had Western titles applied to himself and his bride: *imperator, tsesar'* (caesar), *tsesareva* (caesarina). All these departures from Muscovite norms had a jarring effect on many Russian clerics and laymen and could be viewed as anti-Orthodox provocations.[100]

The marriage was not destined to be a happy one. Even as the celebratory prayers were pronounced, Vasilii Shuiskii and his coconspirators were readying their coup. The laconic chronicler as much as attributed the tsar's demise to his marriage, by ending the list of wedding guests with the bare statement: "And on the 17th day of May the defrocked monk was killed."[101] Just over a week after the wedding, as Dmitrii lay dead in Red Square, the Russian Orthodox Church began to reverse itself again under a new master. Yet the forms of legitimation used for Dmitrii had already fused with the novel strategy created in 1598 for Boris Godunov. As ideologues reverted to vilifying "the pretender" once again, they continued to be influenced by the innovations of 1605–1606. Vox populi and vox feminae had been solidified in the unique legitimacy paradigm of the Smuta. And the Dmitrii saga was far from over.

CHAPTER FIVE

A House Divided

*Russian Orthodoxy under Vasilii IV
and Dmitrii II*

The apostate, heretic, defrocked monk, villain . . . wanted to erase the true
Christian faith and to establish the Lutheran and Latin faith,
and . . . to lead all Christians away from God.

—Tsar Vasilii IV, 1606[1]

I, Tsar and Grand Prince Dmitrei Ivanovich of all Russia . . . chosen by
God . . . and anointed by God . . . made like the Second Israel . . .
the only Christian Tsar under the sun.

—Tsar Dmitrii [II], 1608[2]

The first Tsar Dmitrii might have been the most popular ruler of the Time of Troubles, but he ended up as the most vilified.[3] Overconfidence in his popularity may even have doomed him. From the very outset of his reign, he knew that Vasilii Shuiskii, a prominent boyar, was scheming to overthrow him. In the summer of 1605, he even convicted Shuiskii of treason and condemned him to death. Yet, just before the axe fell at Lobnoe mesto ("Golgotha") in Red Square, word arrived that the sentence had been commuted to exile. Within a few short months Dmitrii pardoned his enemy completely and gave him back his place on the boyar council. Rather than accepting the tsar's clemency gratefully, Vasilii took it as encouragement to persist in his efforts to seize the throne for himself. He succeeded on May 17, 1606. With the Muscovite population already outraged at the reportedly offensive and abusive behavior of some of Dmitrii's foreign wedding guests, Shuiskii and his coconspirators sparked a massive riot by spreading rumors that the Poles were trying to kill the tsar. Benefiting from the chaos, they quickly overpowered a reduced palace guard, chased down "God's anointed," and stabbed and shot him to death.[4]

Meanwhile, the mob that had gathered to "defend the tsar" rampaged through the city, murdering hundreds of Poles, other foreigners, and Russians wearing Polish dress. Hundreds or even thousands of the rioters were themselves killed by armed Poles who fought back. It was a "day of terrible memory," a shockingly "bloody massacre" in the capital city.[5] Shuiskii's assassins dragged Dmitrii's naked and mutilated corpse out onto Red Square and began to vilify him as a "false tsar" and "heretic." According to Claudia Jensen, the conspirators or rioters killed "dozens of Polish musicians" who participated in Dmitrii and Marina's wedding and further denigrated the tsar by piling his body with "musical instruments, a mask, and money, the tools and wages of a sinful musician."[6] The body lay there for three days as a now completely confused populace milled about it. Isaac Massa claimed to have counted twenty-one wounds on the body, which he asserted was definitely the tsar's.[7]

Others who "examined" the body disagreed. Rumors sprang up almost immediately that Dmitrii had escaped (again) and was still alive. Shuiskii ordered further desecration of the body in a kind of religious antifestival aimed at totally delegitimizing the former tsar. The body was removed, thrown into a ditch, then brought back and burned. Various strange "omens," together with trickery on the part of the conspirators, convinced some that Dmitrii had been an evil "sorcerer" who deserved this fate. His ashes were scattered or perhaps fired out of a cannon in the direction of Poland. Yet the damage had already been done. According to Dunning, "outside Moscow, belief in Tsar Dmitrii's survival and opposition to Shuiskii's coup spread like wildfire."[8] Some contemporaries spoke of the burial of a "counterfe[i]t body."[9] After only a brief respite Russia plunged right back into several more years of civil war. Two camps—each with its own tsar, patriarch, and administration—would fight each other until both had been virtually annihilated and the country lay in ruins.

Déjà Vu: Official Orthodoxy at the Accession of Vasilii Shuiskii

By the time that Shuiskii seized power in 1606, Russian Orthodox politics had undergone a remarkable transformation. Hereditary succession (in accordance with "God's will") no longer seemed sufficient as a justification for taking the throne. The innovations of Patriarch Iyov, carried out on behalf of Boris and Fyodor Godunov, had introduced vox populi and vox feminae into the equation. The successful revolt of Dmitrii had brought about a reversion to hereditary forms of legitimacy, but in propounding an Orthodox justification for rebellion, it also revived Byzantine and Russian ideas of "true" and "false" tsars. With the aid of the Orthodox Church, Tsar Vasilii would imitate and combine the legitimation strategies of all three previous rulers of the Time of Troubles.

Shuiskii's propaganda campaign had already begun during the coup of May 17. Dmitrii was vilified as a sorcerer, a worshiper of Satan and idols, and a Catholic. Killing him and overthrowing his regime had allegedly "saved" Orthodox Russia. This was almost exactly the same technique used by Dmitrii against the Godunovs a year earlier. Moreover, just as in that coup against Fyodor Borisovich, Vasilii's next move was to get rid of the patriarch. On May 18 the boyar council announced the deposition of Ignatii. The justification given was that he had supposedly known Dmitrii to be a Catholic. Church hierarchs also contrived ostensible canonical reasons to remove him. Shuiskii and the other aristocrats were probably concerned that, after the precedents of 1598 and 1605, popular perception would accord the patriarch the chief role in choosing a new tsar. Like Iyov before him, Russia's second Orthodox patriarch found himself jailed in a monastery and denounced as a "false patriarch." This cleared the way for Vasilii to maneuver his way onto the throne.[10]

As in 1598 new propaganda had to be invented, and it did not immediately assume a settled form. The first official text justifying the accession appeared on May 19, the same day that Vasilii actually took the throne. In a maneuver much debated in historiography, the new tsar bound himself to consult with the other boyars "in true judgment" (*istinnym sudom*) before expropriating property or condemning anyone to death, "in order that Orthodox Christendom would be our tsarist government, preserving good in quietude and in calmness and in prosperity." This "Record of Accession" also gave a brief statement of the ostensible bases of his legitimacy, beginning as follows:

> By the grace of God, we, the Great Sovereign, Tsar, and Grand Prince Vasilii Ivanovich of all Russia, by the praiseworthy God's bounties and love for humanity, and because of the plea of the whole Sanctified Council, and according to the petition and request of all Orthodox Christendom, have come to be over the hereditary possession [*otchina*] of our forebears, as tsar and grand prince

over the Russian state, which God did grant to our forebear Riurik, who was [descended] from the Roman Caesar—and then for many years and until our forebear the Grand Prince Aleksandr Iaroslavich Nevskii, my forebears were over this Russian state; and after this they separated into the Suzdal appanage principality, not by confiscation and not unwillingly, but according to kinship [*rodstvo*], just as great brothers were accustomed to sit at great places.[11]

The principal elements of this statement may be summarized as follows: (1) Vasilii came to the throne as a result of God's mercy and love (vox Dei). (2) The Church council "pleaded" with Vasilii to accept the throne (ecclesiastic sanction). (3) "All Orthodox Christendom"—i.e., the whole Russian population—petitioned Vasilii to become tsar (vox populi). (4) Vasilii's princely lineage was tied to the old dynasty and therefore could be traced all the way back to Riurik and Caesar Augustus. An emphasis was placed on the new tsar's pedigree, with repeated mention of his "forebears" (*praroditeli*) and their "hereditary possession" (*otchina*) of the Russian state. This was based partly on a genealogical mistake or fabrication, in addition to the fictitious nature of claiming descent from the Roman Caesar. Late medieval chronicles had apparently conflated or confused Andrei Iaroslavich of Suzdal with Andrei Aleksandrovich of Gorodets, perhaps intentionally, thus giving the Shuiskii clan an apparently loftier pedigree. It seems the Shuiskiis actually issued from the first Andrei, but claiming descent from the second instead gave them a direct line to the famous Aleksandr Nevskii.[12] The document thus creatively asserted a combination of divine, ecclesiastic, popular, and hereditary legitimacy for Vasilii.

This first attempt at official legitimization may have been hurriedly composed by a few relatives and allies of the new tsar, rather than by ecclesiastic ideologues.[13] It was noticeably crude, with none of the hallmarks of the Church's extremely careful and subtle manipulation of language. In contrast to the usual style of such official pronouncements, it did not establish any mystical ties between the attributes of God, as understood in Russian Orthodoxy, and the new tsar's legitimacy. It failed to draw grandiose rhetorical connections to religious ritual: there were none of the usual actions of the Holy Spirit, powers attributed to ikons, or prayerful appeals to saints. The authors made use of aristocratic kinship and seniority as a factor in legitimation, but did not specifically link them to Orthodoxy. The compilers of this document had a familiarity with the language of Muscovite Orthodox politics but may have lacked the skills and experience of professional publicists.

At the same time, this document demonstrated how accepted and entrenched the new forms of Smuta legitimation had become in the political culture. As if reflexively, Vasilii's coterie included the now formulaic petitions and requests of the Russian Church and people as a primary justification for his accession—regardless of whether anything resembling these had actually taken place. Forms of accession and legitimation unknown a mere decade earlier had already become de rigueur for the Muscovite government. Although Shuiskii did claim some hereditary right by dint of his family pedigree, he could not afford to ignore the new forms of legitimation—not least because other noble families could potentially challenge his claimed princely seniority.

By the following day, May 20, 1606, Tsar Vasilii's retinue had apparently enlisted the aid of some ecclesiastic literati. An official document released for broad distribution throughout the country manifested a much more thorough consideration of the issues involved and of the best strategies for legitimizing the new tsar. The new document also stuck to the usual style for official publicity. It was much more pious or religious in tone, covering every argument with a thick coating of Orthodox Christian rhetoric. The arguments rested more on God and the Orthodox faith than on alleged royal pedigree. When repeating the claims about Vasilii's descent from Caesar and Riurik and the rule of his "forebears" over the Russian state, this document omitted the excessive comments about princely seniority and the justification of his ancestors' move to Suzdal.[14]

The circular dated or perhaps backdated May 20 also established a single, overriding justification for Vasilii's rule: his alleged defense of the Orthodox faith against an evil, anti-Orthodox, false tsar. This demonization of the previous ruler represented the lynchpin of his official justification. Dunning remarked, "Tsar Dmitrii was denounced as a tool of the devil and as the Antichrist. . . . A dramatic propaganda campaign assert[ed] that the false tsar had been a sorcerer who had profaned icons and crosses and had communicated with unclean spirits. . . . The assassins also referred to the dead tsar as a 'pagan' and as a 'Polish minstrel.'"[15] The official document of May 20 called Dmitrii an apostate, heretic, and murderer who "wanted to erase the true Christian faith and . . . lead all Christians away from God."[16]

What had been at stake, in other words, was nothing other than the very preservation of Russian Orthodoxy. The document continued by stating that God himself had seen what was going on and mercifully decided to intervene, meting out "retribution" (*vozmezdie*) to the false tsar and "liberating all us Orthodox Christians" from his evil plot. In fact, this carefully formulated legitimation text did not even mention Shuiskii's coup at all, maintaining instead that "Grishka" had committed suicide (a sin under Orthodoxy). The authors also claimed that God had "revealed to all people his [i.e., Dmitrii's] villainy and heresy."[17] In other words, divine intervention and popular unanimity represented the rhetorical justifications for what had actually been a secret, narrow conspiracy.

Before turning to Vasilii's accession, the authors of this document sought to adduce further proofs of the former tsar's evil intentions. It was claimed that "many documents" had been found in his chambers, including "villainous correspondences with Poland and Lithuania about the destruction of the Muscovite state" and a letter from the Pope on how to establish "the Roman faith" in Russia. Vasilii's propagandists asserted that these letters proved the former tsar's intention of converting all of Orthodoxy "to the Lutheran and to the Latin faith."[18] In the eyes of Russian Orthodox Christians, there could not be a viler crime imaginable.

Vasilii's supporters did not even have to fabricate the damning evidence. Dmitrii had in fact given the impression to his Polish and papal backers that he would promote Catholicism in Russia. On August 4, 1605, for example, Pope Clement VIII had written the following to King Zygmunt (Sigismund) III: "If Dmitrii, as we hope, maintains inviolate at home the Catholic faith he received while an exile from his native land, we have no doubt that the profession of the Catholic religion will now at last find a home among the Muscovites."[19] Yet Dmitrii may have had no intention of following through with his promises, which had been made in order to secure Catholic support for his campaign. A Polish priest also viewed his grisly demise as divinely ordained but for precisely the opposite reason as Vasilii's publicists: "The Divine Will permitted such blindness and obstinacy while secretly preparing a death for Dmitrii which ultimately proved to be most just. Dmitrii had changed greatly from the man he had been in Poland. He gave scant thought to the Catholic faith and religion in spite of all he had promised."[20] Thus some Orthodox Russians portrayed the tsar as too Catholic, while Polish Catholics seem to have regarded him as not Catholic enough.

Hence, even if Vasilii's charges against the late Dmitrii were not entirely true, they did have some basis in fact and could be supported by pieces of evidence. The new regime soon publicized incriminating letters, purportedly from Dmitrii, in an attempt to establish its new official version of events.[21] With the Union of Brest (1595–1596) still in recent memory, Russians could have no doubt of the Pope's interest in Catholicizing further Slavic territory.

The authors of the May 20 pronouncement expressed praise to God for delivering their country from such an evil plot and for sending Tsar Vasilii to save Russian Orthodoxy. They asserted that his stand for truth appropriately prompted his "selection" (*izbranie*) by the Russian church, nobles, and people. The new tsar declared that representatives of all ecclesiastic and social strata had petitioned him to take up the throne "according to the rank of our forebears, which God granted to the great sovereign Riurik, who was [descended] from the Roman Caesar."[22]

The official account was no doubt fictional; nothing resembling a zemskii sobor had actually taken place.[23] The ecclesiastic ideologues had merely adapted the novel but already accepted norms of Smuta legitimation to the case of Vasilii. Pro forma, they assigned the leading role in choosing a tsar to the Church hierarchy, although the absence of a patriarch could not help but be noticed. In concluding the accession story, the authors of this critical document explicitly listed the alleged sources of the new tsar's legitimacy: the will of God, the "request of the intermediaries to God" (i.e., churchmen), the petition of the whole people, and hereditary right (*po kolenstvu nashemu*). The document ended with instructions for this official version of events to be read publicly throughout the land, for the usual prayers to be offered for the new tsar and his reign, and for the populace to "kiss the cross" and swear loyalty to Vasilii. The prescribed prayers included a striking recognition that the country found itself in the midst of a period of turmoil; special attention was paid to the need to revive Orthodoxy and ensure its survival.[24]

At approximately the same time, the Muscovite boyars issued a document of their own, which described the downfall of Dmitrii and the accession of Vasilii in identical terms. The document claimed that the top Church hierarchs had gathered all the different categories or strata of Russian people in order to "select" a new monarch—a suggestion that a kind of zemskii sobor had convened. The authors further remarked that the new, "God-revealed" tsar was one who had "suffered much" during the reign of the supposed Dmitrii, specifically because he was "a champion [*poboritel'*] for God's Church and for the Orthodox Christian faith."[25]

In addition, the Shuiskii camp moved quickly to utilize the ostensible tsaritsa, Maria Nagaia, for legitimation purposes. A letter purporting to be from her announced to the country that the former tsar was not really her son and that she had recognized him only out of fear of death. Later documents would claim implausibly that Vasilii Shuiskii and the other coup leaders had actually placed themselves under the tsaritsa's judgment, declaring their willingness to die if the former tsar had truly been her son.[26] In this way the new regime gained the requisite vox feminae to augment its facade of legitimacy. Naturally, however, the tsaritsa had no less reason to fear death from Vasilii than she had from Dmitrii for a "wrong" answer.

As in 1598 the flood of arguments to prove the new tsar's legitimacy continued for many months. For a time Tsar Vasilii found himself in an awkward and paradoxical position. He relied even more than his predecessors on the Church and on Orthodoxy for his legitimacy—if such a thing were possible. Yet he lacked a sympathetic patriarch to coordinate the all-important ideological campaign. What exactly transpired next remains partially unclear, but a plausible reconstruction follows. Shuiskii's fellow boyars, who had already prevailed upon him to accept certain limitations to his rule, now pushed through the candidacy of his rival Filaret Nikitich (Fyodor Romanov) for the position of Russia's third Orthodox patriarch. Filaret had long harbored political ambitions, prompting Boris Godunov to have him forcefully tonsured and imprisoned in a monastery. Later he allied with Dmitrii, who rehabilitated him and awarded him the metropolitanate of Rostov. Once "pronounced" or "designated" patriarch, Filaret seemingly maintained his loyalty to the cause of "Dmitrii" and worked actively against Vasilii.[27]

Shuiskii therefore knew that he had to get rid of Filaret if he was to have any chance of shoring up his throne. Such a dangerous adversary could not be allowed to proclaim official truth as head of the Russian Orthodox Church. Near the end of May 1606, Vasilii's coup remained incomplete. In contrast to the tight personal alliance and commonality of interests shared by Tsar Boris and Patriarch Iyov in 1598 or Tsar Dmitrii and Patriarch Ignatii in 1605, now there existed instead a dangerous enmity and conflict of interests between tsar and patriarch. Always a cunning schemer, Vasilii devised yet another multifaceted plot. He appointed the patriarch (or patriarch-designate) head of a delegation tasked with literally unearthing the "real" Dmitrii, now considered officially to have died in 1591. On assignment in Uglich, the patriarch would be away from Moscow for almost a week. In the meantime Vasilii planned to hold his own coronation ceremony, all the while falsely claiming Filaret's sanction. By the time the patriarch-designate returned, his accession would be a fait accompli, and the return of the commission with the boy Dmitrii's body would force Filaret to participate in further legitimizing activity on behalf of the new tsar.

On May 29, Tsar Vasilii issued an edict to transfer "Elder Stefan, who was Tsar Semion Bekbulatov," from his jail cell in the Kirillo Belozersk

Monastery. In 1575 Ivan IV had briefly bestowed the rulership of Russia on this former Tatar khan, thus giving him as legitimate a claim to the throne as anyone else during the Time of Troubles. Bekbulatovich may even have been a candidate for the throne in 1598. The oath of loyalty to Tsar Boris (September 15, 1598) subsequently bound the Russian population to have no contact with "Tsar Semion." Dmitrii had similar concerns and so took the decisive step of having Bekbulatovich tonsured and jailed in the Kirillo Belozersk Monastery, located about 450 kilometers (280 miles) north of Moscow. Vasilii's order of transfer kept the potential competitor's new destination secret, but it turned out to be the Solovetskii Monastery, fully 1,000 kilometers (620 miles) away from the capital. Later Romanov propaganda would twist the story, claiming that Dmitrii had banished Bekbulatovich to Solovki for "telling many people that they should not betray the Orthodox Christian faith for Latinism."[28]

On June 1, Vasilii staged a hasty coronation ceremony. With Patriarch-designate Filaret out of town, the tsar received his diadem and anointing from Metropolitan Isidor of Novgorod instead. Muscovite coronation ceremonies often represented the high point and full expression of legitimization rhetoric. However, the evidence suggests that Vasilii's ideologues were still working out several different approaches and had not yet had the chance to create a final synthesis. The prepared speeches focused on Vasilii's family ties to the old dynasty: ancient princes such as Vladimir of Kiev were termed his "forebears" (*praroditeli*), and more recent grand princes and tsars such as Ivan IV were his "kinsmen" (*srodniki*). Isidor recited a new history of recent Muscovite successions, designed to bolster Vasilii's qualifications. In this version of events, Ivan IV blessed his son Fyodor to rule, but then "by God's righteous judgment" the "root of the tsars" had been cut off. Boris had been "chosen" (*izbran*) according to God's will but significantly had come "not from the root of the tsars." The ideologues also demeaned him as "Boris Godunov," rather than "Tsar and Grand Prince Boris Fyodorovich, Autocrat of all Russia." Dmitrii they vilified imaginatively as "having received the Latin faith abominable to God, revealing himself [to be] a second Julian the Apostate, for he desired to uproot to the end the Orthodox and pious faith."[29]

The speechmakers also denied both Boris and Dmitrii the term "autocrat." They were walking a fine line. They would have liked to consider Boris illegitimate altogether, but then they could not also have portrayed Dmitrii as an illegitimate usurper. Yet they could not justify Vasilii's accession if Dmitrii had been a legitimate tsar. Consequently, they described Boris as an evil murderer—but one legitimately elevated to the throne despite his unsatisfactory pedigree. Aside from his own illustrious descent, Vasilii's only other justification for rule seemed to be vox Dei and his alleged restoration of Orthodoxy. The metropolitan claimed that this accession of the new "great God-chosen sovereign" served to "renew piety" and to "liberate God's holy churches from heretical temptation." Vasilii was said to be "loved" and "chosen" and "honored" and "crowned" and "anointed" by God. "By the grace given to us from the Holy and Life-giving Spirit," the metropolitan then pronounced Shuiskii "Tsar and Grand Prince Vasilei Ivanovich, Autocrat of all Russia." Vox populi and vox feminae remained conspicuously absent.[30]

A few days later, Patriarch-designate Filaret returned to Moscow with the body of a dead child, purportedly the disinterred Dmitrii of Uglich. Inside the Kremlin's Archangel Cathedral the boy was canonized as the "martyr Tsarevich Dmitrii," murdered by Boris Godunov. Since saints' bodies were not supposed to decompose, the tsar may have callously arranged to have another young boy killed in order to play the role of the deceased Dmitrii. The long Orthodox ceremonies included a number of obviously fake "miracles," which disgusted some observers. Dmitrii's unfortunate mother Maria Nagaia "recognized" her "son" this time around, too, probably under duress. Vasilii's intent, of course, was to prove that the self-styled Tsar Dmitrii could not have been who he claimed to be. In Ruslan Skrynnikov's words, "no one" was convinced by the show, although contemporary accounts vary on this score. It appears that the official Church also fell into further disrepute as a consequence of surrounding the many lies and constant revisions of history with pious language and promoting them as part of true Orthodoxy.[31]

The time had now come to combine all the "drafts" into a comprehensive formulation of legitimacy. A long circular released on June 6 imitated and resembled the work of Patriarch Iyov in 1598. Like the Confirmatory Document of that year, this official declaration founded the new tsar's legitimacy on a wide variety of bases. Allegedly, God himself had ended Dmitrii's rule and life because of the extreme threat he posed to Orthodoxy. God then "chose" Vasilii to be the new sovereign, tsar, grand prince, and autocrat of Russia. Vasilii accepted the throne "with the help of the great God" and "according to our forebears' tsarist degree"—i.e., in consequence of his royal pedigree. The accession came about at the "plea" (*molenie*) of the patriarch, metropolitans, archbishops, bishops, and the whole Church council. Following the church hierarchs, "many [vassal] tsars and tsareviches," as well as the whole population, had likewise begged him to rule. Tsaritsa Marfa (Maria) "repented" for helping to legitimize Dmitrii and recognized as her true son the new child saint. She begged the Orthodox tsar, church, and people to forgive her for her error. Vasilii magnanimously pardoned her, and church officials prayed that God would mercifully "free her soul from such an evil sin."[32] Later letters purporting to be from the tsaritsa would urge the Russian populace to obey their new, "God-given" tsar.[33]

Shuiskii now had a standard accession story according to the new paradigm invented for Tsar Boris: that is, "selection" (*izbranie*) according to vox Dei, Church leadership and sanction, vox populi, and vox feminae. He combined this with justifications used by Dmitrii: hereditary right and vilification of the previous "false" tsar. The document of June 6 propounded an expanded version of the Dmitrii story, replete with curses against "that villain and heretic and apostate, the defrocked monk." The authors attached some of the former tsar's correspondence as evidence of his evil plots against Orthodox Russia.[34] In this manner Vasilii's publicity campaign added to the new Smuta paradigm. Intentional rewriting of recent history became a requisite component of political legitimization. It would be similarly prominent at the accession of Mikhail Romanov in 1613—a fact that seriously complicates any historiographic analysis of the period. Ecclesiastic authors played an important role in composing these successive revisions of history. Incidentally, Catherine II the Great would use similar strategies to justify her coup of July 1762, which resulted in the assassination of her husband, Peter III.[35]

Throughout his reign Tsar Vasilii kept up a barrage of propaganda against the "evil Grishka" and his "demonic plots" to destroy Orthodox Russia. Churchmen authored a saint's life (vita) of Tsarevich Dmitrii and other tales about "God's revenge" on Boris Godunov.[36] Such explicitly religious texts attempted to bind Vasilii to the "true faith," just as Iyov's compositions had attempted to do for Boris. Meanwhile, official Orthodoxy consistently portrayed Tsar Vasilii as an upstanding, zealous believer who sought above all to defend Orthodox Russia against her heretical enemies. In early July 1606 Shuiskii managed to have Patriarch-designate Filaret replaced with Hermogen, until then the metropolitan of Kazan. It was a calculated move, and one demonstrating yet again the importance attached to the head of the church in establishing a ruler's legitimacy. During the Time of Troubles, every tsar essentially needed his own patriarch. Russia's fourth patriarch in two years would prove to be a zealous crusader on behalf of the new tsar. Hermogen vehemently insisted on the equation of Orthodox piety with support for Tsar Vasilii.

However, according to I. O. Tiumentsev and some other historians, all such publicity efforts failed miserably, at least outside of Moscow. The Church hierarchy had lost too much credibility in the eyes of both elite and ordinary Russians, who could not help but notice such frequent reversals of official "truth." At least some churchmen also joined the opposition. According to Massa, in January 1607 "a priest from Moscow was beheaded for distributing satirical letters, announcing that Dmitry was still alive." By then rebellion had already spread throughout the country. Another bizarre spectacle in February 1607—the summoning of former Patriarch Iyov from his monasterial cell to endorse Vasilii's rule—may have done as much harm as good. Most of Iyov's prefabricated speech simply repeated the party line about Dmitrii wanting "to destroy our unblemished Christian faith to the end." Oddly, he remarked that the former tsar's staunchly Catholic bride Marina had been a "girl of the Lutheran faith."[37] Muscovites did not always discriminate clearly when it came to the non-Orthodox!

Dmitrii I and Vasilii IV both overthrew the preceding ruler and justified their coups as the defense of the "true faith" against a heretic "false tsar." They claimed that a violent takeover had been necessary to ensure the very survival of Russia and of Orthodoxy—which amounted to the same thing in the Muscovite politico-religious worldview. These choices had serious consequences for the rest of the Troubles. The vital questions—*who is the true tsar?* and *what is true Orthodoxy?*—became essentially up for grabs. The ruler glorified in virtually theophanic terms one day might be lying dead in a ditch the next, denigrated as a vile criminal. Official truth could change at any minute: what had been Orthodoxy yesterday was treason today. Legitimation rhetoric became less effective as each ruler vilified the last but utilized the same arguments to claim the throne. Citing such high stakes as the very preservation from destruction of Russia and of Orthodoxy contributed to an extreme radicalization and destabilization of the country. Such rhetoric even became something of a self-fulfilling prophecy, as violent conflicts that ripped through Russia from the time of Vasilii's accession did indeed place the country's future in doubt.

The always fiery Ivan Timofeev, who did not agree with subjects taking action to overthrow unrighteous tsars, declared that Vasilii's supposed "selection" (*izbranie*) had come about "without God" and "not even from a general popular council of the cities of all Russia." In reality, the new tsar was only "self-selected" (*samoizbran*).[38] In the pre-Smuta order, it would have been unthinkable for a Russian autocrat to found his right to rule primarily on popular election or to suffer criticism for lacking the sanction of vox populi. Now this had become not only commonplace but fully expected and indispensible. The first half of the Time of Troubles had definitely changed the rules and the discourse of politico-religious legitimacy in Muscovy.

The Orthodoxy of Rebellion

Ulianovskii viewed the canonization of St. Dmitrii as an ultimately successful "ban on pretenderism."[39] Yet its immediate effect (at least) was the opposite. Shuiskii's coup and propaganda efforts opened the door to a multitude of rebellions, all ostensibly for the sake of truth and Orthodoxy. Russia had reverted to the Byzantine system, which assigned divine approval to any successful revolt. As Leonora Neville has noted, this ideology really "did not discourage those who felt justified in their disgruntlement from attempting a revolt," with the result that medieval Byzantium faced nearly a rebellion a year.[40] Muscovy would be similarly plagued by a dozen or more "pretenders" during the remaining years of its Troubles. A group of Carmelite monks traveling along the Volga in 1606 had to receive laissez-passer from Dmitrii I, Vasilii, and Dmitrii II, as well as other pretenders and local rulers, before they finally made it to Astrakhan.[41] War now became the only practical test of Orthodox truth.

The southern and southwestern frontier regions rose against Vasilii almost immediately. They had fought enthusiastically for the "true tsar" Dmitrii only a year or two earlier and were only too glad to believe the many rumors that he had again escaped a vile plot. Mikhail Molchanov, a close associate of the former tsar, apparently posed as him for a time, intentionally encouraging the reports. Pro-Dmitrii, anti-Moscow, and anti-Vasilii sentiments easily swirled together in a combustible mix. Shuiskii unwisely appointed a new *voevoda* (commander) of Putivl, Prince Grigorii Shakhovskoi, who promptly sparked open revolt in the name of Tsar Dmitrii and swore the people to take revenge on Tsar Vasilii. Molchanov made contact with the Polish Mniszech family, who again joined the cause, and he and Shakhovskoi appointed Ivan Bolotnikov commander-in-chief of a rapidly growing army. By the fall of 1606, rebel forces were already pressing toward the Russian heartland. Vasilii could barely control Moscow and reinforced the defenses of the moated Kremlin. Molchanov no longer posed as the "resurrected" tsar, but the rebellion mounted even without any "Dmitrii" at its head.[42]

The second or reignited civil war proved to be much bloodier and even more destructive than the first. Incredibly, a rebel army numbering tens of thousands and under the command of Istoma Pashkov besieged Moscow on October 28, 1606, less than half a year after Shuiskii's coup. Despite brutal reprisals "fanatic belief in Tsar Dmitrii's survival persisted, and rumors of his imminent return continued to circulate."[43] In the absence of the original pretender, a group of Terek Cossacks put forward "Tsarevich Petr," an alleged son of Tsar Fyodor I. A simple copy of the popular image of Dmitrii, Petr had supposedly been hidden as a child from the murderous Boris Godunov. Now he materialized to lead a gang of freebooters, who terrorized the Volga region with mass thefts, rapes, and murders. Fighting on behalf of "Petr" and "Dmitrii" merged into a general rebellion that split the country in two. Forced to retreat from Moscow, the rebels established a new headquarters in Tula in February 1607. Tsar Vasilii pressed his advantage and besieged the town in the summer. Tula finally capitulated in October, but by then a man claiming to be Dmitrii had emerged at the head of other rebel forces. In 1608 this "second false Dmitrii" set up his court at Tushino, on the northwest side of Moscow, and persistently tried to take the capital.[44]

Why did the assassination of Dmitrii I cause such an extraordinary outbreak of violence? Platonov spoke of a "social struggle," and Soviet historians tried to explain the whole period in terms of "class warfare." But why did the name of Dmitrii possess such power? Dunning has argued that in fact the civil war split Russian society vertically rather than horizontally. In his interpretation Russians fought each other over a question "as much religious as political: to restore the God-chosen ruler to the throne."[45] In other words, the war amounted to a vicious dispute over who could rightfully claim to be "God's anointed" (*pomazannik Bozhii*).

This perspective does ring true, although a number of other factors must have played their roles. The revolts in Dmitrii's name gave many who felt oppressed an outlet for revenge, even if not via a fully developed social consciousness. Pure brigandage and lawlessness additionally attracted many Cossacks and others, who displayed no regard for men or women as they rampaged. The appearance of "Tsarevich Petr" and several other obviously fictional members of the royal family demonstrated that the true identity of Dmitrii was not the real issue for many combatants. Margeret recorded as common knowledge the fact that the invention of new pretenders was "only a pretext to pillage the land"—and that Petr's Cossacks were actually disgruntled with Dmitrii I.[46] In this context the breakdown of order snowballed, restraints on human behavior disappeared, and a vicious cycle of anarchy took hold. Animalistic instinct and greed for booty may well have played as great a role as ideology in shaping the civil war.

The "Dmitrii" who mounted a massive revolt against Shuiskii was really several different people, some of whom were imaginary. This may be one reason why both Russian and Polish governments encountered great difficulty in attempting to discover who he was! Dmitrii II claimed to be the same person as Dmitrii I but apparently looked nothing like him. Virtually all historians of the period regard the "villain of Tushino" as a conscious impostor, and some believe him to have been a Ukrainian or Belorussian Jew. Whoever he was, he managed to "reunite" with his ostensible wife, Marina Mniszech. She willingly identified him as her husband. The two of them even had a child known as the "little felon" (*vorenok*), who attracted a large Cossack following as a pretender in his own right even as a baby.[47]

The two governments, Moscow and Tushino, mirrored each other in several respects. Each had its tsar, patriarch, boyars, churchmen, military servitors, bureaucrats, merchants, and peasants. Each so-called autocrat held tenuously to his own patchwork of loyal territory scattered around the country, while the rest of Russia degenerated into violent chaos. The ideologues in each camp kept up a stream of vitriolic rhetoric against the other. Both armies brutally humiliated and executed suspected traitors and war captives. Moreover, each side claimed to possess the mantle of true Orthodoxy.

Dmitrii II used the same politico-religious language familiar to Orthodox Muscovites from the proclamations of previous tsars. This is not surprising, for a number of clerics, boyars, and government secretaries came over to his camp and continued their work just as they had in Moscow. In fact, many extant documents from his reign were written *u Moskvy* (beside Moscow), as his rebel armies continued to press the gates of the capital in 1608–1609. The rebel camp consistently spoke and acted just as if it already constituted the authentic government of Russia. After the arrival of Filaret in October 1608, an alternate Russian "patriarchate" and rump Church hierarchy asserted their authority and propagandized on behalf of Dmitrii II. Filaret had been appointed but not canonically enthroned as patriarch; whether he participated willingly or unwillingly at first remains open to debate.[48]

In order to claim legitimacy, this Dmitrii had merely to announce his existence and his identity with the previous one. Like Dmitrii I, he claimed vox Dei, the sanction of Orthodoxy, hereditary right, and vox feminae. If Tsar Vasilii equated Orthodox piety with loyalty to his own government, Dmitrii II insisted that the truly pious must join his camp to overthrow the "false tsar" and reestablish the legitimate tsardom. Vasilii called his enemy a "villian" (*vor*) who wanted to destroy Orthodox Christianity; Dmitrii reciprocated by branding Vasilii a "traitor" (*izmennik*) who wanted to destroy Orthodox Christianity. If Tsar Vasilii trumpeted the witness of Tsaritsa Maria that Dmitrii had died, Tsar Dmitrii countered with the witness of Tsaritsa Marina that he had not. Each side called out to the Russian population to "remember your souls and our Orthodox Christian faith and your cross-kissing [i.e., oaths of loyalty]."[49] Both sides could not be right; the population had to choose which of these opposite "Orthodoxies" to credit.

The relatively few extant documents attributed to Dmitrii II furnish ample evidence of his legitimation strategies. A public letter of October 1608, sent to the city of Suzdal, followed the usual Muscovite form in addressing ecclesiastics first and then all other categories of persons. "Tsar and Grand Prince Dmitrei Ivanovich of all Russia" graciously accepted the "repentance" of his subjects, who had "remembered God and their souls and our cross-kissing." The oath to Dmitrii taken in 1605 was held to be still in force. The rebel tsar made multiple references to the Virgin Mary and St. Nikolai and showed his concern for Christendom by urging the Suzdalians to "live in quietness and peace" and not to beat or rob each other. He looked forward to mounting "the throne of the Russian state of our forebears" and dispensing recompense to his supporters. He mentioned ecclesiastic landholdings and also promised tax exemptions. Finally, Dmitrii urged his allies to seek out and destroy traitors, "as much as the merciful God will give help."[50]

Dmitrii II dispatched letters of this nature in response to the many "petitions" received from towns transferring their allegiance to him. In that autumn of 1608, the residents of Yaroslavl also wrote to Dmitrii, asking him to remove their guilt: namely, "that we stood against you, Sovereign, according to our own sin, not knowing . . . for they told us that you, Sovereign, were killed in Moscow." The petitioners humbly asked Dmitrii to "have mercy" regarding their temporary loyalty to Vasilii. The first of many signatories to this missive was Archimandrite Feofil (Theophilos) of the Spasskii Monastery.[51] Dmitrii's government also received numerous requests for aid from ecclesiastics and others suffering the consequences of war. The tsar generally responded with positive assurances but also remained obsessed about possible "traitors."[52]

Dmitrii's letters referred to his "hereditary possession" (*otchina*) and termed him "heritor" (*dedich*) of many lands. He was styled a "righteous born sovereign" (*pravednyi prirozhenyi gosudar'*). These elements reinforced his claims to rule by right of descent from Ivan IV. In addition to frequent allusions to Orthodox religion, he expressed concern about the shedding of "true Orthodox Christian blood." All this was topos—but important in the Muscovite setting. Dmitrii also showed a propensity for grandiose innovation. Bussow reported that he added the term "second Israel" (a variation of "New Israel") to his title and called himself "the only Christian emperor under the sun." These interesting assertions are borne out by the documentary record (e.g., as in the epigraph to this chapter). Dmitrii also used the title *tsesar'* (caesar) as well as tsar—just as Dmitrii I had. He especially emphasized his sovereignty over "eastern" states, claiming to have been "exalted above all khanates [i.e., steppe empires]" and "all Tatar tsardoms."[53]

While recognizing the essential role of Orthodox Christian rhetoric, Dmitrii II—like Dmitrii I—sometimes manifested a lackadaisical or dismissive attitude toward religion. The Polish condottiere Mikolaj Marchocki reported hearing him utter "blasphemy": that he was glad to be a Russian tsar rather than a Polish king, since the latter could be ordered about by some churchman! Marchocki further recorded the following irreverent-sounding statement on the part of Dmitrii: "Never has such a thing happened to a Muscovite monarch; that he should give up his faithful servants, who have warned him about something. And not only for you I [would not do] this, but if God Himself would come down from high heaven and tell me to do that, I will not do that!"[54] Whether or not they obeyed decrees from on high, the first and second Dmitriis both understood the power of traditional Russian Orthodoxy and also the key innovations of the Smuta period. Otherwise they could not have roused multitudes and left such a mark at this particular time in history.

The Ecclesiastic Economy, 1606–1610

This period of division has sometimes been characterized as political *dvoemyslie* (dual thinking or allegiance). Economic realities reflected and supported the political situation. Both Moscow and Tushino issued the usual charters for land, property, and resource extraction rights. Even during an extreme crisis, the socioeconomic order remained consistent—or perhaps inflexible, hindering potential adjustments that might have lessened the hardships of the period. The competing tsars and the many monasteries continued to cling together to the same system of privileged landholding, tax exemptions, usufructuary rights, and domination of the peasantry. Legally, the copious official documents still guaranteed ecclesiastic economic advantages. Practically, however, increasing disorder pushed the system toward breakdown.

During the years 1606–1608 the government of Tsar Vasilii issued dozens of the ordinary economic charters. In addition, it continued to collect obrok rent and other fees; monasteries did the same in their domains.[55] However, extant documents are fewer in number than for preceding years, a reflection of the endemic disruptions in the country. Moreover, the source material is geographically limited due to the ragged division of Russia into two warring camps that developed soon after Vasilii's accession. As during the first civil war, the conflict took place largely, but not entirely, on north versus south lines. At times the Tushino government was able to assert its authority even in important northern towns like Belozero and Vologda. Tsar Vasilii's government, meanwhile, passed stern legislation attempting to control peasant flight, thus further promoting full-fledged serfdom.[56]

Litigation and conflicts (*spornye dela*) became the rule rather than the exception. Frequent accounts of robbery, corruption, coercion, and other abuses permeate the sources of these years. In the fall of 1607, Tsar Vasilii responded to a complaint from the major Kirillo Belozersk Monastery, to the effect that civil servants were wrongly collecting obrok from peasants in the little town of Kunost. The monastery possessed *gramoty* (charters) showing that it owned the town outright and that no obrok or other fees should be collected. Naturally, the tsar's government agreed with the monastery in a judgment "written in our camp outside Tula, on day 10 of September of the 7116th year [i.e., 1607]."[57]

At this time, the tsar was personally directing an ongoing and difficult siege of the rebel headquarters at Tula, about 170 kilometers (105 miles) south of Moscow. Bolotnikov's men had not only been holding out quite well but also harassing the Muscovite forces, causing considerable frustration in the tsar's camp and rumors of defeat in the territories loyal to Moscow. Starvation seemed a greater threat for Vasilii's army than for the rebels. Moreover, on the same day, September 10, Dmitrii II launched his own military campaign, one intended in part to relieve the siege of Tula.[58] It is thus noteworthy that in the midst of this situation Vasilii's officials ensured a response to the Kirillo Belozersk Monastery. For the time being Moscow was powerless to enforce compliance in the northern territories or anywhere else. However, Shuiskii desperately wanted to maintain the appearance of control and needed to keep the powerful and wealthy monasteries on his side. These factors explain his government's support of the privileged ecclesiastic economy even from the mosquito-infested swamps outside Tula. During his reign Vasilii did manage to retain the support of the major Troitsa Sergiev, Iosifo Volokolamsk, and Kirillo Belozersk Monasteries.[59]

The wealthiest ecclesiastic establishment in the Galich region, the Uspenskii Paisiev Monastery, also complained to Tsar Vasilii about repeated encroachment of its property rights by townspeople and local fishermen. The tsar's response of April 7, 1608, bore witness to the fact that previous appeals had done no good; the problem had been ongoing since at least the reign of "the Unfrocked" (i.e., Dmitrii I). Yet there was little alternative but to issue yet another order. Vasilii's government wrote in part:

> And, [the monks] say, those townspeople [*posadtskie liudi*] and fishermen of Galich do not obey our official document, and they gibe at Archimandrite Isaiia with the brotherhood, and they cut up the [monastery's] fencing, and they trample down the monastery's grain [*khleb*], and they call the [monastery's] fishing grounds their own rented [fishing] grounds; and, [the monks] say, [the townspeople and fishermen] want to cast their servants [working] on the monastery's fishing grounds into the water.[60]

The tsar again forbade the offenders to interfere with the monastery's property but could do no better than to close with the following hollow threat: "And if the townspeople and fishermen of Galich undertake to encroach on any resources, then you should write back about this to us at Moscow, and we will undertake an edict against them for their great disobedience."[61]

Strife caused by intense competition for food and money, against the backdrop of war and an impotent central government, shaped this further stage of the Troubles. Ecclesiastics and others in the Suzdal region continued to complain frequently of abuses. One of Vasilii's judgments from January 1608 concerned local officials' intentional violations of the Pokrovskii Convent's tax exemptions.[62] In Velikii Ustiug a tenant farmer of the Arkhangelskii Monastery appealed to the Troitskii Gledensk Monastery for help in recovering 8.2 rubles worth of rye, hay, and straw.[63] In the midst of the ongoing civil war, gaining the ear or sympathy of any local authority could be more beneficial than relying on either tsar's distant court system.

Alliances and loyalties shifted frequently during these years of dvoemyslie or "dual thinking," with monasteries as with individuals. The Ipatiev Troitskii Monastery in Kostroma had been intimately connected to the Godunov and Romanov families for many years. Until the fall of 1608, it recognized the authority of Tsar Vasilii but then switched to support the Tushino patriarchate under Filaret Romanov.[64] In reality neither Tsar Vasilii nor Tsar Dmitrii had much actual authority except in regions actually occupied by his troops—and not always then, as the armies constantly plundered local populations on their own initiative. The besieged Moscow government was isolated and powerless; the Tushino bureaucracy was ad hoc and weak. In the latter case Patriarch-appointee (*narechennyi patriarkh*) Filaret apparently served as principle liaison for relations with monasteries. This represented a notable modification of the Muscovite system of administration, according to which the patriarch ordinarily played little role in the relations between monasteries and the bureaucracy.[65]

The documentary record for the years 1608–1610 is extremely weak. The national economy seems to have splintered into local units, where the balance of power fluctuated among monasteries, civil servants, townspeople, gangs, and peasants. Agriculture and trade certainly continued to function to some extent; otherwise almost no one could have survived. The extant documents do include a smattering of minor purchases, obrok payments, and other arrangements—all signs of regular economic activity.[66] Isaac Massa reported that in 1608 "bread was cheap except in the besieged towns." Even in besieged Moscow, the "great stores of the monasteries" helped somewhat to alleviate the scarcity of food, although the price of bread remained elevated.[67] It stands to reason that most people went about their usual lives as best they could in a drastic situation. Some towns and regions, particularly in the north, probably fared relatively well.

Table 3

Income of the Vologda Office of the Solovetskii Monastery, 1605–1610

Muscovite year	Sales volume	Average price	Sales revenue
7114 (1605–1606)	61,659 poods	0.0815 rubles/pood	5,026 rubles
7115 (1606–1607)	132,759 poods	0.0721 rubles/pood	9,575 rubles
7116 (1607–1608)	123,137 poods	0.0893 rubles/pood	10,990 rubles
7117 (1608–1609)	53,551 poods	0.0730 rubles/pood	3,912 rubles
7118 (1609–1610)	[data missing]	[data missing]	[data missing]
Total for 4 years	**371,106 poods**	**0.0790 rubles/pood**	**29,503 rubles**

Table 4

Expenditure of the Vologda Office of the Solovetskii Monastery, 1605–1610

Muscovite year	Expenditure
7114 (1605–1606)	6,003 rubles
7115 (1606–1607)	8,669 rubles
7116 (1607–1608)	11,641 rubles
7117 (1608–1609)	5,854 rubles
7118 (1609–1610)	10,206 rubles
Total for 5 years	**42,373 rubles**

Though economic actors often had to fend for themselves in this period of turmoil, powerful monasteries could still turn a profit amid the fragmentation and destruction. Records of the Solovetskii Monastery show that its salt trade did quite well during the civil war, particularly in 1606–1608 (see Table 3).[68] Annual income from salt sales in Vologda exceeded 10,000 rubles only once during the Time of Troubles, during the Muscovite year 7116 (September 1607 to August 1608). Considering the dreadful war and widespread brigandage current at the time, we are again forced to a paradoxical conclusion: national disaster actually increased (some) monasterial incomes. The price of salt remained high in the years 1605–1609, making it easier to turn a profit. Yet revenue had been down somewhat during the first Dmitrii's reign. Surprisingly, the early years of Shuiskii's rule brought prosperity to this monasterial business, although income drooped again in 1609. The records for 1610–1615 are unfortunately missing.

Partly as a result of this business success, the monastery did not lack for money or supplies. The monks on assignment in Vologda actually recorded above-average expenditures.[69] Table 4 shows that the Solovetskii Monastery did not suffer deprivation during the reigns of Dmitrii I, Vasilii IV, and Dmitrii II. Even as the Russian state began to disintegrate completely in 1609–1610, the Solovki monks had plenty of cash on hand for their own needs. In that year they apparently spent over 10,000 rubles on grain, fodder, and other supplies. At the same time Solovetskii was not a typical case. This monastery's location in the extreme north of Russia insulated it from many, though not all, of the catastrophes of the period. In addition, it was strong enough to "pacify" local unrest on its own, even in the absence of any central authority (and it had been accustomed to doing so for decades). One might thus be tempted to dismiss Solovetskii's security amidst the national crisis as an extreme exception.

However, other documentary evidence suggests that the Solovki monks were not unique in continuing to reap profits during the Time of Troubles. Apparently the calamities of the period prompted a wave of increase in donations to monasteries. This trend fit in with longer-term patterns. According to S. V. Nikolaeva, who studied the records of the Troitsa Sergiev Monastery, the last decade of the sixteenth century saw a major shift in the proportion of gifts given by the different sectors of society. Whereas previously "feudal clans" (i.e., nobles) had always been responsible for the majority of vklady (donations) to the monastery, now their share dropped below thirty percent. The gap was taken up by an increased number of contributions from monks, monastic servants, and peasants. These statistics refer to the quantity of donations in absolute terms, not to total donated amounts. Wealthier families and individuals generally gave much larger donations than commoners. Still, the observed trend is quite significant.[70]

During the Time of Troubles the trend continued and became more accentuated. Large donations from tsars, princes, and other noblemen fell off, while smaller donations from commoners continued to rise dramatically. During his reign of 1584–1598, Tsar Fyodor Ivanovich gave a total of 2,961.33 rubles to the monastery, in three separate donations. In the same period the regent Boris Godunov donated 1,320 rubles in five installments. After becoming tsar, Boris gave three more times, for a total of 1,500 rubles over the course of 1598–1605. The wife of Fyodor and sister of Boris, Irina (Aleksandra), herself contributed 3,000 rubles to the Troitsa Sergiev in 1598 in order to commemorate her just-deceased husband. Yet by 1609 the monastery was no longer receiving any gifts of this magnitude. The books show a phenomenal 125 donations in that year. Of these, 117 took the form of money. However, only fourteen (12%) of them comprised fifty rubles or more, and none exceeded two hundred rubles. The vast majority of donations during this most painful moment of the Troubles, when the Troitsa Sergiev Monastery was itself under military siege, amounted to ten rubles or less. These came from monks, monasterial servants, and peasants. In fact, says Nikolaeva, "representatives of feudal clans" gave only four donations, or a mere three percent of the total number of vklady. Nonetheless, the exceptionally high number of gifts meant that the monastery still took in over 2,000 rubles in donations, one of its best years in all of the sixteenth and seventeenth centuries. The total figure for monetary vklady in the years 1584–1612 came to just under 30,000 rubles, or roughly the equivalent of $45–82 million for us today.[71]

Jennifer Spock found similar donation patterns in the case of the most prominent ecclesiastic institution in the north, the salt-trading Solovetskii Monastery. Donations from tsars declined—or rather plummeted precipitously at about the midpoint of the Troubles. The last immense donation came from Tsar Dmitrii on May 19, 1606, in the sum of 2,000 rubles. Assuming that the date was recorded correctly, this bestowal represented one of the last acts of the tsar, and he himself perished while his monies were still in transit to the far-off Solovki archipelago. After Dmitrii, Vasilii Shuiskii and the later Romanov tsars gave much less to the monastery. On the other hand, "gifts from humbly born lay men and women came in at the same rate and approximately the same size from 1582 to 1608. . . . [Near] the end of the Troubles, there was a jump in the real value of donated gifts, which doubled sometime between 1608 and 1614 and then generally remained at the higher level through 1645."[72]

Thus, the records of both the Troitsa Sergiev and the Solovetskii monasteries show a major drop-off in large donations from the very wealthy and a counterbalancing rise in smaller donations from peasants and other members of lower social strata. What explains these trends? The tsars reduced their donations largely because of the wars and other catastrophes of the Time of Troubles, which caused them financial difficulty. Indeed, they now needed to "borrow" from the monastery-banks. Tsar Vasilii appropriated 20,255 rubles from the Troitsa Sergiev Monastery; 5,150 rubles from the Solovetskii Monastery; 3,000 rubles from the Iosifo Volokolamsk Monastery; 3,000 rubles from the Kirillo Belozersk Monastery; 589.68 rubles from the Arkhangelskii Monastery; over 400 rubles from the (Vologda?) Pechenskii Monastery; and 88.52 rubles from the Spaso Prilutsk Monastery. Dmitrii II is said to have collected 7,000 rubles from an unnamed monastery.[73] No doubt there were other forced loans in this period, documentation for which has not survived.

Spock did not observe the same decline in gifts from nonroyal noble families as did Nikolaeva.[74] Yet both Spock and Nikolaeva noted that contributions from peasants, monks, and monastic servants soared. These groups were also affected by the Troubles. How is it that they not only continued to give but gave more and more? In Nikolaeva's opinion high mortality caused by war, famine, cold, and disease, "in conjunction with the absence of prospects for the majority of the population, who had been deprived of dwellings and property, to improve their own situation even after the end of war," prompted many commoners to invest more in the afterlife.[75] In other words, the ubiquitous death and desperation led to increased demonstrations of piety.

However, it should be kept in mind that even five or ten rubles represented a very large sum of money for the majority of the population. A peasant who could freely donate even one ruble was not so desperate as Nikolaeva implies, since that ruble could have bought him quite a lot of food. These donations do not appear to have come from the poorest peasants. The monks who accounted for nearly half of all donations to the Troitsa Sergiev in 1609 were not destitute either. The situation was more complex than a case of utter desperation stimulating religiosity. What seems more likely is that soul-searching and panic caused by the Troubles did lead to higher donations to monasteries, but not from the indigent. The *vkladnaia kniga* or "donations book" of the Iosifo Volokolamsk Monastery recorded the following in 1607:

> Gift of Bogdan Ivanovich Polev for [his] son
>
> On day 27 of June of the 7115th year, Feodor Bogdanovich Polev, killed near Tula in state service, was buried in the House of the Immaculate Mother of God in the Osifov Monastery. And his father, Bogdan Ivanovich Polev, gave as a donation for him to the House of the Immaculate Mother of God and to the wonder-worker Iosif, to Igumen Arsenii with the brotherhood, 50 rubles of money for an eternal remembrance. And for this donation of Fyodor Bogdanovich Polev they wrote in the daily [prayer] lists and in the supplicatory [*liteinye*] ones and in the pulpit [*naloinye*] ones and in the eternal remembrance books [*vechnye senaniki*], and they remember him according to the monasterial custom, as long as the House of the Immaculate [Mother of God] and the wonder-workers also stands. And from the daily lists and from the eternal remembrance books they must not wipe out [his name].[76]

The Polev family were by no means peasants. They were local, established, upper-middle class provincial servitors well connected to the Iosifov Monastery for generations. In this instance their gift was not an ordinary donation given in the natural course of events. It clearly resulted from an unnatural death caused by the ongoing warfare of the Time of Troubles. Half a year later, on January 5, 1608, Afonasei Feodorovich Zinoviev donated eight rubles for his "killed" brother Matfei Fyodorovich Zinoviev and five rubles for his "killed" nephew Vasilii Matfeevich Zinoviev. These gifts went toward their "eternal remembrance" at the Iosifo Volokolamsk Monastery.[77] The human consequences of the Troubles thus led to an increase in donations to monasteries, leaving clear traces in the primary sources.

The general danger of the period led to an increase in pious giving even in the absence of actual death. On November 22, 1605, the boyar Prince Ivan Ivanovich Golitsyn donated one hundred rubles so that the monks would pray "for the health" of him, his wife, and his daughter. Although it was not entirely uncommon to ask for prayers of this nature, the size of the vklad and the wording of its written record suggest the possibility that fear may have played some role. The second half of the entry stated that if fate transpired in such a way that God were to "send for their souls," then the monastery must write their names in the appropriate books and say prayers for them as if a commemorative donation had been given after their death.[78] Interestingly, it was probably right around this very time that the Golitsyn clan joined the conspiracy to overthrow Tsar Dmitrii—a potentially life-threatening occupation.[79] We may surmise that, by donating this considerable sum of money to the Iosifo Volokolamsk Monastery, the Golitsyn family hoped to remain alive despite its involvement in *smutnoe* (rebellious) activity and to have insurance toward salvation in case of death.

The Time of Troubles dried up the normally huge donations from tsars to monasteries. At the same time their subjects—from the elite down to the peasantry—were overtaken by concern for their own lives and souls and therefore gave a great deal more than they had previously. Given the Russian Orthodox worldview, this was a perfectly understandable reaction to the grave uncertainty of the Troubles. Economically speaking, it meant that monasteries could maintain their income levels from donations during the Troubles. Some institutions, such as the Troitsa Sergiev Monastery, actually took in more money from donations the worse the Troubles got! These observations parallel the trends noted above regarding the Solovki salt trade.

The unique nexus that existed in Russia between religion and money played into the hands of the monasteries in a time of extreme crisis. Financially speaking, many ecclesiastics suffered far less than the general population. This probably cultivated many seeds of resentment sown during the Famine. At the same time, however, the relative prosperity of the monasteries may also have benefited some local populations by helping to maintain their economies. The fragmentary sources that have survived seem to indicate a rather sudden collapse of the documented economy sometime around 1610 (when the state also collapsed). Yet the remarkable continuance and augmentation of enormous streams of ecclesiastic revenue through most of the Troubles runs counter to the habitual conceptions of the period and gives a dramatically different impression of the role of the Church in Russian society.

CHAPTER SIX

Death and Resurrection

The Apex and End of the Smuta

How alone sits the city! . . . The great one among the countries has
become like a widow . . . Crying in the night, her tears are on her cheek.
And there is none to comfort her.
—Lamentations 1:1–2 in the Ostroh Bible, 1581[1]

Who will not weep, who will not lament, who will not sigh? . . . How could a
land so great and utterly glorious among all the lands come into destruction?
—*A New Tale about the Most Glorious Russian Tsardom,* ca. 1610–1611[2]

Amidst the extreme turmoil of the Time of Troubles, many Russians
claimed to have seen remarkable signs or prophetic visions (*videniia*). A
common theme running through the visions was that God's wrath (*gnev*)
had come because of sin (*grekh*) and that Russians desperately needed
to repent with prayer and fasting. The written descriptions modeled
themselves after certain biblical visions, such as those of Isaiah, Jeremiah,
Ezekiel, and John. They did not follow the biblical models closely in terms
of content, but the language employed was clearly imitative (as was usual
for Muscovite texts of the period). Such religious vision tales came from
both men and women and from various regions of the country—Moscow,
Vladimir, Novgorod, Nizhnii Novgorod.[3]

Though frequently co-opted and used by the authorities for their own ends, the Smuta visions nonetheless manifested an increasing gap between official ideology and what may legitimately be termed "popular Orthodoxy"; i.e., forms of unofficial and unauthorized belief opposed to the official pronouncements of church and state.[4] The *Povest' o videnii nekoemu muzhu dukhovnu* (*Tale of a Vision [Shown] to a Certain Spiritual Man*), said to date from late 1606, furnishes a remarkable example of this phenomenon. The text consists primarily of a dialogue between "my Master and God" (i.e., Christ) and "our hope, the immaculate *Bogoroditsa*" (i.e., the Virgin Mary). The former, despite his merciful desires, had determined to punish the Russian people thoroughly for their many sins. Yet he had to contend with his mother, as well as "my friend Ivan the Christener" (i.e., John the Baptist) and "all my saints," who pleaded with him to pardon the Russians. The Christ of the vision urged them to stop arguing with him: "*For there is no truth even in the tsar or in the patriarch,* nor in all the priestly [i.e., ecclesiastic] order, nor in all my people, the new Israel, for they do not walk according to my tradition, and my commandments they do not keep [cf., e.g., Lev. 26:3; Dt. 8:6, 11:22, 13:4; Josh. 22:5; 1Kgs. 2:3; Mt. 15:3]."[5]

This statement could not have clashed more sharply with the official Muscovite perspective. Officially, the tsar, the patriarch, and the Church not only possessed but epitomized and conveyed sacred truth. Tsar Vasilii's legitimacy rested on his alleged overthrow of a liar and heretic—that is to say, on his claimed defense of Orthodox truth. Yet a provincial "spiritual man" now dared to call it all a sham. In his vision no less a figure than Christ himself pronounced the tsar and patriarch to be liars and quite possibly frauds and imposters as well![6] According to this view, the Russian government, Church, and people had forsaken the true path and therefore deserved ruin. Having deviated from their calling as "Israel," God's people, they would suffer the consequences like biblical Israel of old.

This coincidence of the New Israel ideology with a denunciation of Russia's top leaders, rather than an endorsement of them, sheds additional light on the "Orthodoxy of rebellion" described in chapter 5. The unofficial version of Orthodoxy reflected in this vision clearly incorporated the official view of Russia as God's chosen people. Just as biblical texts had chastised the original Israel for not keeping the commandments (*mitzvot*), so too the supposed "New Israel" now fell under the same charge. The posited results would also be the same in both cases: wars, exile, devastation.[7] The conjunction of this worldview together with an utter discounting of the politico-religious authorities suggests the formation of a Russian national identity independent of the government itself. Moreover, it shows a type of Russian Orthodoxy not dependent on the pronouncements of the Russian Orthodox Church.

In the heart of the Troubles, the Orthodox faith of many Russians became ever more detached from official Muscovite Orthodoxy. With so many reversals of "truth" emanating continually from Moscow, no one could believe the tsar, the patriarch, or the Church. The people did not give up on "Orthodoxy" (*pravoslavie*), but it was now their own brand(s) of Orthodoxy, quite distinct from official religion. "There is no truth in tsars or patriarchs" became a refrain of the Time of Troubles. It was at once a remarkably subversive and appealingly obvious explanation for the widespread calamity.[8] Popular religion thus arose out of and responded to the needs of the time. It is perhaps no coincidence that the first Russian translations of Aesop's *Fables* also appeared at this time (1607)—with their morality tales of individual wisdom, foolishness, humility, pride, deceit, and self-reliance. Though not explicitly political or religious, they seemed to offer a different, independent option for human conduct.[9]

The split between the Moscow and Tushino governments further reduced the potency of official Orthodoxies. Each side claimed to be "Orthodox"; each ruler claimed to replace a fraudulent, non-Orthodox predecessor. As if the situation were not confusing enough, no matter which tsar they chose, the people had to disregard earlier holy oaths they had sworn. In this context, no ipso facto definition of Orthodoxy presented itself at all. Especially in areas not completely under the control of either government, it was up to every community, family, or individual to decide what "truth" to believe. The notion of vox populi, introduced for reasons of political expediency, had by now become a self-fulfilling prophecy. Only the Russian people could arbitrate "God's voice"—that is to say, perceived Orthodoxy.

Over the course of a few years, the Moscow and Tushino camps virtually destroyed themselves in their wars with each other and with the several foreign armies who intervened in Russia's great crisis. Tsar Vasilii suffered numerous defeats; yet he somehow survived until 1610, when a near-total lack of support led to his forced abdication. The Tushinite government had collapsed a bit earlier. The so-called Dmitrii's inability to pay his troops had caused many of the latter to turn to raiding and brigandage, thus alienating local populations. Particularly in the north, victimized towns and villages rose up against Tushinite rule.[10] Amidst the chaos Polish-Lithuanian forces occupied Moscow, the putative capital of sacred history. For perhaps the first time during the long Troubles, that constant bogeyman—the Catholic takeover of Russia—loomed on the horizon. None of the official Orthodoxies had succeeded; all had failed.

In a manner of speaking, official Russian Orthodox Christianity had ceased to exist because the Russian Orthodox church-state had disintegrated.

At this point in history, the very fate of Russia lay in doubt. Contemporaries wrote of the "final destruction" (*konechnoe razoren'e*) of Russia and of Orthodoxy. The empire purporting to carry the mantle of history had, for all intents and purposes, passed away. One devoted Russian Orthodox historian wrote, "The fatherland and the Church perished."[11] Although somewhat exaggerated, since regional populations continued to conceive of a single Russia even during the Polish-Lithuanian occupation, this type of rhetoric expressed a significant degree of truth. What then enabled Orthodox Russia to rise from the ashes, literally to resurrect itself? As recounted often in historiography, Patriarch Hermogen played a key role by calling for national unity. Yet that must have seemed a chimera after the vicious civil wars and fratricidal strife of the previous decade. What could the patriarch possibly say that would change the situation?

Hermogen, like most Christians of his era, believed that the Jews had been rejected by God and forever dispersed from the land of Israel for their sins. The patriarch saw the same fate looming for Russia, the "New Israel." If God had done this to his people in the past, he might well do it again. Hermogen therefore warned in the starkest terms of this grave danger. Most importantly, he tried desperately to undo the separation that had set in between official and popular Orthodoxies. In his view Russia was God's New Israel both as a *polity* and as a *nation*. The continuation of any form of Orthodoxy therefore depended on the reestablishment of the Russian state centered at Moscow. Orthodoxy could not go it alone, could not survive as merely a popular religion. The patriarch's letters conveyed the idea that the Russian state, religion, and people had to go together. For Hermogen that coalescence defined Russian Orthodoxy. In certain respects his conception foreshadowed official Romanov ideology of the nineteenth century, formulated as "Autocracy, Orthodoxy, Nationality" (*samoderzhavie, pravoslavie, narodnost'*). Richard Wortman has in fact argued that the symbols and rhetoric of power in late nineteenth-century Russia represented a "resurrection of Muscovy."[12]

The patriarch's convictions ultimately prevailed enough to enable Russia to struggle out of the devastating Smutnoe vremia. Yet the history of the period's last years would again be filled with unfathomable suffering and destruction. Many of these events have been recounted over and over in historiography. What has often been overlooked is the extent to which they depended on innovations already introduced into Orthodox rhetoric and practice during the preceding portions of the Troubles. The changes pioneered from 1598 on would continue to exert their influence at every critical juncture during the final years of Russia's great crisis.

The Fragmentation of Russian Orthodoxy

In the fall of 1608, Polish-Lithuanian forces under the command of Hetman Jan-Piotr Sapieha besieged the Troitsa Sergiev Monastery, generally considered the most prestigious in Russia. Sapieha's men were accompanied by an army of several thousand (Orthodox) Russians and Cossacks from the Tushino camp of Dmitrii II. The rebel side hoped to capture this famous and wealthy ecclesiastic fortress and thereby break an important bastion of support for Tsar Vasilii. In what would become one of the most astonishing events of the Troubles, the Moscow-supporting monastery managed to hold out until the siege was lifted in January 1610. According to Miller, this not only bestowed Troitsa Sergiev with "a popular adulation that was unequaled" but contributed to the growth of a real sense of "Russia" and "Russianness."[13]

Yet much lay ahead before any sense of unity could be achieved. The times were violent and complex, pitting tsar against tsar, patriarch against patriarch, monastery against monastery. Each side claimed to represent Orthodox Christianity. Indeed, Orthodoxy itself was a critical battleground in the civil war, as rival armies fought desperately over every ecclesiastic institution and action. Shortly after the siege of Troitsa Sergiev began, the Tushinite Filaret Romanov wrote to Sapieha about the plight of the Kirzhachskii Blagoveshchenskii (also Vvedenskii Troitskii) Monastery. This institution depended heavily on the Troitsa Sergiev and on patronage from the princely Mstislavskii clan.[14] Terming himself "the Great Lord, Most Sanctified Filaret, Metropolitan of Rostov and Yaroslavl', designated [*narechennyi*] Patriarch of Moscow and of all Rus'," the rebel hierarch sent his blessing and summarized the case as follows:

> You wrote, lord, to us, that in our patriarchate, in the Pereslavl district, in the Monastery on the Kirzhach [River], there is a temple of the Annunciation of our Most Holy Sovereign Lady the Mother of God and Eternal Virgin Maria; and that temple, you say, has been destroyed by military people, and the throne is torn down and defiled, and the ecclesiastic vessels [i.e., implements] have been taken; and now, you say, in that temple it is impossible to serve the divine liturgies, and

Orthodox Christians have nowhere to run to; and many, you say, die of sickness without communion; and we should give for the sanctification of that temple a holy communion cloth [*antimis*] and bless the sanctifying of that temple.[15]

The language used here in describing the desecration of an Orthodox "temple" is reminiscent of the books of Kings, Maccabees, Josephus, and other texts of ancient Israel that continually underlay Muscovite politico-religious thought. Most interestingly, it seems the Lithuanian military commander Sapieha had taken the initiative to work with Filaret for the monastery's restoration. Even foreign interventionist forces understood the need to be seen as supporting Orthodoxy and to have as large a portion as possible of Russian Orthodoxy functioning under their aegis. After the Troubles, Patriarch Filaret would preside over a rewriting of history that emphasized the "evil plot" of the Polish-Lithuanians to extirpate Orthodoxy in Russia.[16] However, his own correspondence illustrates that the situation had been much more complicated: a camp of Russians allied with foreigners while rebelling against official Orthodoxy in Moscow; at the same time they worked together with those very foreigners in attempting to wrest control of Orthodoxy from the capital. In divided Russia the "ecclesiastic front" of the war prefigured what contemporaries would term the "final (or complete) destruction" of Orthodox Russia within the next few years.

Toward the end of 1609, faced with a "full-scale popular rebellion" in the north occasioned by his own brutal rule, Dmitrii II fled Tushino, and his camp soon disintegrated.[17] For a brief moment it seemed that Russia might return to a more "normal" state of affairs, with only one government in Moscow. Documents of the time reflected the changing situation. On March 6, 1610, Nizhnii Novgorod's Pecherskii Monastery agreed to terms with Moscow's Simonov Monastery, with which it had been carrying on a typical running feud over natural resources. Three years earlier, the Pecherskii's elders had been ordered to appear in court at the Monasterial Chancellery (*Monastyrskii prikaz*) in Moscow to respond to the Simonov's claims of unlawful seizure of its fishing grounds in the Volga River region. Instead they had managed to settle out of court. According to the statement of Archimandrite Ioil, the Pecherskii had agreed to pay the Simonov 269.5 rubles for use of the resources in question. However, at the time only 69.5 rubles passed hands, together with a promissory note for the remaining 200 rubles due on March 25, 1608. For the next two years, with the country split into warring camps, the Pecherskii Monastery simply ignored this debt and continued to exploit the fishing grounds without payment. Yet by late 1609 or early 1610 the tsar had regained at least a semblance of authority, and so the Simonov Monastery submitted a new complaint concerning this breach of contract. The court of the Monasterial Chancellery found the Pecherskii Monastery liable for the 200 rubles and ordered it to relinquish possession of the contested streams and lakes. Once more the Pecherskii decided to bargain, committing to pay a total of 300 rubles plus 30 rubles in government fees in order to continue using these fishing grounds.[18]

At this critical moment important developments were affecting the national economy and ultimately the state of the country as a whole. Some of Russia's isolated northern monasteries finally experienced the dire effects of the Troubles. On May 2, 1610, Tsar Vasilii's government authorized an exemption for tax debts owed by Velikii Ustiug's Arkhangelskii Monastery. According to the official document the monastery had made conscientious payments in the years 1606–1609, when many institutions had stopped sending funds to Moscow. Moreover, the Arkhangelskii had voluntarily contributed soldiers to fight bandit gangs, thus going beyond its obligations. During those difficult and war-filled years the monastery's outlay to the state and in the interests of the state had amounted to nearly three thousand rubles. Yet suddenly the Arkhangelskii found itself unable not only to meet obligations or contribute to the general security but even to sustain itself on the most basic level. The description of its condition, replete with the usual diminutive forms of expression, sounded truly pathetic:

> But now, they say, there has come to be a failed grain harvest, and in many [of their] little monasterial villages the grains die from frost; and they have no monasterial trading or salt mines or resources or fishing grounds whatsoever . . . and in the treasury there is no money . . . and our taxes and services have come to be great and frequent, and the monastery [has become] a poverty-stricken little place [*mestechko ubogoe*]; and because of that failed grain harvest many little peasants [*krest'ianishki*] wander off away from the little monasterial villages, and our God-prayery [*bogomol'e*], the monastery, grows empty; and [even] the elders, they say, wander off away from the monastery to roam the world, because of the failed grain harvest and because of our great taxes.[19]

The Arkhangelskii Monastery, located in the northern regions of European Russia, had apparently not suffered directly from the endemic military conflicts throughout the country. However, by 1610 it was experiencing indirect economic effects of the general situation. This monastery had faithfully supported Tsar Vasilii during the civil war, from a treasury accustomed to ciphering in the thousands of rubles (millions of dollars in today's terms). Yet a failed harvest and increased burdens imposed by the central government had combined to cause the monastery to fail completely. According to its own account, when the Arkhangelskii tried to pay its tax assessments for the previous fiscal year, it found only ninety rubles in the treasury. This prompted the petition for a special exemption—a kind of bankruptcy filing. The tsar's government granted this loyal monastery a one-year reprieve of all payments and also counted a forced loan of 500 rubles in 1607–1608 against its current outstanding debts.[20]

The case of Velikii Ustiug's Arkhangelskii Monastery highlights the enormous importance of forest and water resources vis-à-vis agriculture at this time. Atypically for a northern monastery, the Arkhangelskii found itself in the undesirable and ultimately ruinous position of having no commerce except in grain. Allegedly it possessed no salt works, even though some of its lands were located in an area rich in salt production, near Solikamsk. Nor did it conduct any trade in furs, honey, fish, or other profitable natural resources.[21] This dependence on agriculture alone led to its sudden decline. One can readily appreciate from this case, as well as that of the Pecherskii Monastery, that forest and water resources occupied a position of vital importance in the ecclesiastic economy. It is obvious why monasteries continually fought to gain and to retain such resources. Even with the country in chaos, monasteries rich in natural resources could continue to survive and even prosper. Unfortunate institutions that lacked such resources were much more vulnerable. This dichotomy almost certainly prolonged the Smuta, since an influential and wealthy segment of the elite often had little or no incentive to take action to end the extreme disruptions. In the last years of the Troubles, that would finally change.

Meanwhile, Tsar Vasilii's unpopularity and perceived illegitimacy eventually caught up with him. His ineffective government could barely raise any troops for the army; he had to cede territory in the northwest to Sweden in exchange for mercenary troops. In 1609 he faced down at least one serious coup. Most significantly, the collapse of the Tushino camp failed to bring relief from the brutal warfare raging throughout Russia. The tsar ordered Tushino burnt to the ground, but the wars only intensified. King Zygmunt (Sigismund) III of Poland-Lithuania personally invaded and besieged Smolensk, seeking the "return" of borderlands taken by Russia in 1494–1514. Hetman Zolkiewski led another Polish-Lithuanian force directly toward Moscow, which Zygmunt hoped to exploit in order to gain the Russian throne for himself. The Crimean Tatars also launched a destructive raid. Moreover, by mid-1610 Dmitrii II and his ostensible wife Marina had managed to reconstitute a formidable army in Kaluga, southwest of Moscow. The tsar now faced the threat of a new siege of the capital without his nephew, the hero-commander Mikhail Skopin-Shuiskii, whom he may have had murdered earlier in the year on suspicion of treason. Only Sweden appeared to offer any meaningful support to Tsar Vasilii—and that not out of altruism.[22]

In July 1610 in a now-familiar pattern, leading Muscovite boyars gathered a rowdy mob in Red Square, staged a popular revolt, and deposed Vasilii Shuiskii. This time around they refrained from killing the tsar. Instead, they forced him to become a monk and locked him up securely in a monasterial prison cell. On July 20, the boyars announced his supposedly voluntary abdication "at the request of all the people" (*po chelobit'iu vsekh liudei gosudar'stvo otstavil*). Their written proclamation was filled with religious rhetoric, portraying the coup as necessary for the preservation of Orthodox Christianity. This was of course exactly what Vasilii had claimed back in 1606, as had Dmitrii I a year earlier. The rest of the document also based itself explicitly on the new Muscovite political norms in force since 1598, especially vox populi.[23]

The boyars cited popular sentiment as the deciding factor in ending Vasilii's rule. They claimed that all the people of the "whole land" had petitioned the tsar to abdicate his throne. The reason given for such an extraordinary action was that otherwise "final destruction" would overtake Orthodox Russia. Vasilii's reign had seen incessant fratricidal bloodletting, with the consequence that the people of the realm "do not love Sovereign, Tsar, and Grand Prince Vasilii Ivanovich of all Russia over the Muscovite state, and do not address him as the sovereign, and do not want to serve him."[24] By 1610 such a statement may have sounded "normal," but it was truly astounding within the broader context of Muscovite politico-religious ideology. To claim that the people could depose a divinely appointed and anointed tsar simply because they did not like him and no longer wished to fulfill their sworn oaths of loyalty completely contradicted the whole orientation of pre-Smuta (and post-Smuta) Muscovite politics.[25] This claim also represented a further development in the exploitation of vox populi as a legitimation device during the Troubles. If the people could supposedly bring tsars to power, now they could also allegedly remove unpopular or ineffectual ones at will.

The document announcing Vasilii's deposition had one glaring omission. Neither Patriarch Hermogen nor the other top ecclesiastics were mentioned by name, as was customary in such texts. The patriarch's role at this key moment remains somewhat unclear. He had been a fiery supporter of Vasilii and staunchly opposed to rebellion, but Platonov argued that Hermogen did withdraw his support at the end. Yet the inability of the boyar conspirators even to allege Church sanction for their actions may be seen as a further sign of the fragmentation of Orthodoxy, which traditionally set great stock in unity and uniformity of doctrine and practice. Once again, Russia had at least two opposing official Orthodox positions—that of the patriarch and that expressed by the boyars. With havoc reigning outside the capital, provincial Russians no doubt developed any number of unofficial views that they also considered "Orthodox."[26]

With both Dmitrii II and Zolkiewski ready to take Moscow, the *Semiboiarshchina* or "Rule of Seven Boyars" had to decide what to do. Their move was curious but perhaps one in which they had little choice. Ostensibly for the defense of Russian Orthodoxy, the boyars opened negotiations for Prince Wladyslaw, son of King Zygmunt, to take the throne. The acute military situation and the boyars' mutual distrust of each other dictated taking such a step—quite unusual in the Muscovite context. The irony of inviting a Polish Catholic crown prince to rule in Moscow in order to protect Russian Orthodoxy from Polish Catholic aggression could not have been missed by many! One contemporary firebrand condemned this proposal as a plot of "internal enemies" (*domashnii vrazi*) to destroy the faith.[27] Such language illustrates how fragmented Russian Orthodoxy had in fact become, with different factions holding different interpretations and condemning each other in the harshest terms.

The idea of inviting Wladyslaw to become tsar had been floated ever since 1606. A couple of years later Patriarch-designate Filaret (in Tushino) made the first concerted attempt to realize this idea. The Tushinites bargained back and forth with Zygmunt's government and actually signed a treaty regarding Wladyslaw's accession—but only in February 1610, after Dmitrii himself had fled the camp. The Polish-Lithuanian king had thus succeeded in concluding a monumental agreement with a defunct government that promptly vanished. Now he disingenuously instructed Hetman Zolkiewski to negotiate with the Muscovite boyars for a similar treaty. The talks were merely a ruse: Zygmunt actually intended to conquer Russia outright and to incorporate it into his own realm. However, the Muscovite elite thought they could secure an arrangement by which Wladyslaw would convert to Orthodoxy before ascending the throne. They therefore announced his "election" in August 1610.[28]

However strange it may seem in retrospect, the unique Smuta legitimation scheme dominated in this matter as well. According to the official record, all the different types or strata of people in the realm had unanimously resolved to serve "Prince Vladislav and his children, whom God will give him, the Sovereign, in the future." In other words the proposed founding of a new dynasty rested explicitly on vox populi. The Russian ideologues gave repeated assurances that this new foreign ruler would preserve Orthodoxy in Russia, heretofore under dire threat. The "holy Orthodox Christian [faith] of the Greek law" would allegedly recover its former glory and unity, and all attempts to convert Orthodox Christians to other religions would cease. Patriarch Hermogen and the Sanctified Council of the Church were to preside over the coronation of the new tsar, "according to former custom and propriety [*po prezhnemu obychaiu i dostoian'iu*], as previous Muscovite great sovereigns were crowned." The Muscovite populace actually swore a conditional oath of loyalty to Wladyslaw on the basis of these justifications.[29]

Yet all this was highly optimistic and premature; final agreement with Poland-Lithuania could not be reached in any event. Aside from King Zygmunt's own intentions there were also several other obstacles. The Russians and Poles disagreed on issues regarding the primacy of Russian Orthodoxy, the building of a Catholic chapel in Moscow, the banning of dogs from entering "Orthodox temples" and Jews from the borders of the Russian state, as well as ecclesiastic property and economic interests. Patriarch Hermogen unwaveringly insisted that Wladyslaw must convert to Orthodoxy prior to actually ascending the throne, and this proved to be a key sticking point even in the sham negotiations. In his memoirs Zolkiewski wrote, "In the scroll [i.e., the Muscovite proposal] there was mention of the re-christening of the Crown Prince in the Muscovite faith and not a few other absurdities. However the Hetman did not wish to offend them by a refusal, but sent them to His Majesty."[30] Indeed, Filaret Romanov was dispatched with other dignitaries and notables on a grand embassy to negotiate directly with King Zygmunt, who promptly arrested the lot of them and kept them in captivity until 1619.

Regardless, documents to and from "Tsar and Grand Prince Vladislav Zhigimontovich of all Russia" circulated through the country toward the end of the year 1610. A theoretical accession had taken place in the capital, now occupied by Polish-Lithuanian forces. There had been as of yet no practical accession of a new tsar. Still, it may be that the boyar rulers did not fail to think prospectively about vox feminae as a necessary prop for Wladyslaw's future reign. One of the few surviving letters written in the name of the new tsar was addressed to Tsaritsa Marfa, the mother of Dmitrii, providing for her welfare and position. Meanwhile, the regular government bureaucracy also functioned as if under the supervision and with the approval of Wladyslaw. Ecclesiastic institutions cooperated with this new regime. For instance, the Tikhvin Uspenskii Monastery addressed its request for exemption from levies to the supposed new sovereign.[31] Yet Wladyslaw never came to rule, and utter confusion had by now displaced habitual certainty about the nature and status of Russian Orthodoxy.

"Final Destruction" and the Beginnings of Rebirth

"The first step in solving any problem is to recognize that it exists." This time-worn adage has some relevance to the last years of Russia's Time of Troubles. Contemporaries viewed these years as a period of utter collapse. Yet that very characterization of the situation helped to spur a painful but effective renaissance. Ecclesiastics, townspeople, and others finally decided that they had had enough of the incessant divisions and internecine warfare. Spontaneous and then organized resistance to the Polish-Lithuanian occupation arose in various regions of the country, completely undermining the collaborationist boyar government in Moscow.

Initially, such action assumed several different forms. First, many northern monasteries that had seen their business profits dwindle and then perhaps vanish during the second half of the Troubles now found themselves under threat of despoiling or even complete destruction from the rampaging armies. Numerous Russian cloisters did in fact suffer these fates at this time; large numbers of smaller and medium-size monasteries were wiped out. Even the great Solovetskii Monastery faced the daunting prospect of a Swedish attack in 1611. Novgorod, the great city of the northwest, had fallen under Swedish control, but Solovki held out against foreign rule. Only a perceived miracle saved the monastery from disaster: according to Roy Robson, "the monks believed the Swedes were rebuffed by Sts. Zosima and Savvatii." Perhaps as a result, monasterial elders often took the lead in organizing resistance to the occupation among northern towns. In this they appear to have been guided by the basic motivations of a need for physical security and the desire to restore stability for economic purposes, as well as zeal for Russian Orthodox Christianity.[32]

Second, tales of anger and woe apparently began to circulate throughout the country, bewailing the "final destruction" (*konechnoe razoren'e*) of Orthodoxy and of Russia. The *New Tale* warned that the Polish-Lithuanian occupiers aimed to dispossess, murder, and subjugate all rightful inhabitants of Russia. The text did not spare harsh language, raging against "co-religionist traitors," "apostates," "blood-shedders and destroyers of the Christian faith," "Satan's firstborn," "brothers of Judas the betrayer of Christ," "soul-slaying wolves," and the like. "More bitter than all," it claimed, the foreign occupiers intended "to eradicate our holy, unblemished faith to the end, and to introduce their fallen-away one, and to live themselves in our rightful possession."[33] Such apocalyptic tales softened the ground for the seeds of a unified Orthodox Russian resistance to the Polish-Lithuanian occupation.

Third, in perhaps the most famous ecclesiastic action of the entire long Troubles, Patriarch Hermogen himself sent out rousing missives in 1611 and early 1612, explicitly calling for the Russian people to unify and rise up in urgent defense of Orthodoxy. The patriarch had become an outspoken opponent of the regime of "Tsar Vladislav" and consequently found himself confined to a monasterial cell. Rejecting the official line of the collaborators, he argued that true Orthodoxy consisted of driving the "heretics" out of the country. For this "treasonous" activity, the Moscow government essentially starved him to death in prison in February 1612. But the letters—smuggled out, copied, distributed, and presumably read aloud to assemblies—would have a powerful effect.[34]

Fourth, other Church leaders, especially the elders of the prominent Troitsa Sergiev Monastery, also issued appeals to the populace to "remember the true Orthodox Christian faith," organize themselves militarily, and destroy the "cursed Latinism" hanging over the country. In the eyes of many Russians this monastery's endurance of a harsh sixteen-month siege at the hands of Polish-Lithuanian and rebel forces, combined with reports of its considerable humanitarian activity, granted its leaders (including the cellarer and author Avramii Palitsyn) a moral authority to speak out. However, a fundamental contradiction distinguished the Troitsa brothers' appeals from Hermogen's missives. The patriarch considered the Cossack armies around Moscow to be the chief enemy to national unity. He denounced their savage banditry and never-ending *samozvanshchina* (pretenderism) in the harshest terms. Fearing that the ruthlessly ambitious Marina would succeed in making her infant son Ivan into a real candidate for the throne, Hermogen called for fighting against the Cossacks as well as the Poles. The Troitsa Sergiev Monastery, on the other hand, had collaborated with some Cossack quasi-governments, regarding them as more legitimate than the "traitors" in Moscow. The Troitsa monks therefore called for uniting with anti-Polish Cossack forces in order to drive out the foreign armies. Platonov termed this a clash between "old" and "new" views of the Cossacks. Yet despite their contradictions, both proposals for action aimed at the reconstitution of an Orthodox Russian state free of foreign domination.[35]

With the Orthodox patriarch and other prominent ecclesiastics calling for open rebellion, it is understandable that broad masses of the population decisively rejected the official Orthodoxy emanating from Wladyslaw's ostensible government in Moscow. Multiple strata of the Russian population heeded the circulated letters and accepted their arguments about what represented true Orthodox action. Most notably in Nizhnii Novgorod, but also elsewhere, the gathering of troops and supplies was accompanied by fasting, prayer, and other expressions of Orthodox Christian piety.[36] As Dunning notes, the assassination of Dmitrii II in December 1610 had "removed the chief obstacle to unifying the Russian people against foreign intervention."[37] Yet the moment had to be seized quickly, before he popped up again (a "Dmitrii III" did in fact appear along with other pretenders at the end of the Troubles). In consequence, Orthodoxy as defined by Patriarch Hermogen became the main rallying cry for a national reunification—in essence, the resurrection of Russia itself.

Just what did Patriarch Hermogen write that had the power to unite Orthodox Russians in the midst of an extremely chaotic and violent situation, after years of civil war and foreign intervention? His letters themselves represented yet another variation on the special legitimation themes of the Time of Troubles. In effect, the patriarch addressed the conflict between different versions of purported "Orthodoxy," appealing to the people to discern the true form despite the declarations of Moscow's government. One of his texts, dated to 1611, began with phrases familiar from earlier official documents. He wrote that all tsars rule only by the will of God. He went on to address his letter to every category of person in the realm, starting with churchmen and ending with tillers of the soil (*pashennye liudi*). All these, according to Hermogen, claimed to be Orthodox and yet had betrayed the faith of their birth. In a word, the population had abandoned the one "crowned by God, and anointed with the holy oil, and selected by the whole world and by you yourselves [*oto vsego mira i ot vas samekh izbrannago*]; [that is,] Tsar and Grand Prince Vasilii Ivanovich of all Russia."[38]

Hermogen's letters warned that by betraying Vasilii the people had betrayed God and Orthodox Christianity. Divine wrath would certainly fall—even more than it had already—unless nationwide repentance took place. The patriarch made reference to the destruction of Jerusalem by the Romans in 70 CE as God's judgment on the "deicidal and rebellious Jewish tribe," noting that the punishment had not been lifted "even until this very day." The enemy of the first Israel had come and destroyed the Holy of Holies in the Temple, burned the city, killed and enslaved its residents. He asked: "Do you envy this? Do you want this? Do you thirst for this?" These apocalyptic warnings made the commonplace rejection of Tsar Vasilii's legitimacy into a crime of epic proportions, one leading inexorably to the complete destruction of Orthodox Russia, God's "New Israel." The patriarch continued with more frightening biblical quotations regarding the last days, such as "Nation will rise against nation, and kingdom against kingdom."[39]

In response to claims that Vasilii had been elected or selected "only by Moscow," Hermogen insisted that all cities and all ranks of the Russian state had participated in 1606. Hence his accession had been legitimate; those not acceding to the results were "rising up against God" and wreaking destruction on all Orthodox Christendom.[40] In Hermogen's interpretation of vox populi, the people could make but could not break a God-given tsar. He thus accepted one supposedly democratic coup "in defense of Orthodoxy" (Vasilii's) but rejected another (nominally Wladyslaw's). In so doing, he amplified an irony inherent in the unique political discourse of the Time of Troubles. Even as tsars, rebels, patriarchs, and invaders alike appealed rhetorically to the voice of the people as the voice of God, they nonetheless sought to restrict and suppress actual popular sentiment. Patriarch Hermogen defended a version of Orthodoxy that depended directly on vox populi, but simultaneously he censured the current "popular voice" most severely.

The patriarch's letters came at a time when the notion of Russia's "final destruction" rang true. Through all the previous horrors of the Troubles, the survival of the country did not seem to be in doubt—only who would rule it and what percentage of the population would remain alive. Yet now the central authority had disintegrated, along with much provisional and local administration; the hated Polish-Lithuanians held Moscow; Russians themselves had splintered into warring factions; and multiple armies roamed

5. Monument to Minin and Pozharskii, heroes of the Time of Troubles, before St. Basil's Cathedral, Red Square, Moscow. Reproduced by kind permission of Elizaveta Skriabina.

about, pillaging wantonly. If ever national-apocalyptic rhetoric appeared to have some relevance, it was now.

During 1611 Prince Dmitrii Pozharskii, the merchant Kuzma Minin, the Cossack leader Ivan Zarutskii, and the *dvorianin* (nobleman) Prokofii Liapunov raised forces to fight against the Polish-Lithuanian interventionists. According to Dunning, this brought them "almost overnight . . . enormous prestige and popularity." A kind of national militia movement developed as rebellion against the collaborationist boyar government in Moscow swept across Russia's provinces. The Orthodox Church continued to play an important role in this religious-patriotic uprising. In Dunning's words, "concerned citizens often crowded into their local church's refectory to discuss strategy, and it is clear that townspeople and peasants regarded their own unprecedented activism as part of a life-or-death religious struggle."[41] When the rebels threatened Moscow itself, the Polish-Lithuanian garrison responded by burning much of the capital and plundering the rest. Many refugees fled to the Troitsa Sergiev Monastery.[42]

Meanwhile, the Swedish invasion continued, as both King Karl IX and his son and successor, Gustav II Adolf, craved complete control of the Baltic Sea. Russia's extreme disorder did not discourage them from attempting to grab as much territory as possible. Liapunov even invited greater Swedish intervention, thinking it would help drive out the Polish-Lithuanian occupiers. For their part the Swedes recognized the central importance of Russian Orthodoxy in Russia. They promised to leave the Church intact—including the vast monasterial holdings. Many Novgorodians appeared ready to accept the rule of Gustav Adolf, though Metropolitan Isidor and some other churchmen may have tried to keep the fires of Russian Orthodox resistance alive.[43]

As during the previous years of war, administrative tasks often had to be met in these years by ad hoc governments constituted from within military encampments. Most of the economy probably functioned by means of inertia and informal arrangements, given the lack of stable official channels. Extant documentation from these years is extremely sparse—so much so that the unearthing of just one brief landholding record from 1611 or 1612 prompted the leading researcher Anton Antonov to remark that the document in question provides "a good factual basis for comparison and evaluation of the activity of the bureaucratic apparatus, [and] its links with local executive powers."[44] The records that do exist correspond to what might be expected in the context of widespread devastation. Several monasteries continued their attempts to regain lands and resources that had been forcefully seized by other parties. Other ecclesiastic institutions applied for tax exemptions based on the damages they had suffered as a result of war, famine, disease, peasant flight, and other blights of the period.

On December 26, 1611, for example, Ivan Zarutskii and the former Tushinite commander Dmitrii Trubetskoi jointly authorized the return of certain lands to the Vladimir region's ancient Rozhdestvennyi Monastery of the Most Holy Mother of God. Prince Ivan Mikhailovich Boriatinskii had allegedly submitted a false petition (*lozhnoe chelobit'e*) effecting the expulsion of all the monastery's personnel from its own lands. When the monastery was able to show its official documents establishing proprietorship, the militia government reversed this action, ordering local officials "to expel Prince Ivan Boriatinskii and his people away from that *votchina,* and to forbid the peasants to obey them in anything." Unlike documents from Vasilii's reign, this judgment did not denigrate either Tsar Boris or Tsar Dmitrii but recognized them fully. With regard to Dmitrii in particular, this may be seen as a sign of Cossack influence on the general political orientation. It was written "in the (army) ranks," which at this time would have been somewhere outside occupied Moscow.[45]

By early 1612 the Cossacks' support of various new pretenders—including the "third false Dmitrii" and the "little brigand" Ivan—had created serious divisions within the various groups seeking to "liberate" Moscow. A competing provisional government coalesced in Nizhnii Novgorod and then moved to Iaroslavl, a city that "linked the Upper Volga region to the far north" and had managed to maintain some degree of economic prosperity, even to this point of the Troubles.[46] The war council also functioned or at least portrayed itself as a kind of "assembly of the land" exerting a measure of authority throughout the country. In mid-May 1612 a document from "the boyars and *voevodas* and Dmitrei Pozharskoi with [his] comrades" instructed civil servants in Galich not to collect taxes or levies of any kind from the Simonov Monastery's salt works and lands in the Soligalich region, "because the Simanov [*sic*] Monastery in Moscow is now in final [i.e., complete] destruction."[47] Muscovite rankings generally listed the Simonov as the sixth most important monastery in Russia, so this was a startling sign of the times.[48]

In September 1612 Trubetskoi and Pozharskii managed to put aside their differences and unite their competing "national militias." This made the fall of the Polish-Lithuanian garrison in Moscow imminent. However, around the country many bureaucratic affairs still had to be conducted on an ad hoc basis. A curious document of September 10, 1612, calls attention to this point. In it a couple of officials in Kazan, the secretaries Nikonor Mikhailovich Shulgin and Stepan Iakovlich Dichkov,[49] claimed to speak on behalf of "the Great Russian Muscovite state and the boyars of all the land." Their proclamation presented itself as a judgment having the power to bring about the return of lands allegedly seized from Viatka's Uspenskii Monastery. This monastery was one of the newer northern monasteries, having been founded in 1580 by

Trifon, who "zealously" propagated Orthodox Christianity among the Ostiak and Vogul tribes of the Viatka region until his death in 1612 or 1613. Prior to his establishment of the Uspenskii Monastery in 1580, reportedly "there were no monasteries at all in the whole Viatka region." Some years earlier the same Trifon had founded the Uspenskii Chusovskoi Monastery approximately eighty kilometers (fifty miles) northeast of Perm, on a mountain considered by the local pagans to be the residence of an evil spirit. Reportedly none of them dared to ascend the mountain when he arrived.[50] The career of this monk thus typifies some important ecclesiastic trends of the late sixteenth and early seventeenth centuries, though his motives appear to have been missionary rather than economic.

The current issues of Viatka's Uspenskii Monastery pertained to the intrusion of certain peasants, who allegedly "hayed their monasterial hay-fields by force, to [the amount of] four hundred fifty haystacks (*kopni*) of hay; and that very Vaska Posokhin with [his] comrades, they say, plowed their monasterial plow-lands by force."[51] One *kopna* or "haystack" generally corresponded to five poods of weight (that is, 82 kilograms or 180 pounds). The amount of hay allegedly stolen by Posokhin and his friends would therefore correspond to nearly 37,000 kilograms or 81,000 pounds. In ordinary times this amount of hay would be worth around 25 rubles, but during the latter years of the Time of Troubles, its retail value, at least in Moscow, could be 500 rubles or more.[52] In addition, "those peasants occupied their monasterial land with their own households and fencings" and "caused great oppression to Archimandrite Iona with the brotherhood." According to the complaint, the peasants would even "burn up and make empty the households" belonging to the monastery. After a complete exposition of the matter, Shulgin and Dichkov issued instructions in the name of the "Great Russian Muscovite state" for the expulsion of the trespassers and squatters, who were commanded to live "on the other side of the river Oshtorma, from the Diudium ravine and up to the Kushak stream." To make this unusual document seem official, the secretaries affixed "the seal of the Kazan tsardom" (*pechat['] ts[a]rstva Kazanskogo*) in black wax.[53]

Ever since the conquests of the 1550s, the official title of the Muscovite monarch had featured "Tsar of Kazan" and "Tsar of Astrakhan" as two of its most prestigious components. They were listed just after "Tsar and Grand Prince, Autocrat of all Russia, of Vladimir, of Moscow, of Novgorod." At least within the boundaries of the former khanate, the exceptional seal utilized by Shulgin and Dichkov likely carried some weight. Although the khanate had not actually included Viatka, the latter had been attached to the new ecclesiastic archdiocese of Kazan when that was established in 1555. Hence these regional officials had some basis for trying to arrange monasterial cases in the territory of Viatka, even though they did go beyond their ordinary authority by doing so. Lacking instruction from Moscow, the secretaries simply took whatever (irregular) steps they deemed best in the midst of a chaotic situation, while claiming to act on behalf of the nation. Documentary evidence from 1613 also suggests that the Kazan secretaries exercised greater leeway at the end of the Troubles to try to maintain order in the absence of regular arrangements.[54]

The collapse of the central government in Moscow thus occasioned unorthodox attempts to maintain the standard economic arrangements with monasteries. Despite the impromptu nature of some bureaucratic actions, a systemic continuity persisted all throughout the Troubles. All the governments and quasi-governments of the period sought the cooperation of monasteries in exchange for endorsing their economic privileges. The secretaries in Kazan overreached their authority in issuing official documents "on behalf of the Russian state" when none really existed as such. Yet had there been a tsar and a central government at this time, the content of the judgment would have been identical. The secretaries probably based their decision on this supposition.[55]

The Troubles thus did not prompt a reconsideration of the system itself. Monasteries of course recognized the advantages of their privileged relationship with political power. With the national militia attempting to reestablish a central government, a number of ecclesiastic institutions contributed to the cause. On December 21, 1612, Prince (and *voevoda*) Roman Petrovich Pozharskoi certified that Suzdal's Pokrovskii Convent had paid 25.005 rubles, 50.25 *cheti* of rye, 1.25 *cheti* of buckwheat, and 1.25 *cheti* of oats "into the treasury of the land" (*v zemskuiu kaznu*).[56] Not all such donations were necessarily voluntary. However, monasteries had a clear interest in preserving or reconstituting the system that gave them exclusive and highly profitable "franchises" on land and resources.

In George Vernadsky's view the national liberation movement "blended religious and national feelings under the pall of religion . . . [and] appealed not only to most Muscovites in various social groups, but to the Cossacks as well."[57] In October 1612 armies of Russians and Cossacks jointly "liberated" Moscow in the name of "all the land." Trubetskoi and Pozharskii sent missives throughout Russia, calling for representatives to come "select" a new tsar, "whom the Lord God will give us [*kogo nam dast Gospod' Bog*]." In contrast to previous supposed assemblies of the land (zemskie sobory) of the Time of

Troubles, this one appears to have had a real electoral intention behind it. When representatives did not arrive from some regions, the militia commanders wrote again, explaining the critical importance of selecting a new ruler quickly, since King Zygmunt still intended to destroy Orthodoxy in Russia, and "to slay all of us from the least to the greatest and not give clemency even to nursing babes." Trubetskoi and Pozharskii proclaimed that the entire patriotic movement had sworn "to stand against him and his son and against the Polish and Lithuanian people to the last man, and to consider them our enemies forever."[58] The new tsar was to lead Russia in this stand.

As seen from these letters, the popular-democratic justifications for rule introduced in 1598 by now dominated the general mindset. Introduced for reasons of political expediency, the notion of vox populi as a legitimizing force had been repeated often enough that it had entered into the popular mindset. At the end of 1612, it seemed obvious that a representative assembly would be the proper way to choose a tsar. Divisions among the variegated patriotic forces threatened to ruin this critical attempt at reestablishing a central government, but all they needed was a candidate acceptable enough to bring an end to incessant civil warfare. The nation desperately needed some relief from the perpetual tribulations of the previous decade. Under strong Cossack influence a compromise led to the "unanimous" selection of Mikhail Romanov, the sixteen-year-old son of Filaret, erstwhile patriarch-designate of Moscow and Tushino.[59]

The Last Reprise of a New Ideology

The accession of Mikhail Romanov in 1613 occasioned a final expression of the novel legitimation paradigm that had taken hold during the Smuta. For one last time Muscovite ideologues again synthesized multiple justifications in order to support the rule of a tsar who had come to power in an untraditional fashion. Their primary technique was to imitate the 1598 documents—or simply to copy them verbatim. Tsar Boris's accession thus acted as a kind of "base text," while intermediary developments of the period served as explanatory "glosses" guiding interpretation. The House of Romanov ascended the throne thoroughly ensconced in the "new orthodoxy" of political discourse; that is to say, in a brand of Russian Orthodoxy completely unique to the Time of Troubles.

The churchmen who formulated Tsar Mikhail's legitimacy made no effort to conceal their reliance on the 1598 prototype. Officially, he came to the throne by the now commonplace "selection of all the land" and "voice of the people" (vox populi). Predictably, the Church led the people in expressing the assumed will of God (vox Dei). Moreover, Tsaritsa Ksenia (Marfa) played the same role for her son Mikhail as had Tsaritsa Irina (Aleksandra) for her brother Boris fifteen years earlier (vox feminae). The additional justifications that had become customary also made their appearance in the documents: family ties to the previous dynasty, seen as bestowing a modicum of hereditary legitimacy; an urgent mission to defend Orthodoxy from grave peril; and so forth.

Although purporting simply to relate what had happened, the 1613 accession record clearly resulted from conscious crafting on the part of the ideologues. Its first section set the stage with ornate Orthodox rhetoric and a typical Muscovite *Reichsgeschichte* beginning from Caesar Augustus and "the first Grand Prince Riurik." After brief accounts of early Russian rulers, the narrative progressed to a much more extensive exposition of the Time of Troubles. For each tsar from Boris to Wladyslaw, the authors furnished a carefully constructed and highly polemical interpretation. The Dmitrii saga in particular appeared in such a light as to bolster Mikhail's legitimacy as much as possible. Dmitrii I was denigrated as "Grishka Otrepiev," a heretic and "son of the devil" who had conspired with that other "demonic" character, Patriarch Ignatii, to destroy "our true undefiled Orthodox Christian faith of the Greek law." Dmitrii's marriage, anointing, and crowning of a Polish Catholic left a particularly bad taste in the mouth of the ideologues—though many of them had no doubt worked for him at the time. Among his many alleged crimes Dmitrii was said to have "defiled" holy churches by allowing pagans (e.g., Siberian Kolvintsy), Catholics, and Lutherans to enter. "And not only these," the document continued in a shocked tone, "but he also brought in deicidal Yids." The rest of the Troubles, according to this interpretation, constituted a life-and-death struggle to defend Russian Orthodoxy against the violent invasions of Polish Catholicism. At key moments Metropolitan Filaret (aka Fyodor Nikitich Romanov, the father of Mikhail) appeared like a shining light to reveal the truth and guide the people toward the true path.[60]

As with all previous Russian rulers of the Time of Troubles, young Tsar Mikhail's government attempted to make his own rule appear indistinguishable from the preservation of Orthodoxy itself. If accepted in the popular mindset, this point would make his accession not only legitimate but also unassailable. The 1613 documents therefore stressed repeatedly what mortal danger had faced the "true faith" over the past several years. With strongly emotional language the ideologues described Patriarch Hermogen's action to rouse the nation. In an allusion to Russia's claimed status as the New Israel, they posited that the "final destruction" facing Russia had been worse even than King Herod's slaughter of the babies of Bethlehem in the first century CE.[61]

Only after this lengthy historical introduction did the ideologues mention Mikhail Fyodorovich Romanov-Iuriev. They first described him as the nephew (*plemiannik*) of Fyodor I, the last tsar of the previous dynasty. Continual references to his relationship to the family of Ivan IV reinforced this minimal hereditary legitimacy.[62] Like previous rulers of the period, Mikhail wanted to portray himself as ruling not only by dint of some single factor but rather by virtue of all possible reasons. Yet these were merely supplementary considerations helping to frame the main argument. As in 1598 the central focus of legitimation rhetoric would be vox populi.

Imitating the formulas introduced by Patriarch Iyov fifteen years earlier, the ideologues asserted that representatives of all categories of the Russian populace had gathered to choose a new tsar. Coming from all the cities of the empire, their expressed goal was simply to preserve "the true Orthodox Christian faith of the Greek law from the Latins and from Lutheran and [other] faiths abominable to God." Led by ecclesiastic hierarchs, the assembly "unanimously" chose Mikhail for this task, just as in 1598. Exactly as before, it became necessary to shed many tears, utter countless prayers, and plead "for many days" for him to accept the throne.[63]

The explication of this process elevated the alleged events of 1598 to the status of a new ritual of legitimation. In that year Patriarch Iyov claimed to have led a delegation to the Novodevichii Monastery to "plead" for Boris to rule. Boris and his sister Irina ostensibly refused until several days of cries and petitions finally swayed their hearts. Supposedly, exactly the same thing happened in 1613. Churchmen led a delegation to Kostroma's Ipatiev Monastery to entreat Mikhail and his mother Marfa to agree to his izbranie. Metropolitans, archbishops, boyars, and "all Orthodox Christians even with nursing babes" flocked there, overcome by the great emotion of their desire for Mikhail to take up the scepter. According to the narrative, Marfa and Mikhail repeatedly declined, just as had Boris and Irina.[64]

In 1598 Boris had almost certainly feigned reluctance to accept the crown in order to bolster the appearance of his suitability to rule. The preset ritual was supposed to demonstrate that he possessed the appropriate Orthodox characteristics of a ruler. In 1613 a part of the Romanovs' hesitation may perhaps have been genuine. After all, a certain danger accompanied the position of "tsar" during the Time of Troubles! Regardless, Marfa and Mikhail *had* to act unwilling to accept the decision of the assembly in order to demonstrate that they did not lust for power. Isolde Thyrêt theorized that Marfa consciously manipulated this scenario in order to better the position of her son.[65] Yet, since the official record largely imitated the 1598 template, it is impossible to know for sure what really took place. Either the Romanovs and the Church hierarchs acted their way through a very long, staged performance with interminable prearranged speeches, or (what is more likely) ideologues simply fictionalized the entire affair after the fact. We are dealing here once again with a propaganda document, not an actual account of how and why Mikhail was chosen. The reasons for his selection had much more to do with kinship politics and competition among different powerful interests, including the Cossacks.[66]

According to the official historical record, the ecclesiastics remonstrated with Marfa and Mikhail at great length, chiding them for rejecting the "will of God." They adduced numerous examples from biblical and imperial history, intended to prove that Mikhail must occupy the throne as had David and Constantine and Theodosius. Patristic and scriptural quotations abounded. The churchmen argued that God had "loved" and "fore-chosen" Mikhail—an allusion to the selection of King David, used also in 1598. They claimed that in fixing on Mikhail as their choice for a new ruler the people had "unanimously" (*edinoglasie imeti*) spoken only what "God placed in their mind." For the first (and perhaps last) time, the Russian Orthodox Church claimed that vox Dei, vox populi had been "written" by divine decree (*iakozhe pishet glas naroda glas bozhii*). However, it remains a mystery where in the entire corpus of Orthodox literature this phrase had been written except in the legitimation documents of 1598.[67]

As in 1598 this whole drama finally ended with the tsaritsa and newly chosen tsar reluctantly "submitting to God's will." Before agreeing, they made sure to say that "God knew their hearts"; i.e., that mounting the throne had never even occurred to them and was the furthest thing from their intentions. The metropolitans, archbishops, and archimandrites immediately lent their sanction to Mikhail's accession and held Orthodox services amidst "joyful tears." Tsaritsa Marfa formally "blessed" her son to become "Great Sovereign, Tsar, and Grand Prince Mikhail Fyodorovich, Autocrat of All Russia." The official record ended with more assertions to the effect that Mikhail's selection would enable "our holy and unblemished true Orthodox Christian faith of the Greek law" to return to a state of prosperity. His reign was expected to return stability and peace to "all Orthodox Christendom." The populace then "kissed the cross" and swore to be loyal to the new tsar, while churchmen chanted prayers for him and his family.[68]

The official record of Mikhail's accession thus obviously followed the 1598 prototype. At the same time it incorporated additions and innovations devised for Boris's successors. The great emphasis placed on the urgent defense of Orthodoxy drew of course from general Orthodox conceptions of the tsar as God's representative on earth but also from recent precedents: Boris's Crimean campaign, the rhetoric of Dmitrii I and II, and especially the arguments advanced by Vasilii Shuiskii after his coup. The powerful role ascribed to the tsaritsa clearly imitated the alleged events of 1598, but vox feminae had also been reinforced and refined by every intermediary accession. Other scholars have also noted the prominent role given to Marfa, taking it as a sign of an upsurge in the political and religious status of Muscovite royal women.[69] The attempt to find an element of hereditary legitimacy for Mikhail, in addition to vox populi and vox feminae, also reflected similar attempts for rulers all throughout the Time of Troubles.

In 1613 the Muscovite government sent an embassy to Emperor Matthias of Habsburg, announcing Mikhail's accession. The justifications given remained the same for foreign as well as domestic consumption: the leading of the Russian Orthodox Church in expressing God's will for preserving Orthodoxy (vox Dei); the "blessing" of Mikhail's mother the "Great Sovereigness" (vox feminae); and the tireless "request and petition of all kinds of people of the Great Muscovite State" (vox populi).[70] This triad had become ubiquitous in political texts of the Time of Troubles. However, the unique Smuta legitimization scheme would prove to be short-lived. Russia's first patriarch had cleverly invented it almost out of thin air in order to legitimize a nonhereditary ruler. Yet no Russian ruler actually wanted to be nonhereditary or to found his right to rule on the will of the people. The end of the Troubles would therefore also put an end to the brief appearance of vox populi, vox Dei within the "canon" of Russian Orthodox politics.

Out with the New, In with the Old?

In retrospect 1613 appears to mark the end of the Time of Troubles. The accession of Tsar Mikhail led to a strong political and economic recovery within a relatively short time. Russia itself had been saved and restored. At the time, however, it was far from clear that the Troubles were over. The country lay in shambles. Swedish and Polish-Lithuanian armies still occupied some regions. Prince Wladyslaw considered himself the rightful ruler, and a number of other potential rivals for the throne waited in the wings. After the events of the previous decade, any observer would have been foolish simply to assume that the young Mikhail's reign would last and bring order to Muscovy.

Given this background it is hardly surprising that the Habsburg Empire at first declined to recognize the new tsar. Much like Boris Godunov fifteen years earlier, Mikhail Romanov promptly sent embassies to Emperor Matthias (as well as King James I of England and other sovereigns) in a bid to shore up his own legitimacy. In 1614 the Russian government was incensed to learn that imperial correspondence termed Mikhail only "Sovereign," omitting "Tsar of all Russia" and other elements of the official title. In 1616–1617, when "brother" Matthias's government did agree to recognize the new tsar, the Russian envoy complained that "our enemy," meaning the Polish-Lithuanians, had falsely reported to the Habsburgs that Mikhail's rule had not yet become established (*eshcho ne utverdilsia*). In fact, according to Muscovite publicity, "our Great Sovereign," whom "God gave," was a "direct heir [*priamoi naslednik*] of the Russian state" and "chosen by all ranks of people of the whole Russian State." Furthermore, Mikhail had allegedly "expelled the Lithuanian people from the Muscovite state and captured cities, those cities that the Lithuanian people had captured during the stateless time [*bezgosudarnoe vremia*] by their falsehood and flattery."[71]

Mikhail was not a direct heir of the previous dynasty, and he certainly had not captured back all the territories lost to Poland-Lithuania during the Troubles. Neither side dealt completely straightforwardly in these critical early years of the new Muscovite regime. Matthias had in fact concluded a secret alliance with Zygmunt III in March 1613. The Habsburg emperor appears to have been at least as open to the candidacy of Wladyslaw, who for his part kept hiring mercenary troops for an invasion and otherwise promoting rebellion against Tsar Mikhail.[72]

Despite the odds stacked against him, Mikhail managed to avoid being toppled and to "pacify" his realm. The war (or standoff) with Sweden continued until the 1617 Treaty of Stolbovo, which represented a compromise. Russia had regained Novgorod and several other major towns but was forced to cede away large sections of Karelia. This meant the loss of any access to the Gulf of Finland and the Baltic Sea. On the western front several renewed Polish-Lithuanian offensives, including Wladyslaw's invasion in 1617, kept the war going longer. In 1618 the two sides agreed to the fourteen-year Truce of Deulino, which did temporarily end the fighting. A large swath of territory including Smolensk passed "back" from Muscovy to its archenemy. Lost too were much of Severia and other sections of the southwestern frontier that had initially sparked the civil war with their support for Dmitrii. Although Wladyslaw would not officially abandon his claims to the Muscovite throne until 1634, these concessions enabled Tsar Mikhail to consolidate his own rule inside the country.[73]

In Dunning's interpretation, Mikhail did this largely "by crushing the very same patriotic cossacks who saved the country and brought him to power." War against Zarutskii and Marina's Cossack forces continued for over a year. Upon their capture the three-year-old "little brigand" Ivan was hanged. The new government also took harsh measures against all other popular movements and potential challengers to Tsar Mikhail's legitimacy. Even (or especially) national heroes like Minin and Pozharskii were viewed with suspicion and jealousy. Land grabs and enserfment of free peasantry brought more conflict with the common people. In other words, coming to power via the election of a zemskii sobor and explicit reliance on vox populi did not at all incline Mikhail's government toward demophilia.[74]

The new regime also took steps to distance itself from any form of popular-democratic legitimacy, meaning that the novel legitimation paradigm of the Time of Troubles would not last. The nascent Romanov regime clearly wanted to return to hereditary forms of legitimacy, and perhaps this enabled it to birth a new dynasty. Official documents exaggerated and emphasized Mikhail's family ties to the pre-Smuta tsars and pretended that Tsar Fyodor had intended to bestow the tsardom on Filaret Romanov. Instead of glorifying vox populi, Moscow now insisted that the people should be as "mute as fish"—their allegedly proper role in times of legitimate rule. In revised versions of his accession story, Mikhail's "selection" owed more to Church prelates and elite boyars than to the Russian population. Official ideology underscored the role of the tsar himself as God's representative on earth and the defender of Orthodoxy. The tsar required only silent, voiceless support from his people. The temporary appearance of vox populi in the Russian canon had in fact coincided with attempts to impose order via increasing serfdom. As expressed from above, it was only a faux demophilia adopted for purposes of legitimization, and it vanished once it was no longer needed.[75]

In 1619 Filaret Romanov returned from captivity in Poland-Lithuania. He got himself properly established as patriarch—documents from the first years of Mikhail's reign still referred to him as "metropolitan"—and apparently assumed practical control of the government. His presence obviously strengthened the Romanov position in Moscow. With father as head of the Russian Orthodox Church and son as head of the Russian Orthodox state, a new dynasty had the authority to entrench itself permanently. Filaret did not fail to appreciate the great significance of historiography in accomplishing this end. He presided over an extensive revision of Smuta accounts that blamed virtually everything on the alleged Polish-Lithuanian desire to extirpate Russian Orthodoxy. His personal history during the Troubles was fictionalized to present him in the best possible light. Concerned about potential sources of disunity, the patriarch also ordered monasteries to send selected religious books to Moscow for checking and correction.[76]

In the economic sphere, the election of Mikhail Romanov was followed almost immediately by a quick upsurge in regular documentation, reflecting the reestablishment of a more normal state of affairs. Charters confirming monasterial privileges abounded, as did new land and boundary surveys (*mezhevye knigi, pistsovye knigi*). The early years of Tsar Mikhail's reign saw more payment exemptions granted to monasteries that had been destroyed or damaged by the events of the Troubles. On the other hand some ecclesiastic institutions were able to retain or recover their wealth quickly and to make large tax payments to the state. The 1620s saw steady improvement across the board, together with the usual conflicts over land and resources. In Hellie's overall evaluation, "The economy seems to have recovered by about 1629."[77]

In certain respects Tsar Mikhail's regime succeeded in reestablishing the "old order" from before the Troubles. The transitory appearance of vox populi in the Orthodox canon would not set Russia on a course toward democracy. Rather, the Romanov dynasty would prove itself persistently antidemocratic over the next three centuries. Yet the popular voice could not be completely suppressed; it would keep cropping up in the most inconvenient ways. Regular rebellions, often accompanied by pretenderism, would test the dynasty throughout its existence and ultimately overcome it. At the same time the new regime was not wholly conservative. Dramatic bureaucratic, ecclesiastic, and legislative reforms of the seventeenth century prepared the way for Peter the Great's "revolution from above." The great trauma of the Time of Troubles thus propelled Russia along the slow path toward modernity. Further painful confrontations lay ahead.

CHAPTER SEVEN

In Retrospect

Russian Orthodoxy in the Time of Troubles and Beyond

And in those days there was no tsar in Israel, and a man did what was fitting in his eyes.

—Judges 21:25 in the Ostroh Bible, 1581[1]

The fact that I have denied the Church that calls itself "Orthodox" is completely correct. But I denied it not because I rebelled against the Lord, but on the contrary, only because I wanted to serve him with all the strength of my soul.

—Lev Tolstoy, Letter to the Holy Synod, 1901[2]

Four main themes pulsate through the shared history of the Russian state, church, and people during the Time of Troubles. Russians perceived themselves literally as God's chosen New Israel and believed that the Troubles represented divine punishment for sin. Monasteries acted like the great economic corporations they were, pursuing profit in ways that both perpetuated and helped to end the Troubles. Ecclesiastic hierarchs introduced key innovations into the discourse of political ideology, prompting a temporary shift toward new and different "voices of legitimacy." Finally, a fragmentation of Orthodoxy took hold as the populace increasingly disregarded the word of the official and institutional Church. The foregoing chapters have shed light on each of these issues. A final retrospective glance may enable us to tie together the multiple strands of evidence.

The New Israel

Russia during the Time of Troubles bore some resemblance to Israel during the days of the biblical Judges. As in that ancient text's refrain: *There was no king (or tsar), and everyone acted as he saw fit.* The occurrence of such a condition did not seem out of place in a society that consciously and endlessly imitated ancient Israel. At the beginning of the "disturbed period," Orthodox Patriarch Iyov equated Boris Godunov's reign over the "New Israel" to the deliverance accomplished by biblical heroes of the "old" Israel. Near its close Orthodox Patriarch Hermogen called on the faithful to repent, rise up, and unite to prevent the same apocalyptic "final destruction" that had seemingly overtaken the Jews of antiquity. In between, a string of rulers seized and lost power as one coup followed another in quick succession. Executions and rabble-rousing regularly took place at the platform in Red Square called *Lobnoe mesto.* A calque of *Golgotha,* the name of an infamous place of execution in Roman Jerusalem, this "place of the skull" drove home in macabre fashion the extraordinary extent of Muscovy's self-identification with ancient Israel.[3]

The theme of Russia as the New Israel increased in prominence over the course of the Time of Troubles. Both the Babylonian captivity and the Roman exile of the Jewish people seemed apt metaphors for the disorder, pain, and destruction all around. Literate Muscovites knew of the first from scripture and of the second from later translated texts such as the *Hellenic Annalist.* Throughout the period successive governments blamed the "Latin" (i.e., Catholic) Polish-Lithuanians for causing all or most of Russia's troubles. Their rhetoric constantly recalled the language of accounts concerning the Roman destruction of Jerusalem. Perhaps this double negative association with "Latins" and "Romans" could even help to explain why the "Third Rome" formulation appeared only irregularly in Muscovite texts, while the association with ancient Israel found much more consistent expression. "Infidel" Jews were in fact worse than "schismatic" Latins from the Muscovite perspective, but at the same time Russians had a much stronger ideational bond to the original Israel than to Rome. Muscovy's national identity was based on its alleged status as "Israel"—a claim constantly reinforced in the

6. Lobnoe mesto (Golgotha or The Place of the Skull), Red Square, Moscow. Reproduced by kind permission of Elizaveta Skriabina.

Time of Troubles through comparisons to Jewish history. This of course did not preclude use of the "Third Rome" idea, but it obviously encouraged a preference for "New Israel" rhetoric.[4]

Aleksandr Filiushkin, one of the contemporary historians who has begun to emphasize the "New Israel" paradigm as a key to understanding the Muscovite worldview, remarks that the Russian ruler of this period was considered no ordinary mortal but rather a "tsar-messiah." He was held to be the "guarantor of *pravda* (justice and truth)"; he stood as the savior of all Orthodox Christians from the *nepravda* (injustice and untruth) of the evil enemy. During the Time of Troubles this enemy, this "other," was usually so-called *bezbozhnaia Litva,* the "godless" Poles and Lithuanians. As Filiushkin explains, Muscovy described all opponents of the "New Israel" as anti-Christian, fighting against God's truth and His holy people.[5]

These Muscovite conceptions had been copied almost directly from biblical depictions of earthly "messiahs" (anointed kings and priests) and later Jewish messianic expectations of the Second Temple period. To this day the notion of a "King Messiah" coming to deliver the righteous people of God from evil oppressors has not lost any of its poignancy within Orthodox Judaism. *Mutatis mutandis,* this same notion furnishes a key to understanding the whole of the

Russian Smuta. During the wars of the period, much blood was shed over the disputed question, Who is *pomazannik Bozhii?* The true "anointed" or "Messiah" of God had to be found in order to bring "salvation" to "Israel." In Chester Dunning's words, "The God-chosen tsar became the one essential element in early modern Russia's completely religious political culture."[6] Meanwhile, once allegedly "false" tsars had been deposed, they occupied a place in Muscovite historiography directly comparable to that of reviled "false messiahs" in the Jewish tradition.

The extreme religious significance assigned to the person of the tsar meant that dynastic breakdown could indeed throw the country into chaos. Yet this was not inevitable. Had a new dynasty been established and gained a position of permanent legitimacy, the Troubles might never have occurred as such. In the actual event, climatic, social, and other factors intervened to prevent the possibility of attaining this all-important legitimacy. The sacred ideal of the "tsar-messiah" notwithstanding, large groups within Russian society came to believe that not every enthroned monarch deserved this exalted status. Rather, some should be resisted, overthrown, and killed! One may view this phenomenon as a "desacralization of the image of the tsar"; or alternately, as a disassociation of specific "false" claimants from a still intact idea of the "true tsar." No doubt elements of both modes of thinking were present during the Smuta; to try to separate them too finely might be an exercise in splitting hairs.

Successive tsars of the Time of Troubles tried ever harder to be seen as "champions" and "defenders" of Orthodox Christianity. Defending the "true faith" from the onslaughts of "false tsars" and "godless" enemies could represent a dominant component of legitimacy in the Muscovite politico-religious system. Yet the perceived "punishment for sin" continued unabated. Russians and foreigners alike interpreted the many catastrophes of the period in this light. Such an explanation was especially penetrating, given that Russians considered themselves God's only "Israel." Though some association with New Israel ideas has been present in all Christian societies, Russia's attachment to this theory assumed a unique form due to its claimed status as the only remaining Christian empire (*tsarstvo*). A Russian friend once suggested to this author that perhaps God had simply taken the country at its word. Russians insisted on being "Israel," and so God allowed them to experience some of what that meant, including the consequences of "breaking His covenant."

Whatever one thinks of that slant, it persists until today. A 2009 article in the online journal *Pravoslavie i mir* (*Orthodoxy and the World*) addressed the topic of what "lessons" Russian Orthodox believers of today should learn from the Time of Troubles. The author, Sergei Perevezentsev, made frequent mention of New Israel ideas and the notion of divine punishment for forsaking the right path. He emphasized the roles of the tsar and the Church as guarantors of pravda. The chief "lessons" of the period turned out to be that in troubled times the Russian nation must repent and return to the "true faith" and that the Russian Orthodox Church should properly exercise authority and leadership in directing the country.[7]

After the Time of Troubles, New Israel and New Jerusalem ideas continued to increase in prominence in Muscovy. Many seventeenth-century monasteries and churches adopted names closely linked to the Holy Land. At mid-century, Patriarch Nikon established a major new monastery, called the New Jerusalem. Its design imitated that of the Church of the Holy Sepulchre in the old Jerusalem. The same Nikon founded another monastery named after the Galilee region in the north of Israel.[8] Despite the unpredictable twists and turns of history, the idea of Russia as the New Israel has even begun to reemerge in the twenty-first century as a potential guiding principle of the Orthodox Christian outlook.

Monetary Pursuits

The pro-Church historian Elena Romanenko wrote: "In any difficult times, monasteries came to the aid of the local population. . . . The Time of Troubles showed very clearly that firm and strong monasteries were not only a military and a spiritual but also an economic support of Russia."[9] The anti-Church historian Nikolai Nikolskii wrote the opposite: that monasteries took in huge profits but very rarely gave anything at all to the poor.[10] The truth lies somewhere in between these two extreme viewpoints but unfortunately closer to Nikolskii's assessment. Careful examination of economic documentation from the Time of Troubles demonstrates that pursuit of profit dominated most ecclesiastic activity, even during the Great Famine. Monks and monasteries generally acted in their own economic interest, a fact that helped to cause and to prolong the Time of Troubles. On the other hand the source base may be somewhat skewed. We have records from a few large, wealthy institutions that often behaved greedily. Yet little or no evidence has survived regarding the behavior of individual hermits and many smaller monasteries. How many of these acted like the elders of the great Solovetskii Monastery—making massive business deals while giving only a few kopecks to the poor—remains unclear.

Perhaps some of them instead sacrificed greatly to help others. However, in general the sources demonstrate that caring for the needy did not figure as a prime motive for monastic life in Muscovy in this period.

Ecclesiastic economic interest played an enormous role in shaping the historical context within which the Troubles occurred. In the preceding decades the lure of profitable forest products attracted Church expansion into the northern and eastern regions of the state, including Siberia. The lack of such resources in the south hindered the establishment of new monasteries and the spread of Church influence. Thus, as peasants, slaves, impoverished landowners, and others fled to the southern and southwestern border regions, they entered an area relatively free of official Muscovite religion and propaganda. Some scholars have proposed that this flight to the periphery provided a "safety valve," diffusing tension in the central regions. Yet the Borderlands (*Ukraina*) soon proved to be a tinderbox, igniting a series of revolts that would shake the very foundations of Russia and place in doubt its continued existence as a state.

Remarkably, some Church institutions were able to maintain and even increase their revenue during the Time of Troubles. Their financial well-being derived both from business ventures and from donations (vklady). The suffering and death caused by the Troubles apparently prompted an upswing in religiosity, including donations to monasteries. Though some have argued for a "decline in monasticism" over the course of the sixteenth century,[11] this does not appear to have been true in an economic sense. As for the "charisma" or appeal of monasteries to the broader population, if it did decline prior to the Troubles then it may have made a partial, mixed recovery during that period. Ecclesiastic economic policies alienated many commoners and produced endless conflict. Yet, at the same time, Orthodox Russians still associated monasteries with the "true faith" enough to increase their contributions on behalf of living and dead relatives. They also may have benefited occasionally from a kind of "trickle-down" effect. For their part the monasteries apparently took action to help end the Troubles once they saw their profit margins dwindle and disappear in the last years of the period.

Like many premodern societies, Muscovite Russia did not conceive of politics or economics as independent of religion. Orthodox Christianity was supposed to constitute an all-inclusive worldview and lifestyle for believers. Studying the economic activity of the Church shows clearly this lack of separation between the "sacred" and the "profane." In order to preserve their businesses and profits, monasteries always supported the government in power, even when this necessitated constant reversals of "Orthodoxy." For their part the governments unfailingly supported the monasteries, giving them tax exemptions and backing them up in disputes with local peasants. This remained true regardless of which tsar or "pretender" held sway at a particular time and place. The unbreakable relationship between ecclesiastic economic interests and political power during this period of extreme chaos and upheaval demonstrates just how central a role the monasteries played in the entire Muscovite system. In future centuries many revolutionary changes would be introduced in response to the unmistakable alignment of church wealth with political patronage.

Voices of Legitimacy

The Time of Troubles introduced a radical shift into the politico-religious ideology of Muscovy. Instead of hereditary seniority and dynastic succession, a new paradigm of legitimacy, invented in 1598 for Boris Godunov, dominated during this turbulent decade and a half. Its main components were vox Dei, represented by the Orthodox patriarch and other top Church hierarchs; vox populi, as expressed by ostensible "councils of the land"; and vox feminae, the validation provided by a tsaritsa. Wittingly or unwittingly, each ruler of the Time of Troubles modified, expanded, and entrenched this novel paradigm of legitimacy. It remains completely anomalous in Russian history to this day.

The ideological innovations of the Time of Troubles sprang up, so to speak, in the soil of puzzling, unresolved issues from the reign of Ivan IV. In 1553 the tsar had fallen gravely ill, prompting strife about who should succeed him. Some Church hierarchs and boyars did not want to swear allegiance to Ivan's infant son Dmitrii, though he would have had both hereditary legitimacy and the right of bestowal from the previous tsar. This experience may have destabilized not only Ivan himself but also the very system of political legitimacy in Russia. In 1564 Ivan appeared to abdicate while claiming to ally himself with the simple people against the corrupt churchmen and boyars. He agreed to take up the scepter again only after an extraordinary procession of "all the people" pleaded with him to "return to his possession." In 1575 Ivan inexplicably appointed Simeon Bekbulatovich grand prince, seemingly in his stead. Then in 1581 he struck and killed his adult son and heir Ivan, reputed to be a capable man.[12]

As seen from these bizarre and tragic episodes, the assumed foundations of the tsar's legitimacy had already begun to wobble, even prior to the accession of

Ivan's "weak-minded" son Fyodor in 1584. For his part Fyodor I ruled in name only. Boris Godunov quickly became the real force behind the government, as both Russian and foreign observers understood quite clearly. This discrepancy further undermined standard conceptions of the tsar's authority. Fyodor's death in 1598 brought an end to a long-standing dynasty. Perhaps it was not the mere fact that the dynasty had died out that mattered so much, but rather *how* it had died. The aberrations of Ivan IV had thrown the gates open to new political configurations in Muscovy.

The official accession documents of 1598–1613 do not tell us what actually happened in the political arena. Without exception they were composed for propagandistic purposes, and they must be understood as such.[13] This necessarily changes the focus of one's historical inquiry and leads to different results than those obtained by reading the texts less critically. Rather than an actual change from "autocratic" to "representative" systems, or hereditary accession to election, we see instead a shift in Orthodox political rhetoric. The Muscovite church-state propagated quasi-democratic rhetoric in order to justify several de facto seizures of power, but the "consumers" of this propaganda may have taken it more seriously than it was intended. The notions of vox populi and vox feminae spiraled out of control in the Time of Troubles, helping to produce endless warfare, coups, and reversals of official "truth."

What did Patriarch Iyov and the other Muscovite ideologues of the Time of Troubles actually mean when they spoke of "electing" new tsars? It is important to recognize that the Russian word *izbranie* did not necessarily imply a representative process at all. A better English translation is "selection." Boris and his successors had allegedly been "selected" in the first instance by God Himself—as indeed Ivan IV, Fyodor, and other previous rulers must have been. The official documents made it clear that God had already "pre-selected" (*pred'izbral*) each ruler—as indeed He had selected other men for other tasks. Hence, all that church and nation could do (theoretically, at least) was to confirm God's own "selection" by their agreement.[14] This implies that the notion of "election" or "selection" was not originally intended in so radical and direct a sense as it came to assume over the course of the Troubles. Moreover, as in ancient Athenian democracy, the elite may not have intended to include most of the population when speaking of "the people." Patriarch Iyov himself thus may not have realized the full consequences of opening this Pandora's box.

In the event, such results included temporarily making popular acclaim a requisite part of rulership in Moscow. By the second half of the Troubles, so-called vox populi could not only make tsars, it could easily break them as well. The "voice of the people" had become an indispensible component of Russian Orthodoxy legitimacy—a double-edged sword used to justify both the elevation and the deposition of successive rulers. A radical change had indeed taken place! Vox populi as expressed in civil warfare became the sole practical determinant of vox Dei, and the official representation of "God's voice" by the Russian Orthodox Church(es) ceased to be credible.

Vox feminae, the authorizing voice of a woman, also formed an indispensible component of political legitimacy during the Time of Troubles. From Tsar Boris's reliance on his sister, Tsaritsa Irina, to Tsar Dmitrii I's dependence on the witness of his ostensible mother, Tsaritsa Maria, from Tsar Dmitrii II's crucial alliance with Tsaritsa Marina to Tsar Mikhail's apparent deference to his mother, Tsaritsa Marfa—women ostensibly bestowed men with a right to the throne. Like vox populi this factor represented an important anomaly in Russian history. The strength of the Virgin Mary and Princess Olga cults in Russia at the time likely nourished the possibility of such a development. At the height of the Troubles, the monasterial founder Galaktion of Vologda pronounced: "[Our] sins called forth the Poles and Lithuanians upon us: let [us] begin fasting and prayer and hurry to build the temple of the Sign of the Mother of God. The heavenly tsaritsa will liberate Vologda!"[15] Great devotion to the "heavenly tsaritsa" and faith in her powers were widespread during the sixteenth and seventeenth centuries in Muscovy; they seem to have contributed to the acceptability and appeal of assigning legitimizing power to an earthly tsaritsa.

The top hierarchs of the Russian Orthodox Church introduced and presided over these ideological innovations. They had to walk a fine line. The Orthodox politico-religious system staked its claims to legitimacy and truth on a posited immutability and unbroken continuity from ancient times. From its conception until today, a major tenet of the Orthodox Church has always been its claim to preserve an unalterable "Apostolic Tradition."[16] Yet clearly adaptation had taken place in the past and would continue to take place in the future. The key was to appear always to be following prior precedent even while introducing radically new perspectives. Virtually everything relating to Church practice in Muscovy—from monastic rules to political ideology—represented not slavish copying but rather a mix of "Greek" (i.e., Byzantine) archetypes with Russian innovations.[17]

Contrary to what some might assume, the prominence assigned to the Russian Orthodox Church in official documents was not merely a formality.

Ample evidence exists that churchmen exercised a great deal of actual power and influence in Muscovy, particularly during the Time of Troubles. Partriarchs Iyov, Hermogen, and Filaret participated not only in kingmaking but also in many other key political decisions. Moreover, dismissing the primacy explicitly ascribed to ecclesiastics would introduce a methodological inconsistency for historians. Muscovite-ordered lists of people, commodities, land, and other items are regularly (and correctly) interpreted as indicative of priorities or "precedence" within the society. Following this same method, an abundance of Muscovite documents indicates that ecclesiastics occupied a place of real prominence within the church-state.[18]

Though soon abandoned as official justifications for power, vox populi and vox feminae continued to exert a significant influence in Russia after the Time of Troubles. In 1682 the death of another childless and nominal Tsar Fyodor (III) sparked a dynastic crisis sharply reminiscent of the Smutnoe vremia. While many feared a repetition of those horrendous events, Russian Orthodox Patriarch Ioakim quickly engineered an "assembly of the land" that "selected" a new ruler. Ten-year-old Peter, half-brother of the previous tsar, was to ascend the throne under the regency of his mother the tsaritsa. Yet another ambitious female member of the dynasty orchestrated a coup of sorts, resulting in the addition of a second tsar, Ivan V, as senior ruler together with the younger Peter. This Tsarevna Sophia took over as regent and assumed actual control until the future Peter the Great built up enough of a power base to oust her.[19]

Thus the event often considered the most important for the development of modern Russia—the accession of Peter I—took place within an immediate context heavily influenced by the Time of Troubles. One of the unforeseen results of Peter's reign would be the succession of a series of empresses in the eighteenth century, up to and including Catherine II the Great. Vox feminae of the Time of Troubles arguably helped to pave the way for this female rule in modern Russia. Reliance on female voices for legitimacy during the Smuta may have gone hand in hand with increased devotion to female saints, which scholars such as Isolde Thyrêt and Gary Marker have identified as important for enabling women to rule in Russia.[20] Meanwhile, vox populi and pretenderism continued to feed into widespread popular revolts throughout the seventeenth and eighteenth centuries.[21]

According to Cynthia Whittaker, the Russian government itself attempted to make use of the idea of popular election or "consensual accession" all the way through the eighteenth century.[22] In general, however, vox populi became a counterideology, not official Orthodoxy. Kept alive every so often by revolts, this alternate tradition from the Time of Troubles ultimately contributed to tortured cycles of reform, reaction, and revolution in nineteenth-century Russia. At that century's end Konstantin Pobedonostsev, Russia's chief ideologue and secular head of the Russian Orthodox Church, was still denouncing vox populi, vox Dei as heresy.[23] Official, pro-autocratic definitions of *narodnost'*—the supposed unique character of the Russian people—clashed harshly with popular *narodnichestvo*—a turn toward "the people" themselves—at around the same time. Perhaps it is not too much to propose that the conflict between these two perspectives was not resolved in the twentieth century and has not yet been in the twenty-first.

Official and Unofficial Orthodoxy

The historian Pierre Pascal suggested that the roots of Russia's Church Schism of the 1660s and beyond could be found in the Time of Troubles. Other students of the *Raskol* and of Russian religious history have advanced similar interpretations but frequently with little explanation.[24] The link probably seemed obvious: the Troubles devastated Russia and affected its religious mindset, so they must have had something to do with producing subsequent religious "troubles" or disturbances within another half-century. Yet this was almost too easy a way out. The interpretation was correct but unsubstantiated. If the Time of Troubles really did play such a significant role in causing the Schism, it should be possible to identify specific factors and points of connection, not merely a generic sense of shock and damage. This can in fact be done.

Recent historiography has already provided many pieces of the puzzle. Dunning determined that the civil wars of the Time of Troubles "allowed even lowly Orthodox subjects to oppose erring or evil rulers" and therefore brought a "growing realization . . . that the Russian land and its people, not just the tsar, had important roles to play in safeguarding the country's sacred mission."[25] Georg Michels has pointed to a "growing conflict between church power and society" during the patriarchate of Filaret, immediately after the Time of Troubles. The erstwhile metropolitanate now flexed its muscles as a full-fledged patriarchate, enriching itself greatly and extending its political power, but thereby also provoking numerous social problems. Documents from this period contain evidence that Russians of all social strata advanced harsh criticisms of the Orthodox patriarch. For his part

Filaret responded with "systematic repression of critics and dissenters" that "set the Russian patriarchate on a path that would inevitably lead to crisis."[26] Other analysts have also pointed to a developing split between elite and population in the Muscovite church-state between the Time of Troubles and the Schism.[27] Paul Bushkovitch described "innovative religious writers" after the Troubles who came from the ranks of nonecclesiastic commoners but nonetheless proposed "new currents of thought" that would eventually influence all of Russian society.[28]

Integrating the findings of this book with the work of other scholars reveals that an important change did indeed take place during the Time of Troubles. In addition to economic, political, and social developments, a shift in mentality seems to have been critical. At this painful moment in history, the official New Israel ideology merged with popular sentiments to create a Russian national identity. The new politico-religious consciousness of the people did not depend on whichever particular ruler happened to be in power in Moscow at any given moment. It incorporated key elements of official ideology from the late sixteenth and early seventeenth centuries: Russia's inheritance of the mantle of ancient Israel and Byzantium; the notion of vox populi; and the nation's sacred role as sole defender of the "true faith." Nevertheless, this formative Russian national identity evolved apart from, and even in opposition to, official power. Its proponents unhesitatingly rebelled against sitting tsars and patriarchs perceived as betrayers of Orthodoxy.

This perspective helps to clarify a number of difficult but compelling questions in Muscovite history. Scholars have long debated such issues: When did the Russian peasants actually become "Christian"? When did official politico-religious ideology "filter down" to the popular level? When did a national identity emerge? Interestingly, a number of studies on such questions have focused on the sixteenth and seventeenth centuries but without being able to define the time frame more precisely. Vladimir Vlasov contended that "analysis of the menology, or popular Christianized agrarian and ritual calendar, reinforced with data from popular astronomy and medieval history, leads to the conclusion that the church (Julian) calendar was adopted by the Russian people in the sixteenth and seventeenth centur[ies]. . . . The transition to the Julian calendar is a reliable indication that the Russian peasantry had adopted the Christian annual ritual cycle at this time, which in turn means that they had joined the church and Christianity."[29] Robert Crummey observed, "It is difficult to determine precisely when these rather esoteric theories [such as translatio imperii] took hold in the popular imagination"; but that by the mid-seventeenth century, "many ordinary Muscovites accepted these ideas as axiomatic."[30] The findings of many scholars thus reinforce the idea that the Time of Troubles cut deeply into the Russian psyche in such a way as to produce a palpable transformation in mentality.

Following an independent path of research, Dmitrii Likhachev similarly concluded that the "land-people" (*zemlia-narod*) of the lower and middle classes manifested a "new political consciousness" during the Time of Troubles.[31] Before him, Kliuchevskii spoke of "new political understandings" arising out of the Smuta.[32] More recently, Bushkovitch also focused on the Time of Troubles in his essay on "The Formation of a National Consciousness in Early Modern Russia."[33] The findings of this book therefore coincide with, reinforce, and refine several earlier conclusions of historiography. Perhaps most intriguingly, Tatiana Bernshtam has written that "a *second stage* of Christianization *shattered* the idea of the church and the upper classes with respect to Orthodox unity and revealed its fluidity and evolution into a 'multifaith' (*mnogoverie*)." Bernshtam dates the "clandestine" development of this "second stage" to the sixteenth and seventeenth centuries and its "public announcement" to the period after the Church Schism.[34] Such a pivotal new socioreligious reality could also be interpreted as a multiplicity of competing views within one "faith," Russian Orthodoxy. Given the extreme fragmentation of Orthodoxy that clearly transpired uniquely during the Time of Troubles, its birth can be traced directly to the beginning of the seventeenth century.

As evidence that a "faith-based national consciousness" formed in the minds of "ordinary folk" during the Time of Troubles, Miller adduced the example of a rebellious celebration of Palm Sunday in 1611. According to the contemporary Konrad Bussow, Muscovite commoners disregarded a decree of the official government (made up of Polish-Lithuanian occupiers and boyar collaborators) and brazenly observed the religious festival as they saw fit. Miller remarked, "What once was an elite affair had become a popular celebration."[35] This comment may be taken as emblematic of the Time of Troubles. It was precisely during this watershed period that "the people" appropriated many previously "elite" ideas and customs, adopted and transformed them, and used them for their own ends. Miller tentatively dates the "formation of the Russian identity" to the period around 1605.[36]

During the Time of Troubles Russian popular religion assumed a paradoxical character—in some points identical with official Orthodoxy, in others diametrically opposed to it. Popular Orthodox piety shared many of the features of Church pronouncements but could now exist completely independently of the latter. This frightened the new Romanov dynasty—and with good reason. According to Dunning, the new regime attempted to crush "any notion of Holy Russia that was separate from the person of the tsar."[37] Yet, in the wake of the Time of Troubles, all popular sentiment must have made some distinction between Orthodox Russia and the "true faith" on the one hand and the occupants of the Muscovite thrones (tsar and patriarch) on the other. This was an unintended result of Patriarch Iyov's innovations, an unavoidable consequence of the chaotic Troubles. The Romanovs would prove unable to root out this thorny problem for all three centuries of their rule.

If this was indeed the nature of the "national consciousness" that formed in Russia during the Time of Troubles, then the connections to the Church Schism of mid-century become readily appreciable. Russia now had a bad case of the old and common conundrum of faith versus religion, or individual (and collective) conscience vis-à-vis the official Church. Avvakum and other Old Believers were willing to suffer persecution and death, all in defense of dissident but conservative opinions about the right way to cross oneself or the correct number of "halleluyahs" to say in the liturgy. Old Believer texts drew explicit parallels to the Time of Troubles. Old Believer authors claimed to speak on behalf of "all the Russian people" as against the official politico-religious elite—language highly reminiscent of the Smutnoe vremia. Furthermore, many *raskol'niki* or "schismatics" rebelled because they considered the policies of tsar and church to be unjust and oppressive, aside from any minute questions of dogma or ritual. ("There is no truth in tsars or patriarchs. . . .") Not least, these rebels and schismatics manifested an apocalypticism not unrelated to interpretations formulated during the cataclysmic Troubles.[38]

From 1550 to 1650, according to Bushkovitch, local miracle cults burgeoned throughout Russia. The Muscovite elite, including the Church hierarchy, generally approved of such popular religious sentiment but remained suspicious that it might take an "unorthodox" turn. In fact, this may have happened. The religious traditions most informing the common people came not so much from official theology, hesychasm, or even scripture, but rather from direct, earthy associations with supernatural help amidst everyday life—including such matters as stopping a nosebleed. No wonder, then, that many different "orthodoxies" appeared in the Time of Troubles and soon after. The Troubles even prompted some writers (Timofeev, Khvorostinin, Shakhovskoi) to move in the opposite direction, away from miracles in favor of an emphasis on morality. The Zealots of Piety also sought to revitalize Russian Orthodoxy in the wake of the Troubles by promoting greater spirituality and morality.

All these differing tendencies helped to create serious religious division and discord by mid-century. Patriarch Nikon himself had been a member of the Zealots and adopted many of their proposals, but most of them would object strenuously to his reforms and become Old Believers.[39]

Other important phenomena contributing to the Raskol were also noticeable already during the Smutnoe vremia. During and just after the Troubles, a monk named Arsenii labored away, correcting errors that had crept into copies of Church service books. Apparently of a naturally inquisitive mind, he had studied for years in the library of the Troitsa Sergiev Monastery and had taught himself Greek. He was joined by a certain Dionisii, who also knew Greek (a rare skill in Muscovy). Together they discovered numerous errors in manuscripts and printed editions, some of them quite obvious. Yet Arsenii and Dionisii, though working per the charge of superiors, faced the jealousy and hatred of other monks who possessed no comparable knowledge but nonetheless fancied themselves experts. In the early years of Tsar Mikhail's reign, the studious pair found themselves insulted and attacked, dragged before a Church council and denounced as heretics, and sentenced to beatings, torture, and confinement. A purely textual matter—whether or not a particular prayer had originally included the words "and by fire" (*i ognem*)—was made into a doctrinal issue of the utmost importance. Simply stating the basic facts of the case became a criminal offense.[40]

As any student of religion knows, such intense controversies over one or two words have figured into numerous ruptures throughout history. (One thinks even of the *filioque* clause in the modified Nicene Creed—one of the few theological differences between Eastern and Western Christianity.) Near the end of the Troubles, the case of Arsenii and Dionisii foreshadowed religious disputes that would break out within another generation. Under the direction of Patriarch Nikon, checking of Russian service books against recent Greek editions (not original manuscripts) prompted both conservatives and reformers to denounce each other for "changing" the prescribed texts. During the Russian Church Schism even the great Solovetskii Monastery would revolt against the Muscovite church-state, apparently supported by masses of peasants.[41]

The list of parallels between the Time of Troubles and the Church Schism could go on. According to Michels, one of the most important factors indicating likeliness to rebel in the mid-seventeenth century was "geographic location in an area that had been poorly integrated into the official structure of the Orthodox Church"—such as the southern and western borderlands.[42] This is precisely the same phenomenon that we have observed for the Time of Troubles. The

Schism, much like the Troubles, also brought with it an increase in brigandage and violent social interaction generally. In both periods the official Church underwent discrediting and faced widespread popular rejection of its supposed monopoly on truth. The Smuta and the Raskol thus shared many common features and may be said to belong to the same genus of Russian crises.

Evaluating the Russian Orthodox Church during the Time of Troubles

Miller remarked, "The Church found the Time of Troubles perplexing."[43] This is probably an understatement of considerable proportions! No doubt anyone who survived the Smuta experienced not only confusion but a dreadful shock and a mortal disorientation. The country's first four Orthodox patriarchs all ended up in jail in this period, meaning that the public "face" of the Church changed continually. For a few years two different Russian Orthodox Churches competed for power and allegiance. The country faced famine, war, brigandage, exploitation, cannibalism, and a host of other disasters. Official religion and dynastic legitimacy, Russia's two main "tools of integration,"[44] both broke down entirely.

The Time of Troubles remains perplexing to this day. Even historians writing after the fact have never been able to resolve many of its extreme contradictions. One of Russia's great historians, Nikolai Karamzin, exemplified this constant dilemma. Influenced by standard Romanov propaganda, he wrote that Boris Godunov reigned as the legitimate tsar according to accepted Muscovite practice—and also that he was a regicide, a Russian Macbeth, the "murderer of a saint." Karamzin termed Boris "sensible and solicitous," "one of the most judicious Sovereigns in the world"—and yet claimed that he could not rule properly because he was motivated by guilt and fear. According to Karamzin, Boris's accession "belonged to the most festive days of Russia in her history"—and simultaneously brought down the wrath of God on the country in the form of the Troubles.[45]

Any unbiased appraiser of the Russian Orthodox Church during the Time of Troubles will be confronted with a similar predicament. Pro-Church historians and many Russian Orthodox believers to this day have been attracted to the simplistic view that the Church "saved" Russia. Mikhail Tolstoi wrote imaginatively, "The wrath of God was turned into mercy by the prayers of the Church, triumphing in the heavens and militant on the earth. . . . Like one time under the Mongol Yoke . . . the Church saved the state!"[46] There is perhaps a grain of truth to this perspective. The Church did play an important role in ending the Troubles and restoring the Russian state. However, it also played an important role in creating the conditions for a crisis, in exacerbating social and political conflicts, and thus in provoking and prolonging the Troubles. The role of the Russian Orthodox Church during the Time of Troubles was a paradoxical one, like that of Tsar Boris and many other figures of the period.

Many of the Church's more questionable actions, especially in the realms of politics and economics, led to an extreme loss of credibility for its leadership during the Time of Troubles. Toward the end of the period, Patriarch Hermogen regained a position of moral authority from which to speak to the people, at least partly because of his own personal suffering for the sake of conviction. Other clerics and laymen saw Russia as a whole attaining redemption through suffering. "Holy Russia" was the "suffering servant of God"—an appropriation of Isaiah 53 that had been used also by Jewish writers in the Second Temple period. The end of the Troubles seemed to indicate that God's wrath had passed and His favor had returned to the "New Israel."[47]

Dunning and Michels agree with most historiography that the Church emerged from the Troubles an apparent "big winner," riding a crest of newfound prestige and popularity, in an excellent position to increase its power and wealth. At the same time they both see this as one of the causes of the Schism, since the Church again became a target of popular resentment. Patriarch Filaret's repressive, power-hungry, and money-grabbing tactics seemingly squandered any credibility regained by Hermogen. Even so, later ecclesiastic writers would lionize Filaret as a paragon of religious virtue, the "true founding father of the Russian patriarchate."[48]

However, the speed with which opposition to the Church hierarchy reemerged during the patriarchate of Filaret suggests that the "high" experienced at the end of the Troubles may have been partly illusory. Throughout the whole period devotion and donations to monasteries had continued—but so had economic conflicts between the monasteries and the population. No one could have expected these problems to disappear with the end of the Troubles. An extraordinarily desperate situation did occasion close collaboration between the official Church and the broader society but only in order to prevent the complete elimination of Russia. It is therefore not at all surprising that a return to more "normal" times came accompanied by the reappearance of similarly "normal" tensions and hostility.

The effects of the Troubles and their aftermath are still with us today. In post-Soviet Moscow, the Russian Orthodox Church prides itself on its ostensibly glorious role in the early seventeenth century. It courts the state and desires remarriage, a new "symphony" of religion and power. In 2009 the newly installed Patriarch Kirill remarked: "We as the Church consider it necessary that the spirit of *symphonia* direct our thoughts and deeds in the construction of a model of church-state relations."[49] Meanwhile, Old Believers who refuse to accept the dicta of the official Church still persist, in communities as far away as Alaska. They even undergo their own microschisms, keeping alive the seventeenth-century tradition of rebellion and dissent.[50]

The "Time of Troubles" began with a power play by Tsar Boris and Patriarch Iyov. They succeeded initially but within a few years lost control of the country. The "elected" and "anointed" Boris died in anguish; his wife and son were killed. Inspired by scripture or liturgy, his daughter apparently embroidered the following reflective epitaph in her family's memory: "For we all shall die: tsars and princes, judges and dignitaries, wealthy and indigent, every substance of earthly ones becoming nothing."[51] The Smutnoe vremia forced Russians to consider what was most important in a difficult and transient life. Some chose personal gain, others the official Orthodoxy of the Church, still others truth as they saw it themselves. The same choice is still being made today in Russia and everywhere else.

Notes

Abbreviations

AAE	Akty, sobrannye v bibliotekakh i arkhivakh Rossiiskoi imperii Arkheograficheskoiu ekspeditsieiu
AFZKh	Akty feodal'nogo zemlevladeniia i khoziaistva
AI	Akty istoricheskie, sobrannye i izdannye Arkheograficheskoiu kommissieiu
AMMS	Akty Rossiiskogo gosudarstva: Arkhivy moskovskikh monastyrei i soborov
ASEI	Akty sotsial'no-ekonomicheskoi istorii severo-vostochnoi Rusi
ASZ	Akty sluzhilykh zemlevladel'tsev
AVK	Akty izdavaemye Vilenskoiu kommissieiu dlia razbora drevnikh aktov
DAI	Dopolnenie k Aktam istoricheskim
DRV	Drevniaia Rossiiskaia Vivliofika
EER	Early Exploration of Russia
GKE	Gramoty Kollegii ekonomii (archival fund 281 of Rossiiskii gosudarstvennyi arkhiv drevnykh aktov)
MERSH	The Modern Encyclopedia of Russian and Soviet History
MES	Monastyri: Entsiklopedicheskii spravochnik
MMR	Monashestvo i monastyri v Rossii
MRP	Moskwa w rękach Polaków
MRPTs	Monastyri Russkoi Pravoslavnoi Tserkvi: Spravochnik-putevoditel'
OAU	Opisanie aktov sobraniia grafa A. S. Uvarova
PDS	Pamiatniki diplomaticheskikh snoshenii drevnei Rossii s derzhavami inostrannymi
PISV	Pamiatniki istorii Smutnago vremeni
PLDR	Pamiatniki literatury drevnei Rusi
PMR	Pravoslavnye monastyri Rossii: Kratkii spravochnik
PSRL	Polnoe sobranie russkikh letopisei
RGADA	Rossiiskii gosudarstvennyi arkhiv drevnikh aktov (Archive)
RIB	Russkaia istoricheskaia biblioteka
RMSC	Russian Manuscript Scrolls Collection (archival collection of the Library of Congress)
RNB	Rossiiskaia natsional'naia biblioteka (Archive)

SGGD   Sobranie gosudarstvennykh gramot i dogovorov
SKKDR   Slovar' knizhnikov i knizhnosti drevnei Rusi
SMERSH   The Supplement to the Modern Encyclopedia of Russian, Soviet, and
          Eurasian History
SPPP   Srednevekovoe pravoslavie ot prikhoda do patriarkhata
SRIa11–17 Slovar' russkogo iazyka XI—XVII vv.
SSDS   Skazaniia sovremennikov o Dimitrii Samozvantse
TODRL   Trudy otdela drevnerusskoi literatury
ZDR   Zbiór dyplomatów rzadowych i aktów prywatnych

Introduction

1. *Ostryz'ka Bibliia*, [2:] *l.* 2; *Biblia sirech knigy*, ed. Turkoniak, 23: 14; *Holy Bible* [KJV *editio princeps*], 3B5*v*. The verse is numbered 9:22 in Greek and Slavonic; 10:1 in Hebrew and English.

2. Vladimirov, "Strategicheskii etiud" (address delivered to the Security Council of the Russian Federation, Dec. 19, 2002).

3. *RIB*, 13: 1372.

4. Ibid., 13: 1381–82. Cf. *Zhitiia sviatykh*, 1: 416; Zabelin, *Minin i Pozharskii*, 302ff.; "Zhizneopisanie," 20–22; M. Tolstoi, *Istoriia russkoi tserkvi*, 483–84.

5. *SKKDR*, 3.1: 62.

6. The *Oxford English Dictionary* (www.oed.com), defines "ideology" as: "A systematic scheme of ideas, usually relating to politics, economics, or society and forming the basis of action or policy; a set of beliefs governing conduct." The definition in the *American Heritage Dictionary*, 4th ed., is: "A set of doctrines or beliefs that form the basis of a political, economic, or other system." *Collins English Dictionary*, 10th ed., refers to "the set of beliefs by which a group or society orders reality so as to render it intelligible." So defined, the term is applicable to a wide range of ideas or beliefs, and I use it in this sense throughout the book. Similarly, I use the word "ideologues" to refer to the church and state officials who formulated political and religious ideas in Muscovy. However, some writers prefer to restrict the terms "ideology" and "ideologue" to a more specialized sense. For further discussion on the term's applicability (or lack thereof) to Muscovy, see Ostrowski, *Muscovy and the Mongols*, 135–43.

7. See Platonov, *Ocherki*.

8. Dunning, *Russia's First Civil War*, 2.

9. See Platonov, *Ocherki*; Platonov, *Smutnoe vremia*; Platonov, *Time of Troubles*; Mirsky, *Russia*, 151; Kliuchevskii, *Sochineniia*, 3: 17; Vernadsky, *History of Russia*, 113–21; Pipes, *Russia*, 107; Ilovaiskii, *Smutnoe vremia*, [ii]; Kaiser and Marker, *Reinterpreting Russian History*, 148; Riasanovsky, *History of Russia*, 157–74; Morozov, "Smutnoe vremia," 461; Dunning, *Russia's First Civil War*; G. Luchinskii, in *Entsiklopedicheskii slovar'*, s.v. "Smutnoe vremia," 30A: 584; Hellie, *Slavery in Russia*, 3; Dmytryshyn, *Medieval Russia*, 357; Kostomarov, *Smutnoe vremia*; Zenkovsky, *Medieval Russia's Epics*, 379; Harcave, *Russia*, 53–58; Skrynnikov, *Rossiia*; Skrynnikov, *Time of Troubles*, xii, passim; Bushuev and Mironov, *Istoriia gosudarstva Rossiiskogo*, 2: 51; Rambaud, *History of Russia*, 1: 327; Spector, *Introduction to Russian History*, 50; Evtuhov et al.,

History of Russia, 147–57; Ul'ianovskii, *Smutnoe vremia.*

10. Cf. Greek *deinos* and *frikôdês.*

11. E.g., Bogatyrev, "Micro-Periodization."

12. E.g., Karamzin, *Zapiska*, 12; Karamzin, *Ancient and Modern Russia*, 112; Platonov, *Ocherki*, 3rd ed., 131–50; Platonov, *Time of Troubles*, 19–25; Bolsover, "Ivan the Terrible," 71–89; Hellie, "What Happened?" 199–224; Hunt, "Ivan," 769–809; de Madariaga, *Ivan the Terrible*, x–xi, 358, 385n.1, passim; Halperin, "Ivan IV's Insanity."

13. Platonov, *Time of Troubles*, 96. Cf. Perrie, *Pretenders*, 95–96.

14. *AAE*, 2: 286–87.

15. The basic history of the Time of Troubles may be found in numerous textbooks, encyclopedias, and monographic works, e.g., Platonov, *Ocherki*; Platonov, *Time of Troubles*; Skrynnikov, *Time of Troubles*; Dunning, *Russia's First Civil War*; Riasanovsky, *History of Russia*, 157–74; Perrie, "Time of Troubles"; Evtuhov et al., *History of Russia*, 139–57; Orchard, "Time of Troubles."

16. Kovalenskii, *Moskovskaia Smuta* (1922), 3.

17. Kliuchevskii, *Course in Russian History*, 69–94. Cf. Eskin, "Smuta," 63.

18. E.g., Nehemiah 9:27; Job 38:23; Psalms 9:9/10, 10:1, 26/27:5, 36/37:39, 40/41:1/2, 58/59:16/17; Proverbs 24:10, 25:19; Isaiah 17:14, 33:2; Jeremiah 2:27, 2:28, 8:15, 11:12, 11:14, 14:8, 14:19, 15:11, 30:7; Ezekiel 7:7; Daniel 12:1.

19. The old catalogs of the Library of Congress and Harvard University included the classification "Epoch of confusion, 1605–1613." The newer subject heading is "Time of Troubles, 1598–1613." (See http://catalog.loc.gov, http://authorities.loc.gov, http://holliscatalog.harvard.edu.)

20. See *SRIa11–17*, 25: 217–25, 311–13; Sreznevskii, *Materialy dlia slovaria*, 3: 751–54; Vasmer, *Wörterbuch*, 2: 179, 678; *STsSRIa*, 2: 697–98, 4: 333–34; A. G. Preobrazhenskii, *Etimologicheskii slovar'*, 1: 572; *Entsiklopedicheskii slovar'*, s.v. "Smuta," 30A: 581–84; P. A. Alekseev, *Tserkovnyi slovar'*, 3: 115; Gribble, *Russian Root List*, 48; D'iachenko, *Polnyi slovar'*, 1050, 1106; Gribble, *Slovarik*, 83; *AAE*, 2: 208 ("Tsarskaia gramota v Vologdu," Feb. 20, 1609).

21. Sadovskii, "Vyborka," 13–16.

22. For several examples, see: *SRIa11–17*, 25: 220.

23. E.g., *AAE*, 2: 107; *Khroniki Smutnogo vremeni*, 295; *Novaia povest'*, 191; Dunning, *Russia's First Civil War*, 481n.1; Dunning, "R. G. Skrynnikov," 72–73.

24. See Kliuchevskii, *Course in Russian History*, 12–13; Chistiakova, "Platonov," 419; Morozova, *Smuta nachala XVII v.*, 3.

25. Kotoshikhin, *O Rossii v tsarstvovanie*, 17, 20, 112–18, 305, 683, passim; Longworth, *Alexis*, 155.

26. *Istoricheskie pesni*, 35. Cf. ibid., 27–44 passim; *Byliny severa*, 2: 515–16.

27. Dunning et al., *Uncensored Boris Godunov*, 3.

28. Cf. Emerson, *Boris Godunov.*

29. Zabelin, *Minin i Pozharskii*, 23.

30. Chistiakova, "Platonov," 419.

31. Shchepkina, ["Introduction"], in Waliszewski, *Smutnoe vremia*, [vii]. Cf. Chistiakova, "Platonov," 419.

32. Kabanov, *Smuta Moskovskogo gosudarstva i Nizhnii Novgorod* [*The Troubles of the Muscovite State and Nizhnii Novgorod*] (1911); Zhukovich, *Smutnoe vremia i votsarenie Romanovykh* [*The Time of Troubles and the Accession of the Romanovs*]

(1913); Bochkarev, Got'e, and Picheta, *Smutnoe vremia v Moskovskom gosudarstve* [*The Time of Troubles in the Muscovite State*] (1913); Figes, *People's Tragedy*, 3–34; Wortman, *Scenarios of Power*, 2: 439–480, 524.

33. Got'e, *Time of Troubles: The Diary of Iurii Vladimirovich Got'e, Moscow, July 8, 1917 to July 23, 1922*; Got'e, *Smutnoe vremia: Ocherk istorii revoliutsionnykh dvizhenii nachala XVII stoletiia* [*The Time of Troubles: An Essay on the History of the Revolutionary Movements of the Beginning of the Seventeenth Century*] (Moscow, 1921); Platonov, *Boris Godunov* (Petrograd, 1921); Kostomarov, *Spasiteli Rossii v XVII v.* [*Saviors of Russia in the Seventeenth Century*] (Berlin, 1921); Kostomarov, *Tsar Mikhail Feodorovich* (Berlin, 1921); Kostomarov, *Geroi Smutnago vremeni* [*Heroes of the Time of Troubles*] (Berlin, 1922); Kovalenskii, *Moskovskaia Smuta XVII veka, ee smisl i znachenie. Istoricheskii ocherk* [*The Muscovite Troubles of the Seventeenth Century, Their Meaning and Significance: An Historical Essay*] (2nd ed., Moscow, 1922); Lokot', *Smutnoe vremia i revoliutsiia. Politicheskiia paralleli 1613–1917 g.* [*The Time of Troubles and the Revolution: Political Parallels of 1613–1917*] (Berlin, 1923); Platonov, *Smutnoe vremia* (Prague, 1924); Plotnikov, *Smuta* (Ufa, 1994); Shkliaev, *Odessa v Smutnoe vremia* [*Odessa in a Time of Troubles*] (Odessa, 2004).

34. De Villiers, *Down the Volga in a Time of Troubles: A Journey Revealing the People and Heartland of Post-Perestroika Russia* (1991); Medvedeva-Khazanova, *Rossiia: Smutnoe vremia* [*Russia: Time of Troubles*] (1994); Baev, *The Russian Army in a Time of Troubles* (1996); Bezborodko, "S Bozh'ei pomoshch'iu—cherez Smutnoe vremia" ["With God's Help—through the Time of Troubles"], *Trud* (1998); Bezborodko, "V preddverii Smuty" ["At the Threshold of the Troubles"], *Nezavisimaia gazeta* (1998); Poltorak, ed., *Smutnoe vremia: Istoriia i sovremennost'* [*The Time of Troubles: History and the Present* (conference proceedings with over forty contributors)] (2000); Zemlianoi, "Kuda idesh'? O Smute kak paradigme konservativnogo myshleniia" ["Where are You Going? On the Troubles as a Paradigm of Conservative Thought"], *Nezavisimaia Gazeta* (2001); Arustamian, *Khroniki Smutnogo vremeni* [*Chronicles of a Time of Troubles*] (2002); Vladimirov, "Strategicheskii etiud" (2002); Strygin, "Vtoraia rossiiskaia Smuta i tserkov'" ["The Second Russian Troubles and the Church"], *Bereg* (2002); Strygin, "A v nyneshnei Rossii Smutnoe vremia uzhe zakonchilos'?" ["And Has the Time of Troubles Yet Ended in Contemporary Russia?"], *Vecherniaia Moskva* (2003); Strygin, "Smutnye vremena" ["Times of Troubles"], *Russkii kur'er* (2003); Akhmedkhanov, *Smuta v moem zerkale* [*The Troubles in My Mirror*] (2003); Aver'ianov, "Smutnoe vremia i mutatsii ideologii" ["The Time of Troubles and Mutations of Ideology"] (2004); Pechenev, *"Smutnoe vremia" v noveishei istorii Rossii (1985–2003): Istoricheskoe svidetel'stvo i razmyshleniia uchastnika sobytii* [*The Time of Troubles in the Contemporary History of Russia (1985–2003): A Historical Witness and Reflection of a Participant in the Events*] (2004); Solzhenitsyn, "Pravoslavnaia tserkov' v eto Smutnoe vremia" ["The Orthodox Church in this Time of Troubles"] (2005); Hedlund, "Vladimir the Great" (2006); Perevezentsev, "Uroki Smuty: narod i vera" ["Lessons of the Troubles: People and Faith"] (2009). See also the Preface.

35. ITAR-TASS, "Sviateishii Patriarkh Aleksii II."

36. Baev, "Invented Holiday"; Baev, "Russian March."

37. E.g., Abramovich, *Kniaz'ia Shuiskie i rossiiskii tron* (1991); Kostomarov, *Smutnoe vremia Moskovskogo gosudarstva v nachale VII stoletiia: 1604–1613* (1994); Skrynnikov, *Krushenie tsarstva: Istoricheskoe povestvovanie* (1995); Fedorov, *Boris*

Godunov (1995); Ryl'nikova, ed., *Vasilii Shuiskii* (1995); Sergievskii and Zarin, *Semiboiarshchina* (fiction, 1995); Ilovaiskii, *Novaia dinastiia* (1996); Shirogorov, *Bezvremen'e: Povesti mezhdutsarstviia i smuty* (drama, 1997); Skrynnikov, *Tsar' Boris i Dmitrii Samozvanets: Illiustrirovannaia entsiklopediia* (1997); Pirling, *Dmitrii Samozvanets* (1998); Morozova, *Smuta nachala XVII v. glazami sovremennikov* (2000); Ul'ianovskii, *Smutnoe vremia* (2006); Tatishchev et al., *Velikie rossiiskie istoriki o Smutnom vremeni* (2007); Skrynnikov, *Smutnoe vremia: Krushenie tsarstva* (2007); Skrynnikov, *Minin i Pozharskii* (2007); Platonov, *Smutnoe vremia* (2007 ed.); Morozova, *Smuta na Rusi: Vybor puti* (2007); Ostrovskii, *Dmitrii Samozvanets i Vasilii Shuiskii* (2007); Tiumentsev, *Oborona Troitse-Sergieva monastyria v 1608–1610 gg.* (2008); Tiumentsev, *Smutnoe vremia v Rossii nachala XVII stoletiia: Dvizhenie Lzhedimitriia II* (2008); Berdyshev, *Smutnoe vremia* (2008); Selin, *Novgorodskoe obshchestvo v epokhu Smuty* (2008); Shokarev, *Moskva v epokhu Smuty: 1604–1613 gg.* (2009); Liseitsev, *Prikaznaia sistema Moskovskogo gosudarstva v epokhu Smuty* (2009).

38. "Kreml'"; "Iaitsa"; "Meropriiatiia"; T. Borisov, "Vzgliad."

39. Cf. Batalden, *Seeking God*; Knox, *Russian Society*; Garrard and Garrard, *Russian Orthodoxy Resurgent*; Daniel, *Orthodox Church*; Stolyarova, "You Scratcheth"; Stolyarova, "Holiest of Water"; Anderson, "Putin."

40. Tatishchev, *Istoriia rossiiskaia*, 7: 367; Shcherbatov, *Istoriia rossiiskaia*, 7.2: 147–48; Karamzin, *Istoriia gosudarstva Rossiiskago*, 11: 7–8, 78–79, 105–6, 118–20, passim, and 12: 3, 25–27, 141–43, *passim*; Karamzin, *Zapiska*, 13–19; Karamzin, *Ancient and Modern Russia*, 113–18. Tsarevich Dmitrii was canonized as a saint in 1606, after the death of both Boris Godunov and the "first false Dmitrii."

41. Vernadsky, *Russian Historiography*, 52–53.

42. Pushkin called his original 1825 drama *A Comedy about Tsar Boris and Grishka Otrepiev*. The later, revised version that became canonical included significant adjustments in its use of Karamzin's *History*. Dunning et al., *Uncensored Boris Godunov*.

43. See Keenan, "Ivan III."

44. Solov'ev, *Istoriia Rossii*, book 4, vol. 8; Kostomarov, *Smutnoe vremia*; Kliuchevskii, *Sochineniia*, 3: 16–84.

45. Platonov, *Ocherki*, 3rd ed., 536–37, passim; Platonov, *Time of Troubles*; Riasanovsky, *History of Russia*, 172. Cf. Dunning, *Russia's First Civil War*, 6, 483n.38.

46. G. Vernadsky, *Russian Historiography*, 373–74. This claim is of uncertain veracity. Cf. Pokrovsky, *History of Russia*, xvi; Chistiakova, "Platonov," 420; N. A. Smirnov, *Tserkov'*, 144.

47. Pokrovsky, *History of Russia*, 161–227.

48. I. I. Smirnov, *Vosstanie Bolotnikova*; Zimin, "Voprosy"; Zimin, *V kanun groznykh potriasenii*; Koretskii, *Formirovanie krepostnogo prava*; I. I. Smirnov et al., *Krest'ianskie voiny*; Cherepnin et al., *Krest'ianskie voiny*; Buganov, *Krest'ianskie voiny*; Alpatov, *Russkaia istoricheskaia mysl'*, 1976, vol. 9, passim; Ovchinnikov, "Ob izdanii"; Dunning, *Russia's First Civil War*, 2–5, 10–11.

49. Skrynnikov, *Time of Troubles*, viii, xiii, 305, passim; Skrynnikov, *Rossia*, 3–5; Skrynnikov, "Civil War"; Perrie, *Pretenders*, 3–5; Stanislavskii, *Grazhdanskaia voina*; Dunning, "R. G. Skrynnikov"; Eskin, "Smuta," 63; Dunning, "Byla li v Rossii"; Dunning, "Crisis, Conjuncture"; Dunning, *Russia's First Civil War*, 4, passim; Dunning; "Terror," 492. For a further summary of historiography on the Time of Troubles, see such works as Dunning, *Russia's First Civil War*, 5–11; Skrynnikov, *Time of Troubles*, viii–xiii; Morozova,

Smuta nachala XVII v., 3–5. Note that dozens of other authors have also weighed in on the Time of Troubles; the above represent only the most prominent examples.

50. Cf. Platonov, *Time of Troubles*, 96; Dunning, *Russia's First Civil War*, 222.

51. Billington, *Icon and Axe*.

52. E.g., Tatishchev, *Istoriia rossiiskaia*, 7: 367; Ilovaiskii, *Smutnoe vremia*, 216–22; Picheta, "Moskovskoe gosudarstvo," 6–7; Platonov, *Ocherki*, 3rd ed., 5–24, 449–60, 491–99; Skrynnikov, *Time of Troubles*, 10, 21–23, 33–35; Dunning, *Russia's First Civil War*, 99–100, 203–7, 213–15.

53. M. Tolstoi, *Istoriia russkoi tserkvi*, 5.

54. Makarii, *Istoriia russkoi tserkvi*; Golubinskii, *Istoriia russkoi tserkvi*; Dobroklonskii, *Rukovodstvo*; N. M. Nikol'skii, *Istoriia russkoi tserkvi*; Kartashev, *Ocherki*; Filaret, *Istoriia russkoi tserkvi*; Shubin, *History of Russian Christianity*; M. Tolstoi, *Istoriia russkoi tserkvi*; P. S. Smirnov, *Istoriia khristianskoi pravoslavnoi tserkvi*; Tal'berg, *Istoriia russkoi tserkvi*; Pospielovsky, *Orthodox Church*; Fennell, *Russian Church*; Ware, *Orthodox Church*; Petrushko, *Istoriia russkoi tserkvi*; Beliaev, *Illiustrirovannaia istoriia*; Znamenskii, *Istoriia russkoi tserkvi*. For further explication of major historiography on the Russian Orthodox Church, see Kartashev, *Ocherki*, 1: 12–39.

55. Makarii, *Istoriia russkoi tserkvi* (1996 ed.), 6 (10): 66–68, 74, 51–146, passim.

56. M. Tolstoi, *Istoriia russkoi tserkvi*, 5, 466–67, passim.

57. Bushkovitch, *Religion and Society*, 52, 128, 177, passim; N. A. Smirnov, *Tserkov'*; Baron and Kollmann, *Religion and Culture*; Kivelson and Greene, *Orthodox Russia*; Himka and Zayarnyuk, *Letters from Heaven*.

58. *SPPP*; Shchapov et al., *Tserkov'*; Ul'ianovskii, *Smutnoe vremia*; Skrynnikov, *Krest i korona*, 331–79.

59. Cf. Baron and Kollmann, *Religion and Culture*, 4–5.

60. *Opisi arkhiva*, 3. Cf. Antonov, "Iz pomestnoi praktiki," 396.

61. Based on a survey of archival and published primary sources, including RGADA, *f.* 281 (GKE), *f.* 1190 (Zlatoustov monastyr'), *f.* 1202 (Solotchinskii monastyr'), *f.* 1207 (Chudov monastyr'), *f.* 1196 (Antoniev-Siiskii monastyr'), *op.* 1–7; *Rossiiskii gosudarstvennyi arkhiv*, 1: 76–77, 81–85, 221–25 and 3.2: [all] and 4: 491, 602–41; *Putevoditel' po arkhivu*, 124–84; Antonov et al., "Materialy k katalogu"; *AFZKh*, vol. 3; *Akty Nizhegorodskago Pecherskago Vosnesenskago monastyria*, viii–xi, 1–56, 60–67, 122–23, 160–61, 240–41, 247–49, 255–56, 265–68, 320–23, 332, 343–44. For a fuller quantitative analysis of the documents, see Gruber, "Russian Orthodox Church," 37–50.

62. Efforts at producing a complete inventory of Russian historical documents are in progress. See Antonov et al., "Materialy k katalogu," and related comments in *Russkii diplomatarii*, passim.

63. Orchard, "Introduction," in Bussow, *Disturbed State*, xxix. Cf. I. I. Smirnov, "Konrad Bussov," in Bussow, *Moskovskaia khronika*, 5; Derzhavina, "K probleme."

64. See Gruber, "Russian Orthodox Church," 66–136; Keenan, "Ivan III," 242–43; R. P. Dmitrieva, "K voprosu."

65. Cf. Ginzburg, *History, Rhetoric, and Proof*; Bloch, *Historian's Craft*; Bloch, *Apologie*; Carr, *What is History?*

66. For a fuller discussion of the relevant primary sources, see Gruber, "Russian Orthodox Church," 30–166. On attempts to define or delineate the field of "Church history," see Shevzov, *Russian Orthodoxy*, 7–8.

67. Pascal, *Avvakum*, xv. Cf. Tschizewskij, *Russian Intellectual History*, 112.

68. Michels, *At War*, 2.
69. Dunning, *Russia's First Civil War*, xii.
70. Pascal, *Avvakum*, xiv.
71. See Michels, *At War*, 2–7, 12, 16, 106–20.

Chapter One

1. *AAE*, 2: 8 (No. 2).
2. Zinoviev, *Gomo sovietikus*, 132. Cf. Zinoviev, *Homo Sovieticus*, 12.
3. Raba, *Ha-t'rumah*, 92–104; Rowland, "Moscow," 604–5.
4. Dagron, *Empereur et prêtre*, 17; Dagron, *Emperor and Priest*, 1.
5. Billington, *Icon and Axe*, 61. Cf. Bennet, "Idea of Kingship," 118.
6. Ostrowski, *Muscovy and the Mongols*, 199–216. Cf. Bogatyrev, "Reinventing," 275, 282.
7. Dunning, *Russia's First Civil War*, 31. Cf., e.g., Bushkovitch, *Religion and Society*, 4; Bernshtam, "Russian Folk Culture," 35.
8. E.g., Pipes, *Russia*, 222–23, 233–34, 244–45; Freeze, "Handmaiden"; Freeze, "Orthodox Church," 361; Freeze, "Subversive Piety," 312; Tschizewskij, *Russian Intellectual History*, 105; Knox, *Russian Society*, 43–44, 202n.11; Angold, ed., *Eastern Christianity*, 351–52; Crummey, *Formation of Muscovy*, 140; Pavlov, "Tserkov[n]aia ierarkhiia," 65; Vlasov, "Christianization," 20.
9. N. M. Nikol'skii, *Istoriia russkoi tserkvi*, 118.
10. Gonneau, "L'église," 44.
11. E.g., Robson, *Solovki*, 49–53; Ostrowski, *Muscovy and the Mongols*, 201–2; M. Tolstoi, *Istoriia russkoi tserkvi*, 414–18; Skrynnikov, *Krest i korona*, 263–88.
12. Evtuhov, "Church," 497, emphasis added. Cf. Billington, *Icon and Axe*, 61; Pavlov, "Tserkov[n]aia ierarkhiia," 79.
13. Cf. Bennet, "Idea of Kingship," iii.
14. Val'denberg, *Drevnerusskiia ucheniia*, 360.
15. Cf., e.g., Filiushkin, "Religioznyi faktor," 178; Ostrowski, *Muscovy and the Mongols*, 203–4.
16. I use the term "literati" to refer to men of letters in Muscovite society—scribes, bureaucrats, ecclesiastic officials, propagandists—and to distinguish these from the mass of Russians, who could not read or write. According to the *Oxford English Dictionary* (www.oed.com), the word "literati" is first attested in English from the early seventeenth century, when Western authors hit on it as a means of distinguishing the learned class in China from the mass of the population.
17. Rowland, "Moscow," 591–92, 595, 612–14, passim; Pankhurst, "Falashas," 567–68, 573–75; Raba, *Ha-t'rumah*.
18. Cf. Raba, "Biblical Tradition," 10.
19. Romans 11, esp. verses 13–21. Cf. Romans 3:1ff.
20. Eusebius, *Life of Constantine*, 522–24. Cf. Dacy, *Separation*, 219-39.
21. E.g., Norwich, *Byzantium*, 56; Ensslin, "Government and Administration," 10; J. Meyendorff, *Byzantine Theology*, 213.
22. Norwich, *Byzantium*, 56. Cf. Flusin, "Structures," 139.
23. See Dubnow, *History of the Jews*, 1916 ed., 1: 242–61; Pereswetoff-Morath, *Grin*.

24. Eusebius, *Life of Constantine*, 525. Cf. Norwich, *Byzantium*, 54; Feissel, "L'empereur," 92; Richardson, "Prolegomena" in Eusebius, *Life of Constantine*, 436.

25. Cf. Bava Metsi'a 59b (Talmud); Midrash Tehilim 81:6 and Y. Rosh Hashana 1:3, 57b, both in Schwartz, *Tree of Souls*, 68; *Midrash on Psalms*, 57; Flusin, "Triomphe," 49–75; Feissel, "L'empereur," 81–82; Norwich, *Byzantium*, 52–56.

26. Ostrowski, *Muscovy and the Mongols*, 200–207.

27. Ostrogorsky, *History*, 30–31. See also Justinian, *Corpus juris civilis*, 7 (16): 303, 310–11, and 7 (17): 152–56; Majeska, "Byzantine Political Theory," 66; Dagron, *Emperor and Priest*, 282–312; Flusin, "Structures," 141; Ostrogorsky, *History*, 48, 75–78; Ensslin, "Government and Administration," 12; Herman, "Secular Church," 105; Hussey, *Orthodox Church*, 299–300; Crummey, *Formation of Muscovy*, 139.

28. Cf. Bernshtam, "Russian Folk Culture," 36.

29. Majeska, "Byzantine Political Theory," 66. See also Dagron, *Emperor and Priest*, 13–53; Ensslin, "Government and Administration," 6–7; Herman, "Secular Church," 104; Bennet, "Idea of Kingship," 118.

30. See, e.g., Thomson, *Reception of Byzantine Culture*, §1: 109–10, §1 addenda: 1; J. Meyendorff, "A Third Rome?," 45.

31. See "Christianization of Rus' according to the Primary Chronicle," in Kaiser and Marker, *Reinterpreting Russian History*, 63- 67.

32. Arkhipov, *Po tu storony Sambationa*, 17–54; Arkhipov, "K izucheniiu"; Noonan, "Khazar Qaghanate." Cf. Ostrowski, "Volodimir's Conversion."

33. Noonan, "Khazar Qaghanate," 89.

34. Shchapov, *State and Church*, 196. Cf. Obolensky, *Byzantine Commonwealth*, 180–201; Obolensky, *Byzantium*; Majeska, "Byzantine Influence," 74–80; Majeska, "Byzantine-Russian Relations," 80–86.

35. See, e.g., Crummey, *Formation of Muscovy*, 132–33.

36. Franklin, *Sermons*, cii, 13. Cf. Ilarion, *Slovo Ilariona*, 87; Lezik, "Slovo," 85–102.

37. J. Martin, *Medieval Russia*, 87–88.

38. Crummey, *Formation of Muscovy*, 116, emphasis added.

39. Halperin, *Tatar Yoke*, 169.

40. E.g., ibid., 25; Halperin, "Russia in the Mongol Empire," 258; Halperin, *Russia and the Golden Horde*, 106, 129; Ostrowski, *Muscovy and the Mongols*, 121–22, 131, 144, 163, 186, 199, 215, 225; Crummey, *Formation of Muscovy*, 117.

41. Halperin, *Tatar Yoke*, 62–63, 167–76, passim; Halperin, *Russia and the Golden Horde*, 5–8, 19–20, 61, 74, 106–8, 118, 127, 131, 163, passim.

42. Ostrowski, *Muscovy and the Mongols*, 146–48.

43. Goldfrank, private correspondence, August 2010; Goldfrank, in Evtuhov et al., *History of Russia*, 72.

44. Ostrowski, *Muscovy and the Mongols*, 144.

45. E.g., Halperin, *Tatar Yoke*, 71–75; Budnovits, *Obshchestvenno-politicheskaia mysl'*, 334; Mil'kov, *Osmyslenie istorii*, 1st ed., 32–43, 75–89, passim; 2nd ed., 50–61, 92ff., 158–59, passim.

46. Crummey, *Formation of Muscovy*, 133; D. B. Miller, "Velikie Minei Chetii," 273, 282, 365; Haney, "Moscow," 355.

47. Pelenski, "Sack of Kiev," 316. Cf. Bogatyrev, "Reinventing," 289–90.

48. Pelenski, "Muscovite Ecclesiastical Claims," 103, 109–12; Franklin,

Byzantium—Rus—Russia, §17: 192; Fennell, *Emergence of Moscow*, 110, passim; Crummey, *Formation of Muscovy*, 132–33; Lincoln, *Conquest of a Continent*, 23; Ostrowski, "Why Did the Metropolitan?"; Ostrowski, *Muscovy and the Mongols*, 168–71; Halperin, "National Identity."

49. E.g., D'iakonov, *Vlast'*, 54–90; Crummey, *Formation of Muscovy*, 133, 136–37; Halperin, *Tatar Yoke*, 175; Duncan, *Russian Messianism*, 11–12; Hosking, *Russia*, 5–6; Ensslin, "Government and Administration," 2; J. Meyendorff, "A Third Rome?," 47–49; Swoboda, "Obraz," 386; Filiushkin, "Religioznyi faktor," 145; Ostrowski, *Muscovy and the Mongols*, 164–65, 176–77, 226.

50. The *Oxford English Dictionary* (www.oed.com) defines "messianism" (def. 2) as "the belief that one's nation is to serve a redemptive role in the history of mankind."

51. Ostrowski, *Muscovy and the Mongols*, 164–98, passim.

52. Crummey, *Formation of Muscovy*, 134; Ostrowski, *Muscovy and the Mongols*, 177. Cf. Duncan, *Russian Messianism*.

53. Crummey, *Formation of Muscovy*, 135; Kartashev, *Ocherki*, 1: 389.

54. Alef, "Adoption," 3.

55. Volotskii, *Prosvetitel'*, 287–88, 488, 546–51, passim; Volotskii, *Poslaniia*, 175–79, 186, 229–32, passim; Majeska, "Moscow Coronation"; Ostrowski, *Muscovy and the Mongols*, 17, 25–26, 176–82; Raeff, "Early Theorist," 77–89; Lur'e, "Iosif Volotskii," 29, 69; Szeftel, "Joseph Volotsky's Political Ideas," 19–20; Goldfrank, in Volotskii, *Monastic Rule*, 29; Rowland, "Muscovite Literary Ideology,"125–55; Pliguzov, "O khronologii," 1051; Fennell, "Attitude of the Josephians," 488–503; Crummey, *Formation of Muscovy*, 136; Bennet, "Idea of Kingship," 71–73; Dykstra, *Russian Monastic Culture*, 195ff.; Bogatyrev, "Reinventing," 271, 274–75, 283–87.

56. E.g., Budovnits, *Russkaia publitsistika*, 167–87; Zernov, *Moscow the Third Rome*; Tschizewskij, *Russian Intellectual History*, 92–93; D'iakonov, *Vlast'*, 66ff.; Duncan, *Russian Messianism*, 10–11; Goldfrank, "Moscow"; J. Meyendorff, "A Third Rome?"; Gol'dberg, "Istoriko-politicheskie idei," 61–62, 68–77.

57. Bushkovitch, "National Consciousness," 358–61; Crummey, *Formation of Muscovy*, 137; Swoboda, "Obraz," 387.

58. Ostrowski, "'Moscow the Third Rome"; Ostrowski, *Muscovy and the Mongols*, 218–43. Note, however, that the idea of "Moscow as the Third Rome" continues to enjoy some popularity even today. (See the Russian website http://3rm.info.)

59. Rowland, "Moscow," 591–95, 613–14. Cf. *SGGD*, 2: 97; Bushkovitch, "National Consciousness," 356, 358–63; Raba, "Biblical Tradition"; Ostrowski, *Muscovy and the Mongols*, 176n.54, 218–43; Ostrowski, "Moscow the Third Rome"; Strémooukhoff, "Moscow the Third Rome," 84–101; Toumanoff, "Moscow the Third Rome," 411–47; Majeska, "Moscow Coronation," 353–61; Dunning, *Russia's First Civil War*, 32; Sinitsyna, *Tretii Rim*; Ul'ianovskii, *Rossiiskie samozvantsy*, 248.

60. *AI*, 1: 291–92 (No. 160), quoted in Filiushkin, "Religioznyi faktor," 151; Riha, *Russian Civilization*, 1: 87; Ostrowski, *Muscovy and the Mongols*, 204; Rowland, "Moscow," 595–97, 612, passim; Duncan, *Russian Messianism*, 15; Levin, "Spor"; Raba, *Ha-t'rumah*, 62–91, 142–57, passim.

61. *PSRL*, 8: 207–13, quoted in Ostrowski, *Muscovy and the Mongols*, 164–65.

62. Trubetskoi, "Staryi i Novyi natsional'nyi messianizm," *Russkaia mysl'* (1912), quoted in Valentinov, "O russkom messianizme," 256–7. Cf. Duncan, *Russian Messianism*, 15.

63. John 4, esp. vv. 19–22.

64. D. B. Miller, "Velikie Minei Chetii," 270, 364–65, passim; Majeska, "Byzantine Political Theory," 68; Howes, *Testaments*, 109; M. Tolstoi, *Istoriia russkoi tserkvi*, 387; Halperin, *Tatar Yoke*, 172–76; Budovnits, *Russkaia publitsistika*, 188–207; Bogatyrev, "Reinventing," 272.

65. E.g., Majeska, "Byzantine Political Theory," 68; Crummey, *Formation of Muscovy*, xiii, Plates 15–16 (between pp. 192–93); Lepakhin, "Voinstvo"; Filiushkin, "Religioznyi faktor," 151–61.

66. E.g., Haney, "Moscow," 354–67; Gol'dberg, "Istoriko-politicheskie idei," 61; Bogatyrev, "Reinventing," 289–90.

67. Pelenski, *Russia and Kazan*, 7, 111–17, 122–23, 139–73, 199–201; Ostrowski, *Muscovy and the Mongols*, 164–65; D. B. Miller, "Velikie Minei Chetii," 270, 364–365.

68. *PSRL*, 14.1: 4–6; Elassonskii, "Opisanie puteshestviia"; Gudziak, *Crisis and Reform*, 168–87; Uspenskii, *Tsar' i patriarch*, 495–517; Jensen, *Musical Cultures*, 1–3; Pavlov, "Tserkov[n]aia ierarkhiia," 66–67.

69. Halperin, *Tatar Yoke*, 175. Cf. Vernadsky, *Tsardom of Moscow*, 1: 192.

70. See Guri, "Bibleizmy," 40; Raba, "Biblical Tradition"; Gruber, "Hebrew Concepts"; Kulik, *Retroverting Slavonic Pseudepigrapha*.

71. Bulanin, "O nekotorykh printsipakh," 6. Cf. Swoboda, "Tradition Reinvented," 175–78.

72. Rowland, "Muscovite Political Attitudes," 116–17. Cf. Raba, "Biblical Tradition"; other works listed in Rowland, "Moscow," 595n.11.

73. *RIB*, 13: 8. See also Jeremiah 25:13–14 (the latter verse is absent from the Septuagint).

74. *RIB*, 13: 11.

75. Ibid., 13: 3.

76. Ibid., 13: 6. See also Matthew 10:4; Mark 3:19; Luke 6:16; John 6:70–71, 12:4.

77. Makarii, *Istoriia russkoi tserkvi*, 1996 ed., 6 (10): 64.

78. Cf. Ginzberg, *Legends of the Jews*, 1: 113; *Penitence of Adam*, 22.2.1–23.3.3; Bonwetsch, "Christliche Litteratur," 913.

79. *Zhitie i podvigi*, 10–14; Crummey, *Formation of Muscovy*, 120.

80. *RIB*, 13: 562. Cf. *RIB*, 13: 629–30.

81. Ibid., 13: 11. Cf. Raba, "Biblical Tradition."

82. *RIB*, 13: 200. Cf. *Novaia povest'*, 197–98.

83. "Molitva," in "Povest' o nekoei brani, nalezhashchei na blagochestivuiu Rossiiu," in *RIB*, 13: 257–60. The word "womb" (*utroba*) was used here in the sense of "insides" or "guts" (heart, stomach, womb, intestines, etc.) compelling emotion and action. The apparent connection between Biblical-Hebrew *rekhem* ("womb") and *rakhamim* ("mercies") was reflected in Slavonic (via Greek) and probably contributed to the type of usage illustrated in the quotation. See Sreznevskii, *Materialy dlia slovaria*, 3: 1315.

84. Ilarion, *Slovo Ilariona*, 78; Franklin, *Sermons*, 3.

85. Kliuchevskii, quoted in Valentinov, "O russkom messianizme," 257.

86. Volotskii, *Monastic Rule*, 241.

87. *AAE*, 2: 286–87. (See chap. 6.)

88. E.g., *AAE*, 2: 78, 100, 277, passim; *RIB*, 13: 181–82, 227, 561, 1182, 1251, passim; "Gramoty preosveshchennogo Filareta," in Kukushkina, "Neizvestnoe 'pisanie,'" 198; *Istoricheskie pesni*, 35; *Pamiatniki Smutnogo vremeni*, 434; Timofeev, *Vremennik*,

14; Massa, *Present Wars in Moscow*, 57, 149; Bussow, *Disturbed State*, 168; Platonov, *Drevnerusskiia skazaniia*, 1888 ed., 350, passim; Swoboda, "Tradition Reinvented," 110; Swoboda, "Obraz," 386; Morozova, *Smuta nachala XVII v.*, 12–13; Dunning, "L. E. Morozova," 237; Dunning, *Russia's First Civil War*, 27, 65, passim; Billington, *Icon and Axe*, 123; M. Tolstoi, *Istoriia russkoi tserkvi*, 483; Pascal, *Avvakum*, 4; Bennet, "Idea of Kingship," 123, 136, passim; Perevezentsev, "Uroki smuty."

89. Psalms of Solomon 17:5/6.

90. See, e.g., Genesis 14; Deuteronomy 20; Joshua 7–8; Judges 2, 3, 6, 10, 13, 20, passim; 1 Samuel 4, 14, 17; 2 Samuel 23; Ezekiel 13:5; Psalms 24:8, 140:7; Proverbs 21:31; 2 Chronicles 20.

91. See, e.g., Psalms of Solomon, 17:25. Cf. Isaiah 52:1.

92. *AAE*, 2: 8 (No. 2). Cf. Iyov's *Life of Fyodor*, in *PSRL*, 14.1: 1–22; Bennet, "Idea of Kingship," 64.

93. Avvakum, *Zhitie*; Avvakum, *Life*; Vinogradov, *O iazyke*, 13, 18, passim.

94. Rowland, "Moscow," 595–612.

95. Gruber, "Hebrew Concepts"; A. A. Alekseev, *Tekstologiia slavianskoi Biblii*; 182–84; Pichkhadze, "K istorii"; Kovtun, *Leksikografiia*; Kovtun, *Russkaia leksikografiia*; Kovtun, *Azbukovniki*; Tseitlin, *Kratkii ocherk*; Raba, *Ha-t'rumah*, 173.

96. Cf. Bennet, "Idea of Kingship," 1–2.

97. E.g., Exodus 28:41, 29:7, 29:21, 29:29, 30:30, 40:12–15; Leviticus 4:3, 4:5, 4:16, 6:20, 6:22, 7:36, 8:12, 8:30, 10:7, 16:32, 21:10–12, Numbers 3:3, 35:25; Judges 9:8, 9:15; 1 Samuel 2:10, 2:35, 9:16, 10:1, 12:3, 12:5, 15:1, 15:17, 16:3, 16:6, 16:12–13, 24:6, 24:10, 26:9, 26:11, 26:16, 26:23, 31:4; 2 Samuel 1:14, 1:16, 2:4, 2:7, 3:39, 5:3, 5:17, 12:7, 19:10, 19:21, 22:51, 23:1; 1 Kings 1:34, 1:39, 1:45, 5:1, 19:15–16; 2 Kings 9:3, 9:6, 9:12, 11:12, 23:30; Isaiah 45:1; Psalms 2:2, 18:50, 20:6, 104/105:15; 1 Chronicles 11:3, 14:8, 16:22, 29:22; 2 Chronicles 6:42, 22:7, 23:11.

98. Bogatyrev, "Reinventing," 272.

99. *SGGD*, 2: 299.

100. Cf., e.g., "Christianization of Rus'," in Kaiser and Marker, *Reinterpreting Russian History*, 65; Haney, "Moscow," 354–67.

101. Majeska, "Byzantine Political Theory," 66. Cf. Dagron, *Emperor and Priest*, 13–53; Ensslin, "Government and Administration," 6–7; Herman, "Secular Church," 104.

102. Majeska, "Byzantine Political Theory," 66.

103. McCormick, "Political Structure," 1693.

104. See Kollmann, *Kinship and Politics*.

105. Neville, *Byzantine Provincial Society*, 44.

106. Majeska, "Byzantine Political Theory," 66. Cf. McCormick, "Legitimacy, Political," 1203.

107. *Letopisets ellinskii*, 386–92, 464–69; *PSRL*, 22.1:300–306, 349–53, and 22.2:115–21, 147–55; *AAE*, 2:16. Cf. Thomson, *Reception of Byzantine Culture*, §1: 114.

108. Gonneau, "L'église," 26–30.

109. Flusin, "Structures," 138, emphasis added.

110. Volotskii, *Prosvetitel'*, 287, 547–49. Cf. Raeff, "Early Theorist," 83–89; Szeftel, "Joseph Volotsky's Political Ideas," 19–29; Rowland, "Muscovite Literary Ideology," 125–55; Kivelson, "Devil Stole His Mind," 736, 745–48, 755; Goldfrank, "Deep Origins," 341–54; Goldfrank, "Recentering Nil Sorskii," 374; Dunning, *Russia's First Civil War*, 107–8, 114–17, 202, 236, 259; Ostrowski, *Muscovy and the Mongols*,

204–6; Bennet, "Idea of Kingship," 104–19; Dykstra, *Russian Monastic Culture*, 26–27; Swoboda, "Obraz," 387–408.

111. *Annotated Justinian Code*, 1.1; Herman, "Secular Church," 104; Flusin, "Structures," 141; Flusin, "Triomphe," 49–75; Feissel, "L'empereur," 81–82; Norwich, *Byzantium*, 52–56.

112. Dunning, *Russia's First Civil War*, 199.

113. Ibid., 207. Cf. Massa, *Present Wars in Moscow*, 125.

114. McCormick, "Legitimacy, Political," 1203; Neville, *Byzantine Provincial Society*, 44.

115. E.g., *PSRL*, 14.1: 1-22; Ostrogorsky, *History*, 31, 69; Norwich, *Byzantium*, 38–41, 51, 205–27; Morrisson, "Les événements," 6; Wolff, "Influence of Constantine." (See also chap. 3.)

116. Ensslin, "Government and Administration," 3, 7–10, 14; Hussey and Hart, "Byzantine Theological Speculation," 185; Ostrogorsky, *History*, 27, 31, 46–48; Majeska, "Byzantine Political Theory," 67; McCormick, "Legitimacy, Political," 1203; Feissel, "L'empereur," 88–89, 92; Medvedev, "Politicheskaia ideologiia Vizantii," 159; Flusin, "Structures," 138–40; Dagron, *Emperor*, 3–4, 54–83, 127–57, passim; Magoulias, *Byzantine Christianity*, 1–16; Abaecherli, "Imperial Cult"; Herman, "Secular Church," 104; Hussey, *Orthodox Church*, 300–302; Bogatyrev, "Reinventing," 275; Duncan, *Russian Messianism*, 12; Uspenskii, *Tsar' i patriarkh*, 114–35.

117. McCormick, "Legitimacy, Political," 1203. Cf. Ensslin, "Government and Administration," 3; E. P. Miller, *Politics of Imitating Christ*; Remensnyder, *Remembering Kings Past*, 171, 171n.88; Reuter, *Medieval Polities*, 98, 98n.22; Maguire, *Byzantine Court Culture*, 103ff.

118. E.g., *RIB*, 13, 227; Bogatyrev, "Reinventing," 275, 282; Ostrowski, *Muscovy and the Mongols*, 218.

119. Makarii, *Istoriia russkoi tserkvi*, 1996 ed., 6 (10): 53–55. Cf. Bennet, "Idea of Kingship," 98.

120. Fletcher, *Of the Rus Commonwealth*, 115–17, 121. Cf. Margeret, *Russian Empire*, 21–22; M. Tolstoi, *Istoriia russkoi tserkvi*, 314; Crummey, *Formation of Muscovy*, 119.

121. Fletcher, *English Works*, 260.

122. Margeret, *Russian Empire*, 21–22.

123. Ibid., 29.

124. Massa, *Present Wars in Moscow*, 70–71.

125. Crummey, *Formation of Muscovy*, 138.

126. Billington, *Icon and Axe*, 123–24. See Isaiah 10, 52, 53; Daniel 9, 11, 12. Unfortunately, Billington gives no specific source for this claim. It seems to be an inference based on his general reading of the chronicles and accounts of the period. The main pro of an "interpretive history" such as his is the inclusion of numerous stimulating insights and proposals; the corresponding con may well be the occasional absence of specific corroboration.

Chapter Two

1. National Archives of the United Kingdom (Kew), Public Record Office, State Papers Foreign 91 [Russia], part 1, folio 250–250v, as transcribed in Dunning, "Richest Place," 309–25. Cf. Robson, *Solovki*, 64–65. Dunning believes the author to be Sir Fulke Conway.

2. Dostoevskii, *Polnoe sobranie*, 14: 10; Dostoyevsky, *Brothers Karamazov*, trans. MacAndrew, 12.

3. For the data underlying this conversion estimate, see Gruber, "Russian Orthodox Church," 607–42; and an article in progress, "Estimating the Value of the Ruble in the Early Seventeenth Century: A New Method."

4. Matthew 6:24; Luke 16:13.

5. Smolich, *Russkoe monashestvo*, 61–72. See also, e.g., Budovnits, *Russkaia publitsistika*, 66–109, 147ff., passim; Dykstra, *Russian Monastic Culture*, 11–13; T. A. Smith, *Volokolamsk Paterikon*, 7–8.

6. Ludo Milos, quoted in Dykstra, *Russian Monastic Culture*, 161; Ostrowski, "Church Polemics"; Goldfrank, "Recentering Nil Sorskii"; Sorskii, *Nil Sorsky*, xi–xii, 31–32, 36, 310n.1, passim; Dykstra, *Russian Monastic Culture*, 15–16, 19–20, 22–24, 155–93, 230–32, passim; M. Tolstoi, *Istoriia russkoi tserkvi*, 315.

7. Russian Orthodoxy has long been viewed as "ritualistic" as opposed to "theological." However, Dykstra argues that monks of the Iosifo-Volokolamsk Monastery "were for the most part not very 'ritualist' in the sense of valuing forms over substance." Dykstra, *Russian Monastic Culture*, 15, 227, passim. See also Thomson, *Reception of Byzantine Culture*, [Intro:] xvii/9, and §6 addenda: 4. The reader may wish to consult overviews of Eastern Orthodox Christianity such as Ware, *Orthodox Church*; French, *Eastern Orthodox Church*; Fairbairn, *Eastern Orthodoxy*; Robert, *Through Western Eyes*.

8. Fletcher, *English Works*, 273.

9. Pascal, *Avvakum*, 2; Crummey, *Formation of Muscovy*, 121; Tiumentsev, "Osada"; Dykstra, *Russian Monastic Culture*, 23–24, 24n.43; I. G. Alekseev, *Agrarnaia istoriia*, 94–96. Cf. Dykstra, *Russian Monastic Culture*, 23–24; D. B. Miller, *Saint Sergius*, 123, 235–39.

10. Picheta, "Moskovskoe gosudarstvo," 18–19.

11. Platonov, *Ocherki*, 5th ed., 9ff.; Savich, *Solovetskaia votchina*; Robson, *Solovki*, 56–61, 68–69; Kliuchevskii, "Khoziaistvennaia deiatel'nost' Solovetskogo monastyria v Belomorskom krae," in his *Sochineniia*, 7: 32.

12. Smolich, *Russkoe monashestvo*, 133.

13. See, e.g., Sinitsyna, "Tipy monastyrei," 116–49; Kliuchevskii, *Kurs russkoi istorii*, 301–55; Kliuchevsky, *History of Russia*, 149–96.

14. Hussey, "Byzantine Monasticism," 182; Constantelos, "Social Services," 1167–69; Sinitsyna, "Tipy monastyrei," 134; N. M. Nikol'skii, *Istoriia russkoi tserkvi*, 120; Romanenko, *Povsednevnaia zhizn'*, 292–300; Sorskii, *Nil Sorsky*, 97. See also Isaiah 58:6–14; Zechariah 7:10; Matthew 19:21, 25:31–46; Mark 10:21; Luke 12:33–34, 14:13–14, 18:22; Galatians 2:10; James [Jacob] 2:6; Rubenson, "Origins"; Derwich, "Origins"; Jorgenson, "Orthodox Monasticism"; Prokurat, "Orthodox Monasticism"; Krawchuk, "Russia"; Alfeyev, "Russia"; Warneke, "Social Services."

15. 1 Timothy 6:9–10 (*New American Standard Bible*, 1977, slightly modified).

16. Zarubina, "Pravoslavnyi predprinimatel'," 100.

17. Bennet, "Idea of Kingship," 111n.93.

18. Cf. I. G. Alekseev, *Agrarnaia istoriia*, 95.

19. Sorskii, *Nil Sorsky*, 97; T. A. Smith, *Volokolamsk Paterikon*, 7–8; Dykstra, *Russian Monastic Culture*, 12, 12n.16, 23–24, 27, 220–26; N. K. Nikol'skii, *Kirillo-Belozerskii monastyr'*, 1.1 (1897 ed.), 218–19, 256; Goldfrank, "Dykstra," 173; Platonov, *Ocherki*, 5th ed., 338. (See also chap. 4.)

20. Dykstra, *Russian Monastic Culture*, 221–23.

21. Ibid., 223–25, emphasis in original.

22. Ibid., 15, 163, 180, 185, 229–30, emphasis in original.

23. E.g., *AI*, 2: 140; D. B. Miller, *Saint Sergius*, 166.

24. Goldfrank, "Dykstra," 173–74.

25. Platonov, *Ocherki*, 3rd ed., 9; Platonov, *Ocherki*, 5th ed., 11. See also Kliuchevskii, "Khoziaistvennaia deiatel'nost' Solovetskogo monastyria v Belomorskom krae," in his *Pravoslavie*, 462–88, or in his *Sochineniia*, 7: 5–32; D. B. Miller, *Saint Sergius*, 235–39.

26. Dykstra, *Russian Monastic Culture*, 37.

27. See the documents cited in chaps. 3–5 and, e.g., Schmähling, "Vom Nutzen der Klausur," 467ff.; D. B. Miller, *Saint Sergius*, 123, 218, 235–39, passim.

28. Cf. Kolycheva, "Pravoslavnye monastyri," 84–89; Picheta, "Moskovskoe gosudarstvo," 22; Robson, *Solovki*, 31; Dykstra, *Russian Monastic Culture*, 224, 232.

29. Hellie, *Economy and Material Culture*, 499, 503; Steindorff, "Donations and Commemoration," 482; R. Martin, "Gifts and Commemoration"; D. B. Miller, *Saint Sergius*, 105–37, 148, 154, 229–35, 247–50, passim.

30. Pavlov, "Tserkov[n]aia ierarkhiia," 74–76. Cf. Tikhomirov and Floria, "Prikhodo-raskhodnye knigi," 331.

31. D. B. Miller, *Saint Sergius*, 218, 235, 239. Cf. Savich, *Solovetskaia votchina*.

32. Thyrêt, "Economic Reconstruction?"

33. Prokhorov, *Nekogda ne narod*, 205–14; Goldfrank, "Nil Sorskii's Following." Cf. Romanchuk, *Byzantine Hermeneutics*.

34. See Gruber, "Russian Orthodox Church," 589–92.

35. See the numerous published collections of archival documents listed in the bibliography and, e.g., RGADA, *f.* 1201 (Solovetskii monastyr'), *op.* 1, *ed. khr.* 7–11; RGADA, *f.* 281 (*GKE*), *op.* 5, No. 8011/70 ("Zhalovannaia gramota tsaria Dmitriia Ivanovicha," Sept. 3, 1605, incorrectly listed in the archival *opis'* as "Gramota Velikago Vasil'ia Ivanovicha," for which see No. 8013); RGADA, *f.* 281 (*GKE*), *op.* 5, No. 8466/25 ("Zhalovannaia gramota tsaria Vasiliia Ivanovicha igumnu Solovetskago monastyria Antoniiu s bratieiu," Jan. 25, 1607); *AMMS*, 387–88 (No. 145); Kliuchevskii, "Khoziaistvennaia deiatel'nost' Solovetskogo monastyria v Belomorskom krae," in his *Sochineniia*, 7: 32.

36. E.g., Kliuchevskii, "O zemel'nykh vladeniiakh vserossiiskikh mitropolitov, patriarkhov i sv. sinoda (988–1738 gg.)," in his *Pravoslavie*, 489–519; Kapterev, *Svetskie arkhiereiskie chinovniki*, 26–30.

37. RGADA, *f.* 1201, *op.* 1, *ed. khr.*7 ("Books of the Volodga Service of the Solovetskii Monastery," Muscovite years 7107–7108), *l.* 43*ob.*, transcribed in Gruber, "Russian Orthodox Church," 647–49. Cf., e.g., RGADA, *f.* 1201, *op.* 1, *ed. khr.* 9, *ll.* 165*ob.*–166; RGADA, *f.* 1201, *op.* 1, *ed. khr.* 11, *l.* 119*ob.*

38. RGADA, *f.* 1201, *op.* 1, *ed. khr.* 11 ("Books of the Volodga Service of the Solovetskii Monastery," Muscovite years 7115–7117), *ll.* 2–119, transcribed in Gruber, "Russian Orthodox Church," 647–53. Cf., e.g., RGADA, *f.* 1201, *op.* 1, *ed. khr.* 7, *ll.* 1–43; RGADA, *f.* 1201, *op.* 1, *ed. khr.* 10, *ll.* 1–57; RGADA, *f.* 1201, *op.* 1, *ed. khr.* 12, *ll.* 1–109.

39. Dykstra, *Russian Monastic Culture*, 30–34, 181–82.

40. RGADA, *f.* 1201 (Solovetskii monastyr'), *op.* 1, *ed. khr.* 7–11; Savich, *Solovetskaia votchina*, 93–169; Bushkovitch, *Merchants of Moscow*, 131–32; Gruber,

"Russian Orthodox Church," 248–67; Gruber, "Black Monks."

41. Kolycheva, "Pravoslavnye monastyri," 103. Cf. Romanenko, *Povsednevnaia zhizn'*, 61–65, passim.

42. Hellie, *Economy and Material Culture*, 498–512; Dykstra, *Russian Monastic Culture,* 182; Steindorff, "Donations and Commemoration"; Steindorff, *Memoria in Altrussland;* D. B. Miller, *Saint Sergius*, 105–17, 125–34, 226–31, passim.

43. Cf. *ASZ*; Antonov et al., *Materialy k katalogu*, parts 5, 8; *Khoziaistvo krupnogo feodala-krepostnika*; Antonov, "Akty sluzhilykh tatar"; Gruber, "Russian Orthodox Church," 50–56; and numerous published collections of documents listed in the bibliography.

44. Dykstra, *Russian Monastic Culture*, 220, 224.

45. Ibid., 230, 232.

46. Cf. D. B. Miller, *Saint Sergius*, 158.

47. "The realities of land ownership transformed the character of the institution itself. Ultimately what we see throughout the sixteenth century is not so much a monastery that happens to own land, but rather a landowner that happens to be constituted as a religious community." Dykstra, *Russian Monastic Culture*, 231.

48. See, e.g., ibid., 230–32.

49. Cf. ibid., 229; D. B. Miller, *Saint Sergius*, 142–46; "Antonii Siiskii."

50. Cf. Romanenko, *Povsednevnaia zhizn'*, 14–16; Romanenko, *Nil Sorskii*, 134–35; Robson, *Solovki*, 28.

51. See Dykstra, *Russian Monastic Culture*, 28; Picheta, "Moskovskoe gosudarstvo," 6–7.

52. E.g., Zverinskii, *Material dlia issledovaniia*, vol. 2 passim; Makarii, *Istoriia russkoi tserkvi*, 1996 ed., 6 (10): 745–51. See also below.

53. Zverinskii, *Material dlia issledovaniia*, 2: Nos. 657, 843, 844, 884, 969, 1143, 1167, 1169, 1184, 1193, 1242, 1299, etc.; *Zhitiia sviatykh*, 10: 89–97, 11: 125–33; M. Tolstoi, *Istoriia russkoi tserkvi*, 388–92, 467; Romaniello, "Mission Delayed"; Romaniello, "Profit Motive"; Romaniello, "Controlling the Frontier."

54. Armstrong, "Foreigners, Furs, and Faith" 146–57.

55. "Natsional'nyi arkhiv Respubliki Buriatiia, f. 316, Pokrovskaia Novo-Udinskaia tserkov'," in *Istoriia Russkoi pravoslavnoi tserkvi*, 16.

56. Avvakum, *Zhitie;* Avvakum, *Life*.

57. Zverinskii, *Material dlia issledovaniia*, 2: Nos. 646, 699, 1101, 1203. Cf. Andreev, *Stroganovy*, 158–91; Longworth, *Cossacks*, chap. 2; Skrynnikov, *Sibirskaia ekspeditsiia;* Lincoln, *Conquest of a Continent*, 41–47; Khodarkovsky, "Non-Christian Peoples," 317ff.

58. *AI*, 2: 59 (No. 48).

59. RGADA, *f.* 1111 (Verkhoturskaia Prikaznaia izba), *op.* 1.3, *ed. khr.* 111 ("Otpiska Neudachi Pleshcheeva ob otpuske emu s Verkhotur'ia denezhnykh i khlebnykh zapasov dlia uplaty zhalovaniia sluzhilym liudiam Tobol'ska, Tiumeni i drugikh sibirskikh gorodov i ob otpuske tserkovnogo imushchestva v ukazannye goroda," 1604–1605). Cf. *AI*, 2: 110–11 (No. 81, "Tsarskaia gramota, v Perm Velikuiu, kniaziu Viazemskomu, ob otpravlenii v Verkhotur'e tserkovnoi utvari, sudovykh snastei i zemledel'cheskikh orudii," June 23, 1607).

60. RGADA, *Ustiuzhskii*, ii, passim; Armstrong, "Foreigners, Furs, and Faith," 147–48; Tiumentsev, "Gosudarstvo i tserkov'," 146; *Zhitiia sviatykh*, 4: 431–46; Likhachev, *Chelovek*, 73–80.

61. According to my comprehensive survey of the data in Zverinskii, *Material dlia issledovaniia.* See especially vol. 2: Nos. 692, 699, 704, 706, 709, 720, 721, 734, 735, 761, 763, 772, 778, 793, 843, 858, 884, 888, 917, 923, 944, 949, 951, 974, 989, 1009, 1029, 1040, 1057, 1058, 1078, 1001, 1094, 1131, 1143, 1152, 1167, 1180, 1199, 1200, 1215, 1223, 1224, 1228, 1232, 1235, 1236, 1242, 1249, 1250, 1258, 1267. Cf. Shveikovskaia, "Traditsionalizm," 165–85.

62. Dunning, *Russia's First Civil War*, 84. Cf. Khodarkovsky, *Russia's Steppe Frontier;* Sunderland, *Taming the Wild Field;* Khodarkovsky, "Non-Christian Peoples," 319ff.

63. See Dunning, *Russia's First Civil War*, 73–108; Platonov, *Time of Troubles*, 33–39; Riasanovsky, *History of Russia*, 6th ed., 159–60; Bochkarev et al., *Smutnoe vremia*, 21–22, 31–32, 41, passim. On the nature of frontier zones in general, see McNeill, *Europe's Steppe Frontier;* Rothenberg, *Austrian Military Border;* Setton, *Venice.*

64. Zverinskii, *Material dlia issledovaniia*, 2: No. 1275; *PMR*, 17; Ratshin, *Polnoe sobranie*, 18; Dubakov, "Obrazovanie," 149, 151, 155–58; Bennet, "Idea of Kingship," 101; Pavlov, "Tserkov[n]aia ierarkhiia," 66; Schmähling, "Vom Nutzen der Klausur"; Steindorff, *Religion und Integration*, passim.

65. Dubakov, "Obrazovanie," 156–57.

66. This cloister was razed by Tatars in 1611 and 1630. Zverinskii, *Material dlia issledovaniia*, 2: No. 883; *MES*, 152.

67. *PMR*, 77. Cf. Zverinskii, *Material dlia issledovaniia*, 2: No. 810; Ratshin, *Polnoe sobranie*, 160.

68. Zverinskii, *Material dlia issledovaniia*, 2: Nos. 765, 934, 978, 1098, 1123, 1243, etc.

69. Ibid., 2: No. 933.

70. Dunning, *Russia's First Civil War*, 76, 83–86.

71. *Zhitiia sviatykh*, 10: 89–97, 11: 125–33; Makarii, *Istoriia russkoi tserkvi*, 1996 ed., 6 (10): 56, 111; M. Tolstoi, *Istoriia russkoi tserkvi*, 388–92, 467; Romaniello, "Mission Delayed."

72. This was the Troitskii Kondinskii or Troitskii Kodinskii Monastery. Zverinskii, *Material dlia issledovaniia*, 2: No. 1269. Cf. *RIB*, 2: 152, 172 (Nos. 68, 79).

73. E.g., Zverinskii, *Material dlia issledovaniia*, 2: Nos. 651, 1099, 1218. In contemporary Russian surveys and censuses the Mordva represented a distinct category of person, separate from ordinary "peasants," "poor peasants," and other social groups. See "Vypis' s pistsovykh," 51–52; *Entsiklopedicheskii slovar'*, 19A: 838–39.

74. Mirsky, *Russia*, 156–57. Cf. Bennet, "Idea of Kingship," 101–4.

75. Sunderland, *Taming the Wild Field*, 21–22.

76. See Naidenova, "Vnutrenniaia zhizn'," 285–301; Romanenko, *Povsednevnaia zhizn';* D. B. Miller, *Saint Sergius*, 138ff.

77. Zverinskii, *Material dlia issledovaniia*, 2: No. 1235.

78. Cf. Robson, *Solovki*, 64.

79. Dubakov, "Obrazovanie," 165.

80. Ibid., 156–57.

81. Ibid., 149.

82. Zverinskii, *Material dlia issledovaniia*, 2: Nos. 735, 989, passim; Budovnits, *Monastyri na Rusi;* A. M. Borisov, *Khoziaistvo.*

83. Berry and Crummey, *Rude and Barbarous Kingdom*, 87; Poe, in *EER*, 1: 219. Cf. Poe, *People Born to Slavery*, 58–81, 177.

84. See Berry, in Fletcher, *English Works*, 92, 105, 149; Alpatov, *Russkaia istoricheskaia mysl'*, 1973 vol., 299–300, 309–10; Schmidt, in Fletcher, *Of the Rus Commonwealth*, xxv–xxvi, xliv; Karamzin, *Istoriia gosudarstva Rossiiskago*, 10: Primechaniia 66n.343; Waliszewski, *Smutnoe vremia*, 21; Berry and Crummey, *Rude and Barbarous Kingdom*, 108; Pipes, in Fletcher, *Of the Russe Common Wealth*, 37–38; Bohuslawsky, "Holie as a Horse," 65–66, 70–71; Gruber, "Russian Orthodox Church," 91–97.

85. Fletcher, *Of the Russe Common Wealth*, 87v. Cf. Fletcher, *English Works*, 272.

86. Karamzin, *Istoriia gosudarstva Rossiiskago*, 10: Primechaniia 66n.343.

87. Sinitsyna, "Tipy monastyrei," 173; Kolycheva, "Pravoslavnye monastyri," 82–84; Zverinskii, *Material dlia issledovaniia*, vols. 1–3.

88. Zverinskii, *Material dlia issledovaniia*, passim; Romanenko, *Povsednevnaia zhizn'*, 14.

89. Bushkovitch, *Religion and Society*, 6, 10–31, passim.

90. See the epigraph and Dunning, "Richest Place"; Dunning, "James I"; Dunning, "Fall of Overbury"; Dunning, "Letter to James I"; Robson, *Solovki*, 64–67, 270nn.15–21.

91. E.g., Dunning, *Russia's First Civil War*, 54; Longworth, *Making of Eastern Europe*, 228–29.

92. Picheta, "Moskovskoe gosudarstvo," 21–22, 31–32; Platonov, *Ocherki*, 5th ed., 81–121; Dunning, *Russia's First Civil War*, 53–59.

93. Goldfrank, "Dykstra," 171. (Cf. his source: N. K. Nikol'skii, *Kirillo-Belozerskii monastyr'*, 2006 ed., 1.2: 271–72n.54.)

94. Vernadsky, *Tsardom of Moscow*, 1: 216.

95. Picheta, "Moskovskoe gosudarstvo," 22.

96. RGADA, *f.* 1196 (Antoniev-Siiskii monastyr'), *op.* 3, *ed. khr.* 1 ("Kniga sbora bobylskogo obroka"; erroneously listed in the archives under the year 1596), *ll.* 1–16.

97. Kliuchevskii, "Proiskhozhdenie krepostnogo prava v Rossii," in his *Sochineniia*, 7: 237–317; Blum, *Lord and Peasant*, 110, 248, passim; Picheta, "Moskovskoe gosudarstvo," 32–42; Dal', *Tolkovyi slovar'*, 4: 669; Vernadsky, *Tsardom of Moscow*, 1: 219; Kliuchevskii, "Pravo i fakt v istorii krest'ianskogo voprosa," in his *Sochineniia*, 7: 155.

98. Picheta, "Moskovskoe gosudarstvo," 41.

99. RGADA, *f.* 1196 (Antoniev-Siiskii monastyr'), *op.* 2, *ch.* 2, *ed. khr.* 1158 ("Gramota tsaria i velikogo kniazia Fedora Ivanovicha novo-khomogorskomu voevode Mikhailovichu Laskarovu . . . ," Mar. 16, 1592); Zverinskii, *Material dlia issledovaniia*, 2: No. 618.

100. *OAU*, 80–82 (§1, No. 72–73).

101. A multiplicity of examples may be found listed in, e.g., *Russkii diplomatarii*, 9: 275–338.

102. *OAU*, 82. Cf. Luke 18:1–8; Schmähling, "Vom Nutzen der Klausur"; Goldfrank, "Sisterhood."

103. See *AAE*, 2: 19 (No. 19).

104. Fletcher, *English Works*, 190.

105. See Nechaev, "Smert' tsarevicha Dmitriia," 58–74; Perrie, *Pretenders*.

106. E.g., Mirsky, *Russia*, 133; RGADA, *f.* 1201, *op.* 1, *ed. khr.* 10, *ll.* 2ob.–3; Gruber, "Russian Orthodox Church," 191n.39.

Chapter Three

1. *AAE*, 2: 14; *PSRL*, 14: 19–22, 129; *SGGD*, 1: 622.

2. Pobedonostsev, *Sochineniia*, 279. Cf. Pobedonostsev, *Moskovskii sbornik*, 29–44; Pobedonostsev, *Reflections*, 30–31.

3. The phrase is from Zabelin, *Minin i Pozharskii*, 23.

4. See Platonov, *Ocherki*, 5th ed., 150–51, 180, passim; Platonov, *Time of Troubles*, 43–44, passim.

5. See the introduction.

6. See Dunning, *Russia's First Civil War*, 93.

7. *DAI*, 1: 44 (No. 39, "Chin venchaniia na tsarstvo tsaria Ioanna Vasil'evicha," Jan. 16, 1547).

8. Cf. biblical blessing from father to son, which coincided with inheritance. E.g., Genesis 27.

9. *DAI*, 1: 41, 44, 50, 52. "With fear and trembling" (*s strakhom i trepetom*) was a biblical expression denoting extreme reverence. At their wedding, Makarii instructed Ivan and his bride Anastasiia to have the same attitude—fear, trembling, and heartfelt love—toward "God's churches." Psalm 2:11; *DAI*, 1: 53–54 (No. 40, "Pouchenie mitropolita Makariia tsariu Ioannu Vasil'evichu i tsaritse Anastasii Romanovne, po sovershenii obriada brakosochetaniia," Feb. 13, 1547).

10. *SGGD*, 2: 75–76 (No. 51, "Chin venchaniia na Vserossiiskoe Tsarsvo Gosudaria Tsaria Feodora Ioannovicha," June 30, 1584).

11. Cf. Bennet, "Idea of Kingship," 2–5.

12. See chap. 1.

13. Gonneau, "L'église," 26–30.

14. Solov'ev, *Istoriia Rossii*, 4 (8): 345; Solov'ev, *History of Russia*, 14: 1, 139n.1.

15. *Rossiia i Angliia*, 188; de Madariaga, *Ivan the Terrible*, 299, 436nn.4–5.

16. Cherepnin, *Zemskie sobory*, 125–32; Ostrowski, "Assembly of the Land," 126–35.

17. *Pentateuch*, 80–81, citing Mayer Sulzberger, *The Am ha-aretz, the Ancient Hebrew Parliament* (Philadelphia, 1910).

18. E.g., Platonov, *Ocherki*, 5th ed., 148–59; Pavlov, "Tserkov[n]aia ierarkhiia," 67.

19. Makarii, *Istoriia russkoi tserkvi*, 1996 ed., 6 (10): 66.

20. Platonov, *Ocherki*, 5th ed., 148.

21. Dunning, *Russia's First Civil War*, 92–93.

22. This term appears in Bogatyrev, "Reinventing," 292.

23. 1 Thessalonians 1:4.

24. *AAE*, 2:13–16; *RIB*, 13: 324; Sreznevskii, *Materialy dlia slovaria*, 1: [Appx.] 6, and 2: 509 (citing *SGGD*, 3: No. 2); Ensslin, "Government and Administration," 2; Feissel, "L'empereur," 83; Ostrogorsky, *History*, 30; Uspenskii, *Tsar' i patriarkh*, 139; Anan'ev, "Ul'ianovskii," 273.

25. *AAE*, 2: 1–2. Cf. *RIB*, 13: 974; Bennet, "Idea of Kingship," 8–10.

26. *AAE*, 2: 2–3.

27. McCormick, "Legitimacy, Political," 1203.

28. *AAE*, 2: 2.

29. Cf. Cherepnin, *Zemskie sobory*, 137.

30. Makarii, *Istoriia russkoi tserkvi*, 1996 ed., 6 (10): 67; Bogdanov, *Russkie patriarkhi*, 1: 59–60.

31. Platonov, *Ocherki*, 5th ed., 146.
32. Dunning, *Russia's First Civil War*, 92, 503n.17.
33. Thyrêt, *Between God and Tsar*, 102. Cf. Bennet, "Idea of Kingship," 9, 12–13, 20; Marker, *Imperial Saint*.
34. See Krom, *Vdovstvuiushchee tsarstvo*.
35. See chap. 7.
36. Margeret, *Russian Empire*, 19–20. Cf. *RIB*, 2: 566–67.
37. Karamzin, *Istoriia gosudarstva Rossiiskago*, 11: 9–12. Cf. ibid., 11: Primechaniia 5–6nn.10, 14, 16.
38. *AAE*, 2: 6–13 (Nos. 2–5).
39. Solov'ev, *History of Russia*, 14: 11–12. The source of Soloviev's quotations from the primary sources may be seen in *AAE*, 2: 13.
40. Platonov, *Boris Godunov: Tsar of Russia*, trans. Pyles, 175.
41. Skrynnikov, *Time of Troubles*, 97–98, 101–2, 126, passim.
42. Skrynnikov, *Boris Godunov*, trans. Graham, 98–99.
43. Skrynnikov, "Boris Godunov's Struggle," 346–47.
44. *AAE*, 2: 57–59, 96–97 (Nos. 10, 41); Platonov, *Ocherki*, 5th ed., 154–56; Dunning, *Russia's First Civil War*, 181.
45. *AAE*, 2:11–12 (No. 4).
46. Dunning, in Margeret, *Russian Empire*, 119n.48. For a slightly modified position, see Dunning, *Russia's First Civil War*, 92.
47. Dunning, *Russia's First Civil War*, 91.
48. Khodarkovsky, *Russia's Steppe Frontier*, 124–25.
49. See, e.g., Karamzin, *Istoriia gosudarstva Rossiiskago*, 10: 32–36; Platonov, *Ocherki*, 5th ed., 54–59; Dunning, *Russia's First Civil War*, 74–85, 402; Liseitsev, "Russko-krymskie otnosheniia," 95, 97.
50. The fuller quote from Makarii on the correspondence between Boris and Iyov includes his opinion on authorship and reads as follows: "These epistles, compiled probably by secretaries [*d'iaki*], are highly scanty in content, but then rich in verbosity and saturation of expressions." Like most scholars, Makarii has overlooked the extraordinary significance of this ostentatious rhetoric in the correspondence. Makarii, *Istoriia russkoi tserkvi*, 1996 ed., 6 (10): 68.
51. Ibid.
52. *AAE*, 2: 6–13. Cf. Bennet, "Idea of Kingship," 94–96, 100.
53. Derived from the name of Ishmael's mother, Hagar. (See Genesis 16 and 21.)
54. *AAE*, 2: 6–8. Cf. Iyov's "Povest' o chestnem zhitii tsaria i velikogo kniazia Feodora Ivanovicha vseia Rusii," in *PSRL*, 14.1: 11, 17, 21.
55. *AAE*, 2: 9–12; *Biblia sirech knigy* [Ostroh Bible], ed. Dergacheva, [4:] *l*. 57. Cf. Massa, *Present Wars in Moscow*, 42.
56. *AAE*, 2: 8.
57. Ibid., 2: 13–16 (No. 6, "Sobornoe opredelenie, ob izbranii Tsarem Borisa Feodorovicha Godunova," 1598). Cf. Bennet, "Idea of Kingship," 14–16, 22; Ostrowski, "Assembly of the Land."
58. Boas, "*Vox populi*," 496–500; Boas, *Vox populi: Essays*, 8–38, passim; Browne, *Pseudodoxia Epidemica*, 1: iii, 8. John Wong of the University of Sydney informs me that an ancient Chinese proverb expresses the Mandate of Heaven in the same sense as vox populi, vox Dei. "*Tian shi zi wo min shi / Tian ting zi wo min ting*"—that is, "Whatever the

people see is what Heaven sees; whatever the people hear is what Heaven hears." Wong, personal interview, March 28, 2011.

59. The question requires further research. Speculatively, it may even be possible that the "monarchical republic" of Elizabethan England influenced Muscovy in significant ways. The English Muscovy Company was quite active in the sixteenth and seventeenth centuries and could have communicated ideas regarding female rule, (quasi-)popular legitimacy, and the role of parliament. Note also that in the seventeenth century "*Vox Populi*" became quite a popular title for English-language books, e.g., Thomas Scott, *Vox populi, or Newes from Spayne* (London, 1620); William Prynne, *Vox Populi, or the Peoples Humble Discovery of His Majesties Ungrounded Jealousies and their own Loyaltie* (London, 1642); *Vox Populi, or, The Supplication and Proposals of the Subjects of this Miserable Kingdome, Languishing and Almost Expiring under the Heavy Burden of Free Quarter* (London: John Playford, Inner Temple, 1647); James I of England, *Vox Regis, or The Difference Betwixt a King Ruling by Law and a Tyrant by his own Will, with the Excellency of the English Laws, Rights, and Priviledges; in Two Speeches of King James to the Parliaments in 1603 and March 21, 1609, and in his Basilicon Doron, which may be an Appendix to Vox Populi* (London: Francis Smith, 1681); *Vox Populi, or, The Peoples Claim to their Parliaments Sitting to Redress Grievances and Provide for the Common Safety, by the Known Laws and Constitutions of the Nation* (London: Francis Smith, 1681); Joseph Boyse, *Vox Populi, or, The Sense of the Sober Lay-Men of the Church of England* (London: Randall Taylor, 1690). Cf. *Rossiia i Angliia*; Hamel, *England and Russia;* Collinson, "Monarchical Republic of Queen Elizabeth I," in his *Elizabethan Essays;* and *Monarchical Republic.*

60. See Genesis 41, esp. verse 40. Here *tsar'stvova* ("reigned") arguably could have meant "ruled" in a general sense, without necessarily implying that Joseph was the chief ruler. Russian translations of the *Slovo o prekrasnom Iosife* attributed to St. Ephraim of Syria assert that "Joseph reigned in Egypt" (*Iosif tsarstvoval vo Egipte*)—although speaking primarily of his coming to rule over his brothers who had betrayed him. A similar usage appears in other Muscovite texts. However, had this been the intended meaning, then the story would not have supported the case of Boris's rising to become chief ruler (tsar) of Muscovy. Sreznevskii, *Materialy dlia slovaria*, 3: 1434, 1465–66; Sirin, *Slovo o prekrasnom Iosife;* T. A. Smith, *Volokolamsk Paterikon*, 125.

61. *AAE*, 2: 15–16.

62. Ibid., 2: 16.

63. On the variants of the "Confirmatory Document" and their dating, see Cherepnin, *Zemskie sobory*, 137–39; Skrynnikov, "Boris Godunov's Struggle," 325–29. The discussion in this section utilizes the version of this document published in: *AAE*, 2: 16–54 (No. 7, "Gramota utverzhdennaia, ob izbranii Tsarem Borisa Feodorovicha Godunova," Aug. 1, 1598).

64. Cherepnin, *Zemskie sobory*, 139. Cf. Anan'ev, "Ul'ianovskii," 273.

65. *AAE*, 2: 34. Cf. Bennet, "Idea of Kingship," 16–17; Pavlov, "Tserkov[n]aia ierarkhiia," 68.

66. *AAE*, 2: 16–41.

67. Cf. *RIB*, 2: 15–16; Platonov, *Ocherki*, 5th ed., 156.

68. *AAE*, 2: 55. Cf. Bennet, "Idea of Kingship," 20.

69. *AAE*, 2: 56; cf. Makarii, *Istoriia russkoi tserkvi*, 1996 ed., 6 (10): 69.

70. *PSRL*, 14.1: 6–7. Cf. Exodus 41:33, 38–40; Daniel 1:19–20.

71. *AAE*, 2: 56–57.
72. Karamzin, *Istoriia gosudarstva Rossiiskago*, 10: 123.
73. *AAE*, 2: 57–61.
74. *RIB*, 13: 344–50.
75. *PDS*, 2: 664–665.
76. Bantysh-Kamensky, *Obzor vneshnykh snoshenii Rossii*, 1: 16; Gruber, "Muscovite Embassy," 63. Cf. Pavlov, "Tserkov[n]aia ierarkhiia," 66.
77. *AAE*, 2: 86–89.
78. Ibid., 2: 86.
79. The English term "cabinet counsel" or "cabinet" was used in the early seventeenth century for the monarch's council of private advisors. An alternate translation of *sigklit* could be "privy council." (See *Oxford English Dictionary*.)
80. *AAE*, 2: 86–87.
81. Dunning, *Russia's First Civil War*, 181, 527n.5.
82. On the term "autocrat," see also chap. 4.
83. *AAE*, 2: 87.
84. Cf. Ul'ianovskii, *Smutnoe vremia*, 55ff; Bussow, *Disturbed State*, 48.
85. See chap. 4. On female rule in early modern Western Europe, see Jansen, *Monstrous Regiment;* Jansen, *Debating Women;* Cruz and Suzuki, *Rule of Women*.
86. *AAE*, 2: 87–88.

Notes to Chapter Four

1. *Ostryz'ka Bibliia*, [1:] *l.* 20*ob.*; *Biblia sirech knigy*, ed. Turkoniak, 1: 92.
2. *AAE*, 2: 78 (No. 28).
3. E.g., Massa, *Histoire des guerres*, 1: 62–63, 2:70; Massa, *Kratkoe izvestie*, 56; Massa, *Present Wars in Moscow*, 57, 134–35, 145; Bussow, *Disturbed State*, 35–36.
4. *PDS*, 2: 656. "Conciliar secretary" is a translation of *dumnii d'iak*.
5. Robert J. W. Evans, *Rudolf II*, 1; Mattingly, *Renaissance Diplomacy*, 158–59; Gruber, "Muscovite Embassy," 8–9; *Istoriia diplomatii*, 1: 292, 307; Tarkovskii, "Tri drevnerusskikh perevoda," 209–10.
6. *PDS*, 1: 1288, 1428, and 2: 511, 516; Szeftel, "Title of Muscovite Monarch," 66; Bantysh-Kamensky, *Obzor vneshnikh snoshenii Rossii*, 1: 16; Gruber, "Muscovite Embassy," 8–10, 33–36, 42–43, 52–55, 63, 68–69; Lappo-Danilevskij, "L'idée de l'état," 357.
7. *PDS*, 2: 692–98; Gruber, "Muscovite Embassy," 45–47, 54, 63–67, 71–77, passim.
8. Dunning, *Russia's First Civil War*, 96.
9. Bantysh-Kamensky, *Obzor vneshnikh snoshenii Rossii*, 2: 190–91, and 4: 266; Karamzin, *Istoriia gosudarstva Rossiiskago*, 11: 52–53; Gruber, "Muscovite Embassy," 70; Ul'ianovskii, *Smutnoe vremia*, 322.
10. Margeret, *Russian Empire*, 59; Dunning, *Russia's First Civil War*, 94; Platonov, *Boris Godunov: Tsar of Russia,* trans. Pyles, 110.
11. *OAU*, 85–86 (§1: No. 76).
12. Ibid., 88–89 (§1: No. 79).
13. RGADA, *f.* 281, *op.* 5, *ed. khr.* 8006/65 ("Ukaznaia gramota ob ostavlenii za monastyrem rybnykh lovel i bobrovykh gonov," Mar. 31, 1601), *ll.* 1–2*ob.*

14. Ibid., *f.* 281, passim; *OAU*; *ASZ*; *AFZKh*; Budovnits, *Monastyri na Rusi*; A. M. Borisov, *Khoziaistvo*; Dunning, *Russia's First Civil War*, 143; Koretskii, "Golod 1601–1603 gg.," 250, passim.

15. Borisenkov and Pasetskii, *Tysiachiletniaia letopis'*, 190, 325–26, 503–04; Dunning, *Russia's First Civil War*, 97; M. Tolstoi, *Istoriia russkoi tserkvi*, 468–69; Grove, *Little Ice Age*; Longworth, *Making of Eastern Europe*, 228–29; Koretskii, "Golod 1601–1603 gg.," 219–21, 229–30.

16. Massa, *Histoire des guerres*, 1: 55–56, and 2: 62–63; Massa, *Kratkoe izvestie*, 51–52; Massa, *Present Wars in Moscow*, 51–52; Borisenkov and Pasetskii, *Tysiachiletniaia letopis'*, 190, 326, 503–4; Dunning, *Russia's First Civil War*, 97–98; Koretskii, "Golod 1601–1603 gg.," 226, 228.

17. *RIB*, 13: 977; Bussow, *Disturbed State*, 32–34; Margeret, *Russian Empire*, 58–59; Borisenkov and Pasetskii, *Tysiachiletniaia letopis'*, 190, 326–27, 503–4; Dunning, *Russia's First Civil War*, 98–108; Skrynnikov, *Boris Godunov*, 115–26; Perrie, *Pretenders*, 29–32; Platonov, *Ocherki*, 3rd ed., 240–44; Platonov, *Time of Troubles*, 73–74; Koretskii, "Golod 1601–1603 gg.," 221–24, 227–28, 230, 246–48.

18. Borisenkov and Pasetskii, *Tysiachiletniaia letopis'*, 190, 327–28; Koretskii, "Golod 1601–1603 gg.," 237–39, 254–56; Dunning, *Russia's First Civil War*, 99–103, 107–8, 181–82.

19. Massa, *Present Wars in Moscow*, 53. Cf. Palitsyn, *Skazanie*, 105–6; Margeret, *Russian Empire*, 58; Bussow, *Disturbed State*, 33–34; Koretskii, "Golod 1601–1603 gg.," 232–34; Dunning, *Russia's First Civil War*, 99–100.

20. Bussow, *Disturbed State*, 36.

21. Margeret, *Russian Empire*, 58; Skrynnikov, *Krest i korona*, 333.

22. Koretskii, "Golod 1601–1603 gg.," 242–43, 248–49, 255–56.

23. Dunning, *Russia's First Civil War*, 99–100, 506n.92. Cf. Koretskii, "Golod 1601–1603 gg.," 237–39, 254–56.

24. RNB, *f.* 351; RGADA, *f.* 1111, *op.* 1.3, *ed. khr.* 111, and *f.* 1201, *op.* 1, *ed. khr.* 7, 9; *AFZKh*, 1: 268 (No. 312); Z. V. Dmitrieva, *Bytnye i opisnye knigi*, 126–39; N. A. Smirnov, *Tserkov'*, 126–27; Gruber, "Russian Orthodox Church," 281; Skrynnikov, *Krest i korona*, 333; Koretskii, "Golod 1601–1603 gg.," 232–35, 239–43.

25. "Povest' ob Uliianii Osor'inoi," in *Russkaia povest'*, 45, 206, 350; Zenkovsky, *Medieval Russia's Epics*, 397; Kaiser and Marker, *Reinterpreting Russian History*, 194–96; Gruber, "Russian Orthodox Church," 147–48. Cf. 1 Kings 17; T. A. Smith, *Volokolamsk Paterikon*, 124.

26. RGADA, *f.* 281 (GKE), *op.* 5, *ed. khr.* 8010/69 ("Kupchaia Obros'eva-Dudina monastyria," 1603–1604); RGADA, *f.* 1192 (Iosifo-Volokolamskii monastyr'), *op.* 1, *ed. khr.* 2133 ("Prikhod i raskhod monastyrskikh deneg," Aug. 28, 1600), *ll.* 1–2; RGADA, *f.* 1192, *op.* 1, *ed. khr.* 908 ("Kupchaia," misnamed in the archival catalogue as "Poruchnaia zapis' po monastyrskom krest'ianine . . . ," 1602), *l.* 1; *AFZKh*, 2: 457–58, 461–63 (Nos. 404, 406, 409–12, 414); Bussow, *Disturbed State*, 32; Margeret, *Russian Empire*, 58; Gorfunkel', "Khronologicheskii perechen'," 280–82; Dunning, *Russia's First Civil War*, 97–98, 505n.74; Borisenkov and Pasetskii, *Tysiachiletniaia letopis'*, 190.

27. RGADA, *f.* 281, *ed. khr.* 31/7173, *ll.* 2–102ob. (quotation from *ll.* 2–5ob.), as transcribed in *AMMS*, 350–86 (No. 144; quotation taken from pp. 350–51). A "living clearing" (*pochinok zhivushchei*) was a forest clearing or very small settlement that had people living in it.

28. *OAU*, 90–91 (§1: No. 82).

29. Ibid., 91–92 (§1: No. 83).

30. Cf. Kivelson, "Devil Stole His Mind," 735; Dunning, *Russia's First Civil War*, 100–101, 106, 115–16.

31. Cf. Dunning, *Russia's First Civil War*, 97–99.

32. Cf. Koretskii, "Golod 1601–1603 gg.," 250–51, passim.

33. RGADA, *f.* 1201 (Solovetskii monastyr'), *op.* 1, *ed. khr.* 7–11; Gruber, "Black Monks"; Gruber, "Russian Orthodox Church," 248–67; Savich, *Solovetskaia votchina*, 147–49; Bushkovitch, *Merchants of Moscow*, 131–32. Cf. Hellie, *Economy and Material Culture*, 142, 157. Note that such figures can vary slightly depending on the method of adding awkward Russian monetary units and calculating averages.

34. Cf. Dunning, *Russia's First Civil War*, 98.

35. RGADA, *f.* 1201, *op.* 1, *ed. khr.* 7, *l.* 43; RGADA, *f.* 1201, *op.* 1, *ed. khr.* 8, *ll.* 35, 57; RGADA, *f.* 1201, *op.* 1, *ed. khr.* 9, *ll.* 39, 77ob., 125ob., 165; RGADA, *f.* 1201, *op.* 1, *ed. khr.* 11, *l.* 119; RGADA, *f.* 1201, *op.* 1, *ed. khr.* 12, *ll.* 4ob., 17ob., 53, 81, 108–108ob.; Gruber, "Russian Orthodox Church," 281–83.

36. Nikolaeva, "Vklady," 81–82, 92–94; Spock, "Solovki Monastery," 213–27; Z. V. Dmitrieva, *Bytnye i opisnye knigi*, 128–30; Koretskii, "Golod 1601–1603 gg.," 254; D. B. Miller, *Saint Sergius*, 136, 247–50.

37. Bussow, *Disturbed State*, 32.

38. Massa, *Present Wars in Moscow*, 70–71; Howe, *False Dmitri*, 1–4, 26, 55; Dunning, *Russia's First Civil War*, 123–37; Ul'ianovskii, *Smutnoe vremia*, 307–12.

39. Dunning, *Russia's First Civil War*, 139–43.

40. Ibid., 169.

41. For biblical precedents, see 2 Kings 21:10–15, 23:25–27.

42. RGADA, *f.* 1192, *op.* 2, *ed. khr.* 395 ("Kniga zapisnaia vkladov Iosifova monastyria" [1530]–1606), *ll.* 21ob., 22, passim; Margeret, *Russian Empire*, 59; Massa, *Present Wars in Moscow*, 95; Bussow, *Disturbed State*, 10; Dunning, *Russia's First Civil War*, 94; Ul'ianovskii, *Smutnoe vremia*, 19–21. Incidentally, Margeret had been recruited by Afanasii Vlasiev. Margeret, *Russian Empire*, xvii.

43. Massa, *Histoire des guerres*, 1: 108, and 2: 118; Massa, *Kratkoe izvestie*, 83; Massa, *Present Wars in Moscow*, 95.

44. See also Pavlov, "Tserkov[n]aia ierarkhiia," 69–70.

45. Ul'ianovskii, "Pravoslavnaia tserkov'," 33; Ul'ianovskii, "Motiv," 195.

46. E.g., Ul'ianovskii, "Motiv," 175–77; Ul'ianovskii, *Smutnoe vremia*, 11, 40–41; Massa, *Present Wars in Moscow*, 78; Makarii, *Istoriia russkoi tserkvi*, 1996 ed., 6 (10): 137–38.

47. *AAE*, 2: 78–79 (No. 28). Cf. Dunning, *Russia's First Civil War*, 125; *AI*, 2: 67–69 (No. 55).

48. Margeret, *Russian Empire*, 23, 123n.63; *AVK*, vols. 28–29; Dubnow, *History of the Jews*, 2000 ed., 28–45, 117–18, passim; Govorun, "Voprosy o tserkvi," 168–92; Bennet, "Idea of Kingship," 99; Pereswetoff-Morath, *Grin*, 2: 21–29.

49. Cf. Ul'ianovskii, *Smutnoe vremia*, 265.

50. Howe, *False Dmitri*, 5–18; Perrie, *Pretenders*, 51, 76–77; Ul'ianovskii, *Smutnoe vremia*, 26–29, 37–39; Anan'ev, "Ul'ianovskii," 281; *AI*, 2: 60–61 (No. 50); Dunning, *Russia's First Civil War*, 125.

51. Dunning, *Russia's First Civil War*, 173–75, 179, 181–82, passim; Pirling, *Dmitrii Samozvanets*, chap. 2.

52. *AAE*, 2: 86 (No. 31); Massa, *Present Wars in Moscow*, 78, 90–96; Ul'ianovskii, "Motiv," 175–77, 205; Ul'ianovskii, *Smutnoe vremia*, 12–23, 53; Dunning, *Russia's First Civil War*, 181; Perrie, *Pretenders*, 76. Cf. 1 Samuel 28.

53. *AAE*, 2: 89 (No. 33); *AI*, 2: 67–69 (No. 55); Massa, *Present Wars in Moscow*, 94.

54. See chap. 3.

55. Ensslin, "Government and Administration," 2.

56. *AAE*, 2: 87–89 (No. 32).

57. "Ukaznaia gramota" (No. 8), in Mashtafarov, "Kashinskii Sretenskii monastyr'," 56–60.

58. Ul'ianovskii, "Pravoslavnaia tserkov'," 36–37. Cf. *AI*, 2: 67–69 (No. 55).

59. Bussow, *Disturbed State*, 48; Karamzin, *Istoriia gosudarstva Rossiiskago*, 11: 118–20; Ul'ianovskii, "Pravoslavnaia tserkov'," 36–37. Cf. *SGGD*, 1: 604 (No. 203).

60. Bussow, *Disturbed State*, 44.

61. *RIB*, 1: 16.

62. *SGGD*, 2: 103–23; Massa, *Present Wars in Moscow*, 68, 90–91; Margeret, *Estat de l'empire*, 1607 ed., 51, in *EER*, 2: 307; Margeret, *Estat de l'empire de Russie*, 1946 ed., 133; Margeret, *Russian Empire*, 85–86; Howe, *False Dmitri*, 225–28; Karamzin, *Istoriia gosudarstva Rossiiskago*, 11: 78–79 and chap. 4n.601; Karamzin, *Zapiska*, 13–14; Karamzin, *Ancient and Modern Russia*, 113; Nechaev, "Smert' tsarevicha Dmitriia," 68; Dunning, *Russia's First Civil War*, 195, 247–48, 259; Skrynnikov, *Time of Troubles*, 3, 9, 16, 48; Perrie, *Pretenders*, 65–67.

63. *AAE*, 2: 89–90, 92–93 (No. 34–35, 37); Makarii, *Istoriia russkoi tserkvi*, 1996 ed., 6 (10): 77; Ul'ianovskii, *Smutnoe vremia*, 71, 160–61, 165, 170, 317, passim; Anan'ev, "Ul'ianovskii," 276.

64. Ul'ianovskii, *Smutnoe vremia*, 159–61. Cf. Makarii, *Istoriia russkoi tserkvi*, 1996 ed., 6 (10): 77.

65. Bussow, *Disturbed State*, 51; Howe, *False Dmitri*, 4; Ul'ianovskii, "Motiv," 200–201.

66. Dunning, *Russia's First Civil War*, 116–17; Ul'ianovskii, *Smutnoe vremia*, 55–106; Swoboda, "Tradition Reinvented," 157; Swoboda, "Obraz," 388–408; Anan'ev, "Ul'ianovskii," 279.

67. E.g., Bussow, *Disturbed State*, 48; Ul'ianovskii, "Motiv," 200–201; Ul'ianovskii, *Smutnoe vremia*, 55, 81–83; Anan'ev, "Ul'ianovskii," 275, 275n.11.

68. *AAE*, 2: 89–90 (No. 34).

69. Massa, *Present Wars in Moscow*, 112; Ul'ianovskii, *Smutnoe vremia*, 55, 73–75, 78, 163; Makarii, *Istoriia russkoi tserkvi*, 1996 ed., 6 (10): 78, 644–45n.17; Dunning, *Russia's First Civil War*, 198, 212; Koretskii, "Golod 1601–1603 gg.," 237–38, 256.

70. E.g., Margeret, *Russian Empire*, 68; Makarii, *Istoriia russkoi tserkvi*, 1996 ed., 6 (10): 80; Anan'ev, "Ul'ianovskii," 275. Cf. Ul'ianovskii, "Pravoslavnaia tserkov'," 37.

71. Isaiah 49:1, 49:5; Jeremiah 1:5; Luke 1:15. Cf. *Zhitie i podvigi*, 10–14.

72. 1 Samuel 24, 26; 2 Samuel 1; Psalm 105:15; 1 Chronicles 16:22; Kovtun, *Russkaia leksikografiia*, 433; McCormick, "Legitimacy, Political," 1203. Cf. chap. 1; Ensslin, "Government and Administration," 3; E. P. Miller, *Politics of Imitating Christ*; Remensnyder, *Remembering Kings Past*, 171, 171n.88; Reuter, *Medieval Polities*, 98, 98n.22; Maguire, *Byzantine Court Culture*, 103ff.

73. *Rukopis' Filareta*, 1. Cf. *RIB*, 13: 536–537; Morozova, *Smuta nachala XVII v.*, 265ff.

74. Makarii, *Istoriia russkoi tserkvi*, 1996 ed., 6 (10): 77; Ul'ianovskii, *Smutnoe vremia*, 110–14, 211–30, passim; Dunning, *Russia's First Civil War*, 212–13; Dubakov, "Obrazovanie," 160–61; Ul'ianovskii, "Pravoslavnaia tserkov'," 60–61, passim; Dunning, "L. E. Morozova," 235; Skrynnikov, *Krest i korona*, 339.

75. E.g., RGADA, *f.* 281 (GKE), *op.* 5, *ed. khr.* 8011/70 ("Zhalovannaia gramota tsaria Dmitriia Ivanovicha," Sep. 3, 1605, but misnamed in the *opis'* or archival catalog as "Gramota Velikago Kniazia Vasil'ia Ivanovicha . . ."); RGADA, *f.* 281 (GKE), *op.* 5, *ed. khr.* 8012/71 ("Gramota tsaria Dmitriia Ivanovicha igumnu Ambrosieva Dudina monastyria Evfimiiu s bratieiu ob osvobozhdenie ikh ot platezha poshlin i vsiakikh podatei s raznykh ugodii," Oct. 15, 1605, incorrectly listed in the *opis'* or archival catalog under item No. 8016/71); *AMMS*, 387–88 (No. 145); "Ukaznaia" (No. 24), in Mashtafarov, "Muromskie monastyri," 70–71.

76. Ul'ianovskii, "Pravoslavnaia tserkov'," 38–42, 61.

77. RGADA, *f.* 1201, *op.* 1, *ed. khr.* 10, *ll.* 1–10*ob.*; Gruber, "Russian Orthodox Church," 654–64.

78. E.g., Mauss, *Essai sur le don;* Godelier, *L'énigme du don;* Malinowski, *Argonauts;* Lévi-Strauss, *Structures*; Titmuss, *Gift Relationship*; Sahlins, *Stone Age Economics*; Gouldner, "Importance of Something"; Parry, "Gift"; Morris, "Gift and Commodity"; Cheal, *Gift Economy;* Parry and Bloch, *Money and Morality;* Gregory, "Gifts to Men"; Carrier, "Gifts in a World"; Carrier, "Gift in Theory"; Clark and Mills, "Communal and Exchange Relationships"; Steindorff, *Memoria in Altrussland;* Komter, *Gift;* Komter, "Reciprocity"; Komter and Vollebergh, "Gift Giving"; Davis, *Gift in Sixteenth-Century France;* Rasmussen, "Alms, Elders, and Ancestors"; Joy, "Gift Giving"; Bogatyrev, "Dary"; Cliggett, "Gift Remitting"; Miyazaki, "From Sugar Cane"; Arel et al., "Gift-Giving"; Marcoux, "Escaping the Gift Economy."

79. RGADA, *f.* 1201, *op.* 1, *ed. khr.* 10, *ll.* 7–8*ob.*; *RIB*, 13: 1296; Gruber, "Russian Orthodox Church," 660–61; Hellie, *Economy and Material Culture*, 539, 567, 569.

80. RGADA, *f.* 1201, *op.* 1, *ed. khr.* 10, *l.* 10*ob.*

81. Ibid., *f.* 281 (GKE), *op.* 5, *ed. khr.* 8011/70, *ll.* 1–1*ob.*

82. *AMMS*, 387–88 (No. 145).

83. Mashtafarov, "Muromskie monastyri," 70–71. Cf. Zverinskii, *Material dlia issledovaniia*, 2: No. 676.

84. RGADA, *f.* 281 (GKE), *op.* 5, *ed. khr.* 8012/71 (incorrectly listed in the *opis'* under item No. 8016/71), *ll.* 1–2. Cf. Zverinskii, *Material dlia issledovaniia*, 2: No. 612.

85. "Poslushnaia gramota" (No. 25), in Mashtafarov, "Muromskie monastyri," 71. Cf. *AI*, 2: 70–80; Dunning, *Russia's First Civil War*, 213.

86. RGADA, *f.* 281 (GKE), *op.* 5, *ed. khr.* 8011/70, *ll.* 1–1*ob.*; Hellie, *Economy and Material Culture*, 2, 242, 439, 501–2, 525, 528, 539, 552, 567, passim. On fees for recertification and rewriting of charters, see the numerous collections of documents listed in the bibliography.

87. See Gruber, "Russian Orthodox Church," 212–13.

88. *AFZKh*, 2: 464 (Nos. 415–16).

89. Makarii, *Istoriia russkoi tserkvi*, 1996 ed., 6 (10): 137–38. Cf. Tiumentsev, "Gosudarstvo i tserkov'," 147–49, 163.

90. Tiumentsev, "Gosudarstvo i tserkov'," 148–49; Spock, "Solovki Monastery," 215–18; RGADA, *f.* 1201, *op.* 1, *ed. khr.* 10, *l.* 2; Dunning, *Russia's First Civil War*, 213.

91. Fonkich, *Grechesko-russkie sviazi*, 6–7.

92. *SGGD*, 1: 604–5 (No. 203); Margeret, *Russian Empire*, 86; Makarii, *Istoriia russkoi tserkvi*, 1996 ed., 6 (10): 81; Dunning, *Russia's First Civil War*, 204–7, 212–13; Ul'ianovskii, *Smutnoe vremia*, 320, 324; Skrynnikov, *Krest i korona*, 339; Filiushkin, "Religioznyi faktor," 147, 173ff.

93. Ul'ianovskii, *Smutnoe vremia*, 265, 307–76; Margeret, *Russian Empire*, 22, 26; Dunning, *Russia's First Civil War*, 212, 219, 221.

94. Makarii, *Istoriia russkoi tserkvi*, 1996 ed., 6 (10): 81–82.

95. Bussow, *Disturbed State*, 52. Cf. Margeret, *Russian Empire*, 70; Karamzin, *Istoriia gosudarstva Rossiiskago*, 11: 125–28; Karamzin, *Zapiska*, 14–15; Karamzin, *Ancient and Modern Russia*, 114–15.

96. *AAE*, 2: 155 (No. 67, Feb. 1607); Uspenskii, "Svad'ba Lzhedmitriia," 410; Ul'ianovskii, "Pravoslavnaia tserkov'," 60–61; Ul'ianovskii, *Smutnoe vremia*, 231–38, 243, 269.

97. *RIB*, 1: 51–72, 412–19; *DRV*, 13: 116–22; Howe, *False Dmitri*, 36ff.; Uspenskii, "Svad'ba Lzhedmitriia," 404–7, 417–18; Makarii, *Istoriia russkoi tserkvi*, 1996 ed., 6 (10): 82–83; Ul'ianovskii, *Smutnoe vremia*, 242.

98. *DRV*, 13: 116.

99. Uspenskii, "Svad'ba Lzhedmitriia," 407–18; Ul'ianovskii, *Smutnoe vremia*, 232, 238–69.

100. Margeret, *Russian Empire*, 72; Massa, *Present Wars in Moscow*, 125-33; Bussow, *Disturbed State*, 58-61; Ul'ianovskii, *Smutnoe vremia*, 244–45, 262–66; Makarii, *Istoriia russkoi tserkvi*, 1996 ed., 6 (10): 83; Uspenskii, "Svad'ba Lzhedmitriia," 408, 418–20; Dunning, *Russia's First Civil War*, 227–30.

101. *DRV*, 13: 122.

Notes to Chapter Five

1. *AAE*, 2: 100 (No. 44, "Gramota Tsaria Vasiliia Ioannovicha v Perm' Velikuiu," May 20, 1606).

2. *AI*, 2: 140 (No. 111, "Zhalovannaia gramota Lzhedimitriia Tsaritse inokine Aleksandre," Dec. 9, 1608). As mentioned in the preface, "Dmitrii II" refers here to the "second false Dmitrii."

3. Due to his subsequent vilification it is impossible to know now how popular or unpopular Dmitrii was during his reign. However, we do at least know that he mounted a widespread revolt against Tsar Boris, one that gained enough adherents to succeed. See Dunning, *Russia's First Civil War*, 1–4, 120, 132, 268, passim.

4. Massa, *Present Wars in Moscow*, 136–37; Bussow, *Disturbed State*, 67; Dunning, *Russia's First Civil War*, 207–11, 225, 232–35.

5. *Récit du sanglant massacre*, 20ff.

6. Jensen, *Musical Cultures*, 11.

7. Massa, *Histoire des guerres*, 2: 181–86, 203. See also Dunning, *Russia's First Civil War*, 234–37; and other historiography.

8. E.g., Massa, *Present Wars in Moscow*, 138; Massa, *Histoire des guerres*, 2: 186, 188, 297–98nn.127–29; Margeret, *Estat de l'empire de Russie*, 1946 ed., 118; Dunning, *Russia's First Civil War*, 237–38, 244–46, 250. Cf. Howe, *False Dmitri*, 79.

9. Brereton, *Present Miseries*, 19.

10. E.g., Dunning, *Russia's First Civil War*, 235–37, 240–44; Makarii, *Istoriia russkoi tserkvi*, 1996 ed., 6 (10): 85, 586n.86.

11. *SGGD*, 2: 299–300 (No. 141, "Zapis' vstupivshago na Vserossiiskii prestol Tsaria Vasiliia Ioannovicha Shuiskago," May 19, 1606).

12. *PSRL*, 10: 146, 11: 4, 14.2: 8–9; *RIB*, 13: 168–69, 227, 1295–96; Tikhomirov, "Skazaniia o nachale Moskvy"; Pudalov, "O proiskhozhdenii suzdal'skikh kniazei"; Goldfrank, private correspondence, 2010; Dunning, *Russia's First Civil War*, 242, 544n.25; Abramovich, *Kniaz'ia Shuiskie;* Ostrowski, *Muscovy and the Mongols*, 150–55.

13. Dunning, *Russia's First Civil War*, 242.

14. *AAE*, 2: 100–1 (No. 44, "Gramota Tsaria Vasiliia Ioannovicha v Perm Velikuiu, o vosshestvii ego na prestol," May 20, 1606).

15. Dunning, *Russia's First Civil War*, 236–37. Cf. Margeret, *Russian Empire*, 72–74; Ul'ianovskii, *Smutnoe vremia*, 267.

16. *AAE*, 2: 100. Cf. Howe, *False Dmitri*, 234–35.

17. *AAE*, 2: 100.

18. Ibid.

19. Quoted in Graham, "Further Sources," 83–84. Cf. Massa, *Present Wars in Moscow*, 70–71, 120; Howe, *False Dmitri*, 1–4, 26, 55.

20. Quoted in Graham, "Further Sources," 88.

21. E.g., *AAE*, 2: 106–15 (No. 48).

22. Ibid., 2: 101 (No. 44).

23. Cf. Dunning, *Russia's First Civil War*, 241.

24. *AAE*, 2: 101.

25. *SGGD*, 2: 300–301.

26. *PSRL*, 14: 68–69; Makarii, *Istoriia russkoi tserkvi*, 1996 ed., 6 (10): 86.

27. Dunning, *Russia's First Civil War*, 244; Makarii, *Istoriia russkoi tserkvi*, 1996 ed., 6 (10): 96; M. Tolstoi, *Istoriia russkoi tserkvi*, 468.

28. *AAE*, 2: 57–59, 96–97, 103 (Nos. 10, 41, 45); *PSRL*, 14: 68; Cherepnin, *Zemskie sobory*, 125–32; de Madariaga, *Ivan the Terrible*, 299, 436nn.4–5; Karamzin, *Istoriia gosudarstva Rossiiskago*, 10: 123; Dunning, *Russia's First Civil War*, 181, 246; Ostrowski, "Simeon Bekbulatovich."

29. *AAE*, 2: 104–5 ("Chin venchaniia na tsarstvo Tsaria Vasiliia Ioannovicha," July 1, 1606).

30. Ibid.

31. Margeret, *Russian Empire*, 74; Massa, *Present Wars in Moscow*, 161; Massa, *Histoire des guerres*, 2: 205–7; *RIB*, 13: 169ff., 1298ff.; Nechaev, "Smert' tsarevicha Dmitriia," 68; Dunning, *Russia's First Civil War*, 247–48; Skrynnikov, *Time of Troubles*, 48; Ul'ianovskii, *Smutnoe vremia*, 377–400. Cf. Howe, *False Dmitri*, 62, 237–38.

32. *AAE*, 2: 110.

33. *PISV*, 31–33.

34. *AAE*, 2: 111–15.

35. See Morozova, *Smuta nachala XVII v.*; Morozova, *Rossiia na puti;* Leonard, *Reform and Regicide*, 138–39.

36. *RIB*, 13: 145–76, 877–922.

37. *DAI*, 1: 255–63; *AAE*, 2: 126–35, 155 (Nos. 57, 67); Massa, *Present Wars in Moscow*, 166; *RIB*, 13: 1296; Tiumentsev, "Russkie samozvantsy," 221–32; Dunning, *Russia's First Civil War*, 249–50, 330. Cf. M. Tolstoi, *Istoriia russkoi tserkvi*, 473–74;

Gonneau, "L'église," 42–43.

38. *RIB*, 13: 389. Cf. Swoboda, "Tradition Reinvented," 155–58.

39. Ul'ianovskii, *Smutnoe vremia*, 377, 399–400.

40. Neville, *Byzantine Provincial Society*, 44. Cf. Dunning, *Russia's First Civil War*, 259.

41. Perrie, *Pretenders*, 132, 144–49. My thanks to Matthew Romaniello for pointing out this incident to me.

42. E.g., Dunning, *Russia's First Civil War*, 250–80.

43. Ibid., 320.

44. See ibid., 321–403; Perrie, *Pretenders*, 90–97, 133–53.

45. Dunning, *Russia's First Civil War*, 3–5, 259–60, passim. See also the section on historiography in the introduction.

46. Margeret, *Russian Empire*, 71; Margeret, *Estat de l'empire de Russie*, 1946 ed., 111–12.

47. See Tiumentsev, "Russkie samozvantsy," 242–44: Perrie, *Pretenders*, 158–59.

48. *AI*, 2: 121, 132–33, 135–36, 140, 154–55, 178, 193–95, 198–99, 229–30, 276–77 (Nos. 89, 100, 105–6, 111, 130, 132, 154, 164–66, 171, 198, 234); Dunning, *Russia's First Civil War*, 394, 443–45; M. Tolstoi, *Istoriia russkoi tserkvi*, 482.

49. *AI*, 2: 132–33, 228–29 (Nos. 100, 197).

50. Ibid., 2: 132–33 (No. 100).

51. Ibid., 2: 133–34 (No. 101). Cf. ibid., 2: 131–32 (No. 99).

52. Ibid., 2: 146–49, 152–54, 194–95, 269, 281–82 (Nos. 119, 121, 126–28, 166, 229, 239).

53. Ibid., 2: 132–33, 140, 143, 152, 154, 231, 343–44 (Nos. 100, 111, 114, 127, 130, 199, 285); *Pamiatniki Smutnogo vremeni*, 346–57; Bussow, *Disturbed State*, 123; Rowland, "Moscow," 605, 605n.43.

54. Marchocki, *Historya wojny moskiewskiej*, 1841 ed., 17–18; *MRP*, 31; Marchocki, *Istoriia moskovskoi voiny*, 32–33. Cf. Gonneau, "L'église," 48; Ostrowski, *Muscovy and the Mongols*, 204.

55. RGADA, *f.* 281 (GKE), *op.* 5, *ed. khr.* 8013/72 [erroneously listed in the *opis'* as 8011/70] ("Gramota Velikogo Kniazia Vasil'ia Ivanovicha, igumnu Ambrosieva Dudina monastyria Evfimiiu s bratieiu, ob otdache im vo vladenie bortnykh ukhozhii i ozera Pyrskago s lesami i sennymi pokosami v Strelitskom stanu," Mar. 18, 1606 [the document bears this date but was written "from Tsar and Grand Prince Vasilii Ivanovich of all Russia," raising the question of intentional backdating or alteration—note that according to its addenda the document did not arrive in Nizhnii Novgorod until July 17, well after Vasilii's coup]); RGADA, *f.* 281 (GKE), *op.* 5, *ed. khr.* 8014/73 [listed in the *opis'* as 8012/71] ("Uslovnaia zapis' Dmitriia Dolgova s tovarishchami, o vziatii imi v obrochnoe soderzhanie u startsa Pecherskago monastyria Andreiana Sushnitsyna s bratieiu mel'nitsy, sostoiachei na reke Vezlome," May 24, 1606); RGADA, *f.* 281 (GKE), *op.* 5, *ed. khr.* 8467/26 ("Ukaznaia gramota o sposobe pol'zovaniia 'ezom,'" Jan. 16, 1608); *AAE*, 2: 139–40, 176–78 (Nos. 62, 84–85); *AI*, 2: 84–100, 103–10 (Nos. 68–74, 77–79); Tikhomirov and Floria, "Prikhodo-raskhodnye knigi"; *OAU*, 96–100 (§1: Nos. 85–88); etc.

56. *AI*, 2: 134 (No. 102); Dunning, *Russia's First Civil War*, 256, 350, 362, 471–72, passim.

57. *OAU*, 96 (§1: No. 85).

58. Dunning, *Russia's First Civil War*, 360–68, 375.

59. Cf. Tiumentsev, "Gosudarstvo i tserkov'," 149.

60. "Ukaznaia" (No. 7) in Avdeev, "Galichskii Uspenskii Pais'ev monastyr'," 332, 346–47.

61. Ibid., 346–47.

62. *OAU*, 97 (§1: No. 86).

63. RGADA, *f.* 1187 (Troitskii-Gledenskii monastyr'), *op.* 1, *ed. khr.* 37 ("Chelobitnaia polovnika ustiuzhskogo Arkhangel'skogo monastyria Ivana Chernogo vlastiam Troitskogo Gledenskogo monastyria na ustiuzhskogo posadskogo Tret'iaka Chiganova, ne otdaiushchego emu vziatykh semian i svezshego 'nasil'stvom' seno i solomu," Jan. 14, 1608 [listed incorrectly in the archival catalog under the year 7116/1606]), *ll.* 1–1*ob.*

64. Zverinskii, *Material dlia issledovaniia*, 2: No. 834; Tiumentsev, "Gosudarstvo i tserkov'," 142–43; "Otpis'" (No. 79), in Antonov, "Kostromskie monastyri," 186.

65. *AI*, 2: 178–79, 191–92 (Nos. 155, 161); Dunning, *Russia's First Civil War*, 394. (For comparison among different periods, see the large corpus of published and archival monasterial documents.)

66. RGADA, *f.* 1201, *op.* 2, *ed. khr.* 1548 ("Knigi prikhodnye. I rozkhodnye cherntsa aili. Solovetskog[o] monastyria. Nenokotskog[o] usol[']ia monastyrskog[o] promysla prikazshchika," 1602–1609), *ll.* 682–83; RGADA, *f.* 1201, *op.* 2, *ed. khr.* 1550 ("Knigi prikhodnye i roskhodnye tsrennog[o] solia nogonenokotskogo promyslu starta semiona," 1608–1613), *ll.* 622–55*ob.*; RGADA, *f.* 281 (GKE), *op.* 6, *ed. khr.* 9039/315 ("Kupchaia igumna Theodorovskago monastyria Gerasima s bratieiu, na prodannyi imi synu boiarskomu Ivanu Volosatomu dvor . . . ," Apr. 15, 1612); *DAI*, 1: 268–69 (No. 155); *AI*, 2: 397–98 (No. 330); *AAE*, 2: 273–76 (No. 161).

67. Massa, *Present Wars in Moscow*, 175–76; *Pamiatniki Smutnogo vremeni*, 435.

68. RGADA, *f.* 1201 (Solovetskii monastyr'), *op.* 1, *ed. khr.* 7–11; Gruber, "Black Monks"; Gruber, "Russian Orthodox Church," 248–67.

69. RGADA, *f.* 1201, *op.* 1, *ed. khr.* 7, *l.* 43; RGADA, *f.* 1201, *op.* 1, *ed. khr.* 8, *ll.* 35, 57; RGADA, *f.* 1201, *op.* 1, *ed. khr.* 9, *ll.* 39, 77*ob.*, 125*ob.*, 165; RGADA, *f.* 1201, *op.* 1, *ed. khr.* 11, *l.* 119; RGADA, *f.* 1201, *op.* 1, *ed. khr.* 12, *ll.* 4*ob.*, 17*ob.*, 53, 81, 108–108*ob.*; Gruber, "Russian Orthodox Church," 281–83. Cf. Robson, *Solovki*, 62–63. The expenditure for Muscovite years 7118 and 7119 (September 1609 to August 1611) was not totalled separately but rather recorded together at 20,412 rubles. Halving this gives the approximate figure of 10,206 rubles for 7118.

70. Nikolaeva, "Vklady," 93.

71. Ibid., 93–94. Cf. Z. V. Dmitrieva, *Bytnye i opisnye knigi*, 128–30.

72. Spock, "Solovki Monastery," 208, 213, 215–18; Robson, *Solovki*, 62–63.

73. Makarii, *Istoriia russkoi tserkvi*, 1996 ed., 6 (10): 137–38; Tiumentsev, "Gosudarstvo i tserkov'," 147–49, 163.

74. Spock, "Solovki Monastery," 218–27.

75. Nikolaeva, "Vklady," 93. Cf. Lopez, "Hard Times."

76. RGADA, *f.* 1192, *op.* 2, *ed. khr.* 395, *l.* 116*ob.*

77. Ibid., *f.* 1192, *op.* 2, *ed. khr.* 395, *ll.* 95–95*ob.* On commemorative gifts in Muscovite society, see especially Steindorff, *Memoria in Altrussland*.

78. RGADA, *f.* 1192, *op.* 2, *ed. khr.* 395, *ll.* 215*ob.*–216.

79. Dunning, *Russia's First Civil War*, 216.

Chapter Six

1. *Ostryz'ka Bibliia*, [2:] *l.* 119*ob.*; *Biblia sirech knigy*, ed. Turkoniak, 31: 9. The subject (Jerusalem) is feminine in the original Hebrew but masculine in Slavonic.

2. *Novaia povest'*, 207–8. This reading includes a textual emendation: the last word of the recorded expression *kto ne vosplachetsia, kto ne vozraduetsia* ("who will not weep, who will not rejoice") is much more plausible as *vozrydaet* ("lament"). Such a modification is supported both by the overall sense of the passage and on the basis of comparison to parallel texts. The May 1613 document announcing the accession of Mikhail Romanov remarked in a virtually identical context, "who will not weep and lament" (*khto ne vosplachet i ne vzrydaet*). Note that the Ostroh Bible's rendition of John 16:20 reads, "You will weep and lament, but the world will rejoice" (*v"splachetesia i v"zrydaete vy, a mir" v"zraduetsia*)—a combination that may explain the presumed scribal error. *SGGD*, 1: 610; *Biblia sirech knigy*, ed. Turkoniak, 53: 115; *Novaia povest'*, 207n.22.

3. *RIB*, 13: 101–5, 177–86, 235–48, 951–56; Platonov, *Ocherki*, 5th ed., 334–35; Dunning, *Russia's First Civil War*, 292, 557n.99; Perevezentsev, "Uroki smuty"; Kuznetsov, "Sobytiia Smutnogo vremeni." I have not seen Kuznetsov's text, but he reportedly discusses dozens of "vision tales" from the Time of Troubles. Cf. also chap. 1, 4. According to Terence Thomas, "There is no single definition of what constitutes 'Popular Religion.' Some scholars have defined it as rural in contrast to urban forms of religion, the religion of the peasant in contrast to that of the ruling classes; or, in a variation of this definition, the religion of the masses as contrasted with that of the intellectual or sophisticated classes. If, however, popular religion is seen in contrast to 'official' religion, the latter defined as religion founded on authoritative documents and propagated and maintained by religious specialists, priests or hierarchy, then the term 'popular' can apply to any layperson, whether peasant or ruling-class, who adopts beliefs and practices which may be at odds with the religious specialist's views." Thomas, "Popular Religion," 386–87.

5. *RIB*, 13: 103–4, 182–83, emphasis added.

6. According to Daniel Rowland, the Smuta author Ivan Timofeev believed that righteous people of all social classes ("the strong in Israel") could and should protest against the misdeeds of illegitimate but not legitimate tsars. Rowland, "Political Ideas," 396.

7. Cf., e.g., Exodus 15:26, 16:28, 20:6–7; Leviticus 22:31, 26:3–4; Deuteronomy 4:2, 4:40, chap. 28; Joshua 22:5; Hosea 4:1; Matthew 19:17; John 14:15, 15:10.

8. Platonov, *Ocherki*, 3rd ed., 452; Tiumentsev, "Gosudarstvo i tserkov'," 163–64; Rowland, "Muscovite Political Attitudes," 135–36; Perevezentsev, "Uroki smuty."

9. Tarkovskii, "Tri drevnerusskikh perevoda."

10. See Dunning, *Russia's First Civil War*, 398–400.

11. M. Tolstoi, *Istoriia russkoi tserkvi*, 477.

12. Wortman, *Scenarios*, 2: 235–70.

13. D. B. Miller, *Saint Sergius*, 218; Pavlov, "Tserkov[n]aia ierarkhiia," 74; Tiumentsev, *Oborona Troitse-Sergieva monastyria;* Tiumentsev, "Osada"; M. Tolstoi, *Istoriia russkoi tserkvi*, 486–92; and a vast literature on the subject.

14. Zverinskii, *Material dlia issledovaniia*, 2: No. 864.

15. *AI*, 2: 136 (No. 106, Nov. 1608).

16. E.g., Morozova, *Smuta nachala XVII v.*; Dunning, "L. E. Morozova," 235–38.

17. Dunning, *Russia's First Civil War*, 400–403.

18. RGADA, *f.* 281 (GKE), *op.* 5, *ed. khr.* 8018/77 ("Dogovornaia zapis' Arkhimandrita Pecherskogo monastyria Ioilia s bratieiu, s Arkhimandritom Simonova monastyria Filafeem, na rybnyia lovli v reke Volge," Mar. 6, 1610), *ll.* 1–3. Historians often aver that the Monastyrskii Prikaz (Monasterial Chancellery or Office) was founded in 1649–1650, in accordance with chapter 13 of the 1649 *Ulozhenie* (law code). However, this document of Nizhnii Novgorod's Pecherskii Monastery clearly speaks of a government organ going by the same name forty years earlier (*i veleno nam stoiati na moskve v monastyrskom prikaze pered gosudarevym boiarinom pered kniazem volodimerom timofeevichem dolgorukovo*). Mikhail Gorchakov opened his well-known study of the institution with a qualified assertion: "In the form of a special, independent institution of the state, the Monastyrskii Prikaz was founded by the Conciliar Ulozhenie of Tsar Aleksei Mikhailovich in 1649." The chancellery did in fact exist in another "form" previously. In his *History of the Russian Church*, Makarii pointed to documents from 1611 referring to the Monastyrskii Prikaz. He surmised that it must have been a department (*otdelenie*) of the Prikaz Bol'shogo Dvortsa (Chancellery of the Grand Court). Peter Brown has also identified documents from the early seventeenth century related to this chancellery. *Sobornoe ulozhenie 1649 goda*, 170; Gorchakov, *Monastyrskii prikaz*, 3; Makarii, *Istoriia russkoi tserkvi*, 1996 ed., 6 (10): 615n.133; Brown, "How Muscovy Governed," 526. Cf. Bushkovitch, *Religion and Society*, 57; Boguslavskii, *Slavianskaia entsiklopediia*, 1: 392–93.

19. *AAE*, 2: 269–71 (No. 158).

20. Ibid., 2: 271–72.

21. Ibid., 2: 271.

22. *RIB*, 13: 228–29, 1323–48; M. Tolstoi, *Istoriia russkoi tserkvi*, 474–75; Dunning, *Russia's First Civil War*, 400–410.

23. *AAE*, 2: 277–78.

24. Ibid.

25. Cf. Ostrowski, *Muscovy and the Mongols*, 216–17.

26. Cf. Platonov, *Ocherki*, 3rd ed., 450; Platonov, *Ocherki*, 5th ed., 336; M. Tolstoi, *Istoriia russkoi tserkvi*, 492–94.

27. *RIB*, 13: 229.

28. Floria, *Pol'sko-litovskaia interventsiia*, 127ff., 200ff.; Vernadsky, *Tsardom of Moscow*, 1: 249–54.

29. *AAE*, 2: 280–84.

30. Żółkiewski, *Expedition to Moscow*, 91; Govorun, "Voprosy o tserkvi," 168–92.

31. *AAE*, 2: 284–86 (Nos. 166, 168).

32. Zverinskii, *Material dlia issledovaniia*, 2: Nos. 763, 822, 857, 879, 903, 911, 915, 918, 933, 934, 964, 973, 988, 1001, 1008, 1026, 1029, 1057, 1104, 1154, 1202, 1216, 1249, etc.; RGADA, *f.* 1196, *op.* 3, *d./ed. khr.* 1549 ("Antonievo-Siiskii monastyr'. Istoricheskoe i arkheologicheskoe opisanie," 1890), *l.* 33; *AI*, 2: 158–60 (No. 137, "Chelobitnaia Iaroslavskago Spasskago monastyria arkhimandrita Theofila getmanu Sapege, ob osvobozhdenii monastyrskoi otchiny ot sbora kormov, po prichine razoreniia eia ratnymi liud'mi," Jan. 13, 1609); *PMR*, 154; *Geografiia Rossii*, 249–50; M. Tolstoi, *Istoriia russkoi tserkvi*, 482–86; Robson, *Solovki*, 63. Cf. the Japanese conception of *kami kaze* ("divine winds") that destroyed an invading Mongol fleet in 1281.

33. *RIB*, 13: 200; *Novaia povest'*, 197–98; Platonov, *Ocherki*, 5th ed., 334–35; Dunning, *Russia's First Civil War*, 351; Perevezentsev, "Uroki smuty." Cf. Filiushkin, "Religioznyi faktor," 159, 165, passim.

34. Makarii, *Istoriia russkoi tserkvi*, 1996 ed., 6 (10): 110; Platonov, *Ocherki*, 5th ed., 337–38.

35. Platonov, *Ocherki*, 5th ed., 334–40; M. Tolstoi, *Istoriia russkoi tserkvi*, 494–96.

36. E.g., *AAE*, 2: 318–27 (No. 188); M. Tolstoi, *Istoriia russkoi tserkvi*, 495.

37. Dunning, *Russia's First Civil War*, 415.

38. *AAE*, 2: 286. Cf. *RIB*, 13: 227.

39. *AAE*, 2: 287–90; Matthew 24:7. Cf. Romans 11:21.

40. *AAE*, 2: 289–90.

41. Dunning, *Russia's First Civil War*, 416.

42. See Makarii, *Istoriia russkoi tserkvi*, 1996 ed., 6 (10): 116.

43. M. Tolstoi, *Istoriia russkoi tserkvi*, 484–85; Vernadsky, *Tsardom of Moscow*, 1: 261–66.

44. Antonov, "Iz pomestnoi praktiki," 7: 396.

45. "Ukaznaia" (No. 45), in Kisterev, "Vladimirskii Rozhdestvenskii monastyr'," 146–47.

46. See, e.g., Dunning, *Russia's First Civil War*, 430–34; Zabelin, *Minin i Pozharskii;* Skrynnikov, *Minin i Pozharskii;* Shishov, *Minin i Pozharskii;* Shamshurin, *Minin i Pozharskii.*

47. *OAU*, 100–101 (§1: No. 89).

48. Pavlov, "Tserkov[n]aia ierarkhiia," 74.

49. On the careers of these two officials, see Veselovskii, *D'iaki i pod'iachie*, 151, 585. On the strength of various contemporary reports, Platonov called Shulgin "unreliable" (*nenadezhnyi*). Platonov, *Ocherki*, 5th ed., 349, 354.

50. Zverinskii, *Material dlia issledovaniia*, 2: Nos. 1223–24. Cf. Ratshin, *Polnoe sobranie*, 87; *MES*, 135, 204; *MRPTs*, 61, 208–9; *PMR*, 42.

51. *OAU*, 101–2 (§1: No. 90).

52. *AI*, 2: 249–50 (No. 212); Hellie, *Economy and Material Culture*, 12, 27–29, 647–48.

53. *OAU*, 103.

54. *PDS*, 2: 690–91; *PSRL*, 13: 249–50; Dmitriev, "Tsarskie nakazy"; Szeftel, "Title of Muscovite Monarch," 59–81; Gruber, "Muscovite Embassy," 42–43; Evtuhov et al., *History of Russia*, 127; Riasanovsky, *History of Russia*, 144; Matthew Romaniello, private correspondence, August 2010. At this time Viatka was the name of the region, with its center in the town of Khlynov. In the later eighteenth century Khlynov itself was renamed as Viatka. Under Stalin the city changed its name again, to Kirov. My thanks to David Goldfrank and Matthew Romaniello for pointing out some of these sources concerning the Kazan administration.

55. Cf. Dunning, *Russia's First Civil War*, 464–65; Vernadsky, *Tsardom of Moscow*, 1: 260.

56. *OAU*, 104–5 (§1: No. 92). One *chet'* of grain usually equaled eight poods (131 kg.; 288 lbs.) but sometimes only four or six poods (66–98 kg.; 144–216 lbs.). Hellie, *Economy and Material Culture*, 646, 648.

57. Vernadsky, *Tsardom of Moscow*, 1: 257.

58. "Vttolckningen vtaf," 2–5.

59. For a review of documents and historiography on the izbranie of Mikhail, see Morozova, *Rossiia na puti*, 5–46, passim.

60. *SGGD*, 1: 599–609 (No. 203, "Izbranie na tsarstvo Gosudaria Tsaria Mikhaila Theodorovicha," May 1613).

61. Ibid., 1: 608–10; Matthew 2.
62. *SGGD*, 1: 610ff.
63. Ibid., 1: 611–15; M. Tolstoi, *Istoriia russkoi tserkvi*, 499.
64. *SGGD*, 1: 615–22.
65. Thyrêt, "Marfa Ivanovna," 110–11, passim.
66. Cf. Bennet, "Idea of Kingship," 42–52; Pavlov, "Tserkov[n]aia ierarkhiia," 68; and numerous works on the Time of Troubles.
67. *SGGD*, 1: 615–26. (Cf. chap. 3.)
68. *SGGD*, 1: 626–36.
69. Thyrêt, *Between God and Tsar;* R. E. Martin, "Choreographing," 813–14; Thyrêt, "Marfa Ivanovna"; Thyrêt, "Blessed."
70. *PDS*, 2: 921–71.
71. Ibid., 2: 1098ff., 1122, 1166, 1257, passim; *Istoriia diplomatii*, 1: 292, 307; Gruber, "Muscovite Embassy," 9, 70; *England and the North.*
72. *PDS*, 2: 1298; Keep, "*Moskau und die Politik*," 541–42; Dunning, *Russia's First Civil War*, 453, 456–57.
73. E.g., Dunning, *Russia's First Civil War*, 450–57; Vernadsky, *Tsardom of Moscow*, 1: 276–91.
74. Dunning, *Russia's First Civil War*, 442, 445–47, 451–59.
75. *PDS*, 2: 927–28, 1166; Rowland, "Political Ideas," 395–96; Dunning, *Russia's First Civil War*, 443, 445, 447, 584n.7. Cf. Gonneau, "L'église," 25.
76. *RGADA, f.* 1192, *op.* 1, *ed. khr.* 4 ("Gramota patriarkha Filareta o vysylke v Moskvu k opravke tolkovogo voskresnogo evangeliia," 1628); *PDS*, 2: 927–28, 1095, 1238, passim; Makarii, *Istoriia russkoi tserkvi*, 1996 ed., 6 (10): 127; Michels, "Power, Patronage, and Repression," 81; Dunning, *Russia's First Civil War*, 443–45; Morozova, *Smuta nachala XVII v.*, passim; Dunning, "L. E. Morozova," 235–38. Cf. Makarii, *Istoriia russkoi tserkvi*, 1996 ed., 6 (10): 114–27.
77. RGADA, *f.* 1196, *op.* 7, *ed. khr.* 9; RGADA, *f.* 1201, *op.* 1, *ed. khr.* 11–12; RGADA, *f.* 1206, *op.* 1, *ed. khr.* 1; RGADA, *f.* 281 (GKE), and other monasterial *fondy;* *AMMS*, 25, 72–73, 82, 396–406 (Nos. 6, 23, 26, 148); Sadovskii, "Vyborka," 13–19; Sadovskii, "Kniga," 17–34; Snezhnitskii, "Kopii," 40–55; *OAU*, 100–101, 158–59, 161 (§1: No. 89; §2: Nos. 123–24, 129); *DAI*, 2: 64, 67–68 (Nos. 34, 37); *AAE*, 2: 374–75 (No. 220); *Dokumenty Pechatnogo prikaza*, 297; Zverinskii, *Material dlia issledovaniia*, 2: Nos. 763, 822, 874, 915, 953, 985, 1001, 1026, 1104, 1202, 1216, 1235; V. I. Ivanov, "Nekotorye voprosy," 126–34; Hellie, *Economy and Material Culture*, 4; Gruber, "Russian Orthodox Church," 281–83. Cf. *OAU*, 111–12, 161 (§2: Nos. 2, 4, 127–29); *AI*, 2: 402–3 (No. 337); *DAI*, 2: 19–24, 36–38, 83–85 (Nos. 10, 17, 49–51); *AAE*, 2: 271 (No. 212); Platonov, *Ocherki*, 5th ed., 366.

Notes to Chapter Seven

1. *Ostryz'ka Bibliia*, [1:] *l.* 121; *Biblia sirech knigy*, ed. Turkoniak, 7: 103.
2. L. N. Tolstoi, "Otvet na opredelenie Sinoda," in his *Sobranie sochinenii*, 17: 201.
3. See, e.g., Mark 15:22 and John 19:17 in the Ostroh or Fyodorov Bible of 1581. *Biblia sirech knigy*, ed. Dergacheva, [3:] *ll.* 27, 54*ob.*
4. See chap. 1.
5. Filiushkin, "Religioznyi faktor," 145, 159, 165, 178, passim.

6. Dunning, *Russia's First Civil War*, 90.

7. Perevezentsev, "Uroki smuty." Cf. Solzhenitsyn, "Pravoslavnaia tserkov'."

8. E.g., Zverinskii, *Material dlia issledovaniia*, 2: Nos. 742, 743, 749, 756, 905, 992, 1189, 1219, passim; Bushkovitch, *Religion and Society*, 125.

9. Romanenko, *Povsednevnaia zhizn'*, 297, 300.

10. N. M. Nikol'skii, *Istoriia russkoi tserkvi*, 120. Cf. Dykstra, *Russian Monastic Culture*, 220–21nn.406–7.

11. Bushkovitch, *Religion and Society*, 11ff., 176, passim.

12. See de Madariaga, *Ivan the Terrible*, 107–11, 174–79, 298–316, 340–43.

13. Cf. Filiushkin, "Religioznyi faktor," 147, 150.

14. See chap. 3; Perevezentsev, "Uroki smuty"; Whittaker, "Chosen," 6.

15. Quoted in M. Tolstoi, *Istoriia russkoi tserkvi*, 483. Cf. Bushkovitch, *Religion and Society*, 104, 213n.4; Thyrêt, *Between God and Tsar*, 102; Shevzov, *Russian Orthodoxy*, 217ff., 329n.151.

16. E.g., T. A. Smith, *Volokolamsk Paterikon*, 7–8; Ware, *Orthodox Church*, 1–2, 8, 195–207, passim; Dagron, *Emperor and Priest*, 158–91; Magoulias, *Byzantine Christianity*, 17–65; Bernshtam, "Russian Folk Culture," 36.

17. E.g., N. K. Nikol'skii, *Kirillo-Belozerskii monastyr'*, 2: 139; Budovnits, *Russkaia publitsistika*, 302; Bernshtam, "Russian Folk Culture," 37, 42; Gruber, "Hebrew Concepts."

18. E.g., Platonov, *Ocherki*, 3rd ed., 450; Gonneau, "L'église," 42; Pavlov, "Tserkov[n]aia ierarkhiia," 77–79.

19. E.g., Hughes, *Sophia, Regent of Russia*, 43–44, 62; Hughes, *Russia*, 2, 8–11; Grey, *Peter the Great*, 36–47.

20. Thyrêt, *Between God and Tsar;* Marker, *Imperial Saint*.

21. See, e.g., Avrich, *Russian Rebels*.

22. Whittaker, "Chosen," 5–6, 18, passim.

23. See the epigraph to chap. 3.

24. See the introduction and, e.g., Crummey, "Orthodox Church," 618–19; Aver'ianov, "Smutnoe vremia."

25. Dunning, *Russia's First Civil War*, 475.

26. Michels, "Power, Patronage, and Repression," 93–96.

27. E.g., Bushkovitch, "National Consciousness," 374–75; Pavlov, "Tserkov[n]aia ierarkhiia," 78; Dunning, *Russia's First Civil War*, 474–77.

28. Bushkovitch, *Religion and Society*, 128ff. Cf. Keenan, "Ivan III," 242–43.

29. Vlasov, "Christianization," 17. Cf. 29.

30. Crummey, *Formation of Muscovy*, 138.

31. Likhachev, *Natsional'noe samosoznanie*, 111–19.

32. Kliuchevskii, *Kurs russkoi istorii*, 3: 82ff.; Kliuchevsky, *History of Russia*, 3: 64ff.

33. Bushkovitch, "National Consciousness."

34. Bernshtam, "Russian Folk Culture," 43–44, emphasis in original.

35. Bussov, *Moskovskaia khronika*, 317–21; Bussow, *Disturbed State*, 160ff.; D. B. Miller, "Orthodox Church," 359.

36. D. B. Miller, *Saint Sergius*, 230.

37. Dunning, *Russia's First Civil War*, 115, 476.

38. Michels, *At War*, 4, 10, 21–22, 45, 54, 77, 84, 195, 199, passim; Michels,

"Ruling without Mercy"; Crummey, *Old Believers*, 14, passim; Crummey, "Orthodox Church," 627; Vlasov, "Christianization," 25. (Cf. chap. 6.)

39. Bushkovitch, *Religion and Society*, 103–24, passim. Cf. Michels, "Patriarch's Rivals," 337.

40. Makarii, *Istoriia russkoi tserkvi*, 1996 ed., 6 (10): 114–27.

41. P. Meyendorff, *Russia, Ritual, and Reform;* Michels, "Patriarch's Rivals," 323, 328.

42. Michels, "Patriarch's Rivals," 340.

43. D. B. Miller, "Orthodox Church," 358.

44. Gonneau, "L'église," 25.

45. Karamzin, *Zapiska*, 13; Karamzin, *Ancient and Modern Russia*, 113; Karamzin, *Istoriia gosudarstva Rossiiskago*, 11: 7–8, 78–79, 105–6, 118–20.

46. M. Tolstoi, *Istoriia russkoi tserkvi*, 466, 492.

47. Billington, *Icon and Axe*, 94, 123–24; Dunning, *Russia's First Civil War*, 475.

48. Dunning, *Russia's First Civil War*, 472; Michels, *At War*, 2, passim; Michels, "Power, Patronage, and Repression," 81–83, 89–91, passim.

49. "Sviashchennosluzhiteli o 'simfonii.'" Cf. Knox, *Russian Society*; Garrard and Garrard, *Russian Orthodoxy Resurgent*; Daniel, *Orthodox Church*; Stolyarova, "You Scratcheth"; Stolyarova, "Holiest of Water"; Anderson, "Putin."

50. Personal interview of local woman in Alaskan Old Belief [*starovery*] Russian Orthodox village, January 2007. Cf. Dolitskii, *Staraia Rossiia*; Robson, *Old Believers*.

51. Quoted in Ul'ianovskii, "Motiv," 202. Cf. Psalms 48/49:2/3; Proverbs 22:2; Jeremiah 44/51:12. My thanks to David Goldfrank for pointing out the similarities to Nil Sorskii's adaptations of John of Damascus (mostly his *Order of the Service of the Dead*). Goldfrank, private correspondence, August 2010; Sorskii, *Nil Sorsky*, 194–96.

Bibliography

Archives

Library of Congress, Law Library—Rare Books, Washington, DC: Russian Manuscript Scrolls Collection (Microfilm 95/10004 RR)

Rossiiskaia natsional'naia biblioteka [Russian National Library], Otdel rukopisei [Manuscripts Division], St. Petersburg:
Fond 351, Kirillo-Belozerskii monastyr'

Rossiiskii gosudarstvennyi arkhiv drevnykh aktov [Russian State Archive of Ancient Acts], Moscow:
Fond 233, Pechatnyi prikaz
Fond 235, Patriarshii kazennyi prikaz
Fond 236, Patriarshii dvortsovyi prikaz
Fond 237, Monastyrskii prikaz
Fond 281, Gramoty Kollegii ekonomii
Fond 1111, Verkhoturskaia prikaznaia izba
Fond 1187, Troitskii-Gledenskii monastyr'
Fond 1188, Danilov monastyr'
Fond 1189, Zaikonospasskii monastyr'
Fond 1190, Zlatoustov monastyr'
Fond 1191, Znamenskii monastyr'
Fond 1192, Iosifo-Volokolamskii monastyr'
Fond 1194, Klopskii-Troitskii monastyr'
Fond 1195, Krestnyi Onezhskii monastyr'
Fond 1196, Antoniev-Siiskii monastyr'
Fond 1197, Novospasskii monastyr'
Fond 1198, Pafnut'ev-Borovskii monastyr'
Fond 1199, Savvo-Starozhevskii monastyr'
Fond 1200, Svenskii-Uspenskii monastyr'
Fond 1201, Solovetskii monastyr'
Fond 1202, Solotchinskii monastyr'
Fond 1203, Spaso-Evfim'evskoi monastyr' v g. Suzdale

Fond 1204, Troitse-Sergievskaia lavra
Fond 1205, Nikolo-Ugreshskii monastyr'
Fond 1206, Ustiuzhskii arkhiereiskii dom
Fond 1207, Chudov monastyr'

Published Primary and Secondary Sources

Abaecherli, Aline L. "The Institution of the Imperial Cult in the Western Provinces of the Roman Empire." Bologna: Zanichelli, 1935. [Extracted from: *Studi e Materiali di Storia delle Religioni* 11 (1935): 153–86.]

Abramovich, G. V. *Kniaz'ia Shuiskie i rossiiskii tron.* Leningrad: Izd-vo Leningradskogo universiteta, 1991.

Adelung, Johann Christoph. *Grammatisch-kritisches Wörterbuch der Hochdeutschen Mundart.* 4 vols. Leipzig: Breitkopf, 1793–1801. Reprinted New York: Georg Olms, 1970.

Akhmedkhanov, Dalgat. *Smuta v moem zerkale.* Makhachkala, 2003.

Akty feodal'nogo zemlevladeniia i khoziaistva. Edited by L. V. Cherepnin. Vols. 1–3. Moscow: Akademiia nauk, 1951–1961.

Akty feodal'nogo zemlevladeniia i khoziaistva. Akty Moskovskogo Simonova monastyria (1506–1613 gg.). Edited by L. I. Ivina. Leningrad: Nauka, 1983.

Akty istoricheskie i iuridicheskie i drevniia tsarskiia gramoty Kazanskoi i drugikh sosedstvennykh gubernii. Edited by Stepan Mel'nikov. Vol. 1. Kazan: Dubrovin, 1859.

Akty istoricheskie, sobrannye i izdannye Arkheograficheskoiu kommissieiu. 5 vols. St. Petersburg: Imp. Velichestva Kantseliariia, 1841–1842.

Akty izdavaemye Vilenskoiu kommissieiu dlia razbora drevnikh aktov [aka *Akty izdavaemye kommissieiu, Vysochaishe uchrezhdennoiu dlia razbora drevnikh aktov v Vil'ne*]. 39 vols. Vilnius, 1865–1915.

Akty Nizhegorodskago Pecherskago Vosnesenskago monastyria. Moscow: Snegirevoi, 1898.

Akty, otnosiashchiesia do iuridicheskago byta drevnei Rossii. Edited by N. V. Kalachov. 4 vols. St. Petersburg: Tip. Imp. akademiia nauk, 1857–1901.

Akty Rossiiskogo gosudarstva: Arkhivy moskovskikh monastyrei i soborov XV–nachalo XVII vv. Edited by T. N. Aleksinskaia, V. K. Baranov, A. V. Mashtafarov, V. D. Nazarov, Iu. D. Rykov, et al. Moscow: Ladomir, 1998.

Akty sluzhilykh zemlevladel'tsev XV–nachala XVII veka. Edited by A. V. Antonov and K. V. Baranov. 3 vols. Moscow: Arkheograficheskii tsentr/Pamiatniki istoricheskoi mysli/Drevlekhranilishche, 1997–2002.

Akty, sobrannye v bibliotekakh i arkhivakh Rossiiskoi imperii Arkheograficheskoiu ekspeditsieiu Imperatorskoi akademii nauk. 4 vols. St. Petersburg: Imp. Velichestva Kantseliariia, 1836–1838.

Akty sotsial'no-ekonomicheskoi istorii severo-vostochnoi Rusi kontsa XIV–nachala XVI v. Edited by B. D. Grekov and L. V. Cherepnin. Vols. 1–3. Moscow: AN SSSR, 1952–1964.

Akty Suzdal'skogo Spaso-Evfim'eva monastyria 1506–1608 gg. Edited by S. N. Kisterev. Moscow: Pamiatniki istoricheskoi mysli, 1998.

Akty vremeni pravleniia tsaria Vasiliia Shuiskago (1606 g. 19 maia–17 iiulia 1610 g.). Edited by A. M. Gnevushev. Moscow: Lissner i Sovko, 1914.

Alef, Gustave. "The Adoption of the Muscovite Two-Headed Eagle: A Discordant View." *Speculum* 41, no. 1 (Jan. 1966): 1–21.

Aleksandrovskii, M. *Ukazatel' moskovskikh tserkvei.* Edited by S. V. Korolev. [2nd ed.] Moscow: MGO VOOPIiK, 1996.

Alekseev, A. A. *Tekstologiia slavianskoi Biblii/Textgeschichte der slavischen Bibel.* St. Petersburg: Dmitrii Bulanin, 1999.

Alekseev, Iurii G. *Agrarnaia i sotsial'naia istoriia severo-vostochnoi Rusi XV–XVI vv.: Pereiaslavskii uezd.* Moscow: Nauka, 1966.

Alekseev, Petr Alekseevich. *Tserkovnyi slovar'/Cerkovnyj slovar', ili istolkovanie slavenskich, takže malovrazumitel'nych drevnich rěčenij.* 4th ed. 5 vols. St. Petersburg: Glazunov, 1817–1819. Reprinted New York: Georg Olms, 1976.

Alfeyev, Hilarion. "Russia: Recent Changes." In *Encyclopedia of Monasticism,* edited by William M. Johnston, 2: 1101–3. Chicago: Fitzroy Dearborn, 2000.

Alpatov, M. A. *Russkaia istoricheskaia mysl' i zapadnaia Evropa: XII–XVII vv.* Moscow: Nauka, 1973.

———. *Russkaia istoricheskaia mysl' i zapadnaia Evropa: XVII—pervaia chetvert' XVIII veka.* Moscow: Nauka, 1976.

Ambrosiani, Per. "Nazvaniia dereven' i sel v Novgorodskom okkupatsionnom arkhive." *Novgorodskii istoricheskii sbornik* 10, no. 20: 309–12.

Anan'ev, V. G. "[Review of] Ul'ianovskii V. I., *Smutnoe vremia.*" *Studia Slavica et Balcanica Petropolitana* 3, nos. 1–2/5–6 (2009): 272–84.

Anastos, Milton V. "Byzantine Political Theory: Its Classical Precedents and Legal Embodiment." In *The "Past" in Medieval and Modern Greek Culture,* edited by S. Vryonis, Jr., 13–54. Malibu, CA: Undena, 1978.

Anderson, John. "Putin and the Russian Orthodox Church: Asymmetric Symphonia?" *Journal of International Affairs* 61, no. 1 (Fall/Winter 2007): 185–201.

Andreev, Aleksandr. *Stroganovy: Entsiklopedicheskoe izdanie.* Moscow: Belyi volk, 2000.

Angold, Michael, ed. *Eastern Christianity. The Cambridge History of Christianity.* Vol. 5. Cambridge: Cambridge University Press, 2006.

Ankersmit, Frank, and Hans Kellner, eds. *A New Philosophy of History.* Chicago: University of Chicago Press, 1995.

Annotated Justinian Code. Translated by Fred H. Blume. Edited by Timothy Kearley. 2nd ed. University of Wyoming Law Library. http://uwacadweb.uwyo.edu/blume&justinian.

"Antonii Siiskii." *MERSH* 2: 46.

Antonov, A. V., ed. "Akty sluzhilykh tatar 1525–1609 godov." In *Russkii diplomatarii*, 7: 219–32. Moscow: Arkheograficheskii tsentr, 2001.

———, ed. "Iz pomestnoi praktiki Smutnogo vremeni." In *Russkii diplomatarii*, 7: 396–402. Moscow: Arkheograficheskii tsentr, 2001.

———, ed. "Kostromskie monastyri v dokumentakh XVI–nachala XVII veka." In *Russkii diplomatarii*, 7: 52–218. Moscow: Arkheograficheskii tsentr, 2001.

———, et al. "Materialy k katalogu aktov Russkogo gosudarstva." Parts 1–9. In *Russkii diplomatarii*. Vols. 1–9. Moscow: Arkheograficheskii tsentr, 1997–2003.

———. "Russkii diplomatarii: Real'nost' i perspektivy." In *Russkii diplomatarii*, 6: 241–46. Moscow: Arkheograficheskii tsentr, 2000.

Apostol, P. N. *Moskoviia v predstavlenii inostrantsev XVI–XVII v.* Edited by G. K. Lukomskii. Berlin: Academia, 1922.

Arakcheev, V. A. "Sobornoe ulozhenie 9 marta 1607 g." In *Rossiiskoe gosudarstvo v XVI–XVII vv.: Sbornik statei, posviashchennyi 75-letiiu so dnia rozhdeniia Iu. G. Alekse-eva*, edited by A. G. Man'kov et al., 98–115. St. Petersburg: Dmitrii Bulanin, 2002.

Arel, Maria Salomon, Erika Monahan, Russell Martin, Janet Martin, and Nikolaos Chrissidis. "Gift-Giving in Muscovy: Forms and Meanings." Panel 5–30 at the 41st National Convention of the American Association for the Advancement of Slavic Studies. Boston: November 13, 2009.

Arkhipov, Andrei. "K izucheniiu siuzheta o vybore very. 'Povest' vremennykh let' i 'evre-isko-khazarskaia perepiska.'" In *Jews and Slavs*, edited by Wolf Moskovich, Shmuel Shvarzband, and Anatoly Alekseev, 1: 20–43. Jerusalem: Hebrew University of Jerusalem, 1993.

———. *Po tu storony Sambationa: Etiudy o russko-evreiskikh kul'turnykh, iazykovykh i literaturnykh kontaktakh v X–XVI vekakh*. Vol. 9 of *Monuments of Early Russian Literature*. Oakland, CA: Berkeley Slavic Specialties, 1995.

Arkhiv russkoi istorii: Nauchnyi istoricheskii zhurnal. Edited by I. A. Tikhoniuk et al. Vols. 3–4. Moscow: RGADA/Arkheograficheskii tsentr, 1993–1994.

Armstrong, Peter C. B. "Foreigners, Furs, and Faith: Muscovy's Expansion into Western Siberia, 1581–1649." PhD diss., Dalhousie University, 1997.

Arustamian, Sergei. *Khroniki Smutnogo vremeni*. Erevan: Izd-vo RAU, 2002.

Atlas avtomobil'nykh dorog ot Atlantiki do Tikhogo okeana. Minsk: Trivium, 1999.

Avdeev, A. G., ed. "Galichskii Uspenskii Pais'ev monastyr' po dokumentam XV–XVII vekov." In *Russkii diplomatarii*, 7: 314–47. Moscow: Arkheograficheskii tsentr, 2001.

Aver'ianov, Vitalii. "Smutnoe vremia i mutatsii ideologii." *Perspektivy: Fond istoricheskoi perspektivy.* [Reprinted from *Novaia politika,* June 18, 2004.] http://www.perspectivy.com/misl/idea/smutnoe_vremya.htm.

Avrich, Paul. *Russian Rebels, 1600–1800.* New York: Norton/Schocken, 1972.

Avvakum, Petrovich, Archpriest. *The Life Written by Himself.* Translated by Kenneth N. Brostrom. Ann Arbor: University of Michigan Slavic Publications, 1979.

———. *Zhitie protopopa Avvakuma, im samim napisannoe, i drugie ego sochineniia.* Gorkii: Volgo-Viatskoe knizh. izd-vo, 1988.

Aydelotte, William O. *Quantification in History.* Reading, MA: Addison-Wesley, 1971.

Baev, Pavel K. "Newly Russian Invented Holiday becomes a Day of Nazi Unity." *Eurasia Daily Monitor* 2.209 (Nov. 9, 2005). http://www.jamestown.org/single/?no_cache=1&tx_ttnews[tt_news]=31078.

———. *The Russian Army in a Time of Troubles.* London: Sage, 1996.

———. "The Russian March That Wasn't: Moscow Avoids a Holiday Pogrom." *Eurasia Daily Monitor* 3.205 (Nov. 6, 2006). http://www.cdi.org/russia/johnson/2006-249–2a.cfm.

Banishko evangelie: Srednob"lgarski pametnik ot XIII vek. Edited by Ekaterina Dogramadzhieva and Bozhidar Raikov. Sofia: B"lgarskata Akad. na Naukite, 1981.

Bantysh-Kamensky, N. N. *Obzor vneshnikh snoshenii Rossii (po 1800 god).* 4 vols. Moscow: Lissner i Roman, 1894–1902.

Barash, Jeffrey Andrew. *Martin Heidegger and the Problem of Historical Meaning.* Dordrecht: Nijhoff, 1988.

Barbour, Philip L. *Dimitry Called the Pretender: Tsar and Great Prince of All Russia, 1605–1606.* Boston: Houghton Mifflin, 1966.

Baron, Samuel H., and Nancy Shields Kollmann, eds. *Religion and Culture in Early Modern Russia and Ukraine.* DeKalb: Northern Illinois University Press, 1997.

Batalden, Stephen K., ed. *Seeking God: The Recovery of Religious Identity in Orthodox Russia, Ukraine, and Georgia.* DeKalb: Northern Illinois University Press, 1993.

Beliaev, Aleksandr. *Illiustrirovannaia istoriia russkoi tserkvi.* Moscow: Voskresnyi den', 1894.

Bennet, Douglas J. "The Idea of Kingship in 17th Century Russia." PhD diss., Harvard University, 1968.

Berdyshev, Sergei N. *Smutnoe vremia.* Moscow: Mir knigi, 2008.

Bernshtam, Tat'iana A. "Russian Folk Culture and Folk Religion." In *Russian Traditional Culture: Religion, Gender, and Customary Law,* edited by Marjorie Mandelstam Balzer, 34–47. London: Sharpe, 1992.

Berry, Lloyd E., and Robert O. Crummey, eds. *Rude and Barbarous Kingdom: Russia in the Accounts of Sixteenth-Century English Voyagers.* Madison: University of Wisconsin Press, 1968.

Beskrovnyi, L. G. *Atlas kart i skhem po russkoi voennoi istorii.* Moscow: VINKVS SSSR, 1946.

Bezborodko, Fedor. "S Bozh'ei pomoshch'iu—cherez Smutnoe vremia." *Trud* 205 (Nov. 5, 1998).

———. "V preddverii smuty." *Nezavisimaia gazeta: Figury i litsa* 4 (1998).

La Bible. Translated by André Chouraqui. Paris: Desclée de Brouwer, 1989.

Biblia Hebraica Stuttgartensia. Accessed via *macBible 3.0* [computer program].

Biblia sirech' knigi sviashchennago pisaniia vetkhago i novago zaveta. Moscow: Synodal, 1914.

Biblia sirech['] knigy vetkhago i novago zaveta, po iazyku slovensku [*Ostroz'ka Bibliia 1581 r.*]. Edited by Rafail (Roman Turkoniak). 61 vols. Lvov: UBT, 2003–2005.

Biblia sirech['] knigy vetkhago i novago zaveta, po iazyku slovensku [Ostroh Bible]. Edited by I. V. Dergacheva. Moscow: Slovo-Art, 1988.

Billington, James H. *The Icon and the Axe: An Interpretive History of Russian Culture.* New York: Vintage, 1966.

Bloch, Marc. *Apologie pour l'histoire, ou Métier d'historien.* 3rd ed. Paris: Colin, 1959. Crit. ed. Edited by Étienne Bloch. Paris: Colin, 1993.

———. *The Historian's Craft.* Translated by Peter Putnam. New York: Knopf, 1963.

Bloom, Harold, ed. *Fyodor Dostoevsky's "The Brothers Karamazov."* New York: Chelsea, 1988.

Blum, Jerome. *Lord and Peasant in Russia, From the Ninth to the Nineteenth Century.* Princeton, NJ: Princeton University Press, 1961.

Boas, George. "*Vox populi.*" In *The Dictionary of the History of Ideas: Studies of Selected Pivotal Ideas*, edited by Philip P. Wiener, 4: 496–500. New York: Scribner, 1974. Available online at http://etext.lib.virginia.edu/cgi-local/DHI/dhi.cgi?id=dv4–67.

———. *Vox Populi: Essays in the History of an Idea.* Baltimore, MD: Johns Hopkins University Press, 1969.

Bochkarev, V. N., Iu. V. Got'e, and V. I. Picheta, eds. *Smutnoe vremia v Moskovskom gosudarstve: Sbornik statei s illiustratsiiami.* Moscow: Zadruga, 1913.

Bogatyrev, Sergei. "Dary angliiskogo posla Tomasa Smita Borisu Godunovu." In *Rossiia i Britania. Mezhdunarodnaia nauchnaia konferentsiia k 450-letiiu ustanovleniia diplomaticheskikh otnoshenii i torgovykh sviazei. Tezisy dokladov*, 17–19. Moscow: Kremlin Museums/British Embassy, 2003.

————. "Micro-Periodization and Dynasticism: Was There a Divide in the Reign of Ivan the Terrible?" *Slavic Review* 69, no. 2 (Summer 2010): 398–409.

————. "Reinventing the Russian Monarchy in the 1550s: Ivan the Terrible, the Dynasty, and the Church." *Slavonic and East European Review* 85, no. 2 (Apr. 2007): 271–93.

Bogdanov, A. P. *Russkie patriarkhi, 1589–1700.* 2 vols. Moscow: Terra, 1999.

Boguslavskii, Vladimir V. *Slavianskaia entsiklopediia: XVII vek.* 2 vols. Moscow: Olma-Press, 2004.

Böhne, Matthias, and Olaf Simmons. "The Marteau Early 18th-Century Currency Converter: A Platform of Research in Economic History." http://www.pierre-marteau.com/currency/converter.html.

Bohuslawsky, Boris. "'Holie as a Horse': English Travellers and the Representation of Russian Orthodoxy, 1553–1614." MA thesis, Queen's University, 1997.

Bolsover, G. H. "Ivan the Terrible in Russian Historiography." *Transactions of the Royal Historical Society,* 5th Ser., 7 (1957): 71–89.

Bonwetsch, D. "Die christliche vornicänische Litteratur (mit Einschluss der jüdisch-hellenistischen und apokalyptischen) in altslavischen Handschriften." In *Geschichte der altchristlichen Literatur bis Eusebius*, edited by Adolf Harnack, 1: 886–917. Leipzig: Verlag, 1958.

Borisenkov, E. P., and V. M. Pasetskii. *Tysiachiletniaia letopis' neobichainykh iavlenii prirody.* Moscow: Mysl', 1988.

Borisov, A. M. *Khoziaistvo Solovetskogo monastyria i bor'ba krest'ian s severnymi monastyriami v XVI–XVII vv.* Petrozavodsk: Karel'skoe knizhnoe izd-vo, 1966.

Borisov, Timofei. "Vzgliad v 2013-i: Parlamentskii forum ob istorii doma Romanovykh." *Rossiiskaia gazeta* 5445/69 (Apr. 1, 2011). http://www.rg.ru/2011/04/01/nasledie.html.

Bradley, Raymond S., and Philip D. Jones, eds. *Climate since A.D. 1500.* London: Routledge, 1992.

Brereton, Henry. *Newes of the Present Miseries of Rushia.* London: Bache, 1614 [facs. repr. Amsterdam: Da Capo, 1968].

Broadribb, Donald. *An Attempt to Delineate the Characteristic Structure of Classical (Biblical) Hebrew Poetry.* Beverley, Australia: Bookleaf, 1995.

Brown, Peter B. "How Muscovy Governed: Seventeenth-Century Russian Central Administration." *Russian History* 36, no. 4 (2009): 459–529.

Browne, Sir Thomas. *Pseudodoxia Epidemica or, Enquiries into Very Many Received Tenets and Commonly Presumed Truths.* 3rd ed. London: Nath. Ekins, 1658.

Budovnits, Isaak U. *Monastyri na Rusi i bor'ba s nimi krest'ian v XIV–XVI vekakh, po "Zhitiiam sviatykh."* Moscow: Nauka, 1966.

————. *Obshchestvenno-politicheskaia mysl' Drevnei Rusi.* Moscow: AN SSSR, 1960.

————. *Russkaia publitsistika XVI veka.* Moscow: AN SSSR, 1947. Reprinted The Hague: Mouton, 1970.

Buganov, V. I. *Krest'ianskie voiny v Rossii XVII–XVIII vv.* Moscow: Nauka, 1976.

————. "Rossiia v epokhu Smuty." In *Smuta v Moskovskom gosudarstve: Rossiia nachala XVII stoletiia v zapiskakh sovremennikov,* edited by A. I. Pliguzov and I. A. Tikhoniuk, 6–20. Moscow: Sovremennik, 1989.

Bulanin, D. M. "O nekotorykh printsipakh raboty drevnerusskikh pisatelei." *TODRL* 37 (1983): 3–13.

Bury, J. B. *A History of the Eastern Roman Empire from the Fall of Irene to the Accession of Basil I.* London: Macmillan, 1912.

Bushkovitch, Paul. "The Formation of a National Consciousness in Early Modern Russia." *Harvard Ukrainian Studies* 10, nos. 3/4 (1986): 355–76.

———. *The Merchants of Moscow, 1580–1650.* Cambridge: Cambridge University Press, 1980.

———. *Religion and Society in Russia: The Sixteenth and Seventeenth Centuries.* New York: Oxford University Press, 1992.

Bushuev, S. V., and G. E. Mironov. *Istoriia gosudarstva Rossiiskogo: Istoriko-bibliograficheskie ocherki.* 2 vols. Moscow: Knizhnaia palata, 1991–1994.

Bussow, Conrad. *The Disturbed State of the Russian Realm.* Translated and edited by G. Edward Orchard. Montreal: McGill-Queen's University Press, 1994.

——— [as Ber, Martin]. "Letopis' moskovskaia." In *Skazaniia sovremennikov o Dimitrii Samozvantse,* edited by Nikolai Ustrialov. 3rd ed. 1: 3–143. St. Petersburg: Imp. akademiia nauk, 1859.

——— [as Bussov, Konrad]. *Moskovskaia khronika, 1584–1613.* Edited by I. I. Smirnov. Moscow: AN SSSR, 1961.

———. "Moskovskaia khronika, 1584–1613." In *Khroniki Smutnogo vremeni,* edited by A. Liberman, B. Morozov, and S. Shokarev, 9–162. Moscow: Fond Sergeia Dubova, 1998.

———. *Zeit der Wirren: Moskowitische Chronik der Jahre 1584 bis 1613.* Edited by Marie-Elisabeth Fritze, Jutta Harney, and Gottfried Sturm. Berlin: Koehler und Amelang, 1991.

Byliny. Istoricheskiia pesni. Edited by M. Speranskii. In *Russkaia ustnaia slovesnost'.* Vol. 2. Moscow: Izd-vo Sabashnikovykh, 1919.

Byliny severa. Edited by A. M. Astakhova. 2 vols. Moscow: AN SSSR, 1938–1951.

Byzantine Monastic Foundation Documents: A Complete Translation of the Surviving Founders' Typika and Testaments. Edited by John Thomas, Angela Constantinides Hero, and Giles Constable. Translated by Robert Allison et al. 5 vols. Washington, DC: Dumbarton Oaks, 2000.

The Cambridge Medieval History. Vol. 4: *The Byzantine Empire.* Part 2: *Government, Church, and Civilisation.* Edited by J. M. Hussey, with the assistance of D. M. Nicol and G. Cowan. Cambridge: Cambridge University Press, 1967.

Canary, Robert H., and Henry Kozicki, eds. *The Writing of History: Literary Form and Historical Understanding.* Madison: University of Wisconsin Press, 1978.

Carr, Edward H. *What is History?* New York: Knopf, 1962.

Carrier, James G. "The Gift in Theory and Practice in Melanesia: A Note on the Centrality of Gift Exchange." *Ethnology* 31, no. 2 (Apr. 1992): 185–93.

———. "Gifts in a World of Commodities: The Ideology of the Perfect Gift in American Society." *Social Analysis* 29 (1990): 19–37.

Cheal, D. *The Gift Economy.* London: Routledge, 1988.

Cherepnin, L. V. *Zemskie sobory Russkogo gosudarstva v XVI–XVII vv.* Moscow: Nauka, 1978.

———, et al., eds., *Krest'ianskie voiny v Rossii XVII–XVIII vekov: problemy, poiski, resheniia.* Moscow: Nauka, 1974.

Cherkasova, M. S. "K izucheniiu monastyrskogo d'iachestva v XV–XVII vv. (po arkhivu Troitse-Sergievoi lavry)." In *Rossiiskoe gosudarstvo v XVI–XVII vv.: Sbornik statei, posviashchennyi 75-letiiu so dnia rozhdeniia Iu. G. Alekseeva,* edited by A. G. Man'kov et al., 242–60. St. Petersburg: Dmitrii Bulanin, 2002.

―――. "Khoziastvennaia dokumentatsiia Troitse-Sergieva monastyria kontsa XVI–per-voi chetverti XVII veka." In *Spornye voprosy otechestvennoi istorii XI–XVIII ve-kov.* Vol. 2. Moscow: Akademiia nauk SSSR, 1990.

Chernykh, P. Ia. *Istoriko-etimologicheskii slovar' sovremennogo russkogo iazyka.* 4th ed. 2 vols. Moscow: Russkii iazyk, 2001.

Chistiakova, E. V. "Sergei Fedorovich Platonov i ego trud 'Ocherki po istorii Smuty v Moskovskom gosudarstve XVI–XVII vv. (Opyt izucheniia obshchestvennogo stroia i soslovnykh otnoshenii v Smutnoe vremia).'" In Sergei F. Platonov, *Ocherki po istorii Smuty v Moskovskom gosudarstve XVI–XVII vv. Opyt izucheniia ob-shchestvennogo stroia i soslovnykh otnoshenii v Smutnoe vremia.* 5th ed., 419–40. Moscow: Pamiatniki istoricheskoi mysli, 1995.

Chodorow, Stanley, MacGregor Knox, Conrad Schirokauer, Joseph R. Strayer, and Hans W. Gatzke. *The Mainstream of Civilization.* 6th ed. Philadelphia, PA: Harcourt Brace, 1994.

Christianity and the Eastern Slavs. Vol. 1: *Slavic Cultures in the Middle Ages,* edited by Boris Gasparov and Olga Raevsky-Hughes. In *California Slavic Studies.* Berkeley: University of California Press, 1993.

Church, Nation, and State in Russia and Ukraine. Edited by Geoffrey A. Hosking. New York: St. Martin's, 1991.

Clark, M. S., and J. Mills. "The Difference Between Communal and Exchange Relation-ships: What It Is and Is Not." *Personality and Social Psychology Bulletin* 19 (1993): 684–91.

Cliggett, Lisa. "Gift Remitting and Alliance Building in Zambian Modernity: Old An-swers to Modern Problems." *American Anthropologist,* n.s. 105, no. 3 (Sep. 2003): 543–52.

Collinson, Patrick. *Elizabethan Essays.* London: Hambledon, 1994.

Constantelos, Demetrios J. "Social Services: Eastern Christian." In *Encyclopedia of Mo-nasticism,* edited by William M. Johnston, 2: 1167–69. Chicago: Fitzroy Dearborn, 2000.

Cracraft, James, ed. *Major Problems in the History of Imperial Russia.* Lexington, MA: Heath, 1994.

Crummey, Robert O. *The Formation of Muscovy, 1304–1613.* New York: Longman, 1987.

―――. *The Old Believers and the World of Antichrist: The Vyg Community and the Rus-sian State, 1694–1855.* Madison: University of Wisconsin Press, 1970.

―――. "The Orthodox Church and the Schism." In *The Cambridge History of Russia,* edited by Maureen Perrie. Vol. 1: *From Early Rus' to 1689,* 618–39. Cambridge: Cambridge University Press, 2006.

Cruz, Anne J., and Mihoko Suzuki, eds. *The Rule of Women in Early Modern Europe.* Chicago: University of Chicago Press, 2009.

Cybulski, Marius L. "Political, Religious, and Intellectual Life in Muscovy in the Age of the Boyar Fedor Nikitich Iur'ev-Romanov a.k.a. The Grand Sovereign The Most Holy Filaret Nikitich, Patriarch of Moscow and All Rus', (ca. 1550–1633)." 2 vols. PhD diss., Harvard University, 1998.

Dacy, Marianne. *The Separation of Early Christianity from Judaism.* Amherst: Cambria, 2010.

Dagron, Gilbert. *Empereur et prêtre: Étude sur le "césaropapisme" byzantin.* Paris: Gal-limard, 1996.

———. *Emperor and Priest: The Imperial Office in Byzantium.* Translated by Jean Birrell. Cambridge: Cambridge University Press, 2003.

Dal', Vladimir. *Tolkovyi slovar' zhivogo velikorusskogo iazyka.* 2nd ed. 4 vols. Moscow: Vol'f, 1880–1882. Reprinted Moscow: Russkii iazyk, 1989–1991.

Daniel, Wallace L. *The Orthodox Church and Civil Society in Russia.* College Station: Texas A&M University Press, 2006.

Davis, Natalie Zemon. *The Gift in Sixteenth-Century France.* Madison: University of Wisconsin Press, 2000.

Deistviia Nizhegorodskoi gubernskoi uchenoi arkhivnoi komissii: Sbornik statei, soobshchenii, opisei i dokumentov. Vols. 4–5. Nizhnii-Novgorod: Konyshev, 1900–1903.

de Madariaga, Isabel. *Ivan the Terrible: First Tsar of Russia.* New Haven, CT: Yale University Press, 2005.

Dem'ianov, V. G. *Inoiazychnaia leksika v istorii russkogo iazyka XI–XVII vekov. Problemy morfologicheskoi adaptatsii.* Moscow: Nauka, 2001.

Demidova, Marina Al'bertovna, ed. "Pis'ma S. F. Platonova S. D. Sheremetevu o Smutnom vremeni." In *Arkhiv russkoi istorii: Nauchnyi istoricheskii zhurnal,* edited by I. A. Tikhoniuk et al., 3: 177–86. Moscow: RGADA, 1993.

Denisov, L. I. *Pravoslavnye monastyri Rossiiskoi imperii.* Moscow: Stupin, 1908.

Derrida, Jacques. *Deconstruction in a Nutshell: A Conversation with Jacques Derrida.* Edited by John D. Caputo. New York: Fordham University Press, 1997.

———. *L'écriture et la différence.* Paris: Seuil, 1967.

Derwich, Marek. "Origins: Western Christian." In *Encyclopedia of Monasticism,* edited by William M. Johnston, 2: 970–74. Chicago: Fitzroy Dearborn, 2000.

Derzhavina, O. A. "K probleme poeticheskogo stilia istoricheskoi povesti nachala XVII v." *TODRL* 14 (1958): 298–303.

De Villiers, Marq. *Down the Volga in a Time of Troubles: A Journey Revealing the People and Heartland of Post-Perestroika Russia.* Toronto: HarperCollins, 1991.

D'iachenko, Grigorii. *Polnyi tserkovno-slavianskii slovar' (so vneseniem v nego vazhneishikh drevne-russkikh slov i vyrazhenii).* Moscow, 1900. Reprinted Moscow: Moskovskii patriarkhat, 1993.

D'iakonov, M. *Vlast' Moskovskikh gosudarei. Ocherki iz istorii politicheskikh idei Drevnei Rusi do kontsa XVI veka.* St. Petersburg: Skorokhodov, 1889. Reprinted The Hague: Mouton, 1969.

The Dictionary of the History of Ideas: Studies of Selected Pivotal Ideas. Edited by Philip P. Wiener. 4 vols. New York: Scribner, 1973–1974. Available online at http://etext. lib.virginia.edu/DicHist/dict.html.

Dmitriev, V. D., ed. "Tsarskie nakazy kazanskim voevodam XVII veka." In *Istoriia i kul'tura Chuvashskoi ASSR: Sbornik statei,* 3: 284–419. Cheboksary: NII ChASSR, 1974.

Dmitrieva, R. P. "K voprosu o meste 'Povesti nekoego bogoliubivogo muzha' v literaturnom razvitii XVI–XVII vv." *TODRL* 14 (1958): 278–83.

Dmitrieva, Z. V. *Bytnye i opisnye knigi Kirillo-Belozerskogo monastyria XVI–XVII vv.* St. Petersburg: Dmitrii Bulanin, 2003.

———, ed. "Ustavnye gramoty Kirillo-Belozerskogo monastyria XVI–XVII vv." In *Rossiiskoe gosudarstvo v XVI–XVII vv.: Sbornik statei, posviashchennyi 75-letiiu so dnia rozhdeniia Iu. G. Alekseeva,* edited by A. G. Man'kov et al., 261–69. St. Petersburg: Dmitrii Bulanin, 2002.

Dmytryshyn, Basil, ed. *Medieval Russia: A Source Book, 850–1700.* 3rd ed. Philadelphia, PA: Harcourt Brace Jovanovich, 1990.

Dnevnik Mariny Mnishek. Translated by V. N. Kozliakov. Edited by D. M. Bulanin. In *Studiorum Slavicorum Monumenta.* Vol. 9. St. Petersburg: Dmitrii Bulanin, 1995.

Dobroklonskii, A. P. *Rukovodstvo po istorii russkoi tserkvi.* Vol. 25, edited by Valentin Chaplin et al. In *Materialy po istorii tserkvi.* Moscow: Krutitskoe patriarshee podvor'e, 1999.

Dobromirovo evangelie: kirilski spomenik od XII vek. Edited by Moshe Altbauer. Vol. 1. Skopje: Makedonska Akad. na Naukite, 1973.

Dokumenty GAF SSSR v bibliotekakh, muzeiakh i nauchno-otraslevykh arkhivakh: Spravochnik. Edited by L. M. Babaeva, I. V. Volkova, V. N. Avtokratov, et al. Moscow: Mysl', 1991.

Dokumenty Pechatnogo prikaza (1613–1615 gg.). Edited by S. B. Veselovskii. Moscow: Nauka, 1994.

Dolitskii, Aleksandr B. *Staraia Rossiia v sovremennoi Amerike: Russkie staroobriadtsy na Aliaske.* 4th ed. Juneau: Alaska-Siberia Research Center, 2007.

Dolukhanov, Pavel Markovich. *The Early Slavs: Eastern Europe from the Initial Settlement to the Kievan Rus.* New York: Longman, 1996.

Domostroi. Edited and translated by V. V. Kolesov, V. V. Rozhdestvenskaia, and M. V. Pimenova. Moscow: Sovetskaia Rossiia, 1990.

Dopolneniia k Aktam istoricheskim, sobrannyia i izdannyia Arkheograficheskoiu kommissieiu. 12 vols. St. Petersburg: Imp. Velichestva Kantseliariia, 1846.

Dostoyevsky, Fyodor [Dostoevskii, Fedor]. *Brothers Karamazov.* Translated by Andrew R. MacAndrew. New York: Bantam Classics, 1984.

———. *The Brothers Karamazov.* [Trans. anonymous.] New York: Macmillan, 1919.

———. *Polnoe sobranie sochinenii v tridtsati tomakh.* Leningrad: Nauka, 1972–1988.

Drevnerusskaia knizhnost': Arkheografiia, paleografiia, kodikologiia. Edited by M. A. Shibaev and E. V. Krushel'nitskaia. In *Opyty po istochnikovedeniiu.* Vol. 2. St. Petersburg: Dmitrii Bulanin, 1999.

Drevnerusskaia knizhnost': Redaktor i tekst. Edited by Iu. G. Alekseev and V. K. Ziborov. In *Opyty po istochnikovedeniiu.* Vol. 3. St. Petersburg: Dmitrii Bulanin, 2000.

Drevne-russkie pamiatniki sviashchennago venchaniia tsarei na tsarstvo, v sviazi s grecheskimi ikh originalami. S istoricheskim ocherkom chinov tsarskago venchaniia, v sviazi s razvitiem idei tsaria na Rusi. Edited and commentary by E. V. Barsov. Moscow: Universitetskaia tipografiia (Katkov), 1883. Reprinted The Hague: Mouton, 1969.

Drevniaia Rossiiskaia Vivliofika. Edited by N. I. Novikov. 2nd ed. 20 vols. Moscow: Tip. Kompanii tipograficheskoi, 1788–1791.

Dubakov, A. V. "Obrazovanie Astrakhanskoi eparkhii v XVI–nachale XVII v." In *Srednevekovoe pravoslavie ot prikhoda do patriarkhata,* edited by N. D. Barabanov, I. O. Tiumentsev, et al., 2: 146–73. Volgograd: Izd-vo Volgogradskogo gosud. universiteta, 1998.

Dubnow, S. M. *History of the Jews in Russia and Poland from the Earliest Times until the Present Day.* Translated by I. Friedlaender. 3 vols. Philadelphia, PA: JPS, 1916; Bergenfield, NJ: Avotaynu, 2000.

———. *History of the Jews in Russia and Poland from the Earliest Times until the Present Day.* Translated by I. Friedlaender. Bergenfield, NJ: Avotaynu, 2000.

Dubois, Jean, René Lagane, and Alain Lerond. *Dictionnaire du français classique.* Paris: Larousse, 1971.

Duncan, Peter J. S. *Russian Messianism: Third Rome, Revolution, Communism, and After.* New York: Routledge, 2000.

Dunning, Chester S. L. "Byla li v Rossii v nachale XVII veka krest'ianskaia voina?" *Voprosy istorii* 9 (1994): 21–34.

———. "Cossacks and the Southern Frontier in the Time of Troubles." *Russian History/ Histoire Russe,* 19, nos. 1–4 (1992): 57–74.

———. "Crisis, Conjuncture, and the Causes of the Time of Troubles." In *Kamen' Kraezhg"l'n": Rhetoric of the Medieval Slavic World*, edited by Nancy Shields Kollmann, Donald Ostrowski, Andrei Pliguzov, and Daniel Rowland. Harvard Series in Ukrainian Studies, vol. 19, pp. 97–119. Harvard: HURI, 1995.

———. *"The Fall of Sir Thomas Overbury and the Embassy to Russia in 1613." Sixteenth Century Journal* 22, no. 4 (Winter 1991): 695–704.

———. "James I, the Russia Company, and the Plan to Establish a Protectorate over North Russia." *Albion: A Quarterly Journal Concerned with British Studies,* 21, no. 2 (Spring 1989): 206–26.

———. "A Letter to James I Concerning the English Plan for Military Intervention in Russia." *Slavonic and East European Review* 67, no. 1 (January 1989): 94–108.

———. "The Preconditions of Modern Russia's First Civil War." *Russian History/Histoire Russe,* 25, no. 1–2 (Spring-Summer 1998): 119–31.

———. "Quand un Français redécouvrait la Russie." *Revue historique,* 272, no. 2 (Oct.–Dec. 1984): 331–51.

———. "[Review of] L. E. Morozova, *Smuta nachala XVII veka glazami sovremennikov.*" *Russian History/Histoire russe,* 27, no. 2 (Summer 2000): 235–38.

———. "R. G. Skrynnikov, the Time of Troubles, the 'First Peasant War' in Russia." *Russian Review* 50 (Jan. 1991): 71–81.

———. "The Richest Place in the World: An Early Seventeenth Century English Description and Military Assessment of Solovetskii Monastery." In *Rude and Barbarous Kingdom Revisited: Essays in Russian History and Culture in Honor of Robert O. Crummey,* edited by Chester S. L. Dunning, Russell E. Martin, and Daniel Rowland, 309–25. Columbus, OH: Slavica, 2008.

———. *Russia's First Civil War: The Time of Troubles and the Founding of the Romanov Dynasty.* University Park: Pennsylvania State University Press, 2001.

———. "Terror in the Time of Troubles." *Kritika: Explorations in Russian and Eurasian History* 4, no. 3 (Summer 2003): 491–513.

———. "Who Was Tsar Dmitrii?" *Slavic Review* 60.4 (Winter 2001): 705-29.

———, with Caryl Emerson, Sergei Fomichev, Lidiia Lotman, and Antony Wood. *The Uncensored Boris Godunov: The Case for Pushkin's Original Comedy, with Annotated Text and Translation.* Madison: University of Wisconsin Press, 2006.

Dykstra, Tom E. *Russian Monastic Culture: "Josephism" and the Iosifo-Volokolamsk Monastery, 1479–1607.* Munich: Verlag Otto Sagner, 2006.

Early Exploration of Russia. Edited by Marshall Poe. 12 vols. London: RoutledgeCurzon, 2003.

Elassonskii, Arsenii. *Memuary iz russkoi istorii.* In *Khroniki Smutnogo vremeni*, edited by A. Liberman, B. Morozov, and S. Shokarev, 211–62. Moscow: Fond Sergeia Dubova, 1998.

———. "Opisanie puteshestviia . . . i uchrezhdeniia Moskovskogo patriarshestva." Translated and edited by Pitirim Volokolamskii. In Moskovskaia patriarkhiia, *Bogoslovskie trudy* 4 (1968): 248–79.

———. "Zhenskie monastyri v Rossii." In *Monashestvo i monastyri v Rossii. XI–XX veka: Istoricheskie ocherki*, edited by N. V. Sinitsyna et al., 245–84. Moscow: Nauka, 2002.

Emerson, Caryl. *Boris Godunov: Transpositions of a Russian Theme.* Bloomington: Indiana University Press, 1986.

Encyclopedia of Monasticism. Edited by William M. Johnston. 2 vols. Chicago: Fitzroy Dearborn, 2000.

England and the North: The Russian Embassy of 1613–1614. Edited by Maija Jansson and Nikolai Rogozhin. Translated by Paul Bushkovitch. Philadelphia, PA: American Philosophical Society, 1994.

Ensslin, W. "The Government and Administration of the Byzantine Empire." In *The Cambridge Medieval History.* Vol. 4: *The Byzantine Empire.* Part 2: *Government, Church, and Civilisation*, edited by J. M. Hussey, with the assistance of D. M. Nicol and G. Cowan, 1–54. Cambridge: Cambridge University Press, 1967.

Entsiklopedicheskii slovar'. Edited by I. E. Andreevskii et al. 43 vols. St. Petersburg: Brokgauz and Efron, 1890–1907.

Eskin, Iurii Moiseevich, ed. "Mestnicheskoe delo K. A. Trusov—kniaz' F. F. Volkonskii kak istochnik po istorii tikhvinskogo vosstaniia 1613 g." In *Rossiiskoe gosudarstvo v XVI–XVII vv.: Sbornik statei, posviashchennyi 75-letiiu so dnia rozhdeniia Iu. G. Alekseeva*, edited by A. G. Man'kov et al., 300–307. St. Petersburg: Dmitrii Bulanin, 2002.

———. "Smuta i mestnichestvo." *Arkhiv russkoi istorii: Nauchnyi istoricheskii zhurnal*, edited by I. A. Tikhoniuk et al., 3: 63–124. Moscow: RGADA, 1993.

Eusebius (Pamphilus). *The Life of the Blessed Emperor Constantine.* Translated by Ernest Cushing Richardson. In *A Select Library of Nicene and Post-Nicene Fathers of the Christian Church*, edited by Philip Schaff and Henry Wace. 2nd series. 1: 481–559. New York: Christian Literature, 1890.

———. "The Oration of Eusebius Pamphilus in Praise of the Emperor Constantine. Pronounced on the Thirtieth Anniversary of His Reign." Translated by Ernest Cushing Richardson. In *A Select Library of Nicene and Post-Nicene Fathers of the Christian Church*, edited by Philip Schaff and Henry Wace. 2nd series. 1: 581–610. New York: Christian Literature, 1890.

Evangeliar Assemanuv: Kodex Vatikansky. Edited by Josef Kurz. Prague: NCSAV, 1955.

Evans, J. A. S. *The Emperor Justinian and the Byzantine Empire.* Westport, CT: Greenwood, 2005.

Evans, Richard J. *In Defense of History.* New York: Norton, 1999.

Evans, Robert J. W. *Rudolf II and His World: A Study in Intellectual History, 1576–1612.* Oxford: Clarendon, 1973.

Evtuhov, Catherine. "The Church in the Russian Revolution: Arguments for and against Restoring the Patriarchate at the Church Council of 1917–1918." *Slavic Review* 50, no. 3 (Autumn 1991): 497–511.

———, David Goldfrank, Lindsey Hughes, and Richard Stites. *A History of Russia: Peoples, Legends, Events, Forces.* Boston: Houghton Mifflin, 2004.

Fairbairn, Donald. *Eastern Orthodoxy through Western Eyes.* Louisville, KY: Westminster John Knox, 2002.

Fedorov, Iurii. *Boris Godunov.* Moscow: Armada, 1995.

Fedotov, G. P. *The Russian Religious Mind.* 2 vols. Belmont, MA: Norland, 1975.

Feissel, Denis. "L'empereur et l'administration impériale." In *Le monde byzantine*, edited by Cécile Morrisson. Vol. 1: *L'Empire romain d'Orient, 330–641*, pp. 79–110. Paris: Presses universitaires de France, 2004.

Fennell, John Lister Illingworth. "The Attitude of the Josephians and the Trans-Volga Elders to the Heresy of the Judaisers." *Slavonic and East European Review* 29, no. 73 (June 1951): 486–509.

———. *The Emergence of Moscow, 1304–1359.* Berkeley: University of California Press, 1968.

———. *History of the Russian Church to 1448.* London: Longman, 1995.

Figes, Orlando. *A People's Tragedy: The Russian Revolution, 1891–1924.* New York: Penguin, 1998.

Filaret, Archbishop of Chernigov (Dmitrii G. Gumilevskii). *Istoriia russkoi tserkvi.* 5 vols. Kharkiv: Universitetskaia tip., 1849–1853.

Filiushkin, Aleksandr. "Religioznyi faktor v russkoi vneshnei politike XVI veka: Ksenofobiia, tolerantnost' ili pragmatizm." In *Religion und Integration im Moskauer Russland*, edited by Ludwig Steindorff, 145–79. Wiesbaden: Harrassowitz Verlag, 2010.

Fletcher, Giles. *The English Works of Giles Fletcher, the Elder.* Edited by Lloyd E. Berry. Madison: University of Wisconsin Press, 1964.

———. *Of the Rus Commonwealth.* Edited by Albert J. Schmidt. Ithaca, NY: Cornell University Press, 1966.

———. *Of the Russe Common Wealth. Or Maner of Gouernement by the Russe Emperour, (commonly called the Emperour of Moskouia) with the manners, and fashions of the people of that Countrey.* London: Thomas Charde, 1591. Reprinted with supplementary materials by Richard Pipes and John V. A. Fine, Jr., Cambridge, MA: Harvard University Press, 1966.

Floria, Boris Nikolaevich. *Pol'sko-litovskaia interventsiia v Rossii i russkoe obshchestvo.* Moscow: Indrik, 2005.

———, ed. "Tri pis'ma o sobytiiakh Smuty." *Arkhiv russkoi istorii: Nauchnyi istoricheskii zhurnal*, edited by I. A. Tikhoniuk et al., 3: 161–76. Moscow: RGADA, 1993.

Flusin, Bernard. "Les structures de l'église impériale." In *Le monde byzantin*, edited by Cécile Morrisson. Vol. 1: *L'Empire romain d'Orient, 330–641*, pp. 111–41. Paris: Presses universitaires de France, 2004.

———. "Triomphe du christianisme et définition de l'orthodoxie." In *Le monde byzantin*, edited by Cécile Morrisson. Vol. 1: *L'Empire romain d'Orient, 330–641*, pp. 49–75. Paris: Presses universitaires de France, 2004.

Fonkich, B. L., ed. *Grechesko-russkie sviazi serediny XVI–nachala XVIII vv.: Grecheskie dokumenty moskovskikh khranilishch; Katalog vystavki.* Moscow: Arkhiv russkoi istorii, 1991.

Foucault, Michel. *Dits et écrits, 1954–1988.* 4 vols. Paris: Gallimard, 1994.

———. *The Foucault Reader.* Edited by Paul Rabinow. New York: Pantheon, 1984.

———. "The Subject and Power." *Critical Inquiry* 8 (Summer 1982): 777–95.

Franklin, Simon. *Byzantium—Rus—Russia: Studies in the Translation of Christian Culture.* Burlington, VT: Ashgate, 2002.

———, trans. and ed. *Sermons and Rhetoric of Kievan Rus'.* Cambridge, MA: Ukrainian Research Institute, Harvard University Press, 1991.

Freeze, Gregory L. "Handmaiden of the State? The Orthodox Church in Imperial Russia Reconsidered." *Journal of Ecclesiastical History* 36 (1985): 82–102.

———. "The Orthodox Church and Serfdom in Prereform Russia." *Slavic Review* 48, no. 3 (Autumn 1989): 361–87.

———. "Subversive Piety: Religion and the Political Crisis in Late Imperial Russia." *Journal of Modern History* 68, no. 2 (June 1996): 308–50.

French, R. M. *The Eastern Orthodox Church.* New York: Hutchinson's, 1961.

Garrard, John, and Carol Garrard, *Russian Orthodoxy Resurgent: Faith and Power in the New Russia.* Princeton, NJ: Princeton University Press, 2008.

Geiman, V. G. "Sochinenie Iu. Videkinda kak istochnik po istorii Smutnogo vremeni." In Johann Widekind, *Thet Swenska i Rußland Tiio Åhrs Krijgz-Historie*/Iukhan Videkind, *Istoriia desiatiletnei shvedsko-moskovitskoi voiny*, translated by S. A. Anninskii, A. M. Aleksandrov, and A. F. Kostina, edited by V. L. Ianina and A. L. Khoroshkevich, 509–20. Moscow: Pamiatniki istoricheskoi mysli, 2000.

Geografiia Rossii. Entsiklopedicheskii slovar'. Edited by A. P. Gorkin. Moscow: Bol'shaia rossiiskaia entsiklopediia, 1998.

Gerkman, Elias. *Istoricheskoe povestvovanie o vazhneishikh smutakh v gosudarstve Russkom, vinovnikom kotorykh byl tsarevich kniaz' Dimitrii Ivanovich, nespravedlivo nazyvaemyi samozvantsem.* In *Khroniki Smutnogo vremeni*, edited by A. Liberman, B. Morozov, and S. Shokarev, 9–162. Moscow: Fond Sergeia Dubova, 1998.

Gesenius, Wilhelm. *Gesenius' Hebrew Grammar.* Edited by E. Kautzsch. Translated by A. E. Cowley. 2nd English ed. Oxford: Clarendon, 1910. Reprinted Mineola, NY: Dover, 2006.

Ginzberg, Louis. *Legends of the Jews.* Translated by Henrietta Szold. 7 vols. Philadelphia, PA: JPS, 1967–1969.

Ginzburg, Carlo. *History, Rhetoric, and Proof.* Hanover, NH: University Press of New England, 1999.

Godelier, Maurice. *L'énigme du don.* Paris: Fayard, 1996.

Gol'dberg, A. L. "Istoriko-politicheskie idei russkoi knizhnosti XV–XVII vekov." *Istoriia SSSR* 4 (Jul.–Aug. 1975): 60–77.

Goldfrank, David M. "The Deep Origins of *Tsar'-Muchitel'*: A Nagging Problem of Muscovite Political Theory." *Russian History/Histoire russe* 31, nos. 3–4 (2005): 341–54.

———. "*Moscow, the Third Rome.*" *MERSH* 23: 118–21.

———. "Nil Sorskii's Following among the Iosifo-Volokolamsk Elders." In *The New Muscovite Cultural History: A Collection in Honor of Daniel B. Rowland*, edited by Valerie Kivelson, Karen Petrone, Nancy Shields Kollmann, and Michael S. Flier. Bloomington, IN: Slavica, 2009.

———. "Recentering Nil Sorskii." *Russian Review* 66 (July 2007): 359–76.

———. "*[Review of]* Dykstra, *Russian Monastic Culture,* and Nikol'skii, *KBMU.*" *Kritika* 10.1 (Winter 2009): 169–75.

———. "Sisterhood Just Might Be Powerful: The Testament-Rule of Elena Devochkina." *Russian History* 34.1–4 (2007): 189–205.

Golubinskii, E. E. *Istoriia russkoi tserkvi.* 2 vols. in 4 books, plus *Arkheologicheskii atlas.* Moscow: Universitetskaia tip., 1901–1906. Reprinted The Hague: Mouton, 1969.

Gonneau, Pierre. "L'église face aux crises dynastiques en Moscovie. XVe–XVIIe s." In *Religion und Integration im Moskauer Russland*, edited by Ludwig Steindorff, 25–48. Wiesbaden: Harrassowitz Verlag, 2010.

Gorchakov, Mikhail I. *Monastyrskii prikaz (1649–1725 g.). Opyt istoriko-iuridicheskago izsledovaniia.* St. Petersburg: Tip. A. Transhelia, 1868.

Gorfunkel', A. Kh. "Khronologicheskii perechen' zemel'nykh priobretenii Kirillo-Belozerskogo monastyria (1601–1700)." In *Rossiiskoe gosudarstvo v XVI–XVII vv.: Sbornik statei, posviashchennyi 75-letiiu so dnia rozhdeniia Iu. G. Alekseeva*, edited by A. G. Man'kov et al., 280–99. St. Petersburg: Dmitrii Bulanin, 2002.

Gosudarev dvor v Rossii (konets XV–nachalo XVIII vv.): Katalog knizhnoi vystavki. Edited by M. A. Strucheva et al. Moscow: Gosud. publichnaia istoricheskaia biblioteka Rossii, 1997.

Got'e, Iu. V. *Smutnoe vremia: Ocherk istorii revoliutsionnykh dvizhenii nachala XVII stoletiia.* Moscow: Gosud. izd-vo, 1921.

———. *Time of Troubles: The Diary of Iurii Vladimirovich Got'e, Moscow, July 8, 1917 to July 23, 1922.* Translated and edited by Terence Emmons. Princeton, NJ: Princeton University Press, 1988.

Gottheil, Richard. "Antwerp." In *The Jewish Encyclopedia.* 1: 658–61. New York: Funk and Wagnalls, 1901.

Gouldner, A. W. "The Importance of Something for Nothing." In *For Sociology: Renewal and Critique in Sociology Today*, edited by A. W. Gouldner, 260–90. London: Allen Lane, 1973.

Govorun, M. A. "Voprosy o tserkvi i vere v russko-pol'skikh peregovorakh 1610 goda." In *Srednevekovoe pravoslavie ot prikhoda do patriarkhata*, edited by N. D. Barabanov, I. O. Tiumentsev, et al., 1: 168–92. Volgograd: Izd-vo Volgogradskogo gosud. universiteta, 1997.

Graham, Hugh F. "Further Sources for the Rule of False Dmitrii I." In *New Perspectives on Muscovite History*, edited by Lindsey Hughes, 80–97. New York: St. Martin's, 1993.

Granstrem, E. E. *Opisanie russkikh i slavianskikh pergamennykh rukopisei: Rukopisi russkie, bolgarskie, modovlakhiiskie, serbskie.* Edited by D. S. Likhachev. Leningrad, 1953.

Gregory, C. A. "Gifts to Men and Gifts to God: Gift Exchange and Capital Accumulation in Contemporary Papua." *Man*, n.s. 15, no. 4 (Dec. 1980): 626–52.

Grey, Ian. *Boris Godunov: The Tragic Tsar.* London: Hodder and Stoughton, 1973.

———. *Peter the Great, Emperor of All Russia.* Philadelphia, PA: Lippincott, 1960.

Gribble, Charles E. *Russian Root List, with a Sketch of Word Formation.* 2nd ed. Columbus, OH: Slavica, 1981.

———. *Slovarik russkogo iazyka 18-go veka/A Short Dictionary of 18th-Century Russian.* Cambridge, MA: Slavica, 1976.

Grove, Jean M. *The Little Ice Age.* London: Methuen, 1988.

Gruber, Isaiah. "Black Monks and White Gold: The Solovetskii Monastery's Prosperous Salt Trade during the Time of Troubles of the Early Seventeenth Century." *Russian History* 37, no. 3 (2010): 238–49.

———. "Hebrew Concepts in the Russian Culture of Muscovy." [In Hebrew: "Musagim 'ivriim ba-tarbut ha-rusit shel nesikhut mosqvah."] *Zmanim* 116.2 (2011): 46-51.

———. "The Muscovite Embassy of 1599 to Emperor Rudolf II of Habsburg." Master's thesis, McGill University, 1999.

———. "On the Practice of Literary-Semiotic History." Unpublished typescript, 2001.

———. "A Preliminary Study of Biblical Misquotation in Ilarion's *Slovo o zakone i o blagodati.*" Conference paper. Sherbrooke, QC: Canadian Association of Slavists, 1999.

————. "The Russian Orthodox Church in the Time of Troubles, 1598–1613." PhD diss., Georgetown University, 2006.

Gudziak, Borys Andrij. *Crisis and Reform: The Kyivan Metropolitanate, the Patriarchate of Constantinople, and the Genesis of the Union of Brest.* Cambridge, MA: Ukrainian Research Institute, Harvard University, 1998.

Guri, Yosef. "Bibleizmy v russkom iazyke (Stat'ia vtoraia)." *Jews and Slavs* 3 (1995): 40–53.

The Hagiography of Kievan Rus'. Translated by Paul Hollingsworth. Cambridge, MA: Ukrainian Research Institute, Harvard University Press, 1992.

Halperin, Charles J. "Edward Keenan and the Kurbskii-Groznyi Correspondence in Hindsight." *Jahrbücher für Geschichte Osteuropas* 46, no. 3 (1998): 376–403.

————. "Ivan IV's Insanity." *Russian History* 34, nos. 1–4 (2007): 207–18.

————. "National Identity in Premodern Rus'." *Russian History* 37 (2010): 275–94.

————. *Russia and the Golden Horde: The Mongol Impact on Medieval Russian History.* Bloomington: Indiana University Press, 1985.

————. "Russia in the Mongol Empire in Comparative Perspective." *Harvard Journal of Asiatic Studies* 43, no. 1 (June 1983): 239–61.

————. *The Tatar Yoke.* Columbus, OH: Slavica, 1985.

Hamel, J. *England and Russia; Comprising the Voyages of John Tradescant the Elder, Sir Hugh Willoughby, Richard Chancellor, Nelson, and Others, to the White Sea, Etc.* Translated by John Studdy Leigh. London: Bentley, 1854.

Haney, J. A. V., trans. and ed. "Moscow—Second Constantinople, Third Rome, or Second Kiev? (The Tale of the Princes of Vladimir)." *Canadian Slavic Studies/Revue canadienne d'études slaves* 2 (1968): 354–67.

Harcave, Sidney. *Russia: A History.* 6th ed. Philadelphia, PA: Lippincott, 1968.

Hart, Simon. "Amsterdam Shipping and the Trade to Northern Russia in the Seventeenth Century." *Mededelinger van de Nederlands Vereniging voor Zeegeschiedenis* 26 (Mar. 1973).

Hedlund, Stefan. "Vladimir the Great, Grand Prince of Muscovy: Resurrecting the Russian Service State." *Europe-Asia Studies* 58, no. 5 (July 2006): 775–801.

Hellie, Richard. *The Economy and Material Culture of Russia, 1600–1725.* Chicago: University of Chicago Press, 1999.

————. *Slavery in Russia, 1450–1725.* Chicago: University of Chicago Press, 1982.

————. "What Happened? How Did He Get Away with It? Ivan Groznyi's Paranoia and the Problem of Institutional Restraints." *Russian History* 14, nos. 1–4 (1987): 199–224.

Herberstein, Baron Sigismund von. *Notes upon Russia, Being a Translation of the Earliest Account of that Country, Entitled Rerum Moscoviticarum commentarii.* Translated and edited by R. H. Major. New York: Franklin, 1963.

Herman, Emil. "The Secular Church." In *The Cambridge Medieval History.* Vol. 4: *The Byzantine Empire.* Part 2: *Government, Church, and Civilisation*, edited by J. M. Hussey, with the assistance of D. M. Nicol and G. Cowan, 104–33. Cambridge: University Press, 1967.

Himka, John-Paul, and Andriy Zayarnyuk, eds. *Letters from Heaven: Popular Religion in Russia and Ukraine.* Toronto: University of Toronto Press, 2006.

Historica Russiae Monumenta, ex antiques exterarum centium archivis et bibliothecis depromptal/Akty istoricheskie, otnosiashchiesia k Rossii, izvlechennye iz inostrannykh arkhivov i bibliotek. Edited by A. I. Turgenev. 2 vols. St. Petersburg: Prats, 1841–1842.

The Holy Bible, Conteyning the Old Testament, and the New. [Original edition of King James (Authorized) Version.] London: Robert Barker, 1611. Schoenberg Center for Electronic Text and Image, University of Pennsylvania. http://sceti.library.upenn.edu.

Hosking, Geoffrey. *Russia: People and Empire, 1552–1917.* London: HarperCollins, 1997.

Howe, Sonia E., ed. *The False Dmitri: A Russian Romance and Tragedy, Described by British Eye-Witnesses, 1604–1612.* New York: Stokes, 1916.

Howes, Robert Craig, trans. and ed. *The Testaments of the Grand Princes of Moscow.* Ithaca, NY: Cornell University Press, 1967.

Hughes, Lindsey. *Russia in the Age of Peter the Great.* New Haven, CT: Yale University Press, 1998.

———. *Sophia, Regent of Russia, 1657–1704.* New Haven, CT: Yale University Press, 1990.

Huguet, Edmond. *Dictionnaire de la langue française du seizième siècle.* 7 vols. Paris: Champion, 1925–1973.

Hunt, Priscilla. "Ivan IV's Personal Mythology of Kingship." *Slavic Review* 52, no. 4 (Winter 1993): 769–809.

Hussey, J. M. "Byzantine Monasticism." In *The Cambridge Medieval History.* Vol. 4: *The Byzantine Empire.* Part 2: *Government, Church, and Civilisation*, edited by J. M. Hussey, with the assistance of D. M. Nicol and G. Cowan, 161–84. Cambridge: Cambridge University Press, 1967.

———. *The Orthodox Church in the Byzantine Empire.* Oxford: Clarendon, 1986.

———, and T. A. Hart. "Byzantine Theological Speculation and Spirituality." In *The Cambridge Medieval History.* Vol. 4: *The Byzantine Empire.* Part 2: *Government, Church, and Civilisation*, edited by J. M. Hussey, with the assistance of D. M. Nicol and G. Cowan, 185–205. Cambridge: Cambridge University Press, 1967.

"Iaitsa Faberge priedut v Kostromu iz Baden-Badena." *Russkaia sluzhba novostei.* Mar. 7, 2011. http://rusnovosti.ru/news/135831.

Ilarion, Mitropolit. "Slovo o zakone i blagodati" Ilariona. Edited by Aleksandr M. Moldovan. Kiev: Naukova Dumka, 1984.

———. *Slovo o zakone i blagodati s pokhvaloi kniaziu Vladimiru: Pouchenie v pravoi vierie/Des Metropoliten Ilarion Lobrede auf Vladimir den Heiligen und Glaubensbekenntnis.* Edited by Ludolf Müller. Wiesbaden: Harrassowitz, 1962.

Ilovaiskii, Dmitrii Ivanovich. *Novaia dinastiia.* Moscow: Algoritm, 1996.

———. *Smutnoe vremia Moskovskago gosudarstva.* Moscow: Tip. Volchaninova, 1894. Reprinted The Hague: Mouton, 1970.

Issledovaniia po istochnikovedeniiu istorii Rossii (do 1917 g.): Sbornik statei pamiati V. I. Buganova. Edited by N. M. Rogozhin, Iu. P. Glushakova, A. I. Aksenov, Iu. A. Tikhonov, and L. V. Razumov. Moscow: IRI RAN, 2001.

Istoricheskie akty Iaroslavskago Spasskago monastyria. Edited by I. A. Vakhrameev. Vol. 1. Moscow: Sinodal'naia, 1896.

Istoricheskie pesni XVII veka. Edited by O. B. Alekseeva et al. Moscow: Nauka, 1966.

Istoriia diplomatii. Edited by V. A. Zorin et al. 2nd ed. 3 vols. Moscow: GIPL, 1959–1965.

Istoriia russkoi pravoslavnoi tserkvi v dokumentakh regional'nykh arkhivov Rossii. Annotirovannyi spravochnik-ukazatel'. Edited by Arkhimandrit Innokentii Prosvirnin et al. Moscow: Novospasskii monastyr', 1993.

Istoriia Sibiri s drevneishikh vremen do nashikh dnei. Edited by A. P. Okladnikov, V. I. Shunkov, et al. 5 vols. Leningrad: Nauka, 1968–1969.

ITAR-TASS. "Sviateishii Patriarkh Aleksii II protiv popytok tserkovnogo razdeleniia naroda Rossii." *Pravoslavnaia gazeta—Ekaterinburg: Ofitsial'noe izdanie Ekaterinburgskoi eparkhii Russkoi Pravoslavnoi Tserkvi* 12 (Mar. 4, 2002). http://orthodox.etel.ru/2002/09/razdel.htm.

Ivanov, P. P. *Materialy po istorii Mordvy VIII–XI vv.: Kriukovsko-kuzhnovskii mogil'nik; Dnevnik arkheologicheskikh raskopok.* Edited by A. P. Smirnov. Morshansk: Morshanskii kraevedcheskii muzei, 1952.

Ivanov, V. I. "Nekotorye voprosy izucheniia pistsovykh materialov XVI veka." In *Issledovaniia po istochnikovedeniiu istorii Rossii (do 1917 g.).: Sbornik statei pamiati V. I. Buganova,* edited by N. M. Rogozhin, Iu. P. Glushakova, A. I. Aksenov, Iu. A. Tikhonov, and L. V. Razumov, 126–34. Moscow: IRI RAN, 2001.

Izotov, A. I. *Staroslavianskii i tserkovnoslavianskii iazyki: Grammatika, uprazhneniia, teksty.* Moscow: IOSO RAO, 2001.

Jansen, Sharon L. *Debating Women, Politics, and Power in Early Modern Europe.* New York: Palgrave Macmillan, 2008.

———. *The Monstrous Regiment of Women: Female Rulers in Early Modern Europe.* New York: Palgrave Macmillan, 2002.

Jenkins, Keith, ed. *The Postmodern History Reader.* New York: Routledge, 1997.

Jensen, Claudia Rae. *Musical Cultures in Seventeenth-Century Russia.* Bloomington: Indiana University Press, 2009.

Johanides, Ján. *Balada o vkladnej knižke.* Bratislava: Slovenský spisovatel', 1979.

Jorgenson, Wayne James. "Orthodox Monasticism: Byzantine." In *Encyclopedia of Monasticism,* edited by William M. Johnston, 2: 974–76. Chicago: Fitzroy Dearborn, 2000.

Joy, Annamma. "Gift Giving in Hong Kong and the Continuum of Social Ties." *Journal of Consumer Research* 28 (Sep. 2001): 239–56.

Justinian. *Corpus juris civilis* [The Civil Law]. Edited and translated by S. P. Scott. 17 vols. in 7 books. Cincinnati, OH: Central Trust, 1932. Reprinted New York: AMS, 1973.

Kabanov, A. K. *Smuta Moskovskogo gosudarstva i Nizhnii Novgorod.* Nizhnii-Novgorod: Volgar', 1911.

Kaiser, Daniel H. "[Review of] *Russia's First Civil War: The Time of Troubles and the Founding of the Romanov Dynasty,* by Chester S. L. Dunning." *Journal of Modern History* 74 (2002): 918–19.

———, and Gary Marker, eds. *Reinterpreting Russian History: Readings, 860–1860s.* Oxford: Oxford University Press, 1994.

Kapterev, N. *Svetskie arkhiereiskie chinovniki v drevnei Rusi.* Moscow: Sovremen. Izvest., 1874.

Karamzin, N. M. *Istoriia gosudarstva Rossiiskago.* 5th ed. 12 vols. in 4 books. St. Petersburg: E. Prats, 1842–1844. Reprinted Moscow: Kniga, 1988–1989.

———. *Memoir on Ancient and Modern Russia.* Translated by Richard Pipes. Cambridge, MA: Harvard University Press, 1959.

———. *Zapiska o drevnei i novoi Rossii/A Memoir on Ancient and Modern Russia: The Russian Text.* Edited by Richard Pipes. Cambridge, MA: Harvard University Press, 1959.

Kartashev, A. V. *Ocherki po istorii russkoi tserkvi.* 2 vols. Paris: YMCA, 1959.

Katalog slaviano-russkikh rukopisnykh knig XV veka, khraniashchikhsia v Rossiiskom gosudarstvennom arkhive drevnikh aktov. Edited by A. A. Turilov, I. L. Zhuchkova, and L. V. Moshkova. Moscow: Drevlekhranilishche, 2000.

Kazakova, N. A. *Zapadnaia Evropa v russkoi pis'mennosti XV–XVI vekov.* Leningrad: Nauka, 1980.

Keenan, Edward L. "Ivan III, Nikolai Karamzin, and the Legend of the 'Casting off of the Tatar Yoke' (1480)." In *The New Muscovite Cultural History: A Collection in Honor of Daniel B. Rowland,* edited by Valerie Kivelson, Karen Petrone, Nancy Shields Kollmann, and Michael S. Flier, 237–51. Bloomington, IN: Slavica, 2009.

———. *The Kurbskii-Groznyi Apocrypha: The Seventeenth-Century Genesis of the "Correspondence" Attributed to Prince A. M. Kurbskii and Tsar Ivan IV.* Cambridge, MA: Harvard University Press, 1971.

———. "Muscovite Political Folkways." *Russian Review* 45.2 (Apr. 1986): 115–81.

Keep, J. L. H. "*Moskau und die Politik des Kaiserhofes im XVII. Jahrhundert. I. Teil: 1604–1654,* by Walter Leitsch." *Slavonic and East European Review* 40, no. 95 (June 1962): 541–43.

Khodarkovsky, Michael. "The Non-Christian Peoples on the Muscovite Frontiers." In *The Cambridge History of Russia,* edited by Maureen Perrie. Vol. 1: *From Early Rus' to 1689,* 317–37. Cambridge: Cambridge University Press, 2006.

———. *Russia's Steppe Frontier: The Making of a Colonial Empire, 1500–1800.* Bloomington: Indiana University Press, 2002.

Khoroshkevich, A. L., A. I. Pliguzov, and G. M. Kovalenko. "Apologiia Iukhana Videkinda." In Widekind, Johann, *Thet Swenska i Rußland Tiio Åhrs Krijgz-Historie/ Iukhan Videkind, Istoriia desiatiletnei shvedsko-moskovitskoi voiny,* translated by S. A. Anninskii, A. M. Aleksandrov, and A. F. Kostina, edited by V. L. Ianina and A. L. Khoroshkevich, 521–61. Moscow: Pamiatniki istoricheskoi mysli, 2000.

Khoziaistvo krupnogo feodala-krepostnika XVII v. Edited by S. G. Tomsinskii. Vol. 1: *Khoziaistvo boiarina B. I. Morozova.* Vol. 8.1: *Materialy po istorii feodal'no-krepostnogo khoziaistva.* Trudy Istoriko-arkheograficheskogo instituta. Leningrad: AN SSSR, 1933.

Khroniki Smutnogo vremeni. Edited by A. Liberman, B. Morozov, and S. Shokarev. Moscow: Fond Sergeia Dubova, 1998.

Kievskaia Psaltir' 1397 goda iz Gosudarstvennoi publichnoi biblioteki imeni M. E. Saltykova-Shchedrina v Leningrade (OLDP F6). Moscow: Iskusstvo, 1978.

Kisterev, S. N., ed. "Vladimirskii Rozhdestvenskii monastyr' v dokumentakh XVI–nachala XVII veka." In *Russkii diplomatarii,* 6: 90–147. Moscow: Arkheograficheskii tsentr, 2000.

Kivelson, Valerie A. *Autocracy in the Provinces: The Muscovite Gentry and Political Culture in the Seventeenth Century.* Stanford, CA: Stanford University Press, 1996.

———. "Devil Stole His Mind: The Tsar and the 1648 Moscow Uprising." *American Historical Review* 98, no. 3 (Jun. 1993): 733–56.

———, and Robert H. Greene, eds. *Orthodox Russia: Belief and Practice under the Tsars.* University Park: Pennsylvania State University Press, 2003.

Kliuchevskii, Vasilii Osipovich. *A Course in Russian History: The Seventeenth Century.* Translated by Natalie Duddington. London: M. E. Sharpe, 1994.

——— [as Kliuchevsky, V. O.]. *A History of Russia.* Translated by C. J. Hogarth. 5 vols. New York: Russell and Russell, 1960.

———. *Kurs russkoi istorii.* 2nd ed. 5 vols. Petrograd: Gosud. izd-vo, 1923.

———. *Pravoslavie v Rossii.* [Multiple articles.] Edited by V. S. Antonov, V. A. Korol'kova, et al. Moscow: Mysl', 2000.

————. *Skazaniia inostrantsev o Moskovskom gosudarstve.* Petrograd, 1918.

————. *Sochineniia.* 8 vols. Moscow: GIPL, 1956–1959.

Kloss, B. M. *Nikonovskii svod i russkie letopisi XVI–XVII vekov.* Moscow: Nauka, 1980.

Knizhnye tsentry Drevnei Rusi: Severnorusskie monastyri. Edited by S. A. Semiachko. St. Petersburg: Dmitrii Bulanin, 2001.

Knizhnye tsentry Drevnei Rusi: Solovetskii monastyr'. Edited by S. A. Semiachko. St. Petersburg: Dmitrii Bulanin, 2001.

Knizhnye tsentry Drevnei Rusi: XVII vek.; Raznye aspekty issledovaniia. Edited by R. P. Dmitrieva and D. S. Likhachev. St. Petersburg: Nauka, 1994.

Knox, Zoe Katrina. *Russian Society and the Orthodox Church: Religion in Russia after Communism.* London: RoutledgeCurzon, 2005.

Kolgushkin, V. V. *Opisanie starinnykh atlasov, kart i planov XVI, XVII, XVIII vekov i poloviny XIX veka, khraniashchikhsia v Arkhive Tsentral'nogo kartograficheskogo proizvodstva VMF.* Moscow: VMF, 1958.

Kollmann, Nancy Shields. *By Honor Bound: State and Society in Early Modern Russia.* Ithaca, NY: Cornell University Press, 1999.

————. *Kinship and Politics: The Making of the Muscovite Political System, 1345–1547.* Stanford, CA: Stanford University Press, 1987.

Kolycheva, E. I. "Pravoslavnye monastyri vtoroi poloviny XV–XVI veka." In *Monashestvo i monastyri v Rossii. XI–XX veka: Istoricheskie ocherki*, edited by N. V. Sinitsyna et al., 81–115. Moscow: Nauka, 2002.

Komter, Aafke E., ed. *The Gift: An Interdisciplinary Perspective.* Amsterdam: Amsterdam University Press, 1996.

————. "Reciprocity as a Principle of Exclusion: Gift Giving in the Netherlands." *Sociology* 30 (1996): 299–316.

————, and Wilma Vollebergh. "Gift Giving and the Emotional Significance of Family and Friends." *Journal of Marriage and Family* 59.3 (Aug. 1997): 747–57.

Koposov, N. E. *Kak dumaiut istoriki.* Moscow: Novoe literaturnoe obozrenie, 2001.

Koretskii, V. I. *Formirovanie krepostnogo prava i pervaia krest'ianskaia voina v Rossii.* Moscow: Nauka, 1975.

————. "Golod 1601–1603 gg. v Rossii i tserkov'." *Voprosy istorii religii i ateizma* 7 (1959): 218–56.

Kormovaia kniga Iosifo-Volokolamskogo monastyria/Das Speisungsbuch von Volokolamsk: Eine Quelle zur Sozialgeschichte russischer Klöster im 16. Jahrhundert. Edited by Russell E. Martin. Cologne: Böhlau, 1998.

Kosheleva, Olga E. "Death: Emotional Undercurrents in the Wills and Letters of 17th Century Russian Aristocrats." In *Das Individuum und die Seinen: Individualität in der okzidentalen und in der russischen Kultur in Mittelalter und früher Neuzeit*, edited by Yuri L. Bessmertny and Otto Gerhard Oexle, 217–30. Göttingen: Vandenhoeck and Ruprecht, 2002.

Kostomarov, N. I. *Geroi Smutnago vremeni: Boris Godunov, Lzhedimitrii, Marina Mnishek, Tsar Vasilii Shuiskii.* Berlin: Detinets, 1922.

————. *Smutnoe vremia Moskovskago gosudarstva v nachale XVII stoletiia: 1604–1613. Istoricheskie monografii i issledovaniia.* Moscow: Charli, 1994.

————. *Spasiteli Rossii v XVII v.* Berlin: Detinets, 1921.

————. *Tsar Mikhail Feodorovich.* Berlin: Detinets, 1921.

Kotilaine, Jarmo, and Marshall Poe, eds. *Modernizing Muscovy: Reform and Social Change in Seventeenth-Century Russia.* London: RoutledgeCurzon, 2004.

Kotoshikhin, Grigorii. *O Rossii v carstvovanie Alekseja Mixajloviča.* Edited by A. E. Pennington. Oxford: Clarendon, 1980.

———. *O Rossii v tsarstvovanie Alekseia Mikhailovicha.* St. Petersburg, 1906.

Kovalenskii, M. N. *Moskovskaia Smuta XVII veka, ee smisl i znachenie: Istoricheskii ocherk.* 2nd ed. Moscow: Gosud. izd-vo, 1922.

Kovtun, Liudmila Stepanovna. *Azbukovniki XVI–XVII vv.: starshaia raznovidnost'.* Leningrad: Nauka, 1989.

———. *Leksikografiia v Moskovskoi Rusi XVI–nachala XVII v.* Leningrad: Nauka, 1975.

———. *Russkaia leksikografiia epokhi srednevekov'ia.* Leningrad: AN SSSR, 1963.

Krawchuk, Andrii S. "Russia: History." In *Encyclopedia of Monasticism,* edited by William M. Johnston, 2: 1097–1101. Chicago: Fitzroy Dearborn, 2000.

"Kreml' i RPTs budut prazdnovat' iubilei votsareniia Romanovykh." *Russkii proekt.* June 2, 2010. http://blagievesti.ucoz.ru/news/edinorossy_s_rpc_gotovjatsja_prazdnovat_jubilej_vocarenija_romanovykh/2010–06–02–52.

Krestnikov, Iurii, Andrei Sannikov, and Aleksandr Stebletsov. *Spravochnik-putevoditel' po monastyriam i sviatyniam.* Vols. 1–2. Moscow: Graal', 2001.

Krom, Mikhail. "Vdovstvuiushchee tsarstvo": Politicheskii krizis v Rossii 30–40-kh godov XVI veka. St. Petersburg: Novoe Literaturnoe Obozrenie, 2010.

Kukushkina, M. V. ed. "Neizvestnoe 'Pisanie' o nachale 'Smuty.'" *TODRL* 21 (1965): 194–99.

Kulik, Alexander. *Retroverting Slavonic Pseudepigrapha: Toward the Original of the Apocalypse of Abraham.* Atlanta, GA: Society of Biblical Literature, 2004.

Kuliugin, A. I. *Praviteli Rossii, 862–1917.* 2nd ed. Cheboksary: Chuvashiia, 2000.

Kul'tura srednevekovoi Moskvy: XVII vek. Edited by L. A. Beliaev, T. I. Makarov, S. Z. Chernov, and B. A. Rybakov. Moscow: Nauka, 1999.

Kurlansky, Mark. *Salt: A World History.* New York: Penguin, 2003.

Kuznetsov, Boris V. "Sobytiia Smutnogo vremeni v massovykh predstavleniiakh sovremennikov (videniia i znameniia, ikh znachenie v etot period)." PhD diss. abstract, Moscow Pedagogical State University, 1997.

Lappo-Danilevskij, A. "L'idée de l'état et son évolution en Russie depuis les Troubles du XVIIe siècle jusqu'aux Réformes du XVIIIe." *Essays in Legal History Read before the International Congress of Historical Studies Held in London in 1913,* edited by Paul Vinogradoff, 356–83. London: Oxford University Press, 1913.

Lavrent'ev, A. V. *Tsarevich—tsar'—tsesar'. Lzhedmitrii I, ego gosudarstvennye pechati, nagradnye znaki i medali, 1604–1606 gg.* St. Petersburg: Dmitrii Bulanin, 2001.

LeDonne, John P. *Absolutism and Ruling Class: The Formation of the Russian Political Order, 1700–1825.* New York: Oxford University Press, 1991.

Leonard, Carol S. *Reform and Regicide: The Reign of Peter III of Russia.* Bloomington: Indiana University Press, 1993.

Leont'eva, G. A. *Paleografiia, khronologiia, arkheografiia, geral'dika.* Moscow: Vlados, 2000.

Lepakhin, Valerii V. "Voinstvo v drevnerusskoi literature i ikonopisi." *Internet-zhurnal Sretenskogo monastyria.* http://www.pravoslavie.ru/jurnal/296.htm.

Letopisets ellinskii i rimskii. Edited by O. V. Tvorogov and E. A. Gol'dich. Vol. 1. St. Petersburg: Dmitrii Bulanin, 1999.

Levin, Evgenii. "Spor o sud'be Novogo Izralia. [Review of] Aleksandr Filiushkin, *Andrei Kurbskii.*" *Booknik.ru (evreiskie teksty i temy).* http://booknik.ru/reviews/non-fiction/?id=30141.

Lévi-Strauss, Claude. *Les structures élémentaires de la parenté*. Paris: Presses universitaires de France, 1949.

Levshun, Liubov'. *Istoriia vostochnoslavianskogo knizhnogo slova XI–XVII vekov.* Minsk: Ekonompress, 2001.

Lezik, E. V. "'Slovo o zakone i blagodati' mitropolita Ilariona v otechestvennoi istorio- grafii." In *Srednevekovoe pravoslavie ot prikhoda do patriarkhata*, edited by N. D. Barabanov, I. O. Tiumentsev, et al., 1: 85–102. Volgograd: Izd-vo Volgogradskogo gosud. universiteta, 1997.

Likhachev, Dmitrii S. *Chelovek v literature Drevnei Rusi.* Moscow: Nauka, 1970.

———. *Natsional'noe samosoznanie drevnei Rusi: Ocherki iz oblasti russkoi literatury XI–XVII vv.* Moscow: Akademiia nauk SSSR, 1945.

Lincoln, W. Bruce. *The Conquest of a Continent: Siberia and the Russians.* New York: Random House, 1994.

Liseitsev, Dmitrii V. *Posol'skii prikaz v epokhu Smuty.* 2 vols. Moscow: IRI RAN, 2003.

———. *Prikaznaia sistema Moskovskogo gosudarstva v epokhu Smuty.* Moscow: IRI RAN, 2009.

———. "Russko-krymskie otnosheniia v epokhu Smuty." *Rossiia* 21, no. 1 (2000): 94–123.

Literatura Drevnei Rusi: Biobibliograficheskii slovar'. Edited by O. V. Tvorogov and L. V. Sokolova. Moscow: Prosveshchenie, 1996.

Liusen, Irina. *Grechesko-staroslavianskii konkordans k drevneishim spiskam slavianskogo perevoda evangelii* (codices Marianus, Zographensis, Assemanianus, Ostromiri). Uppsala: AUU, 1995.

Lobanov, N. A. "Obraz Rossii v germanskom obshchestve XVI–XVII vekov." In *Issledo- vaniia po istochnikovedeniiu istorii Rossii (do 1917 g.): Sbornik statei pamiati V. I. Buganova*, edited by N. M. Rogozhin, Iu. P. Glushakova, A. I. Aksenov, Iu. A. Tikhonov, and L. V. Razumov, 135–52. Moscow: IRI RAN, 2001.

Lokot', T. *Smutnoe vremia i revoliutsiia: Politicheskiia paralleli 1613–1917 g.* Berlin: Dvuglavyi orel, 1923.

Longworth, Philip. *Alexis: Tsar of All the Russias.* London: Secker and Warburg, 1984.

———. *The Cossacks.* New York: Holt, Rinehart, and Winston, 1970.

———. *The Making of Eastern Europe: From Prehistory to Postcommunism.* 2nd ed. New York: St. Martin's, 1997.

———. *The Three Empresses: Catherine I, Anne and Elizabeth of Russia.* New York: Holt, Rinehart, and Winston, 1972.

Lopez, Roberto S. "Hard Times and Investment in Culture." In *The Renaissance: A Sym- posium*, edited by S. A. Callisen, 19–32. New York: Metropolitan Museum of Art, 1953. Reprinted in *The Renaissance: Medieval or Modern?*, edited by Karl H. Dan- nenfeldt, 50–63. Boston: Heath, 1959.

Luk'ianov, V. V. *Opisanie kollekstii rukopisei Gosudarstvennogo arkhiva Iaroslavskoi oblasti XIV–XX vekov.* Yaroslavl: Iaroslavskoe knizhnoe izd-vo, 1957.

Lunt, Horace Gray. *Old Church Slavonic Grammar.* 7th ed. New York: Mouton de Gruyter, 2001.

Lur'e, Ia. S. "Iosif Volotskii kak publitsist i obshchestvennyi deiatel'." In *Poslaniia Iosifa Volotskogo*, by Iosif Volotskii, edited by A. A. Zimin and Ia. S. Lur'e. Moscow: AN SSSR, 1959.

Madariaga, Isabel de. *Russia in the Age of Catherine the Great.* New Haven, CT: Yale University Press, 1981.

Magoulias, Harry J. *Byzantine Christianity: Emperor, Church, and the West.* Detroit, MI: Wayne State University Press, 1982.

Maguire, Henry, ed. *Byzantine Court Culture from 829 to 1204.* Washington, DC: Dumbarton Oaks, 2004.

Majeska, George P. "Byzantine Influence on Russia." In *The Modern Encyclopedia of Russian and Soviet History*, edited by Joseph L. Wieczynski, 6: 74–80. Gulf Breeze, FL: Academic International, 1978.

———. "Byzantine Political Theory." In *The Supplement to The Modern Encyclopedia of Russian, Soviet and Eurasian History*, edited by Bruce F. Adams, 5: 66–68. Gulf Breeze, FL: Academic International Press, 2004.

———. "Byzantine-Russian Relations." In *The Modern Encyclopedia of Russian and Soviet History*, edited by Joseph L. Wieczynski, 6: 80–86. Gulf Breeze, FL: Academic International, 1978.

———. "The Moscow Coronation of 1498 Reconsidered." *Jahrbücher für Geschichte Osteuropas,* 26, no. 3 (1978): 353–61.

Makarii (Bulgakov), Mitropolit. *Istoriia russkoi tserkvi.* 3rd ed. 12 vols. St. Petersburg: Golike, 1883–1903. Reprinted The Hague: Europe, 1968–1969.

———. *Istoriia russkoi tserkvi.* [New ed.] Book 6 (vols. 10–11). Moscow: Izd-vo Spaso-Preobrazhenskogo Valaamskogo monastyria, 1996.

Malinowski, Bronislaw. *Argonauts of the Western Pacific: An Account of Native Enterprise and Adventure in the Archipelagoes of Melanesian New Guinea.* London: Routledge, 1922.

Marchocki, Mikołaj Ścibor. *Historia moskiewskiej wojny.* In *Moskwa w rękach Polaków: Pamiętniki dowódców i oficerów garnizonu polskiego w Moskwie w latach 1610–1612*, edited by Marek Kubala, Tomasz Ściężor, and Andrzej Nowosad, 13–84. Liszki: Platan, 1995.

———. *Historya wojny moskiewskiej.* Poznan: Oredownik, 1841.

——— [as N. Markhotskii]. *Istoriia moskovskoi voiny.* Edited and translated by E. Kuksina. Moscow: Rosspen, 2000.

Marcoux, Jean-Sébastien. "Escaping the Gift Economy." *Journal of Consumer Research* 36, no. 4 (Dec. 2009): 671–85.

Margeret, Jacques. *Estat de l'empire de Russie et Grand Duché de Muscovie.* Paris, 1607. Reprinted in *Early Exploration of Russia*, edited by Marshall Poe. 2.2. London: RoutledgeCurzon, 2003.

———. *Estat de l'empire de Russie et Grand Duché de Moscovie, avec ce qui s'y est passé de plus mémorable et tragique pendant le règne de quatre Empereurs: à sçavoir depuis l'an 1590 jusques en l'an 1606, en Septembre.* Paris: Genet, 1946.

———. *The Russian Empire and Grand Duchy of Muscovy: A 17th-Century French Account.* Translated and edited by Chester S. L. Dunning. Pittsburgh, PA: University of Pittsburgh Press, 1983.

Mariinskoe chetveroevangelie s primechaniiami i prilozheniiami. Edited by I. V. Iagich. Graz: Akad. Druck, 1960.

Marker, Gary. *Imperial Saint: The Cult of St. Catherine and the Dawn of Female Rule in Russia.* DeKalb: Northern Illinois University Press, 2007.

Martin, Janet. *Medieval Russia, 980–1584.* Cambridge: Cambridge University Press, 1995.

Martin, Russell E. "Choreographing the 'Tsar's Happy Occasion': Tradition, Change, and Dynastic Legitimacy in the Weddings of Tsar Mikhail Romanov." *Slavic Review* 63, no. 4 (2004): 794–817.

————. "Gifts and Commemoration: Donations to Monasteries, Dynastic Legitimacy, and Remembering the Royal Dead in Muscovy (7159/1651)." In *Religion und Integration im Moskauer Russland*, edited by Ludwig Steindorff, 499–525. Wiesbaden: Harrassowitz Verlag, 2010.

Martynov, V. *Kul'tura, ikonosfera i bogosluzhebnoe penie Moskovskoi Rusi.* Moscow: Russkii put', 2000.

Mashtafarov, A. V., ed. "Kashinskii Sretenskii monastyr' v dokumentakh XV–nachala XVII veka." In *Russkii diplomatarii*, 3: 45–61. Moscow: Arkheograficheskii tsentr, 1998.

————, ed. "Muromskie monastyri i tserkvi v dokumentakh XVI–nachala XVII veka." In *Russkii diplomatarii*, 6: 43–89. Moscow: Arkheograficheskii tsentr, 2000.

Maskiewicz, Samuel. *Dyjariusz Samuela Maskiewicza. Początek swój bierze od roku 1594 w latach po sobie idących.* In *Moskwa w rękach Polaków: Pamiętniki dowódców i oficerów garnizonu polskiego w Moskwie w latach 1610–1612*, edited by Marek Kubala, Tomasz Ściężor, and Andrzej Nowosad, 119–210. Liszki: Platan, 1995.

————, and Bogusław Maskiewicz. *Pamiętniki Samuela i Bogusława Kazimierza Maskiewiczów (wiek XVII).* Edited by Alojzy Sajkowski and Władysław Czapliński. Wroclaw: Zakład narodowy im. Ossolińskich, 1961.

Massa, Isaac. *Histoire des guerres de la Moscovie (1601–1610).* Edited by Michel Obolensky and A. Van der Linde. 2 vols. Brussels: Fr. J. Olivier, 1866. [Vol. 1 contains the Dutch original: *Een cort verhael van begin en oorspronck deser tegenwoordighe oorloogen en troeblen in Moscouia totten jare 1610 onder 't gouuernement van diuerse vorsten aldaer.*]

————. *Kratkoe izvestie o nachale i proiskhozhdenii sovremennykh voin i smut v Moskovii, sluchivshikhsia do 1610 goda za korotkoe vremia pravleniia neskol'kikh gosudarei.* Translated by A. A. Morozov (1937). In *O nachale voin i smut v Moskovii*, edited by A. Liberman, 13–150. Moscow: Rita-Print, 1997.

————. *A Short History of the Beginnings and Origins of These Present Wars in Moscow under the Reign of Various Sovereigns down to the Year 1610.* Translated by G. Edward Orchard. Toronto: University of Toronto Press, 1982.

Materialy po istorii, arkheologii i etnografii Mordovii: Trudy. Vol. 54. Edited by V. I. Kozlov, M. V. Dorozhkin, V. N. Mart'ianov, and I. I. Firstov. Saransk: Mordovskoe knizhnoe izd-vo, 1977.

Materialy po istorii feodal'no-krepostnogo khoziaistva. Vol. 1. *Trudy istoriko-arkheograficheskogo instituta,* vol. 8. Leningrad: AN SSSR, 1933.

Materialy po istorii krest'ian v Rossii XI–XVII vv.: Sbornik dokumentov. Edited by V. V. Mavrodin. Leningrad: Izd-vo Leningradskogo universiteta, 1958.

Materialy po istorii Nizhegorodskogo kraia iz stolichnykh arkhivov. Edited by A. K. Kabanov. Vol. 4. Nizhnii-Novgorod, 1915.

Mathiesen, Robert. *The Ostrih Bible, 1580/81–1980/81: A Quadricentennial Exhibition.* Cambridge, MA: Houghton Library (Harvard University), 1980.

Mattingly, Garrett. *Renaissance Diplomacy.* Baltimore, MD: Penguin, 1955.

Mauss, Marcel. *Essai sur le don: Forme et raison de l'échange dans les sociétés archaiques.* Paris: Alcan, 1925.

McCormick, Michael. "Legitimacy, Political." In *The Oxford Dictionary of Byzantium*, edited by Alexander P. Kazhdan, Alice-Mary Talbot, Anthony Cutler, Timothy E. Gregory, and Nancy P. Ševčenko, 2: 1203. Oxford: Oxford University Press, 1991.

———. "Political Structure." In *The Oxford Dictionary of Byzantium*, edited by Alexander P. Kazhdan, Alice-Mary Talbot, Anthony Cutler, Timothy E. Gregory, and Nancy P. Ševčenko, 3: 1692–94. Oxford: Oxford University Press, 1991.

McNeill, William H. *Europe's Steppe Frontier, 1500–1800*. Chicago: University of Chicago Press, 1964.

The Meaning of Historical Terms and Concepts: New Studies on "Begriffsgeschichte." Edited by Hartmut Lehmann and Melvin Richter. Occasional Paper No. 15. Washington, DC: German Historical Institute, 1996.

Medlin, William-Kenneth. *Moscow and East Rome: A Political Study of the Relations of Church and State in Muscovite Russia.* Thèse No. 144, Université de Genève, Faculté des lettres. Neuchatel: Delachaux et Niestlé, 1952.

Medvedev, I. P. "Politicheskaia ideologiia Vizantii: Istoriograficheskii ekskurs." In *Rossiiskoe gosudarstvo v XVI–XVII vv.: Sbornik statei, posviashchennyi 75-letiiu so dnia rozhdeniia Iu. G. Alekseeva*, edited by A. G. Man'kov et al., 154–66. St. Petersburg: Dmitrii Bulanin, 2002.

Medvedeva-Khazanova, Marina. *Rossiia: Smutnoe vremia.* St. Petersburg: Astra-Liuks, 1994.

Mel'nikov, A. P. "K istorii blizhaishikh okrestnostei Nizhniago-Novgoroda." *Deistviia Nizhegorodskoi gubernskoi uchenoi arkhivnoi komissii: Sbornik statei, soobshchenii, opisei i dokumentov*, 4: 69–75. Nizhnii-Novgorod: Konyshev, 1900.

"Meropriiatiia v ramkakh 'Romanovskogo festivalia' mart 2011 g." *Kontsertno-vystavochnyi tsentr "Gubernskii."* http://www.kvc-kos.ru/afishamart_10–11(2).html.

Meyendorff, John. *Byzantine Theology: Historical Trends and Doctrinal Themes.* 2nd ed. New York: Fordham University Press, 1979.

———. *"Was There Ever a Third Rome? Remarks on the Byzantine Legacy in Russia."* In *The Byzantine Tradition after the Fall of Constantinople*, edited by John J. Yiannias, 45–60. Charlottesville: University Press of Virginia, 1991.

Meyendorff, Paul. *Russia, Ritual, and Reform: The Liturgical Reforms of Nikon in the 17th Century.* Crestwood, NY: St. Vladimir's Seminary Press, 1991.

Michels, Georg B. *At War with the Church: Religious Dissent in Seventeenth-Century Russia.* Stanford, CA: Stanford University Press, 1999.

———. "The Patriarch's Rivals: Local Strongmen and the Limits of Church Reform during the Seventeenth Century." In *Modernizing Muscovy: Reform and Social Change in Seventeenth-Century Russia*, edited by Jarmo Kotilaine and Marshall Poe, 317–42. London: RoutledgeCurzon, 2004.

———. "Power, Patronage, and Repression in the Church Regime of Patriarch Filaret (1619–1633)." In *Religion und Integration im Moskauer Russland*, edited by Ludwig Steindorff, 81–96. Wiesbaden: Harrassowitz Verlag, 2010.

———. "Ruling without Mercy: Seventeenth-Century Russian Bishops and their Officials." *Kritika: Explorations in Russian and Eurasian History* 4, no. 3 (Summer 2003): 515–42.

———. *Self-Immolation during the Russian Church Schism.* Pittsburgh, PA: Carl Beck Papers, 1999.

The Midrash on Psalms. Translated by William G. Braude. New Haven, CT: Yale University Press, 1959.

Mil'kov, V. V. *Osmyslenie istorii v Drevnei Rusi.* 1st ed. Moscow: IF RAN, 1997. 2nd ed. St. Petersburg: Aleteiia, 2000.

Miller, David B. "The Orthodox Church." In *The Cambridge History of Russia*, edited by

Maureen Perrie, Vol. 1: *From Early Rus' to 1689*, pp. 338–59. Cambridge: Cambridge University Press, 2006.

———. *Saint Sergius of Radonezh, His Trinity Monastery, and the Formation of the Russian Identity.* DeKalb: Northern Illinois University Press, 2010.

———. "The Velikie Minei Chetii and the Stepennaia Kniga of Metropolitan Makarii and the Origins of Russian National Consciousness." In *Forschungen zur osteuropäischen Geschichte*, 26: 263–382. Berlin: Harrassowitz, 1979.

Miller, Eric Patrick. *The Politics of Imitating Christ: Christ the King and Christomimetic Rulership in Early Medieval Biblical Commentaries.* Charlottesville: University Press of Virginia, 2001.

Miroslavljevo Jevangelje: Kritichko izdanje. Edited by Nikola Rodich, Gordana Jovanovich, and Dimitrije Bogdanovich. Belgrade: Srpska Akad. Nauka, 1986.

Mirsky, D. S. *Russia: A Social History.* Edited by C. G. Seligman. London: Cresset, 1942.

Miyazaki, Hirokazu. "From Sugar Cane to 'Swords': Hope and the Extensibility of the Gift in Fiji." *Journal of the Royal Anthropological Institute* 11, no. 2 (June 2005): 277–95.

The Modern Encyclopedia of Russian and Soviet History. Edited by Joseph L. Wieczynski et al. 60 vols. Gulf Breeze, FL: Academic International, 1976–1995.

The Monarchical Republic of Early Modern England: Essays in Response to Patrick Collinson. Edited by John F. McDiarmid. Burlington, VT: Ashgate, 2007.

Monashestvo i monastyri v Rossii, XI–XX veka: Istoricheskie ocherki. Edited by N. V. Sinitsyna et al. Moscow: Nauka, 2002.

Monastyri: Entsiklopedicheskii spravochnik. Edited by Tikhon (Arkhiepiskop Bronitskii). Moscow: Moskovskaia Patriarkhiia/Respublika, 2001.

Monastyri Russkoi Pravoslavnoi Tserkvi: Spravochnik-putevoditel'. Edited by L. G. Rudin and P. V. Kuznetsov. Moscow: Izd-vo Moskovskoi Patriarkhii, 2001.

Morozov, B. "Smutnoe vremia glazami russkikh i inostrantsev." In *Khroniki Smutnogo vremeni*, edited by A. Liberman, B. Morozov, and S. Shokarev, 461–70. Moscow: Fond Sergeia Dubova, 1998.

Morozova, L. E. *Rossiia na puti iz Smuty: Izbranie na tsarstvo Mikhaila Fedorovicha.* Moscow: Nauka, 2005.

———. *Smuta na Rusi: Vybor puti.* Moscow: AST-Press Kniga, 2007.

———. *Smuta nachala XVII v. glazami sovremennikov.* Moscow: IRI RAN, 2000.

Morris, Ian. "Gift and Commodity in Archaic Greece." *Man*, n.s. 21, no. 1 (Mar. 1986): 1–17.

Morrisson, Cécile. "Les événements/perspective chronologique." In *Le monde byzantin*, edited by Cécile Morrisson. Vol. 1. *L'Empire romain d'Orient, 330–641*, pp. 3–47. Paris: Presses universitaires de France, 2004.

———, ed. *Le monde byzantin.* Vol. 1. *L'Empire romain d'Orient, 330–641.* Paris: Presses universitaires de France, 2004.

Moskovskie kirillovskie izdaniia XVI–XVII vv. v sobraniiakh RGADA. Katalog. Edited by A. A. Guseva, E. V. Luk'ianova, and L. N. Gorbunova. Vol. 1: *1556–1625 gg.* Moscow: Arkheograficheskii tsentr, 1996.

Moskwa w rękach Polaków: Pamiętniki dowódców i oficerów garnizonu polskiego w Moskwie w latach 1610–1612. Edited by Marek Kubala, Tomasz Ścięźor, and Andrzej Nowosad. Liszki: Platan, 1995.

Naidenova, L. P. "Vnutrenniaia zhizn' monastyria i monastyrskii byt (po materialam Solovetskogo monastyria)." In *Monashestvo i monastyri v Rossii, XI–XX veka: Istoricheskie ocherki*, edited by N. V. Sinitsyna et al., 285–301. Moscow: Nauka, 2002.

Nechaev, B. "Smert' tsarevicha Dmitriia." In *Smutnoe vremia v Moskovskom gosudarstve: Sbornik statei s illiustratsiiami*, edited by V. N. Bochkarev, Iu. V. Got'e, and V. I. Picheta, 58–74. Moscow: Zadruga, 1913.

Neville, Leonora Alice. *Authority in Byzantine Provincial Society, 950–1100*. Cambridge: Cambridge University Press, 2004.

New Perspectives on Muscovite History. Edited by Lindsey Hughes. New York: St. Martin's, 1993.

Nikolaeva, S. V. "Vklady i vkladchiki v Troitse-Sergiev monastyr' v XVI–XVII vekakh (po vkladnym knigam XVII veka)." In *Tserkov' v istorii Rossii,* 2: 81–93. Moscow: IRI RAN, 1998.

Nikol'skii, N. K. *Kirillo-Belozerskii monastyr' i ego ustroistvo do vtoroi chetverti XVII veka*. 2 vols. St. Petersburg: Sinodal'naia, 1897–1910; new ed. St. Petersburg: Dmitrii Bulanin, 2006.

Nikol'skii, N. M. *Istoriia russkoi tserkvi*. 3rd ed. Edited by N. S. Gordeinko. Moscow: Izd-vo politicheskoi literatury, 1985.

Noonan, Thomas S. "The Khazar Qaghanate and Its Impact on the Early Rus' State: The *Translatio Imperii* from Itil to Kiev." In *Nomads in the Sedentary World*, edited by Anatoly M. Khazanov and André Wink, 76–102. Richmond, Surrey: Curzon, 2001.

Norwich, John Julius. *Byzantium: The Early Centuries*. New York: Knopf, 1989.

———. *A Short History of Byzantium*. New York: Knopf, 1997.

Novaia povest' o preslavnom rosiiskom tsarstve i sovremennaia ei agitatsionnaia patrioticheskaia pis'mennost'. Edited and commentary by N. F. Droblenkova. Moscow: AN SSSR, 1960.

Novgorodskii istoricheskii sbornik. Vols. 9 (19)–10 (20). Edited by B. V. Anan'ich, E. A. Gordienko, D. M. Bulanin, G. M. Kovalenko, V. N. Pleshkov, V. Iu. Cherniaev, and V. L. Ianin. St. Petersburg: Dmitrii Bulanin, 2003–2005.

Novokhatko, O. V. *Zapisnye knigi Moskovskogo stola Razriadnogo prikaza XVII veka*. Moscow: Pamiatniki istoricheskoi mysli, 2001.

Novyi letopisets. In *Khroniki Smutnogo vremeni*, edited by A. Liberman, B. Morozov, and S. Shokarev, 263–410. Moscow: Fond Sergeia Dubova, 1998.

Novyi zavet na grecheskom iazyke s podstrochnym perevodom na russkii iazyk. St. Petersburg: Rossiiskoe bibleiskoe obshchestvo, 2002.

Obolensky, Dimitri. *The Byzantine Commonwealth: Eastern Europe, 500–1453*. London: Weidenfeld and Nicolson, 1971.

———. *Byzantium and the Slavs*. Crestwood, NY: St. Vladimir's Seminary Press, 1994.

Olearius, Adam. *The Travels of Olearius in Seventeenth-Century Russia*. Edited and translated by Samuel H. Baron. Stanford, CA: Stanford University Press, 1967.

Oman, Charles. *A History of the Art of War in the Sixteenth Century*. London: Methuen, 1937.

Opisanie aktov sobraniia grafa A. S. Uvarova: Akty istoricheskie. Edited by I. M. Kataev, A. K. Kabanov, and M. V. Dovnar-Zapol'skii. Moscow: Lissner i Sovko, 1905.

Opisi arkhiva Razriadnogo prikaza XVII v. Edited by K. V. Petrov. St. Petersburg: Dmitrii Bulanin, 2001.

Opisi Solovetskogo monastyria XVI veka. Edited by M. I. Mil'chik, Z. V. Dmitrieva, and E. V. Krushel'nitskaia. St. Petersburg: Dmitrii Bulanin, 2003.

Opisi Tsarskogo arkhiva XVII v. i Arkhiva Posol'skogo prikaza 1614 g. Edited by S. O. Shmidt. Moscow: Izd-vo vostochnoi literatury, 1960.

Orchard, G. Edward. "Time of Troubles (1598–1613)." In *The Modern Encyclopedia of Russian and Soviet History*, edited by Joseph L. Wieczynski, 39: 49–57. Gulf Breeze, FL: Academic International Press, 1985.

Ostrogorsky, George. *History of the Byzantine State.* Translated by Joan Hussey. Rev. ed. New Brunswick, NJ: Rutgers University Press, 1969.

Ostromirovo evangelie 1056–57 goda. Edited by A. Vostokov. St. Petersburg: Imp. akademiia nauk, 1843.

Ostrovskii, A. *Dmitrii Samozvanets i Vasilii Shuiskii.* St. Petersburg: Azbuka-klassika, 2007.

Ostrowski, Donald. "The Account of Volodimir's Conversion in the *Povest' vremennykh let:* A Chiasmus of Stories (Revised and Updated)." Unpublished typescript. Revision of article previously published in *Harvard Ukrainian Studies* 28 (2006): 567–80.

———. "The Assembly of the Land (*Zemskii sobor*) as a Representative Institution." In *Modernizing Muscovy: Reform and Social Change in Seventeenth-Century Russia*, edited by Jarmo Kotilaine and Marshall Poe, 117–42. London: RoutledgeCurzon, 2004.

———. "Church Polemics and Monastic Land Acquisition in Sixteenth-Century Muscovy." *Slavonic and East European Review* 64, no. 3 (July 1986): 355–79.

———. "'Moscow the Third Rome' as Historical Ghost." In *Byzantium: Faith and Power (1261–1557): Perspectives on Late Byzantine Art and Culture*, edited by Sarah T. Brooks, 170–79. New Haven, CT: Yale University Press, 2006.

———. *Muscovy and the Mongols: Cross-Cultural Influences on the Steppe Frontier, 1304–1589.* Cambridge: Cambridge University Press, 1998.

———. "Simeon Bekbulatovich: Tatar Khan, Grand Prince of Rus', Monastic Elder." *Russian History* [forthcoming].

———. "Why Did the Metropolitan Move from Kiev to Vladimir in the Thirteenth Century?" In *Christianity and the Eastern Slavs.* Vol. 1: *Slavic Cultures in the Middle Ages.* Edited by Boris Gasparov and Olga Raevsky-Hughes, 83–101. California Slavic Studies. Vol. 16. Berkeley: University of California Press, 1993.

Ostryz'ka Bibliia: The Ostroh Bible 1581. Winnipeg: St. Andrew's College, 1983.

Ovchinnikov, R. V. "Ob izdanii istochnikov po istorii krest'ianskoi voiny v Rossii nachala XVII veka (Istoriko-bibliograficheskii obzor publikatsii)." In *Issledovaniia po istochnikovedeniiu istorii Rossii (do 1917 g.): Sbornik statei pamiati V. I. Buganova*, edited by N. M. Rogozhin, Iu. P. Glushakova, A. I. Aksenov, Iu. A. Tikhonov, and L. V. Razumov, 153–73. Moscow: IRI RAN, 2001.

Oxford Dictionary of Byzantium. Edited by Alexander P. Kazhdan, Alice-Mary Talbot, Anthony Cutler, Timothy E. Gregory, and Nancy P. Ševčenko. 3 vols. Oxford: Oxford University Press, 1991.

Palitsyn, Avraamii. *Skazanie Avraamiia Palitsyna.* Edited by L. V. Cherepnin. Moscow: AN SSSR, 1951.

Pamiatniki diplomaticheskikh i torgovykh snoshenii Moskovskoi Rusi s Persiei. Edited by N. I. Veselovskii. Vol. 1. St. Petersburg: Iablonskii i Perott, 1890.

Pamiatniki diplomaticheskikh snoshenii drevnei Rossii s derzhavami inostrannymi. 10 vols. St. Petersburg: Imp. Velichestva Kantseliariia, 1851–1871.

Pamiatniki diplomaticheskikh snoshenii Krymskago khanstva s Moskovskim gosudarstvom v XVI i XVII vv., khraniashchiesia v Moskovskom glavnom arkhive ministerstva inostrannykh del. Edited by F. Lashkov. Simferopol: Krym, 1891.

Pamiatniki istorii Smutnago vremeni. Edited by A. I. Iakovlev. Moscow: Klochkov, 1909.

Pamiatniki literatury Drevnei Rusi. 10 vols. in 12 books. Moscow: Khudozhestvennaia literatura, 1978–1994.

Pamiatniki Smutnogo vremeni. Tushinskii vor: Lichnost', okruzhenie, vremia. Dokumenty i materialy. Edited by V. I. Kuznetsov and I. P. Kulakova. Trudy Istoricheskogo fakul'teta MGU, vol. 10. Istoricheskie istochniki, vol. 2. Moscow: MGU, 2001.

Pankhurst, Richard. "The Falashas, or Judaic Ethiopians, in their Christian Ethiopian Setting." *African Affairs* 91 (1992): 567–82.

Parry, J. "The Gift, the Indian Gift, and the 'Indian Gift.'" *Man* 21, no. 3 (1986): 453–73.

———, and M. Bloch, eds. *Money and the Morality of Exchange.* Cambridge: Cambridge University Press, 1989.

Pascal, Pierre. [1938.] *Avvakum et les débuts du Raskol.* Paris: Mouton, 1963.

Pashkova, T. I. "Tiuremnoe zakliuchenie v zakonodatel'stve Moskovskoi Rusi." In *Rossiiskoe gosudarstvo v XVI–XVII vv.: Sbornik statei, posviashchennyi 75-letiiu so dnia rozhdeniia Iu. G. Alekseeva,* edited by A. G. Man'kov et al., 82–98. St. Petersburg: Dmitrii Bulanin, 2002.

Pavlishchev, N. I. *Istoricheskii atlas Rossii.* Warsaw: Tip. Stanislava Strombskago, 1845.

Pavlov, Andrei. "Tserkov[n]aia ierarkhiia v sisteme gosudarstvennoi vlasti Rossii i uchrezhdenie patriarshestva." In *Religion und Integration im Moskauer Russland,* edited by Ludwig Steindorff, 65–79. Wiesbaden: Harrassowitz Verlag, 2010.

Pechenev, V. A. *"Smutnoe vremia" v noveishei istorii Rossii (1985–2003): Istoricheskoe svidetel'stvo i razmyshleniia uchastnika sobytii.* Moscow: Norma, 2004.

Pelenski, Jaroslaw. "The Origins of the Muscovite Ecclesiastical Claims to the Kievan Inheritance (Early Fourteenth Century to 1458/1461)." In *Christianity and the Eastern Slavs.* Vol. 1: *Slavic Cultures in the Middle Ages,* edited by Boris Gasparov and Olga Raevsky-Hughes, 102–15. California Slavic Studies, vol. 16. Berkeley: University of California Press, 1993.

———. *Russia and Kazan: Conquest and Imperial Ideology (1438–1560s).* The Hague: Mouton, 1974.

———. "The Sack of Kiev of 1169: Its Significance for the Succession to Kievan Rus'." *Harvard Ukrainian Studies* 11, no. 3/4 (Dec. 1987): 303–16.

The Penitence of Adam: An Apocryphal Armenian Adam Book. Edited and translated by Michael E. Stone. Hebrew University of Jerusalem. http://micro5.mscc.huji. ac.il/~armenia/website/index.html.

The Pentateuch and Haftorahs. Edited by J. H. Hertz. 2nd ed. London: Soncino, 1971.

Pereswetoff-Morath, Alexander. *A Grin without a Cat.* Vol. 1: *"Adversus Judaeos" Texts in the Literature of Medieval Russia.* Vol. 2: *Jews and Christians in Medieval Russia.* Lund: Lund University Slavonic Studies, 2002.

Perevezentsev, Sergei Viacheslavovich. "Uroki smuty: narod i vera." *Pravoslavie i mir* (Nov. 4, 2009). http://www.pravmir.ru/uroki-smuty-narod-i-vera.

Perrie, Maureen, ed. *The Cambridge History of Russia.* Vol. 1: *From Early Rus' to 1689.* Cambridge: Cambridge University Press, 2006.

———. *Pretenders and Popular Monarchism in Early Modern Russia: The False Tsars of the Time of Troubles.* Cambridge: Cambridge University Press, 1995.

———. "The Time of Troubles (1603–1613)." In *Cambridge History of Russia,* edited by Maureen Perrie. Vol. 1: *From Early Rus' to 1689,* pp. 409–31. Cambridge: Cambridge University Press, 2006.

Petrei, Petr. *Istoriia o velikom kniazhestve Moskovskom, proiskhozhdenii velikikh russkikh kniazei, nedavnikh smutakh, proizvedennykh tam tremia Lzhedimitriiami, i o moskovskikh zakonakh, nravakh, pravlenii, vere i obriadakh.* Translated [1867] by A. N. Shemiakin. In *O nachale voin i smut v Moskovii*, edited by A. Liberman, 151–464. Moscow: Rita-Print, 1997.

Petrov, K. V. "K izucheniiu opisei arkhiva Razriadnogo prikaza pervoi poloviny XVII veka." In *Issledovaniia po istochnikovedeniiu istorii Rossii (do 1917 g.): Sbornik statei pamiati V. I. Buganova*, edited by N. M. Rogozhin, Iu. P. Glushakova, A. I. Aksenov, Iu. A. Tikhonov, and L. V. Razumov, 174–87. Moscow: IRI RAN, 2001.

———. "K izucheniiu sbornikov s dokumentami XVI–nach. XVII v. iz sobraniia RNB (Q.IV.70. Ch. 1–4)." In *Drevnerusskaia knizhnost': Arkheografiia, paleografiia, kodikologiia*, edited by M. A. Shibaev and E. V. Krushel'nitskaia, 77–99. St. Petersburg: Dmitrii Bulanin, 1999.

———. "K izucheniiu teksta razriadnykh zapisei za Smutnoe vremia." In *Drevnerusskaia knizhnost': Redaktor i tekst*, edited by Iu. G. Alekseev and V. K. Ziborov, 3: 127–47. St. Petersburg: Dmitrii Bulanin, 2000.

Petrushko, Vladislav. *Istoriia russkoi tserkvi s drevneishikh vremen do ustanovleniia patriarshestva.* Moscow: Pravoslavyi Sviato-Tikhonovskii gumanitarnyi universitet, 2005.

Philipse, Herman. *Heidegger's Philosophy of Being: A Critical Interpretation.* Princeton, NJ: Princeton University Press, 1998.

Phipps, Geraldine Marie. "Britons in Seventeenth-Century Russia: A Study in the Origins of Modernization." PhD diss., University of Pennsylvania, 1971.

———. *Sir John Merrick, English Merchant-Diplomat in Seventeenth-Century Russia.* Newtonville, MA: Oriental Research Partners, 1983.

Picheta, V. "Moskovskoe gosudarstvo vo vtoroi polovine XVI veka." In *Smutnoe vremia v Moskovskom gosudarstve: Sbornik statei s illiustratsiiami*, edited by V. N. Bochkarev, Iu. V. Got'e, and V. I. Picheta, 3–44. Moscow: Zadruga, 1913.

Pichkhadze, A. A. "K istorii chet'ego teksta slavianskogo Vos'miknizhiia." *TODRL* 49 (1996): 10–21.

Pipes, Richard. *Russia under the Old Regime.* New York: Penguin, 1979.

Pirling, Pavel O. *Dmitrii Samozvanets.* Rostov-on-Don: Feniks, 1998.

Pisarev, N. *Domashnii byt russkikh patriarkhov.* Kazan: Tip. Imp. universiteta, 1904. Reprinted Moscow: Khudozhestvennaia literatura, 1991.

"Pisateli i poeti XVII v." *TODRL* 44 (1990): 3–160.

Placek, Joseph Anthony. "Grigorii Karpovich Kotoshikhin's *O Rossii v tsarstvovanie Alekseia Mikhailovicha:* A Translation and Linguistic Commentary." Master's thesis, Georgetown University, 1965.

Platonov, Sergei F. *Boris Godunov.* Petrograd: Ogni, 1921.

———. *Boris Godunov: Tsar of Russia.* Translated by L. Rex Pyles. Gulf Breeze, FL: Academic International, 1973.

———. *Drevnerusskiia skazaniia i povesti o Smutnom vremeni XVII veka, kak istoricheskii istochnik.* St. Petersburg: 1888; 2nd ed. St. Petersburg: Aleksandrov, 1913.

———. *Moscow and the West.* Edited and translated by Joseph L. Wieczynski. Hattiesburg, MS: Academic International, 1972.

———. *Moskva i Zapad.* Berlin: Obelisk, 1926. Reprinted The Hague: Europe, 1966.

———. *Ocherki po istorii Smuty v Moskovskom godusarstve XVI–XVII vv.: Opyt izuche-*

niia obshchestvennago stroia i soslovnykh otnoshenii v smutnoe vremia. 3rd ed. St. Petersburg: Bashmakov, 1910. Reprinted The Hague: Europe, 1967; 5th ed. Moscow: Pamiatniki istoricheskoi mysli, 1995.

———. *Smutnoe vremia.* Prague: Plamia, 1924.

———. *The Time of Troubles: A Historical Study of the Internal Crisis and Social Struggle in Sixteenth- and Seventeenth-Century Muscovy.* Translated by John T. Alexander. Lawrence: University Press of Kansas, 1985.

Pliguzov, Andrei Ivanovich. "O khronologii poslanii Iosifa Volotskogo." In *Russkii feodal'nyi arkhiv.* Vol. 5: *XIV–pervoi treti XVI veka,* edited by V. I. Buganov, 1043–61. Moscow: Akademiia nauk, 1992.

———, and Anna Leonidovna Khoroshkevich. "Iukhan Videkind kak istoriograf russkoi Smuty." In *Arkhiv russkoi istorii: Nauchnyi istoricheskii zhurnal,* edited by I. A. Tikhoniuk et al., 3: 7–28. Moscow: RGADA, 1993.

Plotnikov, Ivan Fedorovich. *Smuta: Revoliutsionnye sobytiia v Beloretskom okruge v 1918 g.* Ufa: Kitap, 1994.

Pobedonostsev, Konstantin Petrovich. "Constantine Pobedonostsev Attacks Democracy, 1896." In *Major Problems in the History of Imperial Russia,* edited by James Cracraft, 390–97. Lexington, MA: Heath, 1994.

———. *Moskovskii sbornik.* Moscow: Sinodal'naia, 1896.

———. *Reflections of a Russian Statesman.* London: G. Richards, 1898.

———. *Sochineniia.* St. Petersburg: Nauka, 1996.

Poe, Marshall. *Foreign Descriptions of Muscovy: An Analytic Bibliography of Primary and Secondary Sources.* Columbus, OH: Slavica, 1995.

———. "Izobretenie kontseptsii 'Moskva—Tretii Rim.'" *Ab Imperio: Teoriia i istoriia natsional'nostei i natsionalizma v postsovetskom prostranstve* 1, no. 2 (2000): 61–86.

———. "Moscow, the Third Rome: The Origins and Transformations of a 'Pivotal Moment.'" *Jahrbücher für Geschichte Osteuropas* 49, no. 3 (2001): 412–29.

———. "A People Born to Slavery": Russia in Early Modern European Ethnography, 1476–1748. Ithaca, NY: Cornell University Press, 2000.

Pokrovsky, Mikhail N. *History of Russia from the Earliest Times to the Rise of Commercial Capitalism.* Edited and translated by J. D. Clarkson and M. R. M. Griffiths. New York: Russell and Russell, 1966.

Polnoe sobranie russkikh letopisei. 43 vols. Moscow: 1843–1997.

Poltorak, S. N., ed. *Smutnoe vremia: Istoriia i sovremennost': Materialy dvadtsatoi Vserossiiskoi zaochnoi nauchnoi konferentsii.* St. Petersburg: Nestor, 2000.

Poslaniia Ivana Groznogo. Edited by D. S. Likhachev, Ia. S. Lur'e, and V. P. Adrianova-Peretts. Moscow: AN SSSR, 1951.

Pospielovsky, Dimitry V. *The Orthodox Church in the History of Russia.* Crestwood, NY: St. Vladimir's Seminary Press, 1998.

Possevino, Antonio. *The Moscovia of Antonio Possevino, S.J.* Translated by Hugh F. Graham. Pittsburgh, PA: University Center for International Studies, 1977.

Pozdeeva, I.V., V.I. Erofeeva, and G.M. Shitova. *Kirillicheskie izdaniia XVI vek–1641 god. Nakhodki Arkheograficheskikh ekspeditsii 1971–1993 godov, postupivshie v Nauchnuiu biblioteku Moskovskogo universiteta.* Moscow: Izd-vo Moskovskogo universiteta, 2000.

Pravoslavnye monastyri Rossii: Kratkii spravochnik. Novosibirsk: Sibirskii khronograf, 2000.

Preobrazhenskii, A. A. "'Zapasy' dvorianskoi znati na sibirskoi sluzhbe v nachale XVII v." In *Rossiiskoe gosudarstvo v XVI–XVII vv.: Sbornik statei, posviashchennyi 75-letiiu so dnia rozhdeniia Iu. G. Alekseeva*, edited by A. G. Man'kov et al., 274–79. St. Petersburg: Dmitrii Bulanin, 2002.

Preobrazhenskii, A. G. *Etimologicheskii slovar' russkogo iazyka.* 2 vols. Moscow: Lissner i Sovko, 1910–1914. Reprinted Moscow: Gosud. izd-vo inostrannykh i natsional'nykh slovarei, 1959.

Prikhodo-raskhodnye knigi moskovskikh prikazov 1619–1621 gg. Edited by S. B. Veselovskii, V. I. Buganov, and B. V. Levshin. Moscow: Nauka, 1983.

Prokhorov, G. M. *"Nekogda ne narod, a nyne narod Bozhii . . .": Drevniaia Rus' kak istoriko-kul'turnyi fenomen.* St. Petersburg: Oleg Abyshko, 2010.

Prokurat, Michael. "Orthodox Monasticism: Slavic." In *Encyclopedia of Monasticism*, edited by William M. Johnston, 2: 976–83. Chicago: Fitzroy Dearborn, 2000.

Pudalov, B. M. "K voprosu o proiskhozhdenii suzdal'skikh kniazei." *Drevniaia Rus'* 4, no. 18 (2004): 46-53.

Putevoditel' po arkhivu Leningradskogo otdeleniia Instituta istorii. Leningrad: AN SSSR, 1958.

Quattuor Evangeliorum: Codex Glagoliticus olim Zographensis nunc Petropolitanus. Edited by V. Jagich. Graz: Akademie Druck, 1954.

Raba, Joel. "The Biblical Tradition in Old Russian Chronicles." *Forschungen zur osteuropäischen Geschichte* 46 (1992): 9–20.

———. *Ha-t'rumah v'ha-t'murah: Eretz Yisrael v'am Yisrael ba-olamah ha-rukhani shel Rusiya b'yamei ha-beinayim.* Tel Aviv: Tel Aviv University, 2003. [Forthcoming English translation: *The Gift and Its Wages: The Land of Israel and the Jewish People in the Spiritual Life of Medieval Russia.* Brepols, 2011.]

Raeff, Marc. "An Early Theorist of Absolutism: Joseph of Volokolamsk." *Slavic and East European Review* 8, no. 2 (Apr. 1949): 77–89.

———. "Joseph Volotsky's Political Ideas in a New Historical Perspective." *Jahrbücher für Geschichte Osteuropas* 13, no. 1 (1965): 19–29.

———. *Understanding Imperial Russia: State and Society in the Old Regime.* Translated by Arthur Goldhammer. New York: Columbia University Press, 1984.

Rambaud, Alfred. *History of Russia from the Earliest Times to 1882.* Translated by L. B. Lang. Edited by Nathan Haskell Dole. 3 vols. Boston: Page, 1879–1882.

Rasmussen, Susan J. "Alms, Elders, and Ancestors: The Spirit of the Gift among the Tuareg." *Ethnology* 39., no. 1 (Winter 2000): 15–38.

Ratshin, Aleksandr. [1852.] *Polnoe sobranie istoricheskikh svedenii o vsekh byvshikh v drevnosti i nyne sushchestvuiushchikh monastyriakh i primechatel'nykh tserkvakh v Rossii.* Moscow: Knizhnaia palata, 2000.

Razzhivin, V. F. "Nekotorye demograficheskie aspekty gorodov Mordovskoi ASSR." *Materialy po istorii, arkheologii i etnografii Mordovii. Trudy.* Vol. 54. Edited by V. I. Kozlov, M. V. Dorozhkin, V. N. Mart'ianov, I. I. Firstov, 106–13. Saransk: Mordovskoe knizhnoe izd-vo, 1977.

Récit du sanglant et terrible massacre arrivé dans la ville de Moscou, ainsi que de la fin effrayante et tragique du dernier duc Démétrius, 1606. Translated by Augustin Galitzin. Paris: J. Techener, 1859.

Remensnyder, Amy G. *Remembering Kings Past: Monastic Foundation Legends in Medieval Southern France.* Ithaca, NY: Cornell University Press, 1996.

Reuter, Timothy. *Medieval Polities and Modern Mentalities.* Edited by Janet L. Nelson. Cambridge: Cambridge University Press, 2006.

Riasanovsky, Nicholas V. *A History of Russia.* 6th ed. New York: Oxford University Press, 2000.

Ricoeur, Paul. *Temps et récit.* 3 vols. Paris: Seuil, 1983–1985.

Riha, Thomas, ed. *Readings in Russian Civilization.* Vol. 1: *Russia before Peter the Great, 900–1700.* Rev. ed. Chicago: University of Chicago Press, 1969.

Robert, Letham. *Through Western Eyes: Eastern Orthodoxy—A Reformed Perspective.* Fearn: Mentor, 2007.

Robinson, N. F. *Monasticism in the Orthodox Churches, being an Introduction to the Study of Modern Hellenic and Slavonic Monachism and the Orthodox Profession Rites, together with a Greek Dissertation on the Monastic Habit.* London: Cope and Fenwick, 1916. Reprinted New York: American Review of Eastern Orthodoxy, 1964.

Robson, Roy R. *Old Believers in Modern Russia.* DeKalb: Northern Illinois University Press, 1995.

———. *Solovki: The Story of Russia Told through Its Most Remarkable Islands.* New Haven, CT: Yale University Press, 2004.

Rogozhin, N. M. "The 'Ambassadorial Book on the Ties between Russia and England 1613–1614' as a Historical Source." In *England and the North: The Russian Embassy of 1613–1614,* edited by Maija Jansson and Nikolai Rogozhin, xxix–xxxvi. Translated by Paul Bushkovitch. Philadelphia, PA: American Philosophical Society, 1994.

———. *Obzor posol'skikh knig iz fondov-kollektsii, khraniashchikhsia v TsGADA (konets XV–nachalo XVIII v.).* Moscow: Akademiia nauk, 1990.

———. "Posol'skie knigi nachala XVII v. kak istoricheskii istochnik." PhD diss., Moscow, 1983. [As cited in Rogozhin, *Posol'skie knigi Rossii;* and Liseitsev, *Posol'skii prikaz.*]

———. *Posol'skie knigi Rossii kontsa XV–nachala XVII vv.* Moscow, 1994.

Romanchuk, Robert. *Byzantine Hermeneutics and Pedagogy in the Russian North: Monks and Masters at the Kirillo-Belozerskii Monastery, 1397–1501.* Toronto: University of Toronto Press, 2007.

Romanenko, Elena V. *Nil Sorskii i traditsii russkogo monashestva.* Moscow: Pamiatniki istoricheskoi mysli, 2003.

———. *Povsednevnaia zhizn' russkogo srednevekovogo monastyria.* Moscow: Molodaia gvardiia, 2002.

Romaniello, Matthew. "Controlling the Frontier: Monasteries and Infrastructure in the Volga Region, 1552–1682." *Central Asian Survey* 19, nos. 3–4 (2000): 429–43.

———. "Mission Delayed: The Russian Orthodox Church after the Conquest of Kazan'." *Church History* 76, no. 3 (Sept. 2007): 511–40.

———. "The Profit Motive: Regional Economic Development in Muscovy after the Conquest of Kazan'." *Journal of European Economic History* 33, no. 3 (Winter 2004): 663–85.

Rossiia i Angliia, 1553–1593/England and Russia/Pervyia sorok let snoshenii mezhdu Rossieiu i Anglieiu, 1553–1593/First Forty Years of Intercourse between England and Russia, 1553–1593. Edited by Iurii V. Tolstoi. St. Petersburg: Transhelia, 1875.

Rossiia v srednie veka i novoe vremia: Sbornik statei k 70-letiiu chl.-korr. RAN L. V. Milova. Edited by M. B. Bulgakov, L. N. Vdovina, A. A. Gorskii, V. A. Kuchkin, and B. N. Floria. Moscow: ROSSPEN, 1999.

Rossiiskii gosudarstvennyi arkhiv drevnikh aktov: Putevoditel'. Edited by Iu. M. Eskin et al. 4 vols. in 5 books [includes 2 vols. under the title: *Tsentral'nyi gosudarstvennyi arkhiv drevnikh aktov SSSR: Putevoditel'*]. Moscow: Glavarkhiv/Drevlekhranili-shche /Arkheograficheskii tsentr, 1991–2000.

Rossiiskii gosudarstvennyi arkhiv drevnikh aktov (RGADA). *Ustiuzhskii arkhiereiskii dom, f. 1206, op. 1*. Archival guide (internal). Moscow, 1976.

Rossiiskoe gosudarstvo v XVI–XVII vv.: Sbornik statei, posviashchennyi 75-letiiu so dnia rozhdeniia Iu. G. Alekseeva. Edited by A. G. Man'kov et al. St. Petersburg: Dmitrii Bulanin, 2002.

Rothenberg, Gunther Erich. *The Austrian Military Border in Croatia, 1522–1747*. Urbana: University of Illinois Press, 1960.

Rowland, Daniel Bruce. "Did Muscovite Literary Ideology Place Limits on the Power of the Tsar (1540s-1660s)?" *Russian Review* 49, no. 2 (Apr. 1990): 125–55.

———. "Moscow: The Third Rome or the New Israel?" *Russian Review* 55.4 (Oct. 1996): 591–614.

———. "Muscovite Political Attitudes as Reflected in Early Seventeenth Century Tales about the Time of Troubles." PhD diss., Yale University, 1976.

———. "Towards an Understanding of the Political Ideas in Ivan Timofeyev's *Vremennik*." *Slavonic and East European Review* 62, no. 3 (July 1984): 371–99.

Rubenson, Samuel. "Origins: Eastern Christian." In *Encyclopedia of Monasticism*, edited by William M. Johnston, 2: 968–70. Chicago: Fitzroy Dearborn, 2000.

Rublack, Hans-Christoph. "New Patterns of Christian Life." In *Handbook of European History, 1400–1600: Late Middle Ages, Renaissance and Reformation*, edited by Thomas A. Brady, Jr., Heiko A. Oberman, and James D. Tracy. Vol. 2: *Visions, Programs and Outcomes*, 585–605. Leiden: Brill, 1995.

Rukopis' Filareta, patriarkha moskovskago i vseia Rossii. Edited by Pavel Mukhanov. Moscow: Tip. Lazarevykh Instituta vostochnykh iazykov, 1837.

Rumiantseva, V. S. "Monastyri i monashestvo v XVII veke." In *Monashestvo i monastyri v Rossii, XI–XX veka: Istoricheskie ocherki*, edited by N. V. Sinitsyna et al., 163–85. Moscow: Nauka, 2002.

Rusinov, N. D. *Drevnerusskii iazyk*. 3rd ed. Moscow: Vysshaia shkola, 1999.

Russia under Western Eyes, 1517–1825. Edited by Anthony Glenn Cross. New York: St. Martin's, 1971.

Russian Embassies to the Georgian Kings, 1589–1605. Edited by W. E. D. Allen. Translated by Anthony Mango. 2 vols. Cambridge: Cambridge University Press, 1970.

The Russian Orthodox Church: 10th to 20th Centuries. Edited by Alexander Preobrazhensky. Moscow: Progress, 1988.

Russkaia istoricheskaia biblioteka. 39 vols. St. Petersburg, 1872–1927. [For vol. 13 I have used the 2nd ed. (St. Petersburg: Aleksandrov, 1909).]

Russkaia povest' XVII veka. Edited by Mikhail Osipovich Skripil'. Moscow: Gosud. izd-vo khud. lit., 1954.

Russkii diplomatarii. Vols. 1–9. Moscow: Arkheograficheskii tsentr, 1997–2003.

Ryl'nikova, N. A., ed. *Vasilii Shuiskii*. Moscow: Armada, 1995.

Rywkin, Michael, ed. *Russian Colonial Expansion to 1917*. New York: Mansell, 1988.

Sadovskii, A. Ia., ed. "Kniga Nizhegorodskago uezda boiarskikh, dvorianskikh, i detei boiarskikh, i inozemtsov dozoru Sily Mikiticha Grekova da pod"iachago Klementiia Kozodavleva: Leta [7]121 godu." In *Deistviia Nizhegorodskoi gubernskoi uchenoi arkhivnoi komissii: Sbornik statei, soobshchenii, opisei i dokumentov*, 5: 17–34. Nizhnii-Novgorod: Konyshev, 1903.

————, ed. "Vyborka iz pistsovykh i platezhnykh knig Nizhegorodskago uezda o sobytiiakh i deiateliakh epokhi smutnago vremeni. V pistsovoi knige 'Nizhegorodtskago uezda Boiarskikh, Dvorianskikh i detei Boiarskikh i inozemtsev dozoru Sily Nikiticha Grekova, da ponod'iachego [*sic*] Klementiia Kozodavleva leta 121 godu.'" *Deistviia Nizhegorodskoi gubernskoi uchenoi arkhivnoi komissii: Sbornik statei, soobshchenii, opisei i dokumentov*, 4: 13–19. Nizhnii-Novgorod: Konyshev, 1900.

Sahlins, Marshall D. *Stone Age Economics*. Chicago: Aldine-Atherton, 1972.

Salimov, Aleksei Maratovich. *Tverskoi Spaso-Preobrazhenskii sobor*. Edited by V. A. Bulkin. Tver: RIF, 1994.

Savich, A. A. *Solovetskaia votchina XV–XVII v. Opyt izucheniia khoziaistva i sotsial'nykh otnoshenii na krainem russkom severe v drevnei Rusi*. Perm: Permskii gosud. universitet, 1927.

Schaller, Helmut Wilhelm, Karla Günther-Hielscher, and Victor Glötzner. *Real-und Sachwörterbuch zum Altrussischen*. Neuried: Hieronymus Verlag, 1985.

Scheltema, H. J. "Byzantine Law." In *The Cambridge Medieval History*. Vol. 4: *The Byzantine Empire*. Part 2: *Government, Church, and Civilisation*, edited by J. M. Hussey, with the assistance of D. M. Nicol and G. Cowan, 55–77. Cambridge: Cambridge University Press, 1967.

Schmähling, Angelika. "Vom Nutzen der Klausur: Religiöse und gesellschaftliche Funktionen der Frauenklöster im Moskauer Reich." In *Religion und Integration im Moskauer Russland*, edited by Ludwig Steindorff, 461–76. Wiesbaden: Harrassowitz Verlag, 2010.

Schwartz, Howard. *Tree of Souls: The Mythology of Judaism*. Oxford: Oxford University Press, 2004.

A Select Library of Nicene and Post-Nicene Fathers of the Christian Church. Edited by Philip Schaff and Henry Wace. 2nd series. 14 vols. New York: Christian Literature, 1890–1900.

Selin, Adrian Aleksandrovich. *Novgorodskoe obshchestvo v epokhu Smuty*. St. Petersburg: BLITS, 2008.

The Septuagint with Apocrypha: Greek and English. Edited by Sir Lancelot C. L. Brenton. Peabody, MA: Hendrickson, 1987.

Seredonin, S. M. *Sochinenie Dzhil'sa Fletchera "Of the Russe Common Wealth" kak istoricheskii istochnik*. St. Petersburg: Skorokhodov, 1891.

Sergievskii, Nikolai, and Andrei E. Zarin. *Semiboiarshchina*. Moscow: Armada, 1995.

Setton, Kenneth M. *Venice, Austria, and the Turks in the Seventeenth Century*. Philadelphia, PA: American Philosophical Society, 1991.

Shamshurin, Valerii, ed. *Minin i Pozharskii——spasiteli Otechestva*. Moscow: Novator, 1997.

Shchapov, Yaroslav N. *State and Church in Early Russia, 10th–13th Centuries*. Translated by Vic Shneyerson. New Rochelle, NY: Caratzas, 1993.

————, P. N. Zyrianov, et al., eds. *Tserkov' v istorii Rossii*. Vols. 1 and 2. Moscow: IRI RAN, 1997–1998.

Shcherbatov, M. M. *Istoriia rossiiskaia ot drevneishikh vremian*. 7 vols. St. Petersburg: Imp. akademiia nauk, 1770–1791.

Shestakov, A. V. *Krest'ianskie voiny i vosstaniia ugnetennykh narodov v XVII veke: Khoziaistvo, gosudarstvennyi stroi, kul'tura i byt v Rossii vo vtoroi polovine XVII veka.* Leningrad: Polit. upr. KBF, 1938.

Shevzov, Vera. *Russian Orthodoxy on the Eve of Revolution.* Oxford: Oxford University Press, 2004.

Shirogorov, Vladimir Vladimirovich. *Bezvremen'e: povesti mezhdutsarstviia i smuty.* Moscow: Molodaia gvardiia, 1997.

Shishov, A. V. *Minin i Pozharskii.* Moscow: Voen. izd-vo, 1990.

Shkliaev, Igor' N. *Odessa v Smutnoe vremia.* Odessa: Studiia "Negotsiant," 2004.

Shokarev, S. Iu. *Moskva v epokhu Smuty: 1604–1613 gg.* Moscow: Interreklama, 2009.

Shubin, Daniel H. *A History of Russian Christianity.* 4 vols. New York: Algora, 2004–2006.

Shumilov, V. N. *Obzor dokumental'nykh materialov Tsentral'nogo gosudarstvennogo arkhiva drevnikh aktov po istorii SSSR perioda feodalizma XI–XVI vv.* Edited by M. N. Tikhomirov. Moscow, 1954.

Shvatchenko, O. A. "Sluzhilaia votchina i pomest'e v Moskovskom uezde XVI–XVII vv." In *Rossiia v srednie veka i novoe vremia: Sbornik statei k 70-letiiu chl.-korr. RAN L. V. Milova*, edited by M. B. Bulgakov, L. N. Vdovina, A. A. Gorskii, V. A. Kuchkin, and B. N. Floria, 137–64. Moscow: ROSSPEN, 1999.

Shveikovskaia, E. N. "Traditsionalizm kak tip sotsial'no-ekonomicheskogo razvitiia: Russkii Sever v XVI—XVII vv." In *Rossiia v srednie veka i novoe vremia: Sbornik statei k 70-letiiu chl.-korr. RAN L. V. Milova*, edited by M. B. Bulgakov, L. N. Vdovina, A. A. Gorskii, V. A. Kuchkin, and B. N. Floria, 165–85. Moscow: ROSSPEN, 1999.

Sinitsyna, Nina V. "Tipy monastyrei i russkii asketicheskii ideal (XV–XVI vv.)." In *Monashestvo i monastyri v Rossii, XI–XX veka: Istoricheskie ocherki*, edited by N. V. Sinitsyna et al., 116–49. Moscow: Nauka, 2002.

———. *Tretii Rim: Istoki i evoliutsiia russkoi srednevekovoi kontseptsii (XV–XVI vv.).* Moscow: Indrik, 1998.

Sirin, Efrem. *Slovo o prekrasnom Iosife.* Sergiev Posad: STSL, 2001.

Sivkov, K. "Tsar' Fedor Ioannovich i Boris Godunov." In *Smutnoe vremia v Moskovskom gosudarstve: Sbornik statei s illiustratsiiami*, edited by V. N. Bochkarev, Iu. V. Got'e, and V. I. Picheta, 45–57. Moscow: Zadruga, 1913.

Skazaniia sovremennikov o Dimitrii Samozvantse. Edited by Nikolai Ustrialov. 3rd ed. Vols. 1–2. St. Petersburg: Tip. Imp. akademiia nauk, 1859.

Skrynnikov, Ruslan G. *Boris Godunov.* Moscow: Nauka, 1978.

———. *Boris Godunov.* Translated by Hugh F. Graham. Gulf Breeze, FL: Academic International, 1982.

———. "Boris Godunov's Struggle for the Throne." *Canadian-American Slavic Studies* 11, no. 3 (Fall 1977): 325–53.

———. "The Civil War in Russia at the Beginning of the Seventeenth Century (1603–1607): Its Character and Motive Forces." Translated by Maureen Perrie. In *New Perspectives on Muscovite History*, edited by Lindsey Hughes, 61–78. New York: St. Martin's, 1993.

———. *Krest i korona: Tserkov' i gosudarstvo na Rusi IX–XVII vv.* St. Petersburg: Iskusstvo-SPB, 2000.

———. *Krushenie tsarstva: istoricheskoe povestvovanie.* Moscow: Armada, 1995.

———. *Minin i Pozharskii.* Moscow: Molodaia gvardiia, 1981.

———. "Nestiazhateli i osifliane na sobore 1503 g." In *Srednevekovoe pravoslavie ot prikhoda do patriarkhata*, edited by N. D. Barabanov, I. O. Tiumentsev, et al., 1: 126–42. Volgograd: Izd-vo Volgogradskogo gosud. universiteta, 1997.

———. *Rossiia v nachale XVII v.: "Smuta."* Moscow: Mysl', 1988.

———. *Samozvantsy v Rossii v nachale XVII veka: Grigorii Otrep'ev.* Edited by A. P. Derevianko. Novosibirsk: Nauka, 1987.

———. *Sibirskaia ekspeditsiia Ermaka.* Novosibirsk: Nauka, 1982.

———. *Smutnoe vremia: Krushenie tsarstva.* Moscow: Khranitel', 2007.

———. *The Time of Troubles: Russia in Crisis, 1604–1618.* Translated by Hugh F. Graham. Gulf Breeze, FL: Academic International, 1988.

———. *Tsar' Boris i Dmitrii Samozvanets: Illiustrirovannaia entsiklopediia.* Smolensk: Rusich, 1997.

Slovar' istoricheskikh terminov. Edited by V. S. Simakov. St. Petersburg: Lita, 1998.

Slovar' knizhnikov i knizhnosti drevnei Rusi. Edited by D. S. Likhachev. 3 vols. in 7 books to date. Leningrad: Nauka, 1987–2004.

Slovar' russkogo iazyka XI—XVII vv. 26 vols. to date. Moskva: Nauka, 1975–.

Slovar' tserkovno-slavianskago i russkago iazyka, sostavlennyi Vtorym otdeleniem Imperatorskoi akademii nauk. 2nd ed. 4 vols. St. Petersburg: Tip. Imp. akademii nauk, 1867–1868. Reprinted Leipzig: Zentralantiquariat, 1972.

Smirnov, I. I. *Vosstanie Bolotnikova, 1606–1607.* Moscow: Gosud. izd-vo polit. lit., 1951.

———, A. G. Man'kov, E. P. Pod"iapol'skaia, and V. V. Mavrodin. *Krest'ianskie voiny v Rossii XVII–XVIII vv.* Moscow: Nauka, 1966.

Smirov, N. A., ed. *Tserkov' v istorii Rossii (IX v.–1917 g.): Kriticheskie ocherki.* Moscow: Nauka, 1967.

Smirnov, P. A. *Dvoeverie v russkikh prostonarodnykh prazdnikakh.* Moscow: Gosud. akademiia slavianskoi kul'tury, 2001.

Smirnov, Petr Semenovich. *Istoriia khristianskoi pravoslavnoi tserkvi.* Jordanville, NY: Sviato-Troitskago monastyria, 1957.

Smith, T. Allan, [trans. and ed.]. *The Volokolamsk Paterikon: A Window on a Muscovite Monastery.* Toronto: Pontifical Institute of Mediaeval Studies, 2008.

Smith, William. *Smith's Bible Dictionary.* Old Tappan, NJ: Spire, 1980.

Smolich, Igor Kornilevich. *Russkoe monashestvo 988–1917; Zhizn' i uchenie startsev: prilozhenie k "Istorii russkoi tserkvi."* Moscow: Pravoslavnaia entsiklopediia, 1997.

Smuta v Moskovskom gosudarstve: Rossiia nachala XVII stoletiia v zapiskakh sovremennikov. Edited by A. I. Pliguzov and I. A. Tikhoniuk. Moscow: Sovremennik, 1989.

Snezhnitskii, A., ed. "Kopii s dvukh zhalovannykh tsarskikh gramot i s pistsovykh i mezhevykh knig selenii Nizhegorodskoi gubernii, byvshikh izdrevlu v Kurmyshskom, Nizhegorodskom i Arzamasskom uezdakh, v Zakudemskom i Zavadskom stanakh i proch." In *Deistviia Nizhegorodskoi gubernskoi uchenoi arkhivnoi komissii: Sbornik statei, soobshchenii, opisei i dokumentov*, 5: 35–70. Nizhnii-Novgorod: Konyshev, 1903.

Sobornoe ulozhenie 1649 goda. Edited by M. N. Tikhomirov and P. P. Epifanov. Moscow: Izd-vo Moskovskogo universiteta, 1961.

Sobranie gosudarstvennykh gramot i dogovorov, khraniashchikhsia v Gosudarstvennoi kollegii inostrannykh del. 5 vols. Moscow: Vsevolozhskii/Selivanovskii/Lissner i Roman, 1813–1894.

Solov'ev, S. M. *History of Russia.* 48 vols. to date. Gulf Breeze, FL: Academic International, 1976–2002.

———. *Istoriia Rossii s drevneishikh vremen.* 29 vols. in 15 books. Moscow: ISEL, 1959–1966.

Solzhenitsyn, Aleksandr. "Pravoslavnaia tserkov' v eto Smutnoe vremia." *Rodina* 11 (2005). http://www.istrodina.com/rodina_articul.php3?id=1743&n=90.

Sorskii, Nil. *Nil Sorsky: The Authentic Writings.* Edited and translated by David M. Goldfrank. Kalamazoo, MI: Cistercian Publications, 2008.

Spector, Ivar. *An Introduction to Russian History and Culture.* 4th ed. Princeton, NJ: Nostrand, 1965.

Spock, Jennifer. "The Solovki Monastery, 1460–1645: Piety and Patronage in the Early Modern Russian North." 2 vols. PhD diss., Yale University, 1999.

Srednevekovoe pravoslavie ot prikhoda do patriarkhata: Sbornik nauchnykh statei. Edited by N. D. Barabanov, I. O. Tiumentsev, et al. 2 vols. Volgograd: Izd-vo Volgogradskogo gosud. universiteta, 1997–1998.

Sreznevskii, I. I. *Materialy dlia slovaria drevne-russkago iazyka po pis'mennym pamiatnikam.* 3 vols. St. Petersburg: Tip. Imp. akademiia nauk, 1893–1912. Reprinted Graz: Akademische Druck-u. Verlagsanstalt, 1971.

Stanislavskii, A. L. *Grazhdanskaia voina v Rossii XVII v.: Kazachestvo na perelome istorii.* Moscow: Mysl', 1990.

Staroslavianskii slovar' (po rukopisiam X–XI vekov). 2nd ed. Edited by R. M. Tseitlin, R. Vecherki, and E. Blagova. Moscow: Russkii iazyk, 1999.

Steindorff, Ludwig. "Donations and Commemoration in the Muscovite Realm—A Medieval or Early Modern Phenomenon?" In *Religion und Integration im Moskauer Russland: Konzepte und Praktiken, Potentiale und Grenzen, 14.-17. Jahrhundert. (Forschungen zur osteuropäischen Geschichte,* vol. 76.), edited by Ludwig Steindorff, 477–98. Wiesbaden: Harrassowitz Verlag, 2010.

———. *Memoria in Altrussland: Untersuchungen zu den Formen christlicher Totensorge.* Stuttgart: F. Steiner Verlag, 1994.

———, ed. *Religion und Integration im Moskauer Russland: Konzepte und Praktiken, Potentiale und Grenzen, 14.-17. Jahrhundert. (Forschungen zur osteuropäischen Geschichte,* vol. 76.) Wiesbaden: Harrassowitz Verlag, 2010.

Stites, Richard. *Revolutionary Dreams: Utopian Vision and Experimental Life in the Russian Revolution.* New York: Oxford University Press, 1989.

Stoglav: Issledovanie i tekst. Edited by E. B. Emchenko and N. V. Sinitsyna. Moscow: Indrik, 2000.

Stolyarova, Galina. "The Holiest of Water." *Transitions Online* (Oct. 14, 2010). http://www.tol.org.

———. "You Scratcheth my Back . . ." *Transitions Online* (Jan. 21, 2010). http://www.tol.org.

Strémooukhoff, Dimitri. "Moscow the Third Rome: Sources of the Doctrine." *Speculum* 28, no. 1 (Jan. 1953): 84–101.

Strygin, Vladimir. "A v nyneshnei Rossii smutnoe vremia uzhe zakonchilos'?" *Vecherniaia Moskva* 83 (May 12, 2003).

———. "Smutnye vremena." *Russkii kur'er* (2003).

———. "Vtoraia rossiiskaia smuta i tserkov'." *Bereg* 34 (Aug. 23, 2002).

Subtelny, Orest. *Ukraine: A History.* 2nd ed. Toronto: University of Toronto Press, 1994.

Sunderland, Willard. *Taming the Wild Field: Colonization and Empire on the Russian Steppe.* Ithaca, NY: Cornell University Press, 2004.

The Supplement to the Modern Encyclopedia of Russian, Soviet, and Eurasian History. Edited by George N. Rhyne et al. 9 vols. to date. Gulf Breeze, FL: Academic International, 1995–2008.

Supplementum ad Historica Russiae Monumenta, ex archivis ac bibliothecis extraneis deprompta, et a Collegio Archaeographico edita/Dopolneniia k Aktam istoricheskim, otnosiashchimsia k Rossii: Sobrany v inostrannykh arkhivakh i bibliotekakh i izdany Arkheograficheskoiu kommissieiu. St. Petersburg: Prats, 1848.

Svetil'nik: Tserkovnoe iskusstvo i arkheologiia. Edited by Vladimir Silov'ev, Nikolai Nikolaevich Vizzhilin, et al. Vol. 1. Moscow: Izdatel'skii sovet Russkoi Pravoslavnoi Tserkvi, 2001.

"Sviashchennosluzhiteli o 'simfonii' gosudarstva i tserkvi." Regions.ru: Novosti federatsii. Feb. 4, 2009. http://www.regions.ru/news/2194403.

Swoboda [Svoboda], Marina. "Obraz tsaria vo 'Vremennike' Ivana Timofeeva." *TODRL* 52 (2001): 385–408.

———. "Tradition Reinvented: The Vision of Russia's Past and Present in Ivan Timofeyev's *Vremennik*". PhD diss., McGill University, 1997.

Szeftel, Marc. "Joseph Volotsky's Political Ideas in a New Historical Perspective." *Jahrbücher für Geschichte Osteuropas* 13, no. 1 (Apr. 1965): 19–29.

———. "The Title of the Muscovite Monarch up to the End of the Seventeenth Century." *Canadian-American Slavic Studies* 13, nos. 1–2 (1979): 59–81.

"Tak nazyvaemoe Inoe skazanie." In *Russkaia istoricheskaia biblioteka.* Vol. 13: *Pamiatniki drevnei russkoi pis'mennosti, otnosiashchiesia k Smutnomu vremeni*, cols. 1–144. 2nd ed. St. Petersburg: Imp. Arkheogr. Kommissiia/Aleksandrov, 1909.

Tal'berg, N. D. *Istoriia russkoi tserkvi.* Jordanville, NY: Holy Trinity Monastery, 1959.

Talmud: Tractate Bava Metsia. Edited by Hersh Goldwurm. 3 vols. Brooklyn, NY: Mesorah, 1992–1999.

Tarkovskii, P. B. "Tri drevnerusskikh perevoda Ezopa: Ideologicheskii ocherk." *TODRL* 49 (1996): 187–223.

Tatishchev, Vasilii Nikitich. *Istoriia rossiiskaia.* Edited by S. N. Valk and M. N. Tikhomirov. 7 vols. Leningrad: Nauka, 1962–1968.

———, et al. *Velikie rossiiskie istoriki o Smutnom vremeni.* Moscow: Khranitel', 2007.

Taube, Moshe. "A Jewish Conspiracy to Proselytize Muscovy as Solution to the Y7K Problem?" Lecture. Dumbarton Oaks, Washington, DC, May 12, 1999.

Tazbir, Janusz. *Poland as the Rampart of Christian Europe: Myths and Historical Reality.* Warsaw: Interpress, 1983.

Thomas, Terence. "Popular Religion." *A New Dictionary of Religions.* Edited by John R. Hinnells. 2nd ed. Oxford: Blackwell, 1995.

Thomson, Francis J. *The Reception of Byzantine Culture in Mediaeval Russia.* Brookfield, VT: Ashgate, 1999.

Thyrêt, Isolde. *Between God and Tsar: Religious Symbolism and the Royal Women of Muscovite Russia.* DeKalb: Northern Illinois University Press, 2001.

———. "'Blessed is the Tsaritsa's Womb': The Myth of Miraculous Birth and Royal Motherhood in Muscovite Russia." *Russian Review* 53, no. 4 (Oct. 1994): 479–96.

———. "Economic Reconstruction or Corporate Raiding? The Borisoglebskii Monastery in Torzhok and the Ascription of Monasteries in the 17th Century." *Kritika: Explorations in Russian and Eurasian History* 11, no. 3 (Summer 2010): 490–511.

————. "Marfa Ivanovna and the Expansion of the Role of the Tsar's Mother in the 17th Century." In *Rude and Barbarous Kingdom Revisited: Essays in Russian History and Culture in Honor of Robert O. Crummey*, edited by Chester S. L. Dunning, Russell E. Martin, and Danie Rowland, 109–29. Bloomington, IN: Slavica: 2008.

Tikhomirov, M. N. *Istochnikovedenie istorii SSSR*. Vol. 1. Moscow: ISEL, 1962.

————, and B. N. Floria, eds. "Prikhodo-raskhodnye knigi Iosifo-Volokolamskogo monastyria 1606/07 g." In *Arkheograficheskii ezhegodnik za 1966 god,* 331–83. Moscow: Nauka, 1968.

————. "Skazaniia o nachale Moskvy." *Istoricheskie zapiski* 32 (1950): 233–41.

Timofeev, Ivan. *Vremennik Ivana Timofeeva*. Edited and translated by O. A. Derzhavina and V. P. Adrianova-Peretts. Moscow: AN SSSR, 1951.

Titmuss, R. *The Gift Relationship*. London: Allen and Unwin, 1970.

Tiumentsev, I. O. "Gosudarstvo i tserkov' v Rossii v 1608–1610 gg." In *Srednevekovoe pravoslavie ot prikhoda do patriarkhata*, edited by N. D. Barabanov, I. O. Tiumentsev, et al., 1: 142–68. Volgograd: Izd-vo Volgogradskogo gosud. universiteta, 1997.

————. *Oborona Troitse-Sergieva monastyria v 1608–1610 gg.* Moscow: Tseikhgauz, 2008.

————. "Osada." *Rodina* 11 (2005). http://www.istrodina.com/rodina_articul.php3?id=1729&n=90.

————. "Russkie samozvantsy 1606–1607 godov i narodnaia religioznost'." In *Srednevekovoe pravoslavie ot prikhoda do patriarkhata*, edited by N. D. Barabanov, I. O. Tiumentsev, et al., 2: 212–67. Volgograd: Izd-vo Volgogradskogo gosud. universiteta, 1998.

————. *Smutnoe vremia v Rossii nachala XVII stoletiia: Dvizhenie Lzhedimitriia II*. Moscow: Nauka, 2008.

Tolochko, O. P. "*Istoriia rossiiskaia" Vasiliia Tatishcheva: Istochniki i izvestiia*. Moscow: Novoe literaturnoe obozrenie, 2005.

Tolstoi, Lev N. *Sobranie sochinenii v 22 tomakh*. Moscow: Khudozhestvennaia literatura, 1978–1985.

Tolstoi, Mikhail. *Istoriia russkoi tserkvi: Rasskazy iz istorii russkoi tserkvi*. Sortavala: Spaso-Preobrazhenskii Valaamskii monastyr', 1991.

Torop, F. *Populiarnaia entsiklopediia russkikh pravoslavnykh imen*. Moscow: Belyi volk, 1999.

Toumanoff, Cyril. "Moscow the Third Rome: Genesis and Significance of a Politico-Religious Idea." *Catholic Historical Review* 40, no. 4 (Jan. 1955): 411–47.

Troeltsch, Ernst. *The Social Teaching of the Christian Churches*. Translated by Olive Wyon. 2 vols. London: Allen, 1931.

Tschizewskij, Dmitrij. *Russian Intellectual History*. Translated by John C. Osborne. Edited by Marin P. Rice. Ann Arbor, MI: Ardis, 1978.

Tseitlin, Ralia M. *Kratkii ocherk istorii russkoi leksikografii (slovari russkogo iazyka)*. Moscow: GUPIMP RSFSR, 1958.

Tserkovnye drevnosti: Sbornik dokladov konferentsii (27 ianvaria 2000 g.). Edited by Ioann (Ekonomtsev) et al. Moscow: Prosvetitel', 2001.

Ul'ianovskii, Vasilii Irinarkhovich. "Motiv 'Proneseniia chashi' v religiozno-tserkovnoi deiatel'nosti Borisa Godunova 1604–1605 gg." In *Srednevekovoe pravoslavie ot prikhoda do patriarkhata*, edited by N. D. Barabanov, I. O. Tiumentsev, et al., 2: 174–211. Volgograd: Izd-vo Volgogradskogo gosud. universiteta, 1998.

————. "Pravoslavnaia tserkov' i Lzhedmitrii I." In *Arkhiv russkoi istorii: Nauchnyi istoricheskii zhurnal*, edited by I. A. Tikhoniuk et al., 3: 29–62. Moscow: RGADA, 1993.

————. *Rossiiskie samozvantsy: Lzhedmitrii I.* Kyiv: Libid', 1993.

————. *Smutnoe vremia.* Moscow: Evropa, 2006.

Uspenskii, B. A. *Istoriia russkogo literaturnogo iazyka (XI–XVII vv.).* 3rd ed. Moscow: Aspekt Press, 2002.

————. "Svad'ba Lzhedmitriia." *TODRL* 50 (1997): 404–25.

————. *Tsar' i patriarkh: Kharizma vlasti v Rossii. Vizantiiskaia model' i ee russkoe pereosmyslenie.* Moscow: Iazyki russkoi kul'tury, 1998.

Vainshtein, O. A. *Rossiia i Tridtsatiletniaia voina 1618–1648 gg.: Ocherki iz istorii vneshnei politiki Moskovskogo gosudarstva v pervoi polovine XVII v.* Leningrad: OGIZ, 1947.

Val'denberg, Vladimir. *Drevnerusskiia ucheniia o predelakh tsarskoi vlasti: Ocherki russkoi politicheskoi literatury ot Vladimira Sviatogo do kontsa XVII veka.* Petrograd: Benke, 1916. Reprinted The Hague: Europe, 1966.

Valentinov, N. "O russkom messianizme." *Novyi zhurnal* 90 (1968): 256–64.

Vasmer, Max [as Fasmer, Maks]. *Etimologicheskii slovar' russkogo iazyka.* Translated and edited by O. N. Trubachev and B. A. Larin. 4 vols. Moscow: Progress, 1986–1987.

————. *Russisches etymologisches Wörterbuch.* 3 vols. Heidelberg: Carl Winter—Universitätsverlag, 1950–1958.

Vavilin, V. F. "Nekotorye voprosy tipologicheskoi klassifikatsii i metodiki issledovaniia sel'skikh poselenii." In *Materialy po istorii, arkheologii i etnografii Mordovii: Trudy*, edited by V. I. Kozlov, M. V. Dorozhkin, V. N. Mart'ianov, and I. I. Firstov, 54: 33–57. Saransk: Mordovskoe knizhnoe izd-vo, 1977.

Veisman, A. D. *Grechesko-russkii slovar'.* 5th ed. St. Petersburg: Veisman, 1899. Reprinted Moscow: Shichalin, 1991.

Verduin, Leonard. *The Anatomy of a Hybrid: A Study in Church-State Relationships.* Grand Rapids, MI: Eerdmans, 1976.

Vereshchagin, E. M. *Tserkovnoslavianskaia knizhnost' na Rusi: Lingvotekstologicheskie razyskaniia.* Moscow: Indrik, 2001.

Vernadsky, George. *A History of Russia.* 5th ed. New Haven, CT: Yale University Press, 1961.

————. *Russian Historiography: A History.* Edited by Sergei Pushkarev. Translated by Nickolas Lupinin. Belmont, MA: Nordland, 1978.

————. *The Tsardom of Moscow, 1547–1682.* 2 vols. [Vol. 5 of *A History of Russia.*] New Haven, CT: Yale University Press, 1969.

Veselovskii, S. B. *D'iaki i pod'iachie XV–XVII vv.* Moscow: Nauka, 1975.

Vinogradov, V. V. *O iazyke khudozhestvennoi prozy: Izbrannye trudy.* Edited by M. P. Alekseev et al. Moscow: Nauka, 1980.

Vkladnaia kniga Serpukhovskogo Vysotskogo monastyria. Edited by S. S. Ermolaev, E. E. Lykova, and V. V. Shilov. Materialy i issledovaniia po istorii Serpukhovskogo kraia. Moscow: Arkheograficheskii tsentr, 1993.

Vkladnyia i kormovyia knigi Rostovskago Borisoglebskago monastyria v XV, XVII i XVIII stoletiiakh. Edited by A. A. Titov. Yaroslavl: TGZU, 1881.

Vladimirov, Aleksandr I. "Strategicheskii etiud: Tezisy k logike etnogeneza i possionarnosti osnovnykh sovremennykh geopoliticheskikh igrokov, i imperativy natsional'noi strategii." *Rossiiskie kadety.* http://www.cadet.ru/vlad_v/etd4.htm.

Vlasov, V. G. "The Christianization of the Russian Peasants." In *Russian Traditional Culture: Religion, Gender, and Customary Law*, edited by Marjorie Mandelstam Balzer, 16–33. London: Sharpe, 1992.

Volotskii, Iosif. *The Monastic Rule of Iosif Volotsky*. Translated and edited by David M. Goldfrank. 2nd ed. Kalamazoo, MI: Cistercian, 2000.

———. *Poslaniia Iosifa Volotskogo*. Edited by A. A. Zimin and Ia. S. Lur'e. Moscow: AN SSSR, 1959.

———. *Prosvetitel', ili oblichenie eresi zhidovstvuiushchikh*. Kazan: Imp. univ., 1903.

Voskoboinikova, N. P. *Opisanie drevneishikh dokumentov arkhivov moskovskikh prikazov XVI–nach. XVII vv.* Edited by N. F. Demidovaia and N. Shields Kollmann. Moscow: Arkheograficheskii tsentr', 1994.

"Vttolckningen vtaf dett bref som ifra Muskou åhr skriffwet till Ostaskof, och till alle andre befästninger som vnder dett Maskouské herskapet ahr./K istorii izbiratel'nago sobora 1613 goda. Izlozhenie pis'ma, otpravlennago iz Moskvy v Ostashkov i drugie goroda Moskovskago gosudarstva." Edited by A. K. Kabanov. [Istoricheskaia biblioteka (Moscow), catalogue number 42 b/5b. Stamped by the library Apr. 28, 1925. Source possibly belongs to *Deistviia Nizhegorodskoi gubernskoi uchenoi arkhivnoi komissii* or a similar serial publication.]

"Vypis' s pistsovykh i mezhevykh knig votchiny Nizhegorodskogo Pecherskogo monastyria—selu Iagodnomu, s prikhodskimi k nemu derevniami, v nyneshnem Kniagininskom uezde, 1621 i 1622-go godov." In *Deistviia Nizhegorodskoi gubernskoi uchenoi arkhivnoi komissii: Sbornik statei, soobshchenii, opisei i dokumentov*, 5: 40–55. Nizhnii-Novgorod: Konyshev, 1903.

Waliszewski, Kazimierz [as Valishevskii, K.]. *Smutnoe vremia*. Translated by E. N. Shchepkina et al. St. Petersburg: IVOKNSPVZhK, 1911. Reprinted Moscow: IKPA, 1989.

Ware, Timothy. *The Orthodox Church*. New York: Penguin, 1993.

Warneke, Sara. "Social Services: Western Christian." In *Encyclopedia of Monasticism*, edited by William M. Johnston, 2: 1169–71. Chicago: Fitzroy Dearborn, 2000.

White, Hayden. *The Content of the Form: Narrative Discourse and Historical Representation*. Baltimore, MD: Johns Hopkins University Press, 1987.

———. *Metahistory: The Historical Imagination in Nineteenth-Century Europe*. Baltimore, MD: Johns Hopkins University Press, 1973.

———. *Tropics of Discourse: Essays in Cultural Criticism*. Baltimore, MD: Johns Hopkins University Press, 1978.

Whittaker, Cynthia H. "Chosen by 'All the Russian People': The Idea of an Elected Monarch in Eighteenth-Century Russia." *Acta Slavica Iaponica* 18 (2001): 1–18.

Widekind, Johann. *Thet Swenska i Rußland Tiio Åhrs Krijgz-Historie/Iukhan Videkind. Istoriia desiatiletnei shvedsko-moskovitskoi voiny*. Translated by S. A. Anninskii, A. M. Aleksandrov, and A. F. Kostina. Edited by V. L. Ianina and A. L. Khoroshkevich. Moscow: Pamiatniki istoricheskoi mysli, 2000.

Wilson, Francesca. *Muscovy: Russia through Foreign Eyes, 1553–1900*. New York: Praeger, 1971.

Wolff, Renata. "The Influence of Constantine on the Church." Conference paper. Miami, FL: American Catholic Historical Association, Apr. 16, 2004. For conspectus, see Francis J. Sicius, "The Spring Meeting of the American Catholic Historical Association," *Catholic Historical Review* 90, no. 4 (Oct. 2004): 839.

Wortman, Richard S. *Scenarios of Power: Myth and Ceremony in Russian Monarchy.* 2 vols. Princeton, NJ: Princeton University Press, 1995–2000.

Zabelin, Ivan Egorovich. *Domashnii byt russkikh tsarei v XVI i XVII stoletiiakh.* 3rd/4th ed. 3 vols. 1901–1918. Reprinted Moscow: Iazyki russkoi kul'tury, 2000.

———. *Minin i Pozharskii: Priamye i krivye v Smutnoe vremia.* New ed.; following the 3rd ed. (1896). Edited by D. M. Volodikhin. Moscow: AGRAF, 1999.

Zarubina, N. N. "Pravoslavnyi predprinimatel' v zerkale russkoi kul'tury." *Obshchestvennye nauki i sovremennost'* 5 (2001): 100–112.

Zavariukhin, N. V., and A. S. Luzgin. "Iz istorii zaseleniia Saranskogo uezda russkimi v XVII–nachale XVIII veka." In *Materialy po istorii, arkheologii i etnografii Mordovii: Trudy,* edited by V. I. Kozlov, M. V. Dorozhkin, V. N. Mart'ianov, and I. I. Firstov, 54: 73–87. Saransk: Mordovskoe knizhnoe izd-vo, 1977.

Zbiór dyplomatów rządowych i aktów prywatnych, posługujących do rozjasnienia dziejów Litwy i złączonych z nią krajów (od 1387 do 1710 r.)/Sobranie gosudarstvennykh i chastnykh aktov, kasaiushchikhsia istorii Litvy i soedinennykh s nei vladenii (ot 1387 do 1710 goda). Edited by Maurycy Krupowicz. Vol. 1. Vilnius: Tip. Osipa Zavadzkago, 1858.

Zemlianoi, Sergei. "Kuda idesh'? O Smute kak paradigme konservativnogo myshleniia." *Nezavisimaia gazeta* (2001).

Zenkovsky, Serge A., ed. and trans. *Medieval Russia's Epics, Chronicles, and Tales.* Rev. ed. New York: Meridian, 1974.

Zernov, Nicolas. *Moscow the Third Rome.* London: Society for Promoting Christian Knowledge, 1937.

———. *The Russians and their Church.* 3rd ed. London: SPCK, 1978.

Zhitie i podvigi prepodobnogo i bogonosnogo ottsa nashego Sergiia, igumena Radonezhskago i vseia Rossii chudotvortsa. Edited by Nikon (Rozhdestvenskii). Sergiev Posad: STSL, 2003.

Zhitiia sviatykh, na russkom iazyke, izlozhennyia po rukovodstvu Chet'ikh-Minei. Edited by Dimitrii Rostovskii. 12 vols. Moscow: Sinodal'naia, 1902–1911. Reprinted Borovsk: Rozhdestva Bogoroditsy Sviato-Pafnut'ev Borovskii monastyr', 1997.

"Zhizneopisanie prepodobnogo Irinarkha, zatvornika Rostovskogo." In *Svetil'nik: Tserkovnoe iskusstvo i arkheologiia,* edited by Vladimir Silov'ev, Nikolai Nikolaevich Vizzhilin, et al., 1: 20–22. Moscow: Izdatel'skii sovet Russkoi Pravoslavnoi Tserkvi, 2001.

Zhukovich, P. *Smutnoe vremia i votsarenie Romanovykh.* Moscow: Tip. Sytina, 1913.

Zimin, A. A. *V kanun groznykh potriasenii: Predposylki pervoi krest'ianskoi voiny v Rossii.* Moscow: Mysl', 1986.

———. "Nekotorye voprosy istorii Krest'ianskoi voiny v Rossii v nachale XVII v." *Voprosy istorii,* no. 3 (1958): 97–113.

Zinoviev, Aleksandr. *Gomo sovietikus: Moi dom, moia chuzhbina.* Moscow: KOR-INF, 1991.

———. *Homo Sovieticus.* Translated by Charles Janson. London: Paladin Grafton, 1985.

Znamenskii, Petr V. *Istoriia russkoi tserkvi: Uchebnoe rukovodstvo.* Moscow: Krutitskoe patriarshee podvore, 1996.

Żółkiewski, Stanisław [Stanislas]. *Expedition to Moscow.* Translated by Jedrzej Giertych. London: Polonica, 1959.

———. *Początek i progres wojny Moskiewskiej.* Paris: Księgarnia Luxemburgska [1866].

———. *Początek i progres wojny Moskiewskiej.* Edited by Jarema Maciszewski. Warsaw: Państwowy Instytut Wydawniczy, 1966.

————. *Rękopism Hetmana Żółkiewskiego (Początek i progres woyny Moskiewskiey za panowania K. I. M. Zygmunta III°, Za Regimentu I. M. P. Stanisława Żółkiewskiego, Woiewody Kijowskiego, Hetmana Polnego Koronnego)/Rukopis' Zholkevskago (Nachalo i uspekh Moskovskoi voiny v tsarstvovanie E. V. Korolia Sigizmunda III-go, pod nachal'stvom Ego Milosti, Pana Stanislava Zholkevskago, Voevody Kievskago, Napol'nago Koronnago Getmana).* Edited by Pavel Mukhanov. Moscow: Universitetskaia tip., 1835.

Zverinskii, V. V. *Material dlia istoriko-topograficheskogo issledovaniia o pravoslavnykh monastyriakh v Rossiiskoi imperii, s bibliograficheskim ukazatelem.* 3 vols. St. Petersburg, 1890–1897.

Index

posadskie liudi. *See* townsfolk

Posokhin, Vaska, 170

Posolskii prikaz. *See* international relations

possessors, 52

poverty, 52–53, 64, 69–74, 104, 158, 185

power (and force), 4–6, 11, 15, 21, 24–26, 32, 44–46, 49–50, 60–61, 69, 78, 89, 98, 105, 117–18, 121–22, 134, 146–47, 149, 154–55, 168, 170, 186, 189, 190, 196–97. *See also* army; rape; violence

Pozharskii, Dmitrii, 8, 10, 12, 15, 167–72, *167*, 178

Pozharskoi, Roman, 171

pravda (truth, justice), xi, 4, 14, 16, 28, 40, 74, 87, 92, 109, 114–15, 117, 124, 132–34, 138–39, 153–54, 173, 180, 182, 184, 187–88, 193, 195, 197. *See also* nepravda

prayer, 3–4, 21, 41–42, 49–50, 54, 59–60, 67–68, 81, 92, 100, 110–12, 114–15, 126, 130, 133, 137, 150–52, 158, 165, 174, 176, 188, 194–95. *See also* commemoration; liturgy; petitions

preaching, 30–31, 49

predestination, 77, 88–90, 175. *See also* God; izbranie

prelates. *See* Russian Orthodox Church, hierarchy

pretenders (samozvantsy), 4, 6–7, 10, 74, 108–110, 112–14, 116, 119, 121, 126, 139–41, 164–65, 169, 179, 186, 189. *See also specific individuals*

prices (and speculation), 16, 59, 102–7, 119–21, 146–47

pride, 12, 30, 86, 154, 197. *See also* humility

priests. *See* clergy; deacons; *and under* monasteries; Russian Orthodox Church

prikazy (government offices). *See* bureaucracy; *and specific departments*

primogeniture, 40, 76–78, 164

prisons, 4, 8, 15–16, 21, 37, 51, 67–68, 85, 113, 129, 134–35, 138, 160, 164, 195

profit, 51–74, 98, 100, 102, 105–7, 109–10, 120–22, 146–48, 151, 159, 163, 171, 180, 184–86. *See also* commerce

propaganda, x, 6, 21, 74, 79, 83, 90, 92, 109–11, 115–16, 118, 129, 131–32, 135, 137, 139, 141, 175, 185, 187, 195, 205n16

property, 9, 19, 53, 55, 63, 70, 100, 104, 108–9, 119, 122, 129, 143, 145, 149, 162. *See also* destruction; landholding; *and under* monasteries

prophecy, 3, 8–9, 20, 34, 39, 41, 47–48, 86, 118, 138, 152, 154. *See also* Bible; visions; *and specific individuals*

Protasei (Protasii, elder monk), 58, 119–21

Protestantism, 24, 42, 110, 123–24, 127, 132, 138, 173–74

Psalms of Solomon, 42

Psalms, x, 3, 8, 41, 48. *See also* Bible

Pskov, 33, *65*

punishment (for sin). *See* God; sin; *and under* Time of Troubles

Pushkin, Aleksandr, 10, 14, 203n42

Putin, Vladimir, 12

Putivl, *37*, 108, 139

Pyskorsk Spaso Preobrazhensk monastery, 63

Qipchaq khanate. *See* Crimea; Mongol-Tatar empire

quotation, 18, 30, 38–42, 90, 166, 175, 208n83, 217n39. *See also* imitation

quriltai, 78. *See also* parliament; zemskii sobor

Raba, Joel, 34

raiding, 4, 6–7, 9, 11, 52, 57, 68–69, 85, 102, 105, 108, 112, 140–41, 146–47, 154, 158, 160, 164–69, 178, 194–95

rape, 108–9, 113, 140

Raskol (church schism), 21–22, 43, 50, 53, 62, 190–97, 233n50; pre-Russian, 181, 194

Razboinyi prikaz, 112. *See also* raiding

Razin, Stenka, 10

real estate. *See* landholding; property

rebellion. *See* uprisings

Red Square, 10, 114, 126–28, 160, *167*, 181, *182*. *See also* Moscow

reforms, 21–22, 124, 179, 189–90, 194. *See also* revolution